Challenge to Leadership

Project Director   CHARLES M. DARLING, III

Associate Project Director   THEODORE A. SMITH

Editor   EDWARD C. BURSK

This project, a study of the management of institutions in future years, was carried out through the Public Affairs Research Division of The Conference Board—Walter Hamilton, Vice President.

Challenge
to Leadership

MANAGING IN A CHANGING WORLD

THE CONFERENCE BOARD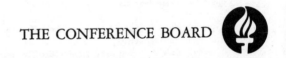

The Free Press, New York
Collier–Macmillan Publishers, London

Copyright © 1973 by The Conference Board, Inc.

Printed in the United States of America
All rights reserved. No part of this book may be
reproduced or transmitted in any form or by any
means, electronic or mechanical, including photo-
copying, recording, or by any information storage
and retrieval system, without permission in writing
from the Publisher.

The Free Press
A Division of Macmillan Publishing Co., Inc.

Collier–Macmillan Canada Ltd.

Library of Congress Catalog Card Number: 73–1861

printing number
1   2   3   4   5   6   7   8   9   10

Copyright Acknowledgments

Grateful acknowledgment is made to the following for use of material
reprinted in Chapter Ten:

Chart C, page 312: Reprinted from Haus Thirring, *Energy for Man,*
© 1958, Indiana University Press, Bloomington. Reprinted by permission
of the publisher.

Chart F, page 313: Figure 3.1, "Changes in Industrial Composition of
the U.S. Labor Force, 1870–1960," from INDUSTRIAL SOCIOLOGY,
2nd edition, by Delbert C. Miller and William H. Form. Copyright ©
1964 by Delbert C. Miller and William H. Form. Reprinted by permission of Harper & Row, Publishers, Inc.

Chart G, page 313: Reprinted from *Report of the National Goals Research Staff,* QUANTITY WITH QUALITY, p. 183 (1970), courtesy of
U.S. Government Printing Office.

Chart H, page 313: Figure 19.1, "Average Hours of Work per Week
from 1850 to 1960 with Estimated Projections from 1960 to 2000," in
INDUSTRIAL SOCIOLOGY: THE SOCIOLOGY OF WORK ORGAN-
IZATIONS, 2nd edition, by Delbert C. Miller and William H. Form
(Harper & Row, 1964, p. 815).

Chart L, page 315: Reprinted from TECHNOLOGICAL FORECAST-
ING AND LONG RANGE PLANNING by Robert U. Ayres. Copyright
© 1969 by McGraw-Hill Book Company. Used with permission of
McGraw-Hill Book Company.

Chart R, page 356: Reprinted from Anthony J. N. Judge, "The World
Network of Organizations," in INTERNATIONAL ASSOCIATIONS
Journal No. 1 (January, 1972), by permission.

Contents

Preface

Most societies, but particularly technically advanced ones such as the United States, are undergoing major transitions—social, political, economic, and philosophical. Possibly the most compelling of these is the one taking us from an "Industrial" to a "Post-Industrial" age—a transformation that is being fueled by developments in information and communications technology.*

Some important characteristics of the new age may already be evident. As individual or independent institutions become more global, more interrelated and interactive, they will give way to systems and networks. Delayed decision-making will yield to real-time management. Preoccupation with short-term limits to growth will yield to a more appropriate balance between short-term tactics and long-term strategy. Anything less will mean a failure to employ our new managerial capabilities. Attention must be paid to the implications of man's own decisions relating to his environment, to man's rapidly changing aspirations and satisfactions, and to man's perception of himself and of his society.

The recognition of the transition to the "Post-Industrial" society is helping us to see with increasing clarity the short and long term necessity for the introduction of more effective social management into our affairs. Yet such a transition poses real problems for leaders. We are being ushered into a significantly new era before we have begun to manage, much less resolve, problems thrown up by the outgoing "Industrial" era. Critical elements in our basic "guidance" and "measuring" systems are perhaps neither guiding as to where we want to go nor measuring what we want to measure. Perceptual and communication gaps exist between the leadership of the "Industrial" era and the "Post-Industrial" era.† As yet, we have only limited means for viewing and assessing change and its implications and for organizing our resources and developing social management concepts.

In the past, U.S. management has met most of the nation's needs for goods and services, thus making it materially possible for the United States to move in a philosophical sense from the "Industrial" to the "Post-Industrial" society.

* *Information Technology; Some Implications for Decision Makers.* 1972 The Conference Board, Inc.

† Even our symbols, as Max Ways of *Fortune* has noted, are anywhere from 25–50 years behind real-time events. For example, we still use early industrial era symbols in our attempt to characterize Post-Industrial phenomena.

Through the 1970's and 1980's management faces the challenge of self-renewal. Japan, for example, is today in the interesting position of financing Americans to go to Japan to study Japanese concepts of management.

The gradual emergence and acceptance of sophisticated foreign management practice is related to the re-emergence of business concern for the whole society. This concern will call forth a more comprehensive view of management requirements confronting business, government, education, and the voluntary sectors of our society.

In 1971, the Senior Executives Council, a group of 37 chief executives from business, universities, foundations, and public institutions, meeting periodically to consider major issues of our day, commissioned a major study. The objectives were to determine the more important characteristics of the managerial context of the Post-Industrial era; the character of top management likely to be required in our major institutions; the ways in which top management is likely to inter-relate; and the steps necessary to confront the challenges and maximize the opportunities for management during the final years of this century.

The authors who contributed to the study, and their associated panelists who provided counsel and who reviewed the draft papers, were asked to engage in responsible conjecture. What follows is a set of statements dealing with likely "significant developments" in management over the next 20 years.

The intention of The Conference Board and the Senior Executives Council was to initiate candid, public discussion on "Challenge to Leadership." It is their earnest hope that, through this report, they may further advance the dialogue on the character, shape, and extent of management in the Post-Industrial era.

The study of the future trends in management and the papers which are contained in this book were sponsored and financed by the Senior Executives Council of The Conference Board. The Council has exerted no control over the material, and the papers do not necessarily reflect the views of the Senior Executives Council or of any of its individual members. The names of the members of the Senior Executives Council may be found at the back of this book.

Robert O. Anderson, Chairman
Senior Executives Council of
The Conference Board

New York City
January, 1973

About the Contributors

Henry M. Boettinger   is Director of Planning, American Telephone and Telegraph Company. In addition to his duties at A. T. & T., he is Adjunct Professor of Management Philosophy at Pace College. He is also the author of "Moving Mountains, or the Art and Craft of Letting Others See Things Your Way," Macmillan, 1969.

H. Igor Ansoff   is Dean of the Graduate School of Management, Vanderbilt University. He is presently engaged in establishing an institute of strategic management at Vanderbilt. He is the author of numerous publications, including "Corporate Strategy" (McGraw-Hill, 1965).

William D. Carey   is Vice President, Arthur D. Little, Inc. Mr. Carey, who is located in Washington, has occupied various positions in the Federal government, serving as Assistant Director of the Budget from 1966 to 1969. He has been the recipient of the Rockefeller Public Service Award.

Marvin Bower   is presently a Director of McKinsey & Company, Inc., having previously been Managing Director. Aside from his consulting duties to industry, he has served as executive consultant to a number of government agencies. He is the author of "The Will to Manage."

C. Lee Walton, Jr.   is Managing Director of McKinsey & Company, Inc. Mr. Walton serves on the respective business advisory groups for the Graduate School of Business, University of Chicago, and the Graduate School of Industrial Administration, Carnegie–Mellon University.

Ernest L. Boyer   is Chancellor of the University of the State of New York. He is in an excellent position to discuss educational management since the structure of which he is the head consists of some 72 institutes of higher learning—one of the two large state systems in the United States.

Kenneth E. Boulding   has distinguished himself in economics and in the humanities generally. An Oxford graduate, he is presently Professor of Economics at the University of Colorado and makes his headquarters at the Institute of Behavioral Sciences there. He has served as President of the American Economics Association.

David Horton Smith and *John Dixon* are respectively Director of Research and Director of the Center for a Voluntary Society in Washington, D.C. Dr. Smith is Editor of the *Journal of Voluntary Action Research* and an Associate Professor at Boston College.

Peter F. Drucker   left his native Vienna to engage in banking in London prior to coming to the United States in 1937. He is known as both management consultant and writer. His book "The Age of Discontinuity" (Harper and Row, 1969) has been cited as a reference in many of these chapters. He is Professor of Management, Graduate Business School, New York University, and Clarke Professor of Social Science, Claremont Graduate School (California).

William Simon   is the Director, Institute for Juvenile Research in Chicago. He has previously taught at Indiana University and at the University of Chicago.

John McHale   is Director, Center for Integrative Studies, State University of New York at Binghamton. An artist and designer as well, he has been concerned with long range implications of science and technology on social and cultural developments. Magda Cordell McHale, his wife, is also associated with the Center.

Management Study Project   Charles M. Darling, III, Project Director, was, during much of the study program, Director, Planning and Forecasting, Public Affairs Research, The Conference Board. Theodore A. Smith, the Associate Project Director, was formerly an Executive Vice President of RCA. Edward C. Bursk, Editor, was for many years Editor of the *Harvard Business Review*.

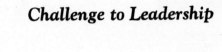

Challenge to Leadership

One

HENRY M. BOETTINGER

The Management Challenge

NOTHING fails like success" was the central lesson Dean Inge digested from his ruminations on our civilization's history. Received as a clever paradox, his shrewd insight finds only too-vivid confirmation in our own time. Nearly every vision that men at the turn of the century battled for has been achieved in the Western world. Democracy based on universal suffrage, compulsory education, the harnessing of science to expanding industries, greatly increased incomes, control of infectious diseases, workmen's protection, social insurance, cheap transportation, communications and power, and widespread material amenities, all are accomplished facts.

The problems facing every institution in our society are so formidable . . .

Yet, in spite of this success, every institution of our society is "in trouble." Leaders, perplexed as to purpose and subjected to ever-escalating expectations, experience barrages of criticism and demands to justify their every move. Sundry pundits compare the worst examples of current practice with the best of theoretical ideals. And numberless books, articles, and broadcasts entreat those in charge either to change their ways or prepare to face annihilation and breakdown of society as we know it.

But why add another volume to this already tottering pile? Our answer is both simple and confident: these apocalyptic works offer men of affairs almost no concrete help in understanding the interactive forces at work. And they particularly fail those leaders who must actually invent, evaluate, select, and make the changes necessary to bring their institutions into a workable congruence with the society they are designed to serve. Yet these are the crucial tasks facing those charged with managing business, government, education, churches, voluntary groups, and new forms of hybrid organizations.

Unlike the pundits, leaders cannot be content to lament or point fingers of scorn; they are responsible for the fates of their organizations and the people associated with them. They know they are judged on performance, not promises; on the concrete effects of their acts, not on the elegance of their visions. Such harsh tests make them receptive to any knowledge which can either narrow the inevitable uncertainties of their worlds, or suggest new departures they can embrace.

We have passed the point-of-no-return when individuals can live without institutions, and everyone increasingly recognizes that his own future is linked to their fates. This enhanced awareness has annihilated the former mood of resigned indifference. Frustrations with the symptoms of institutional disorder are now rapidly transformed into pressures on those in leadership positions. Just as an increasing reliance on high technology makes a society more vulnerable to sabotage, so new instruments for communication and mobilization of opinion allow—and stimulate—new values to emerge and inject their power into our social and political systems more quickly than before.

Every manager, in every sector of society, will face the clash of new values with his current perceptions and accustomed behavior. He will also face greater uncertainty in forming his judgments of appropriate response, because the members of our society have a far wider range of options as to where they can deploy their energies and incomes than in the past.

One thing seems indispensable: an improvement in our anticipatory powers, which must be based on an increased sensitivity to changing conditions before their infiltrated effects surface as crises. "Crisis management" may exhilarate its practitioners, but the entire spectrum of our population—from students to the aged—are now intolerant of the turbulence, disappointments, and dislocations which attend their unwelcome role of victims to it.

. . . that the only solution is through brave, brainy decision making . . .

Gone are those nostalgic days of purposeful serenity, where expectations were both predictable and clear, where stability of relationships among institutions could be taken for granted, and where small increments of improvement were seen as sufficient.

Dangerously large numbers no longer perceive our nation as the Land of Opportunity and—without knowing how or when it happened—expect most changes in their lives to be for the worse. This is not the first time such conditions have existed, but history grants the accolade of "great" only to those persons who arrested the pessimistic momentum of their times and channeled existing and emerging forces into new, purposeful directions.

To manage is to lead. But leadership today requires both reorientation of our institutions in directions conducive to viability in the Post-Industrial Age, and adapting our management methods—and their teaching—to attain the new goals consistent with such alterations in direction. Popular clamor cannot do this. If it can be done at all, many approaches will have to be explored by pioneers willing to commit their reputations and positions to the task. Leadership is a quality of character and intellect, not a condition or empty honor.

Seldom in our history have there been more things that need doing and more resources to do them with. But the indispensable ingredient remains that precious ability to perceive the aspirations of followers, discern the true limits of possibilities, and select the lines of advance which hold maximum promise of success.

Leaders will be judged, in this period of discontinuity, not by tactical nimbleness but by the robustness of their strategic designs for the organizations they head. Good designs will be new, because they must contend with novel circumstances. The organization of any successful institution is a monument to old problems successfully solved. Their very existence is proof of a good design in the past. But unchanging conduct and progressively changing conditions result in both logical muddle and exasperating symptoms of breakdown.

Every manager's judgment is—or soon will be—taxed with this question: Do we need only retune the system we have, or must we rethink our basic purposes and methods? The upward-turning points of an institution's progress have usually been accompanied by a successful rethinking, and by subsequent marriage of action to new insights.

. . . but such decision making, in turn,
requires deep knowledge, cool judgment.

Reexamination of the shared premises which hold any organization together is hazardous unless productively constrained by deep knowledge and cool judgment.

This book undertakes to marshal knowledge useful to leaders, and combines contributions of seasoned observers, expert on the management of various sectors of our society. One of the themes connecting each chapter is the similarity of management problems in all institutions—and the differences. The experience and techniques attending each one's development offer lessons for the others, especially at present when the various management cultures of different origins seem to be converging in important respects.

In the United States, we think of "management" as something related solely to business, but, as the following pages will show, management now pervades every kind of organization experiencing division of labor and hierarchic structures—which leaves precious little unaffected. The simple idea that others need only learn what business has to teach in order to put things right will be seen to have outlived its time. In fact, the ways that others have found to deal with multiple constituencies and criteria of effectiveness over their history offer business a rich source of derived experience as to what may work and what may not. Bismarck's view, "Fools say they learn by experience. I prefer to profit by other people's experience," underlies the rationale of this effort.

All institutions are now linked in one over-all "social ecology."

All sectors of society face problems generated from previous success. All institutions are linked together in such a way that failure of any one drags others down with it, and causes still others to pick up its burden. At the least, leaders in one sector should have some understanding of the potential fallout they can expect from issues and crises now current in other sectors; at the most, their future decisions could take greater account of reverberations sent beyond the boundaries of a specific organization's domain.

As Drucker demonstrates (see p. 271), we can no longer be as sure as Adam Smith that single-minded pursuit of individual self-interest will result in the greatest possible good for all, but we have yet to find an alternative most leaders and individuals can embrace. Exposure to the history, practices, and philosophies which permeate this work may help trigger those creative explosions of leadership necessary to the quest.

One thing seems certain: there will be no "best" or "final" state, because such a view is at least antievolutionary, if not fanatical. What is required is to find new *processes* which are strong enough to stand up to wide swings in what happens to planning assumptions. The elder von Moltke's wisdom that "no plan can survive contact with the battle" illustrates the uncertainty attending unfolding reality with which management must cope. In making plans, managers treat as fixed things which are essentially variable, but they must also be ready to change as evidence of this variability advances upon them. Those who can't change their *minds,* can't change anything else.

This may call for a rediscovery of the flexible, entrepreneurial outlook which attends the early phases of any institution's history of success. Ansoff (see p. 35) develops this idea in depth, and suggests ways to break the crust of custom in order to pass from conditions of the Industrial Era across the discontinuity which marks entrance to the Post-Industrial Society. He also contrasts those characteristics and qualities of persons and institutions which make for success in the two modes of competitive and entrepreneurial environments.

Some Management Aspects of Institutions

The philosopher, Scott Buchanan, toward the end of his life, regretted his relative neglect of the central roles played by the institutions of society. He called them the stately galleons which carried the members of a society toward unknown destinations. Some were in the lead, others straggled behind, but the entire population served in some ship under individual captains. "How did they set the course of the fleet?" was the question which bemused him—and he found no answer to it. Could there be a grand design, or must they merely "follow the leaders"? Would they wander and drift, or could they somehow agree on where all wish to go?

These over-all design decisions in our culture are the tasks and reasons for political governance, whose processes and traditions display fractures and strains under ever-increasing stress.

Carey estimates the immutable proportions of ingredients in public management as 60 per cent policy, 30 per cent execution, and 10 per cent administration (see p. 64), almost inversions of business management as set out by Bower (see p. 94). This may account for a great deal of mutual misunderstanding between these great institutions as they seem to talk past one another so often. Yet all leaders face the central problems of making choices under constraints.

If they see their task as one of managing these choices, they must deal with some unfortunate connotations of the very word "management." To unions, "management" is seen as the people they struggle with; to lower managers, "management" begins two levels above them; to the counter-culture, "management" is synonymous with "The Establishment"; and the verb "to manage" carries to most people a heavy whiff of manipulation, something considered not quite to be trusted. Yet to managers themselves, the word means the act of combining and directing energies of human beings, facilities, tools, and materials in ways that accomplish some useful purpose. A great deal of barren controversy springs from such elementary lack of agreement on terms.

Similarly with the manager's preoccupation with *control,* which he uses in the cybernetic sense of trying to keep a dynamic activity, subject to disturbances, both stable and "on course." But others see the quest for "control" as evil intention, prevention of progress, deprivation of talent opportunities, and a Machiavellian conservatism pledged to the status quo. The introduction of certain management techniques to deal with administration of higher education and government has encountered resistance from those who hold such views.

Ansoff, Boyer, and Bower present ideas of how such conflicts can be resolved, and analyze the inadequacy of older responses developed under far different conditions.

*Our businessmen have much to learn from
unconventionally organized institutions . . .*

The rise of voluntary organizations, based on changing motivation, methods, and alliances, constitutes a phenomenon not well understood. But Smith and Dixon show how they promise to quicken the pace of change in other institutions as they mobilize discontents and aspirations of people willing to discipline their lives to the service of certain ideals (see p. 205). Not least affected by this shift will be the venerable voluntary organizations in our society which have channeled energies of altruism in ways possibly no longer attractive to their traditional sources of recruits.

The management of voluntary institutions under present conditions is in a yeasty state, but managers in more hierarchically ordered groups may be interested in knowing how leaders denied classic disciplinary methods forge effective organizations from a wide variety of heterogeneous personalities.

Some of Bower's suggestions for business management (see p. 127) appear to converge with the methods of voluntary organizations, especially as business attempts to persuade its members to bring their heretofore latent energy into new purposeful outlets which can harmonize the drives of individuals with the goals of a specific business.

Another type of institution has quietly emerged over the last 50 years, almost unnoticed by the general public, yet enjoying vast resources and charged with filling demands which existing organizations have found awkward or impossible to meet. Boulding addresses this development of such "intersect organizations," whose characteristics are a variable blend of government and business (see p. 181). They include government corporations and private foundations, transcendent financial operations, transportation authorities, and NASA—a motley collection of increasing influence in the daily lives of all of us. Their methods, legitimacy, authority, and appraisal may offer a glimpse of the future shape of a Post-Industrial era.

. . . and from business managers in other nations around the world.

The United States has developed, until the recent past, in relative isolation from the intellectual and cultural currents in the rest of the world. Our most spectacular invisible export was the "management boom," whose end Drucker announces (see p. 265). Just as business has lost its dominant position in our country, forced to the status of a major planet and not that of the sun (there is no sun any longer), so has management as an American monopoly been absorbed, and transformed, to meet the requirements of cultures different from our own. As we leave our youthful innocence behind, when growth alone was the major measure of success, we can learn lessons of adaptation from other nations whose criteria of excellence differ from our own.

The dimensions of managing any institution are many, and other intelligent people throughout the world have surpassed us in several of those which now loom in importance in our own country. Exposure to their views can cause us to begin that reexamination of our inarticulate premises and myths long taken-for-granted which usually accompanies the triumphs of leadership during a discontinuity in human affairs. We may be as reluctant to acknowledge this as medieval men were to hear that the earth was no longer the center of the universe. But a polycentric view of excellence and power may allow us to make greater progress than possible under stubborn adherence to an outworn faith, however comfortable it may once have been.

Needed: awareness of change in individual
values and in institutional structures.

Ralph Waldo Emerson once wrote that "an institution is the lengthened shadow of one man." That may have been true in his day, but only a rash, egoistic leader would claim that today. An institution is a combination of individual persons, and its health and value depend on the qualities and ability of the individuals who are willing to harness their thought and action to its aims.

Simon reports the shift in outlook and values that young persons are bringing to the organizations they join (see p. 288). Those who manage organizations should be as aware of the changes in this most precious of assets as an architect would be if he could no longer acquire traditional, well-known products of construction. That architecture of human effort we call management is, in the words of Servan-Schreiber, "the art of arts because it is the organizer of talent." These new people will not—or cannot—do some of the things their fathers did, but they can also do many things that their fathers could not. Changes in the structural design of institutions may be more influenced by this thrust of social evolution than by any other factor.

At the very least, an openness to new knowledge and its application is the best defense against "resting on the oars" after a period of primacy—the phenomenon that Toynbee says has accounted for the failures of self-determination throughout human history. The nemesis of creativity, in his view, has been the idolization of an ephemeral technique that has been allowed to ossify because of its brilliant past success.

Management of institutions could experience that fate, but this book rests on a foundation of belief that a blend of thought, information, and action can develop new strategies for managing our institutions. Effective strategies will not squander our heritage in romantic anarchism, but they may need to be unchained from those traditions and behavior whose erstwhile usefulness has disappeared.

A Trinity of Principles

Every human institution, from a family to a nation, develops along three strands. The three strands, or principles of development, are *competition, cooperation,* and *innovation.* In America, we tend to think of competition as the antithesis of cooperation, or innovation as always progressive and the inevitable accompaniment of competition. But close observation of any organized effort will show all three present simultaneously, though in varying degrees of strength at different periods or situations.

Each principle contributes to increased excellence only when the various sets of activities involved are channeled to the principle most appropriate for it. When a specific activity is guided by the *wrong* principle, chaos, absurdity, decline, or other forms of disorganization develop. Also, experienced practical men, as well as historians, know that not every innovation lives up to its initial promise.

We like cooperation and innovation—for the sake of competition.

Let me illustrate this somewhat abstract idea, because its comprehension is one of the underlying themes of the rest of this book, even though none of the individual authors makes it explicit.

Consider a rowing race, where each boat contains eight oarsmen and a coxswain. Each crew is in absolute competition with other crews, yet each member of a single crew must cooperate in iron conformity to the beat set by the cox, and their improvement over previous performance is due to innovations in training, technique, or equipment. Team sports of every type employ simultaneous operation of the three principles, and such idealized forms of human effort make them beloved by leaders struggling to communicate grand visions to their organizations. The theme, baldly put, is "We must all cooperate and innovate so that we can compete."

But notice how these words take important assumptions for granted. Suppose all of the competition energy is *internal* to the organization (office or campus politics) and cooperation means satisfaction with a "share of market" or "share of resources" status quo. Innovation will then be diverted to serve perverse ends—primarily individual or departmental advancement. It is as though our crew members bent all their efforts to supplant their leader on the stroke oar, regardless of how their boat did against other crews.

History is littered with examples of such human tragedy. Heads of governments, university deans, factory foremen, and even bishops are not innocent of such experiences. Ansoff (see p. 57) notes that the most moribund organizations—moribund, that is, from an entrepreneurial point of view—are usually seething political cauldrons where all energy is focused to acquisition of *internal* power and perquisites.

On a somewhat higher plane, but still pertinent, Drucker notes that the United States is the only nation in the world where government and business are seen as adversaries (see p. 249). This may be the logical consequence of our faith and doctrine in the Constitution's separation of powers, but when old markets take on global dimensions of supply and demand, such postures may not be the best-tailored for the nation's modern interests. Conversely, in institutions where cooperation and maintenance of equilibrium were the traditional desiderata, allowing the role of rivalry to be increased may be the proper prescription for new expeditions toward excellence.

We seek contradictory goals—and reasonableness in compromising them.

Thus the great pendulum swings—in education of the young, in agriculture, churches, military affairs, government, philanthropy, and business—in ways far more complex than easily understood sports and games; and each age begins the debate anew. Excesses of cooperation sound the call for competition, and excesses of competition raise the cry for cooperation—both insisting, often rightly, that their advocated reforms will spur needed and possible innovations. In a society as variegated as the United States, we are not surprised to hear the shouts of recruiters to both standards simultaneously. Ecologists for more cooperation, consumer advocates for more competition, are only two current examples.

We call our society a "pluralistic" one—which means we are content to enunciate and strive for contradictory goals without embarrassment, because we know that compromise between extreme views is the practical way our development has occurred. Our favorite adjective is "reasonable." Few of us are comfortable with a highly refined ideology, where preprogrammed answers to every problem are processed on demand. That has not been our way. Instead, we prefer a certain looseness in our systems, but not *too* much for discomfort or collapse. Knowing where the boundary lies makes a person a candidate for the pinnacle of wisdom.

The argument over liberty and equality rages at the same intensity as it has for two hundred years, and we are not daunted by the historical fact that large-minded and decent-hearted men, like John Stuart Mill, carried their struggle to reconcile the two goals to their graves. We still want *both,* and perhaps the best course is to keep on trying, even if logic tells us we are assaulting infinity with bare fists. We must search for that "harmony in opposites," so irritating to the Western mind.

Leadership is not a game for ideologues—at least not today.

To manage any institution in periods of intensified change, a leader should be aware that these great surging currents of human aspirations will still toss his ship about. In taking initial steps toward rectifying the deplorable effects of past social discrimination, a pioneer will be accused of tokenism. If this causes him to hesitate, he will meet the charge of chauvinism. There is no room for ideologues today.

In making the adaptations necessary, leaders will have to examine which profile of the three principles of competition, cooperation, and innovation is best for a particular situation, internal or external to their institutions. Multiplication of the constituencies of every manager will make this choice more difficult than it was in the past, and explanations of why a particular choice is made will have to face new, larger, and more critical audiences.

The two essential requirements for a successful man-of-affairs still remain: (1) he must be *positive* about what he wants to do, and (2) he must be able to explain what he wants to do both to potential allies and to hostile critics. Those tests of leadership will be with us for a long, long time.

Management in the "Learning" Society

We do not "know it all"; and know we never can. The race between incessant demands to act and our enclaves of ignorance calls for that condition of mingled curiosity and faith in the power of knowledge which we call "learning."

It is hard enough for an individual, but when institutions themselves are told they must learn, we are carried beyond frontiers of optimism and common sense. Institutions are created by humans, and when we use the metaphor of "education of an institution" we mean that the individuals who give allegiance to it undergo a transformation under the guidance of enlightened leaders.

Revolutionists, of course, believe this to be absurd or impossible, and seek ways to supplant existing leaders in order to seize their chambers of policy and instruments of discipline. Even the most cursory reading of history shows that revolutions are successful only when existing leaders demonstrate beyond doubt that they have exhausted their capacity to learn—in short, they could not develop new abilities to handle new types of problems.

Yet, as H. A. L. Fisher wrote in his *History of Europe,* "The fact of progress is written plain and large on the page of history; but progress is not a law of nature. The ground gained by one generation may be lost by the next. The thoughts of men may flow into the channels which lead to disaster and barbarism." The engines of history are leaders *plus* ideas. Leaders barren of ideas are caretakers; but ideas uncoupled to the will, passion, and skills of leaders are merely intellectual toys. Progress requires both, especially when new problems engulf an old bastion of success.

Today's leaders are faced with the most
obdurate and complex obstacles to progress . . .

Consider some conclusions drawn from a number of nationwide studies conducted by Daniel Yankelovich in the recent past. *More than half* our population now believe the following three statements, which represent a startling shift in attitudes of great significance to those in leadership positions throughout our country:

1. "You cannot trust statements made by leaders in our society."
2. "You no longer 'get what you pay for'." (unreliability, poor quality, service deterioration, deficient corrections)
3. "Environmental problems could be solved if those in charge really wanted to solve them."

Another survey of college students disclosed that a majority believe: "Hard work no longer pays off."

Were this array of beliefs to grow and be sustained, they would dissolve the social glue that has held our society together. What can one do to disprove or dispel these feelings? It can only be done by demonstrated performance over a considerable span of time, not by public relations tricks, which will be counterproductive.

. . . but they also have unparalleled resources
with which to overcome those obstacles.

Think of the available resources: an educated population, a body of relevant technology and science, superb methods of information and communication, and an economic base of proven capacity.

But resources themselves are not enough. Today's leaders must find new ways of combining these resources so that they become mutually supportive, rather than mutually disruptive as they now so often seem to be. Such new approaches will be found—if at all—by acquiring new perceptions of reality. Flight to the fantasies of nostalgia, of a "world that never was," will not do; nor will wishful thought without commitment.

Hardheaded men who have made their perilous ascents to leadership naturally possess unbounded faith in those structures and systems to which they owe their success. How difficult it must be for them to entertain heresies! But the undulant curve of human progress shows that the great ones can and do so—in fact, are remembered *because* they did. Whether in politics, business, science, education, religion, or war, their chronicles are illuminated by men blessed with "the seeing eye"—which penetrated the surface events and techniques of their time and caused them to rearrange old concepts and materials to break through rigidities they inherited. They were, admittedly, few, but they were enough.

The immodest purpose of this book is to assist in that "seeing."

Managers must be on guard against an overdeveloped sense of skepticism . . .

As healthy as skepticism is in stable times, it needs to be held in check when novel circumstances surface—at least for a decent interval of hearing. To offset this bias, statisticians distinguish two major classes of error in framing hypotheses:

1. Assuming *true* that which is *false*.
2. Assuming *false* that which is *true*.

The habits of a lifetime seldom allow a leader to make the first class of error, but can make him excessively vulnerable to those of the second. If one refuses to act on information or intelligence until it is absolutely proven beyond doubt, he will find himself constantly behind others in both tactical response and strategic innovation. The exasperating behavior of lower functionaries and officials here finds its roots: the paralyzing fear of being wrong. It is exactly the inverse behavior of the entrepreneur, whose driving force is the hope of profit by assumption of risk. Even law courts insist that only proof beyond a *reasonable* doubt be required for decisions.

Management in all periods must make decisions, which are choices made under conditions of uncertainty. But the uncertainty in our current situation has been magnified to such an extent that C. P. Snow reports a general malaise throughout the world, expressed as, "We know so much, but feel we can do so little." [1] Our information technology promises to let us know even more, but until these new floods of information are patterned by a human intelligence and coupled to courage, they contribute only additional loads for already burdened leaders.

. . . and must take a positive, integrated, multidimensional view.

Donald Schon states that every institution can be characterized by three aspects: (1) its *theory,* doctrine, or philosophy, (2) its *structure,* or relationships among its members; and (3) its *technology,* or the processes, tools, and materials it uses.[2] In the past, managers have felt they could treat each of these as separate functions without undue harm, but under today's conditions the three aspects all *interact* with one another. Simply put, a change in one puts stress on the other two, these stresses cause change with reactive effects on the others, and so on, in a continuous adaptation.

If Schon is right, the interventions managers make in altering their organizations must take account of all three dimensions simultaneously. A routinely assigned division of labor with severely partitioned tasks—which works so well in a factory—will produce disappointment.

Many of our present troubles can thus be seen to have their origins in great successes in one dimension whose propagated stresses were not matched or allowed for in the others. Whether in the international monetary system, urban renewal, new technologies in industry, new sources of pupils and teachers in education, taxation, military supply, welfare, medicine, transportation—on through the whole agenda of difficulty—rapid alterations in one dimension have not been matched by adaptations in others. "Seeing" an institution in this way, of course, is called "systems thinking," where one tries to improve the over-all operation, not merely one part of it.

But what do we mean when we say *"improve"* it?

*Central problem: selecting criteria of
effectiveness—and getting them accepted . . .*

This brings us to the antecedent problem of managing in a changing world: the selection of criteria of effectiveness, and securing acceptance of them by those constituencies that can assert a legitimate interest. Without clear criteria, the entire process of management becomes absurd, because a manager cannot rationally develop those objectives and goals necessary to lead large numbers of individuals engaged in a common effort. A manager without them must stand mute when asked, "Just what are you trying to do?"—or at least be unresponsive.

The stereotyped capitalist dismisses this with a mocking smile, "After all the bunk is cleared away, it's only earnings-per-share that count." Admittedly, such ice-pick concentration can often produce apparent miracles of short-term results, sometimes achieved by robbing past investments and mortgaging the future. But such a manager purchases his single-mindedness by confusing ends and means.

Profits are one means by which a society's larger purpose is served. They are one test of effectiveness—a harsh one, indeed—but they are a constraint, not an *end in themselves* from society's point of view. Profits are the igniters needed to fire the engines of private enterprise. They are both the test of past decisions and the spur to assume new risks. Also, research, development, and innovation depend on current profits for their support and furnish the strategic "cultural reserve" for future adaptation to changed demands and opportunities. Without profits a business fails, but merely having them does not make it a success in the eyes of increasingly powerful constituencies.

Long-term results, achieved in support of—at least without harm to—other objectives of society, are a far sterner test and one which now dominates the minds of business leaders. Yet the existence of fairly clear criteria of performance has accounted for a great deal of the vigor, responsiveness, and drive one finds in business management.

The large question ahead is how to maintain that vigor with an expanded set of criteria, of far less precision than profits. These, hopefully, are to be precipitated from the cloud of currently raging controversies over the dimensions of "public interest"—a murky phrase which now seems to mean something different to everyone.

Also, business leaders have found it extremely difficult—if not impossible—to have all of the persons throughout their organizations embrace corporate profits as a criterion of their individual effectiveness. Profit centers, decentralization, statistical surrogates of operational quality and efficiency, and other forms of incentives have proved very useful, but still cannot do the entire job. People now want—and need—to feel that their time and contributions have been put to worthwhile use, and seek daily reinforcement that their presence makes a difference. Employees petition not only "Treat me well," but also "Use me well, and trust me." It is here that new performance criteria may find their most fertile ground. Ansoff, Bower, Drucker, and Simon all offer take-off points for managers faced with this emerging attitude.

. . . and the problem is particularly difficult in nonbusiness management.

Let us leave the relatively crystalline world of business for a moment, and turn to other areas of management. What criteria of performance exist or are possible? We do not find—and cannot hope to find—anything like the litmus tests of balance sheets, but instead an enormous range that seems to comprehend every aspiration and anxiety known to human beings.

Demand for services is certainly no problem—in fact, most institutions are in conditions of overload, where simply handling each day's crises requires prodigies of energy. Both Boyer and Carey describe in eloquent detail the need for redesign in education and government, where many previous activities, acquired somewhat mindlessly, must be shed to lighten the unbearable loads which prevent innovations and discourage hopes for advance.

Certainly all must feel concern at Carey's estimate (see p. 69) that if present momentum is not arrested, perhaps one half of GNP in 25 years will be committed to governmental activities. The effect on capital markets alone of accompanying preemptive drains will constitute a social revolution of the most subtle kind, yet nonetheless authentic. We have had no experience in allocations of capital which were not, to some extent, "market-tested," with the possibilities of observing results and altering decisions, which is the only way to keep systems stable and "on course."

Until criteria of performance for nonprofit areas like education and government activity can be developed and accepted, all attempts to "manage" them—in the sense of purposeful control—will probably founder. The nonprofit sectors are now subject to *positive* feedback, where a deviation from intention produces *further* deviation in the same direction. This is the most unstable mode for any system—human, mechanical, or biological. When failure of a program triggers *additional* appropriations, and success *reduces* them, we have an inversion of the speculator's wisdom, "Let gains run; cut losses."

This pathology is well known to serious, dedicated managers in the nonprofit areas and dominates their concerns. George Schultz, in his capacity as the first head of the Office of Management and Budget, put it this way in a recent address: [3]

[There is] an overwhelming need in Government to have terminal facilities on activities or programs. It seems to be practically impossible to stop something once Government starts it. No matter how bad it is, it just keeps going. The only question is whether it should be bigger, but never whether or not it should just be eliminated. I think this is a problem that has been around for a long while and it certainly needs our continuing attention.

The fear of this sickness so paralyzed the heads of European governments in the nineteenth century that they refused involvement in anything not proven absolutely necessary to their nation's survival or to prevent domestic revolutions. Their evil was toleration of economic and social injustice; but the belated attempts of their successors to rectify undue postponement of reform resulted in the complete turnabout whose results baffle us today. When political candidates use quantitative lists of bills *introduced* as a measure of competence, we should expect legislative overload, contradictory programs, and government inefficiency. It is a melancholy political fact that making an old program actually *work* is not as glamorous as wrapping old ideas in new bills.

The age-old question remains: Who does what for whom, and who pays?

The last century's single criterion of performance in foreign affairs was maintenance of balance of power; in domestic affairs, maintenance of an uneasy equilibrium. And the *leaders* in these two areas felt that they performed quite well. But the slow revolution in rising expectations and the rapid revolution in industrial and military technology found them unprepared. We cannot turn to them for guidance—except in things to avoid. New approaches may have to be forged by the hammers and anvils of a dialectical process between those leading and those led; between those who pay for services and those who provide them.

When Plato was an old man, rich in experience, observation, and thought, he wrote *The Laws*. His compromised ideal for the best practical arrangement of power was: *personal* authority subject to *popular* control. It may still not be a bad place to begin in redesigning our institutions today. Personal authority is needed to fix responsibility and secure efficiency, but popular control is necessary to prevent tyranny. How that authority can be made legitimate and how popular control can be made operative without paralyzing leadership are the central questions of managing in a changing world.

Boulding's discussion (see p. 179) of "intersect" organizations illustrates one response, but an "intersect" organization *is* a hybrid, which draws its resources in the form of grants (personal or government) and disburses them in modes normal to business. The problem of control remains as unsolved there as in the original species which formed the hybrids.

One thing seems clear. A manager of any organization will not be able to function well if every decision he makes is subject to second-guessing and new performance criteria brought up *after the fact* by his constituencies, superiors, and people in his charge. That is a fool's game, but many are forced to play it today. It produces a disorientation remarkably similar to the effects of scientific "brainwashing," where a succession of unpredictable stimuli, of unpredictable intensity, finally disables the ability to perceive and act by destroying those purposeful cause-and-effect relations which a normal mind seeks and needs to remain rational.

Consider the constituencies which a president of a great university must somehow find ways to satisfy today: undergraduates, graduate students, minority groups, young untenured faculty, tenured faculty, his administrative people, alumni, foundations, state legislators, city councils, Federal grant officers, community groups and leaders, and his governor and mayor. Is there *any* set of practical goals, much less methods, which he can find to bring their legitimate concerns to some focus which can energize their contributions toward achieving those goals? If not, how can any suggestions or innovations be judged? How can his performance be judged by each of these constituencies?

The president presides over an institution at the center of a learning society, and his problems of management are similar to those faced by every other leader today. Only their constituencies differ.

When the old fashioned alternatives
(à la Machiavelli, or Luther) don't work . . .

If after-the-fact appraisal is unworkable, what alternatives are left?

A scholar might flee in desperation to Machiavelli, and try to play off each faction against another, but this requires a nimbleness and lack of principle, as well as ultimate powers of enforcement and discipline, not usual to leaders in our society.

A leader who believes he enjoys charismatic gifts might emulate Luther, and nail his personally revealed goals to the college door with this implication: "All who agree, get in; all who don't, get out." It is a course of great manly appeal, but he must be sure the best remain. This sort of behavior today is more likely to produce the reverse effect. Pascal's insight hints why:

People are generally better persuaded by the reasons they have themselves discovered than by those which have come into the mind of others.

Postures of history's great captains were appropriate when leaders were born to rule—an aristocracy's imperative—and iron discipline could be enforced. They are inconsistent with both the traditions and realities of our country where the "consent of the governed" is the legitimizing principle—never more so than today. That consent can only be gained by persuasion, and to secure it a leader needs a full armory of its weapons for the range of engagements in which he must contend.

As Churchill said of Lord Birkenhead's forensic equipment, he must have "the bludgeon for the platform; the rapier for personal dispute; the entangling net and trident for the courts of law; and a jug of clear spring water for an anxious perplexed conclave." Quite an order, but a lack of any one constitutes a serious handicap today.

. . . the only recourse is the planning process (with an overriding purpose) . . .

One remaining alternative to a state of random criticism of past actions lies in the use of the *planning process,* where agreement on *what is to be done* and *how its effects will be judged* is the overriding purpose. It is not safe to begin the arduous tasks of implementation of any program without establishing these twin beacons of decision. As a purposeful program cuts its way through the tangle of events and errors, continual reference to their constant beams allows all involved to fix their positions with an accuracy which now eludes us.

Planning is thinking ahead with a view toward present action and, when done seriously, is management's most demanding task. It is unfortunate that planning has become an antonym for democratic processes, but we should not deny ourselves its use because of a tyranny of obsolete controversy. Our present methods of "planning by existing momentum" are taking us to unwanted destinations.

At stake may be the survival and enhancement of real democracy, where the views of many voices are listened to with respect before a course of action is embraced. But an appropriate planning process must traverse a path atop the two slippery slopes of demagoguery and "consensus" management. The one panders to base instincts and grievances; the other settles for the least-common-denominator of agreement, drowning progress in lethargy.

A planning process geared to modern managerial needs will have two attributes: (1) it will not underestimate the intelligence of its participants, and (2) it will not overestimate their information. Much of the barren controversy we observe today flows from attitudes the reverse of these.

Special knowledge, techniques, and information have much to contribute, but without the nexus of a planning process on which to home, they are now consigned to arid journals, where barriers of langauge and readership make them ciphers in decision. Ansoff (see p. 38) shows how managers in the Post-Industrial Era can tap this accumulated reservoir in direct and relevant ways, and Drucker (see p. 267) contends that making proper use of the "knowledge worker" is one of the unsolved riddles of our age.

We can do better, but old antagonisms first must wither, and the joy of battle with long-standing adversaries must be forsworn. A temporary guide during our passage toward the Post-Industrial Society might well be that of experienced diplomats: "Treat every enemy as though he may become your friend, and every friend as though he may become your enemy." The price of luxuries like permanent allies and antagonists will soon be beyond our means.

Experienced men, rich in disappointments and poor in triumphs, will rightly turn skeptical eyes toward a planning process patterned after once-fashionable Planning-Programming-Budgeting systems. These philosopher's stones promised to solve all problems of previously intractable areas at one stroke. Their seeds of failure lay in an inability—or their elitist practitioners' unwillingness—to give appropriate weight to those nonquantifiable, but vital, factors in programs designed to deal with human aspirations and human nature. Of course they could not deliver, except in those limited affairs where only technological considerations prevailed.

Required, instead, are methods by which the neglected, but essential, *antecedent* steps of deciding *what* is to be done, before one turns to *how,* and securing wide consent as to the purpose of a proposal for improvement. Impatient men may be attracted to methods of *compelling* agreement, but history gives compulsion low marks for success.

. . . and not adaptation or correction through legislation (the old way).

Since de Tocqueville, foreign observers have remarked on a reflex in Americans to remedy any and all ills with rapid, specific legislation. "There ought to be a law!" is the citizen's initial outburst in situations where his interests are harmed or frustrated. The edifice of our law is a marvelous collective accomplishment, a monument to generations of its thinkers and practitioners, a shield for rights dearly purchased. But the law's roots are found in *sanctions,* and make it too rough an instrument for the cultivation of the kind of progressive planning processes and managerial systems we need today.

As Holmes said, "If you want to know the law, and nothing else, you must look at it as a bad man," but we now need forms and guides which can mobilize the creative energies of *good* men. We can no longer take those energies for granted and see the task of progress as one of constraining them. B. H. Liddell-Hart analyzed what he called "The Fallacy of Compulsion" [4] in the following lines:

We learn from history that the compulsory principle always breaks down in practice. It is practicable to *prevent* men doing something; moreover that principle of restraint, or regulation, is essentially justifiable insofar as its application is needed to check interference with others' freedom. But it is not, in reality, possible to *make* men do something without risking more than is gained from the compelled effort. The method may appear practicable, because it often works when applied to those who are merely hesitant. When applied to those who are definitely unwilling it fails, however, because it generates friction and fosters subtle forms of evasion that spoil the effect which is sought. The test of whether a principle works is to be found in the product.

Efficiency springs from enthusiasm—because this alone can develop a dynamic impulse. Enthusiasm is incompatible with compulsion—because it is essentially spontaneous. Compulsion is thus bound to deaden enthusiasm—because it dries up the source. The more an individual, or a nation, has been accustomed to freedom, the more deadening will be the effect of a change to compulsion.

The harsh realism of this passage gives clues as to why hopes of social progress based solely on legislative acts are so often disappointed in their implementation. Managers of our institutions should not expect to find the primary solution to their problems primarily on the legal path. Much can be done in rearrangements of existing legal relationships, such as Carey (see p. 85) proposes for the tangle of eighty thousand local and state governments—and the task is awesome. But these rearrangements and rationalizations can at the most only set up the conditions for enthusiasm and new ideas to flourish, not guarantee them.

One remarkable aspect of the following chapters is their lack of emphasis on adaptation through legislation. Until the recent past, legislative issues and their attendant factional slogans would have dominated any discussion of programs for progress. Is this due to a collective disenchantment with a once-bright weapon that now so often breaks in the hands of those who try to use it in good causes? Or does it reflect a subtle, growing realization that it is far harder to *make* persons do the right thing than to *prevent* them from doing wrong to others?

Older societies tried to furnish positive motivation by inculcating the concept of *duty* in their members. But this was only successful in penetrating the layers of those trained for—and usually born in—existing governing elites. In retrospect, we can see that it led to excessive conservatism, as the baton of "duty" was passed unchanged from generation to generation, continually raising the pressure for political and social upheavals. Our nation was born in one of them.

We must find another principle for our particular conditions and their future configurations. This may be the most important strategic problem confronting managers in the next decade or two: discovery of new arrangements, organizational forms, relationships, and processes which can persuade persons throughout our institutions to volunteer their minds and energies to purposes both they and society consider worthwhile. Drucker once defined the task of management as "to organize the work, and organize people to do the work." In our mid-passage to the Post-Industrial Society, the last phrase may have to be revised as: " . . . and *finds ways to get* people to do the work."

The Quest for Style

Appreciation of new motivational needs is found in Bower's chapter on business management (see p. 130), where the various ways managers present themselves to subordinates and colleagues—their choice of management style—greatly influence the behavior and effectiveness of their organizations. Styles once superbly geared to older conditions have become obsolete as the characteristics and special skills of subordinates have changed.

But managers are not professional actors; they cannot "try on" different roles until they get a good fit—at least, not without appearing comical. Buffon, the great French naturalist, concluded, "Style is the man himself." If he is right, a change of style requires a change in the man—or, at least, a change in the way he perceives himself and his people.

Much may frighten us, appear paradoxical,
but still be creative.

Simon's perceptions of how persons will adapt to the Post-Industrial Age may frighten, puzzle, or provoke many in leadership positions. His discernments, if correct, shake the foundations of traditional management practice, beliefs, recruitment, and motivations. Viewed from current perspectives, his findings appear paradoxical, but from another point of vantage they may suggest new exploratory expeditions for discovery of a new management dynamics. If so, it will not be the first time that a clash of two contradictory but internally consistent "logics" has set off a creative explosion.

Consider the effects if potential increase in status, conformity with higher authority, long tenure of employment with a single organization, and fear of failure all decrease as employee drives. What if the changes Simon predicts actually result in: (1) greater involvement with the job *as an experience in itself,* instead of as a burden tolerated for future promotion; (2) a desire for collegial relations; (3) an increase in assertiveness; and (4) a demand for supervision to demonstrate competence and cooperation rather than allowing it to rest on hierarchic authority? Who would want to—or could—manage such people whose motivations are so different from those assumed today?

Readers of Bower and Simon can see that existing management and post-industrial-minded persons are all searching for new styles, the one to adapt an institution to new conditions, the others to allow individuals a realization of new self-images made possible by those conditions. Some form of congruence of these two styles with each other is necessary if the social system of which both groups are overwhelmingly important parts is to maintain stability and achieve some progress—however defined. The examples from other nations in Drucker's analysis show how some of them are already attempting to work out such congruences.

Land of Promise or Slough of Despond?

A landmark in the history of ideas was that of Vico (1668–1744), who said for the first time: "The social world is the work of men." Today, we find the statement banal, but in an age when all events and relationships among mankind were ascribed to Divine Will, it was a notion correctly seen as heretical and dangerous. If society were man-made, then other men could remake it.

Here lies the foundation for the ideas both of human progress and of revolution. All later concepts of management flow from this view. If one embraces it, the effects can be ennobling or terrifying. When blame for existing conditions cannot be placed elsewhere, man himself must assume responsibility for changing them. Responsibility is the great developer of people, and managers *are* managers because they carry burdens of responsibility. *How* they carry them, dictates their own development and that of our society; what they *believe* dictates how they decide to carry them.

Will the managers of our institutions be commanders of ships, not rafts?

If managers of our institutions believe that responsibility is limited to keeping their organizations merely afloat on currents of change, they are commanders of rafts, indifferent to the fate or problems of other managers or institutions, and we should abandon hope for progress. If managers believe that their responsibility requires concern with how their organizations affect—and are affected by—the development of others, we stand a chance.

All managers will make decisions in the face of forces and events discussed in the following chapters. As Harold Lasswell [5] has pointed out, every policy decision involves five intellectual tasks, which may be done consciously or unconsciously: (1) clarification of goals, (2) description of trends, (3) analysis of conditions underlying the trends, (4) projection of future developments, and (5) invention, evaluation, and selection of alternative courses of action.

No book can choose goals or select alternatives to achieve them—those will remain the central tasks of leadership—but other aspects of decision making supporting those tasks will be found in abundance in the following pages, touching most concerns of managerial life in our society. McHale's graphic presentations, for example, offer a source of future reference for anyone in need of "Maps for the Mind" in matching a proposed decision against past and future trends.

Can good men find ways to combine their knowledge, energies, skills?

But someone who can be satisfied only by a handy list of "rules for success in managing the future" is best warned of the disappointment that awaits him. Cocksureness is not an attribute of these discussions. They intend, instead, to bring together in convenient form a great deal of information, ideas, and expert opinion significant to managers across the spectrum of our major institutions.

Future progress may demand that managers find ways to work together in guiding this nation's course along the strands of cooperation, competition, and innovation. A common appreciation of relevant facts, trends, and discontinuities would then be indispensable to any effective dialogue. Narrow-minded indifference would poison or prevent the process; but this country was not founded and nurtured by indifference, and narrow-mindedness has not been characteristic of our best leaders. Therein lies hope and promise.

It is one of history's ironies that evil men find it so easy to combine in order to gain their ends, and that good people have so often found it impossible. On whether or not good men find ways to combine their knowledge, energies, and skills may rest the future of us all. This book is justified if such persons glimpse even dimly some possible paths—not just one, because vitality springs from diversity, and exploration remains the most fruitful response to uncertainty. Frontiers of geography have disappeared, but those of management and society, delineated hereafter, are as wide as any adventurer could want.

Notes

1. C. P. Snow, *Public Affairs* (New York: Scribners, 1971), p. 202.
2. Donald Schon, *Beyond the Stable State* (New York: Random House, 1971), pp. 33–36.
3. George Schultz, "Improving Management for More Effective Government," 50th Anniversary Lectures, General Accounting Office, Washington, D.C., 1971.
4. B. H. Liddell-Hart, *Why Don't We Learn From History?* (New York: Hawthorn Press, 1971), p. 46.
5. Harold Lasswell, *International Encyclopedia of the Social Sciences* (New York: The Macmillan Company, Volume 12, p. 181.

Management in Transition

> The dogmas of the quiet past are inadequate to the stormy present. The occasion is piled high with difficulty, and we must rise with the occasion. As our case is new, so we must think anew and act anew.
>
> —Abraham Lincoln
> *Second Annual Message,*
> December 1, 1862

IN the next thirty years most organizations will be confronted by drastically new and unprecedented challenges, and there are management gaps that must be filled if we are to meet these challenges. The focus of this paper is on these gaps.

Has our management system, once so successful, become inadequate now?

At the outset we have to resolve an apparent paradox. During the first fifty years of this century, the challenges and problems that had to be met and overcome were formidable indeed, yet American industry did meet them, did elaborate and perfect a system of management that has been fabulously successful in creating national wealth. Why is it, then, that modern American management may not be adequate for coping with the new challenges?

The answer is twofold: (1) we are moving into a period marked by social challenges so distinct and different that it can be called a new era—the "Post-Industrial Era"; (2) modern management developed only over a long period of time—first it was learning by trial and error; then it accumulated enough know-how to become a practicioner's art; and finally it evolved, if not into a full-blown science, at least into a systematic technology. And we can expect a similar lag between the upsurge of a whole new set of forces and problems and the emergence of managerial techniques to handle them. That is, unless we anticipate today the directions in which management technology must develop to be ready for tomorrow.

But before we do that, we must gain a clearer idea of where we stand today and how we got there. Only then can we look at management critically and constructively—management, first and primarily, in the business firm and, secondly but with less detail, in the institution of higher learning and in other purposive (nonprofit) organizations.

Management in the Business Firm

THE RISE OF THE BUSINESS FIRM

The history of the business firm in the United States can be roughly divided into three distinct periods: the Industrial Revolution, the Mass-Production Era, and the Post-Industrial Era (see Figure 1).

Swift, Firestone, Carnegie, Ford—the
great entrepreneurs laid the groundwork.

The Industrial Revolution, having commenced in the 1820's with construction of canals and railroads, was vastly accelerated by a series of major technological inventions that eventually gave birth to the modern firm and the modern marketplace. At the outset, however, the social mechanisms for matching the technology to the marketplace did not exist. Most of the great inventions were brainchildren of talented individuals who, having given birth to new ideas, had no ready mechanism for converting them into reality.

This role was performed by the great entrepreneurs—like Swift, Firestone, Carnegie, Ford. On one hand, they identified the match between market and product and, on the other, marshalled human, physical, and monetary resources necessary to convert a potential match into commercial reality. These were entrepreneurial managers who focused on harnessing the vast strategic opportunities, rather than devote their efforts to elaborating structures or directing daily opera-

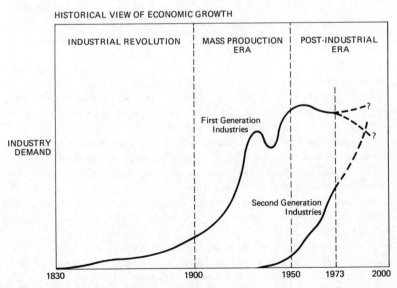

tions. They laid the groundwork for the profit- and efficiency-seeking social organization known today as the business firm.

In the following Mass-Production Era, attention shifted from strategy to commercial exploitation, to development of organizational capabilities, and to use of these capabilities to make profits. The period was characterized by several overlapping phases from production orientation.

From production orientation (Ford's "any color as long as it's black") . . .

The first, the *production-oriented* phase (in which Henry Ford I was the legendary pioneer), focused on elaboration of the productive mechanisms: purchasing, inventory control, manufacturing, distribution. The goal was to maximize economies of scale and to minimize the unit cost (and hence the price). The price was seen as the primary attraction to customers, who were hungry for goods, but not affluent enough to satisfy all of their wants.

The tools of the production-oriented phase were three: (1) standardization of the product, (2) subdivision of labor into most effective tasks, and (3) automation of production (substitution of capital for labor). Standardization reduced prices but also induced uniformity. In this production-oriented phase, the lower price to the customer was worth that sacrifice. Hence Ford's famous motto, "Give it to them in any color as long as it's black," which by the 1920's earned for him 65 per cent of the automotive market.

. . . to marketing orientation (GM's multimodel, multicolor strategy).

In the late 1920's growing affluence of the consumer began to rob production emphasis of its competitive edge. General Motors with its multimodel, multicolor strategy was steadily overtaking Ford. By the 1930's, shares of the market between Ford and GM had been reversed. Emphasis shifted to *market* rather than product orientation. Responsiveness to consumer wants and preferences, rather than to the lowest price or greatest durability, became the determinant of the success of the firm. Not long thereafter, the two viewpoints were integrated into a "total marketing concept," which sought balanced attention to both production and marketing.

The effectiveness of the total marketing concept began to reach its limits as consumer demand became saturated. Industry's answer was twofold:

(1) *Stimulate demand:* The consumer was now affluent enough to be able to replace his still usable car, refrigerator, vacuum cleaner, or clothes with new ones which offered convenience features, greater esthetic appeal, or enhanced social prestige. The introduction of annual model changes by General Motors in 1932 symbolized and triggered the era of artificial obsolescence;

(2) *Create new demand through technology:* Seeds of diversification were sown earlier in the century when firms based on technologically complex products began to build research and development laboratories. By contrast with the

Industrial Revolution, when inventions were made by outsiders, the laboratories internalized the inventive process. Their early focus, however, was on the improvement of efficiency, quality, and durability of the firm's traditional products. (Substitutions of artificial fibers for cotton and wool, synthetic rubber for natural, and plastics for steel are but a few examples of this trend).

The important departure came when R&D laboratories began, at the same time, to develop substitute technologies for traditional products and, also, to create new products and industries. (The birth of the electronics industry, and of computer industry, radio, and television, exemplifies this later trend.)

Shift of focus: from managing the firm to expanding its scope.

Throughout industrial history, acquisition of other firms has been used as an alternative form of growth. The pattern, however, has changed over time. During the Industrial Revolution, the purpose of acquisitions was either to increase market share through acquisition of competitors or to control production costs through acquisition of sources of raw materials. Around the break of the century, a relatively brief but violent period of financial manipulation and empire building through acquisitions and mergers evolved. This development led to a public outcry against "smash-grab imperialism" and resulted in the enactment of the original antitrust laws.

In the late stages of the Mass-Production Era, acquisitions became a tool of growth through horizontal integration—rounding out of the firm's product line. This direction was followed by a shift to concentric diversification: diversification into new industries which were related to the parent business either through common technology, marketing, or production capability. The philosophy of these largely *synergistic* acquisition phases was in contrast with the *conglomerate* phase that arrived in the late 1960's. Under the latter phase, relationship among parts of the conglomerate was almost exclusively financial. Synergy was held to be an irrelevant and unrealistic concept. The emphasis was on "creative financing," an attitude reminiscent of the trust-building days of the 1890's.

Some of the concentric acquisition activity and almost all of the conglomerates resulted in a major shift in the focus of top management. Whereas before the main emphasis was on growth from within, with acquisition being a secondary balancing or remedial activity, the new emphasis was just the reverse. Top management began to shift its attention from managing the existing firm to creating new horizons and expanding the firm's scope.

The mass-production industries give way to technology-driven newcomers.

The Great Depression undermined confidence in the self-regulatory mechanisms of the economy and broke the upward trend of the Mass-Production genius of the business firm. Then came World War II; a four-year hiatus in consumer goods production accumulated a demand which could not be satisfied out of existing capacities. For a period, the ability to buy a car of any color so long as one could get it shifted emphasis from marketing to expansion of capacity and enhancement of internal productivity (shades of the 1920's!).

By the early 1950's, however, signs of saturation again began to appear. The total marketing concept did less and less to revive demand. Accelerated product substitution through R&D became more and more the key competitive tool; so did expansion to foreign markets. (For an increasing number of traditional industries, though, not even these tools could stem a strong trend of saturation.)

At the same time, new R&D-based industries hungry for investment began to emerge, with rapid growth rates. It became increasingly apparent that a "changing of the guard" was in progress. Industries which were the chief engines of the Mass-Production Era were being replaced as growth leaders by the technology-driven newcomers. This shift alone would have been enough to cause a fundamental change in the problems and concerns of management. Sixty years of concentration on gaining the customers' favor through competition, of struggle for growth, and of increased market shares were yielding progressively poorer results and promised, at best, modest growth and profitability prospects.

Economic demand shifts were not the only signs of drastic change. The firm progressively had to confront a different world: expansions of the marketplace from nation-state to virtually global dimensions, accelerated rates of change, the threat of sudden technological obsolescence, different attitudes of consumers, the changing nature of the labor force, pressures of consumerism, and growing governmental regulations. The Mass-Production Era was drawing to a close and a new era was in the making. We shall look at the shape of this new era in another section. In the meanwhile, we need to appraise the managerial capabilities that developed in response to the challenges of the Mass-Production Era.

ACHIEVEMENT OF MANAGERIAL COMPETENCE

When, after World War II, U.S. industry began a massive invasion of the European market, the ability of American firms to outperform local industries had caused much local concern and puzzlement. An initial explanation, offered by both European and American observers, gave credit to the superior American industrial technology. Yet American firms seemed to succeed against competitors across a range of industries, only some of which were heavily technologically based. In seeking to explain this, the French journalist Servan-Schreiber argued that American superiority lay not so much in its technology but in a superior managerial competence.[1]

Individuals who have been exposed to management in the United States and abroad agree that the managerial capabilities of American firms on the average tend to be superior to those of European firms, and yet the average American manager does not appear to be a more intelligent or capable person than his counterpart. If anything, he is more likely to be narrower in outlook, less socially, politically, and culturally sensitive, than many of his counterparts. The explanation for the difference appears to lie less in inherent qualities of the individual and more in the culture which surrounds him.

A favorable social climate fed the growth of management efficiency.

Throughout the first half of the twentieth century a central characteristic of the American scene was society's commitment to the accumulation of physical wealth. The doctrine of political populism on which the Republic was founded found a congenial philosophical companion in the doctrine of economic populism. Formulated by an Englishman, Adam Smith, the laissez-faire doctrine, which asserts that social welfare is maximized when business is encouraged to maximize its profits under a minimum of external constraints, found a fuller acceptance in the United States than in its country of origin, or in other European countries. When a senior industrial executive said, "What's good for General Motors is good for the country," his remarks may have been perceived as indelicate, but they were not far from the popular consensus of the times.

This centrality of the firm greatly simplified the environmental perspective of the manager. His unique focus was to be on the markets and the customers of the firm, his attitude toward government attempts to regulate the firm's behavior was justifiably negative, and any concern with issues other than single-minded pursuit of profit was an unwarranted diversion.

The benevolent social climate made the managerial profession the most respected and aspired-to in American society—a situation unmatched elsewhere in the world. The best of national brainpower was attracted by the profession's prestige, its challenges, and its promise of high economic rewards within the prevailing social ethic. To be rich was both prestigious and righteous.

While social contrality of the firm and homogeneity of its environment encouraged a single-minded commitment to the "business of business," the prevailing growth ethic supplied a universal yardstick for success. To grow was both necessary and good; not to grow was to stagnate and die. Rationalizations for growth were many: economies of scale and hence enhanced productivity, control of market behavior through dominant market share, managerial motivation and growth potential in an expanding organization, and "critical mass" for research, development, and other investments made available through size.

Personal prestige, centrality of the firm, social endorsement of profitability, commitment to growth, and ethnocentric market perspective—all provided an environment highly conducive to development of efficient management practices in American industry.

Changes in the economy bred changes in managerial practices.

At the same time, the environment presented a number of absorbing challenges: the new directions needed when, as we saw in the preceding section, the focus shifted from developing mass-production technology through better use of

workers and of capital, to developing goods and services in response to consumers' wishes, and stimulating their desire to buy, and then to creating new demands through artificial obsolescence and new product development.

The major achievements of management during the Mass-Production Era were
the development of know-how and techniques for structuring, planning, super-
vising, motivating, and controlling the productive processes of the firm. The
crowning success was "the Miracle of Mass Production" in World War II.
Management was seen as "the art of getting things done through others," the
"others" being mostly workers and not fellow managers. As firms grew and
became complex, however, difficult and pressing problems began to arise in
managing managers: structuring, planning, and controlling managerial work.

The separation of ownership and management was successfully made.

One of the early trouble spots was the differentiation between managers and
owners of the firm. In the early days of industry, owners of assets were also the
key managers. As firms grew large and went public, ownership became widely
distributed among outsiders who bought stock as an investment and had neither
the expertise nor the interest in management. Management increasingly passed
into the hands of professionals. A twofold problem arose: (1) how to motivate
the managers to give their best effort to the firm, and at the same time (2) how
to ensure that these efforts are unselfishly devoted to the owners' interests.

The first problem was solved through development of a cultural norm which
may be called "surrogate ownership," which coalesced the managerial class, and
which effectively set it apart from the workers. When a new manager, after a
trial period, was given the symbolic "key to the executive washroom," and was
admitted to the "in" group, he was henceforth expected to treat the firm as his
own and devote all of his energies to the pursuit of its goals. In return, he was
rewarded with prestige, power, stock options, and bonuses—all of which were
tied in with continued success of the firm and hence reinforced his allegiance.
In the United States, this norm became so ingrained that it survived many years
of increasing managerial mobility among firms. In most Western European
countries and in Japan it has remained even stronger, since the manager still
typically spends his entire career in a single firm, as Drucker has noted (see
p. 246).

Solution to the second problem of ensuring that managers acted in the interest
of the owners was sought through a legal requirement for an elected board of
directors empowered and required to guard the owners' interests. Wide distribution of ownership in a majority of firms, the lack of communication between
directors and owners, management's control of information to outside directors,
the practice of packing the board with "inside" directors—all these factors
increasingly mitigated against this solution. Throughout the Mass-Production Era,
management increasingly came to exercise virtual control over selection of the
firm's growth thrusts as well as the conduct of operations. So long as the firm

operated profitably, the board and the owners had a minimal influence on the course of the firm. The board of directors stepped in and took control only when substantial and chronic losses were incurred.

Interestingly enough, this benign neglect of responsibility seldom incurred social or public censure against the board for allowing the situation to get out of control. It was not until the late 1960's and early 1970's, well into the succeeding Post-Industrial Era, that the liability of the directors was reasserted through a proliferation of stockholder suits.

The problem of large, heterogeneous, dispersed organizations was solved.

As firms grew in size and diversified geographically, management changed from a small, closely-knit group to a large, heterogeneous, dispersed organization. Three related problems arose: (1) ensuring uniform adherence to a common goal, (2) motivating managers through a far-flung organization, and (3) responding expeditiously to local problems and opportunities.[2]

A dual solution evolved through trial and error early in the twentieth century and became widely adopted. First, each manager was not only made responsible for the performance of his unit but also given sufficient authority and control to exact that performance. Secondly, this authority and responsibility was decentralized to levels at which the best information was available for proper and expeditious response to local challenges. The principle of authority commensurate with responsibility and the principle of decentralization of authority both became important and distinctive cornerstones of American management culture. (This principle does not have similar importance in either European or Japanese managerial cultures, which place strong emphasis on collegiality—a sharing of authority among several persons.)

Decision making was decentralized—even passed to staff experts.

The growth in the size of management was accompanied by growth and change in role of quasi-management commonly called "staff." The early function of this group was to collect, arrange, and transmit information on behalf of management, but not to participate in or to make decisions. Growth in complexity of operations and in specialized technical knowledge forced managers increasingly to involve staff and technical experts (legal, financial, engineering, public relations, etc.) in the process of decision making.

In distinction from the days of the Industrial Revolution, when a manager could justifiably consider himself expert on all important aspects of a decision, he was increasingly forced to use the expertise of others. Some observers have pointed out that this trend, together with decentralization, deprives top management of control not only over operational decisions but even over the fundamental strategic thrusts of the firm.[3] When this occurs, a coalition of technocrats takes over the decisions and leaves top management to "rubber stamp" their consensus.

(In fact, many firms have now reached the point of "management by technocracy." As we look at the scene today, we see that the role of top management in large firms has become increasingly ambiguous and less powerful; corporate staff have become the symbol of "lean" efficient corporate management; and goal setting for major strategic thrusts has been progressively delegated to lower management levels. Top management limits its scope to budgeting review, public relations, and management development.)

During the Mass-Production Era, abdication of strategic control by top management did not often spell disaster for the firm, but it did represent a further step in the loss of owners' control over the direction of the firm's fortunes. To the question, "In whose interests is the firm managed?" the answer became increasingly "In the interests of those who work in it," and less "In the interests of the owners."

Systematic arrangements were made for managerial work.

The decentralization of managerial control, together with the size, complexity, and geographic dispersion of firms, increasingly emphasized the need for systematic arrangements of managerial work.

Early progress was made in the elaboration of structural management through more explicit assignment of authority, responsibility, and accountability. The fuctional organizational structure, which first emerged in response to demand for internal efficiency of the production-oriented phase, was not adequate to the later demands of market responsiveness. So this structure was gradually replaced by the more responsive divisional form. As firms diversified abroad and as the environment became more dynamic, the divisional forms, in turn, were found to be increasingly inadequate. Various hybrid forms emerged, and as the firm entered the Post-Industrial Era, the appropriate and effective organizational structure was yet to be discovered.[4]

Systematic control of operations was augmented by budgeting and profit planning. After World War II, long-range planning and control and its simpler version, management by objectives, found increasing acceptance. By the mid 1950's, however, it became increasingly clear that long-range planning, which is based on an assumption of a great deal of environmental stability, would have to be replaced by more advanced forms of planning.[5]

As for the manager himself (as an individual), the dynamics of the Mass-Production Era offered a favorable environment for his training. Amid rapid change there was continuity. In a smoothly growing world, past experience was a reliable guide to the future. It was possible to train a manager by moving him upward through an organization. The problems encountered at any managerial level were likely to be a repetition on a larger scale of problems experienced earlier.[6] The over-all character of the manager's problem world remained stable for the length of his managerial career. His world was built on a stable technological base, known customers, a familial internal organizational structure, and a familiar, if dynamic, competition. The problems and surprises, the risks and the opportunities that challenge him, came from changes in familiar variables (sales, inventory, costs, competition) and not from structural changes such as a major influx of foreign competition or drastic obsolescence of technology.

Thus, in response to the challenges, American industry has been very successful in developing an effective manager capable of dealing with challenges of the Mass-Production Era. His profile can be described by the following characteristics:

1. He is profit-minded, relates all of his decisions and actions to the over-all profitability of the enterprise.
2. He equates his personal success with the success of the enterprise.
3. He is experienced and familiar with the traditional business of the firm and has developed a feel for the critical variables which affect the success of the enterprise.
4. His problem-solving perspective is primarily a technological and economic one. He has had little exposure to the political, societal, and cultural influences which affect business decisions.
5. Within his perspective, he is an incisive *convergent* problem-solver. He is quick to relate a problem to a previous precedent, to isolate the critical variable, to devise an appropriate solution.
6. He is preconditioned to prefer the familiar solution to a novel one, an incremental change to a large one, a familiar risk to a gambler's plunge.
7. He is a skillful communicator and leader of men. In exercising leadership, he is preconditioned to exploit the historical dynamics of the organization. He is skillful in timing the introduction of a needed change in the organization. He is a skillful crisis manager so long as the options available to him include familiar solutions.
8. He has only limited skills in solving novel problems which have no precedent in his previous experience. Nor is he skilled in leading the organization on major departures from historical organizational development.

Of course not every firm had all the attributes described above, or had the right kind of managers, or achieved dynamic growth. Some led the way; some trailed, oriented more toward comfortable survival than toward vigorous competition.

Now, as society moves into the Post-Industrial Era, these two classes of firms face different problems. The leaders will need to adapt, not because of past imperfections, but because of drastic changes in challenges; while laggards, if they are not to go down completely, will have to leapfrog the whole way from a conservative past into a turbulent future.

CHALLENGE OF THE POST-INDUSTRIAL ERA

During the Mass-Production Era, an outside observer of the firm would perceive the manager's world as relatively simple. His almost undivided attention was on "the business of business." He had a willing pool of labor (so long as the wage was right), and he catered to a receptive consumer. He was only secondarily troubled by such esoteric problems as tariffs, monetary exchange rates, differential inflation rates, cultural differences, and political barriers between markets. Research and development was a controllable tool for increased productivity and product improvement. Society and government, though increasingly on guard against monopolistic tendencies and competitive collusion, were essentially friendly partners in promoting economic progress.

From the insider's viewpoint, however, the manager found his life very complex, challenging, and demanding. Outside the firm, he had to fight constantly for market share, anticipate customers' needs, provide timely delivery of superior products priced below competitors, and ensure the retention of customer loyalty. Internally, he had to struggle constantly for increased productivity through better planning, more efficient organization of work, and automation of production. Continually, he had to contend with demands from labor unions for an increasing share of profits. He had to meet these demands and still maintain the level of productivity, retain his competitive position on the market, pay confidence-inspiring dividends to stockholders, and generate sufficient retained earnings to meet the company's growth needs.

Thus, it was natural for busy management to treat environmental changes, such as periodic economic recessions, inflation, growing governmental constraints, dissatisfaction of consumers, and changing work attitudes, as *distractions* from "the business of business," to be weathered and overcome within a basically sound framework of relationships with the environment. It took almost twenty years to bring about an awareness that such distractions signaled a fundamental transformation of society—the emergence of a new social era, which posed unfamiliar problems to the firm and thrust management into new roles.

The population is assured of economic wealth to meet its needs.

The most significant element is a level of economic wealth adequate to meet the basic physiological and survival needs of the population. The Mass-Production Era was uniquely focused on a *search* for this level of affluence. The Post-Industrial Era *is* an age of affluence. Here are some of its parameters:

1. The arrival of affluence casts doubt on economic growth as the critical instrument of social progress. Social aspirations shift away from "quantity" to "quality" of life. Industrial bigness increasingly appears as a threat both to economic efficiency through monopolistic practices, and to society through "government-industrial" complexes. Large enterprises are challenged on their change-resisting bureaucratic tendencies, their lack of creativity, their failure to

produce increased efficiency while increasing size. Acquisition of other firms is challenged on the grounds of bigness per se and not on the traditional antitrust rationale. Studies are prepared for dismemberment of giant firms. The growth ethic, which had provided a clear guiding light to social behavior, begins to decline. "Zero growth" alternatives are advanced, but without a clear understanding of how social vitality is to be retained when growth stops.

2. Realignment of social priorities focuses attention on the negative side-effects of profit-seeking behavior: environmental pollution, fluctuations in economic activity, inflation, monopolistic practices, "manipulation" of the consumer through artficial obsolescence, blatant advertising, incomplete disclosure, low-quality after-sale service. All these effects begin to appear to be too high a price to pay for the laissez-faire conditions of "uncontrolled competition." The firm is now assumed to be able not only to maintain affluence under stringent constraints (which only 20 years ago would have been considered fundamentally subversive and socially destructive) but also to undertake "social responsibility." Thus, one of the consequences of affluence is the loss of social centrality for the institution that created it.

3. Having "filled their bellies," individuals begin to aspire to higher levels of personal satisfaction both in their buying and in their working behavior. They become increasingly discriminating—increasingly demanding "full disclosure" about their purchases, demanding "post-sales" responsibility from the manu-facturer, unwilling to put up with ecological pollution as a by-product. They begin to lose faith in the wisdom of management and its knowledge of "what is good for the country." They challenge the firm directly through "consumerism" and put pressure on government for increased controls.

Managers begin to reject the role of "surrogate owners" of the enterprise expected to work for the "good of the firm." Workers begin to refuse technology-defined roles (no matter what the economic rewards) which are boring and monotonous, and which are not congruent with their new higher-level value systems.[7]

4. Satisfaction of survival needs, on the one hand, and an increase in discre-tionary buying power, on the other, produce fundamental changes in demand patterns. Buying attitudes change. Possession of material goods loses social prestige. The great American love affair with the automobile comes to an end. An increasing proportion of spenders are nonearners—the young and the old.

On the aggregate demand level, many industries that fueled progress in the Mass-Production Era reach saturation. These industries do not necessarily decline, but their growth slows down and their accumulated resources exceed their oppor-tunities for reinvestment. New industries emerge that cater to the affluent consumer—luxury goods, recreation, travel, services, etc.

5. As a result of its affluence, the nation feels that it can afford to turn its attention to social problems that remained unsolved, or were even caused by profit-seeking activity: social justice, poverty, housing, education, public trans-portation, environmental pollution, ecological imbalance. The private sector is

now called upon to perform a twofold role: (a) to restrain and remove its problem-causing activities (such as pollution), and (b) to take responsibility for positive social progress. New demands for social services create potential new markets, but they are not easy to serve because the government replaces the consumer as an intermediate buyer. Nor is it easy to make a profit in them, because they have remained previously unattended precisely because they could not attract profit-seeking capital.

6. Technology fundamentally affects both supply and demand. Triggered by wartime demand and made possible by postwar affluence, massive investment in research and development spawns new technology-based industries on the one hand, and brings about obsolescence in others.

(As an offshoot of the growth ethic, the Mass-Production Era spawned an "R&D" ethic: i.e., to develop and change products is to remain competitive, to restrain new product introduction is to stagnate. As a result, from the firm's internal perspective, technology becomes an "R&D monster," with a dynamic of its own, which determines a firm's growth thrusts independently of, and sometimes in spite of, the aspiration of management.) [8]

7. Aided by vast improvements in communication and transportation, the marketplace loses its national identity and becomes global. In addition to the pains of saturation, many of the mature industries in the United States (e.g., steel, consumer electronics, consumer durables, automobiles) find themselves confronted with a foreign invasion of their traditional markets. The pressure becomes strong to expand to foreign markets that have not yet reached saturation.

Initially (1960–1970), U.S. technologically intensive industries held a commanding competitive advantage and were presented with lucrative growth opportunities abroad. But in the 1970's some U.S. industries will be increasingly confronted with a disadvantageous competitive gap in Europe and Japan.

The manager faces a very different world full of vexing problems.

Thus, a manager who has been brought up in the Mass-Production Era, peering uneasily outward through the windows of the corporate office at the world of the 1970's, perceives a very different world full of vexing things.

It is a world which lost little of the original competitive complexity and acquired many others; a world of discontinuity in which it is dangerous to predict the future through reliance on history; a world full of novel problems and challenges for which past experience is a poor guide. In this world, the business firm has lost its Ptolemaic centrality. It is no longer the social sun around which revolve other less important planets. It has become a part of a Keplerian system of many interacting and independent planets.

To understand the world, new terminology and concepts are needed. The predominant emphasis during the Mass-Production Era was on *competitive behavior* and the profitable exploitation of the current markets of the firm. Externally to the firm, this behavior called for advertising, selling, distributing, purchasing;

internally, for managing production, controlling various inventories, maintaining motivation and morale of the organization, developing organizational and human capabilities, maintaining, expanding, and improving facilities.

In the background, another distinctive mode of behavior has been concerned, not with exploitation of the current business posture, but with developing and maintaining viable and potentially profitable relationships with the environment.

Externally to the firm, this behavior calls for setting the organizational objectives, determining the major growth and expansion thrusts of the firm, securing financial and human resources—internally, for developing new products, acquiring new physical, human, and financial capabilities; and, externally, test marketing and introducing new products/services to the customers. This interface maintenance and development behavior—we shall call it *entrepreneurial behavior*—received relatively minor attention in the Mass-Production Era. The major emphasis then was on competitive behavior.

New priority: not competitive behavior, but entrepreneurial behavior.

In the Post-Industrial Era, the relative importance of the two modes shifts. Vigorous competitive behavior remains essential and becomes more challenging and complex. Externally to the firm, new problems include coping with a disaffected and increasingly recalcitrant consumer, competing against foreign competition at home, penetrating foreign cultures and markets abroad, coping with complexities of international monetary, economic, and political barriers. Internally, it requires accommodation to the new values and aspirations of both the management and the labor force, changing the basis of managerial authority (and still retaining control of operations), redesigning work roles to make them fulfilling and satisfying, and retaining productive efficiency.

These changes alone would have been enough to strain and challenge managerial capabilities of the Mass-Production Era. But the priority shifts to the previously secondary entrepreneurial behavior. Saturation in many industries, birth of new ones, product proliferation, shortening of product life-cycles, expanding opportunities abroad—all make vigorous entrepreneurial behavior a precondition for success and a prerequisite for survival.

Growing noneconomic interactions between the firm and society require broadening the decision horizon to include not only economic (competitive), but also technological, sociological, political, demographic trends and variables. Within this horizon, the environment calls for an ability to discern discontinuities which pose threats and opportunties to the firm and to translate these into growth thrusts and skills to develop new financial and other resources. The accelerating rate of death and birth of both industries and products moves entrepreneurial behavior to the forefront of continuous managerial attention.

The primary focus is no longer on exploiting the firm's business, it is on *changing* the business, including products-markets-industries-technologies which no longer offer the best potential.

The manager must have a new set of organizational capabilities.

As one scans the list of the managerial capabilities of the Mass-Production Era presented earlier, it becomes apparent that major changes are needed to meet the new requirements of entrepreneurial behavior. The differences are in every element—individual skills, organizational capabilities, and value systems. A summary of the distinctive attributes for the respective modes of behavior is presented in Table 1. It suggests very strongly that the Post-Industrial Era requires development of a new set of organizational capabilities.

CAPABILITY FOR ENTREPRENEURIAL BEHAVIOR

The entrepreneurial manager is distinctive from his Mass-Production counterpart in the following respects:

1. He is globally profit-minded both in time and in space. His concern is both with immediate and with long-term profitability. He has no emotional attachment to the traditional business of the firm. All opportunities are to be weighed against the over-all profitability of the enterprise. He applies Alfred P. Sloan's creed: "The strategic aim of the enterprise is to produce a satisfactory return on the

Table 1. Comparison of Organizational Modes

ATTRIBUTE	MODE	
	COMPETITIVE	ENTREPRENEURIAL
Objective	Optimize profitability	Optimize profitability potential
Goals	Extrapolation of past goals modulated by performance	Determined through interaction of opportunities and capabilities
Reward & Penalty System	(1) Rewards for stability, efficiency	(1) Rewards for creativity and initiative
	(2) Rewards for past performance	(2) Penalties for lack of initiative
	(3) Penalties for deviance	
Information Space	(1) Internal: performance; External: historical opportunity space	(1) Internal: capabilities
		(2) Global opportunity space
Problem Space	Repetitive, familiar	Nonrepetitive, novel
Leadership Style	(1) Popularity	(1) Charisma
	(2) Skill to develop consensus	(2) Skill to inspire people to accept change
Organizational Structure	(1) Stable or expanding	(1) Fluid, structurally changing
	(2) Activities grouped according to resource conversion process	(2) Activities grouped according to problems

resources invested in it and if the return is not satisfactory, either the deficiency must be corrected *or resources allocated elsewhere"* (italics mine).[9]

2. He tempers his devotion to profitability with social awareness. He is a responsible citizen who does not believe that what is good for business is good for the country. On the other hand, he is clear-minded about protecting the primary wealth-generation purpose of the firm from erosion by unacceptable constraints or by diversionary or depressing activities.

3. He finds his satisfaction, not only in the extrinsic rewards of money and power, but also in the intrinsic satisfaction of creative managerial work.

4. His familiarity with his business firm is less on terms of what it has done and more in terms of what it can do: based upon its resources, strengths, and weaknesses, and the constraints on its behavior. He has a continuing interest in, and broad knowledge of, opportunities outside the traditional business of the firm.

5. His problem-solving perspective is broad: technological, competitive, economic, political, cultural, sociological. In the words of another paper, he is a man of many archetypal talents—entrepreneur, planner, administrator, system architect, politician, and statesman. (The difficulties of breeding this paragon

Table 1. (*Continued*)

ATTRIBUTE	MODE	
	COMPETITIVE	ENTREPRENEURIAL
	(3) Search for economics of scale	(3) Activities closely coupled
	(4) Activities loosely coupled	
Management Problem Solving		
(a) Recognition of action need	(1) Reactive in response to problems	(1) Active search for opportunities
	(2) Time lagged behind occurrence of problems	(2) Anticipatory
(b) Search for alternatives	(1) Reliance on experience	(1) Creative search
	(2) Incremental departures from status quo	(2) Wide ranging from status quo
	(3) Single alternative generated	(3) Multiple alternative generated
(c) Evaluation of alternatives	(1) Satisficing-first satisfactory accepted	(1) Optimizing-best of a set of alternatives is selected
(d) Risk attitude	(1) Minimize risk	(1) Risk propensive
	(2) Consistency with past experience	(2) Risk portfolio

of all virtues are formidable; perhaps group management is the only possible way to bring all these talents together.) [10]

6. He is a divergent creative problem solver. He continually searches for new alternatives; he is a habitual learner, quick to assimilate new information and isolate the controlling variables and devise novel solution procedures.

7. He is a skillful leader of group and organizational problem solving. Where he lacks personal expertise, he is skilled in the art of using experts.

8. His risk propensities are not biased in favor of the familiar, nor is he a habitual gambler on the unknown. He attempts to develop a balanced portfolio of risks commensurate with possible gain.

9. His leadership skills lie in inducing the organization to take bold departures from the past tradition.

The manager can only operate within a new organizational environment.

Just like the skilled competitive manager, the entrepreneurial manager can only operate within a conducive organizational environment. In entrepreneurial behavior, the design of this environment is focused not only on efficiency but also on over-all long-term effectiveness—not so much on strategic steady-state as on utilizing the best fields of opportunity open to the firm.

Some of the features of this environment are:

1. Authority based not on power but on knowledge, in which work is designed to the dual criteria of task effectiveness and intrinsic motivation of the individual.

2. An organizational structure which accommodates both stability of competitive behavior and fluidity of entrepreneurial behavior—a combination of efficiency-seeking bureaucracy and innovative "adhocracy." (The multidivisional, multinational structure prevalent today does not accommodate these demands; hence the search is on for new organizational forms.)

3. A decentralized substructure of "strategic business units" (a term used in the General Electric Company to describe such substructure) matched to the distinctive segments (demand-technology life cycles) of the firm's environment, with maximum entrepreneurial freedom for managers of each segment.

4. A top level corporate substructure devoted to balancing the firm's strategic portfolio of distinctive segments and to integrating entrepreneurial and competitive activities.

5. A surveillance system which scans the environment beyond limits of current business for major trends, projects these into the future, translates them into threats and opportunities to the firm, and injects this information into appropriate action points—a forecasting system, which does not assume the future to be an extrapolation of the past, but explores structural changes underlying current trends.

6. An information system which is rich beyond current operating data, which communicates up, down, as well as sideways, to link people according to common tasks.

7. A reward and motivation system which rewards both current profitability and imaginative investment in future profitability, which is tolerant of meaningful failure and risk-taking behavior, which builds rewards into the content of jobs, and which recognizes the changed personal values of both workers and managers.

8. A control system which is future-oriented, based on "remaining cost to complete and remaining performance to accomplish" rather than on historical performance.

9. A closely coupled entrepreneurial management system (similar to an extension of PPBS) to be based on entrepreneurial analysis of multiple novel alternatives, which matches planning, programming, budgeting, implementation, and control into a coherent whole.

10. A career-long management development system which combines career planning, job rotation, and education, which is married neither to promotion from within nor hiring from without, and which develops managers through exposure both to the current operations and to the opportunities and challenges of the unfolding socio-political-cultural environment.

We have just looked at an aggregate description of entrepreneurial management. A more detailed analysis is presented in Table 2, where the profile of entrepreneurial management is compared with the profile of competitive management developed during the Mass-Production Era.

The comparison suggests that the two profiles are indeed very different, and that a major capability-building task is ahead for firms entering the Post-Industrial Era where the emphasis is on enterpreneurial behavior.

Management must grow, expand—must manage management.

But beyond the problem of building the capability, lie equally different problems of accommodation and integration. Successful managements of the Mass-Production Era were built on the minimal-management principle, with managerial capacity just adequate to accommodate demands of competitive behavior. The addition of entrepreneurial problems requires a reevaluation of the minimal management concept. Experience shows that minimally managed organizations cannot anticipate discontinuities, cannot span them except through painful and lengthy trial and error. Entrepreneurial responsiveness requires much greater managerial capacity than competitive behavior, as well as new skills, both in line and staff. Thus, as new entrepreneurial skills are developed, management will have to grow and expand.

As this growth occurs, the two managerial processes—competitive and entrepreneurial—will come in conflict. In fact, the conflict occurs not only in management but also within the firm's logistic process. This conflict is familiar to everyone who has tried to introduce a major new product line to replace a previously successful one. It is a conflict of values, skills, work habits, risk attitudes, reward systems. Thus, a major managerial challenge will be to accommodate what has been called "bimodal behavior" within the firm.[11] The current emergence of innovative forms of organizational structure is one sign of search for such accommodation.[12]

Another sign is the observable reversal of the trend toward "rubber stamp" top management. The reversal signifies a newly recognized need for *integrative management,* which can only take place at the top, which balances, accommodates, and guides the coexistence of the competitive and the entrepreneurial modes. Even in the early stages of the Post-Industrial Era one can observe top management in leading firms turning from operational-type concerns, such as budgeting, toward new nonoperational concerns. Some of these concerns are balancing resource allocation between competitive and entrepreneurial investments, the selection of the optimal strategic portfolio of demand-technology life cycles, the development of managers, and new structures and systems for successful coexistence and cooperation of the two modes.

During the Industrial Revolution, top managers were lonely entrepreneurial trail-blazers; in the Mass-Production Era, they became coordinators of complex organizations; in the Post-Industrial Era, they are reemerging as influential entrepreneurs.

Thus, the greatly increased complexity of choices and the recent rapid strides in technology of management make nonsense of the minimal-management principle. In the Post-Industrial world, to skimp on management will be to invite disaster through loss of the firm's relevance to its environment. Maximal management, however, can invite equal disaster through sluggishness, inefficiency, and unresponsiveness. A major focus of the early stages of the Post-Industrial Era has already become the *management of management,* the development and application of techniques or practices for efficient handling of the enlarged and expanded responsibility of management.

The question is: What is the ability of management technology to meet this challenge?

Table 2. Comparison of Managers in the Mass-Production and Post-Industrial Eras

MANAGER IN THE MASS-PRODUCTION ERA	MANAGER IN THE POST-INDUSTRIAL ERA
Values and Attitudes	*Values and Attitudes*
Surrogate Owner	Professional
Committed to laissez faire	Committed to social value of free enterprise
Profit optimizer	Social-value-optimizer
Seeks economic rewards and power	Seeks job satisfaction
Seeks stability	Seeks change
Prefers incremental change	Prefers entrepreneurial change

Table 2. *(Continued)*

MANAGER IN THE MASS-PRODUCTION ERA	MANAGER IN THE POST-INDUSTRIAL ERA
Skills	*Skills*
Experientially acquired	Acquired through career-long education
Familiar problem solver	Novel problem solver
Intuitive problem solver	Analytic problem solver
Conservative risk taker	Entrepreurial risk taker
Convergent diagnostician	Divergent diagnostician
Lag controller	Lead controller
Extrapolative planner	Entrepreneurial planner
Change control leadership	Change generation leadership
Action Perspective	*Action Perspective*
Intrafirm	Environmental
Intraindustry	Multiindustry
Intranational (regional)	Multinational
Intracultural	Cross-cultural
Economic	Economic
Technological	Technological
	Social
	Political
ORGANIZATIONAL ENVIRONMENT	ORGANIZATIONAL ENVIRONMENT
Basis of Managerial Authority	*Basis of Managerial Authority*
Surrogate asset ownership	Knowledge ownership
Power to hire and fire	Expertise
Power to reward and punish	Ability to challenge
	Ability to persuade
Organizational Rewards	*Organizational Rewards*
Rewards: Past contribution to profitability "Total profit awareness" Cooperation Loyalty	Rewards: Creativity Innovation Novelty Meaningful failure
Penalties: Failure Deviance	Penalties: Lack of initiative
Structure	*Structure*
Activities: Aggregation by function for economies of scale Aggregation by product for competitive response Entrepreneurial activity embedded in structure	Activities: Aggregated by task for entrepreneurial response Entrepreneurial activities segregated from competitive activities

Table 2 (*Concluded*)

MANAGER IN THE MASS-PRODUCTION ERA	MANAGER IN THE POST-INDUSTRIAL ERA

Power: Unity of authority-responsibility
        Structured authority
        Decentralization for competitive response
        Centralization for decision optimality
Roles designed for task effectiveness
	Power: Decentralization for entrepreneurial response
	        Strategic authority
	        Decentralization for job enrichment
	        Centralization for strategic portfolio control
	Roles designed for task effectiveness and job satisfaction

Information Environment	*Information Environment*

External surveillance: traditional environment
External information from competitive results
Internal information generated by incurred costs
Management information derived from logistic information
Communication: along authority structure
       results and problems upward
       instructions downward
	External surveillance: global environment
	Dedicated surveillance system
	Internal information generated by activities capabilities and skills
	Management information directly generated
	Communication: problem lines
	       opportunities and threats expertise upward
	       guidelines downward

Management Decision-Making	*Management Decision-Making*
Change absorbing Risk minimizing Triggered by problems Serial diagnosis Convergent Consistent with experience Incremental Sequential attention to goals Satisficing	Change generating Risk propensive Triggered by opportunities Parallel diagnosis Divergent Novel Global Simultaneous attention to goals Optimizing

Systems	*Systems*
Financial accounting Capital budgeting Expense budgeting Historical control Long-range (extrapolative) planning	Human resource accounting Capability accounting Capability budgeting Action budgeting Strategic entrepreneurial planning Forward control

CAN WE MEET THE CHALLENGE?

Having progressed from a practitioner's art to an experientially based technology, management now needs to become a science-based technology. The trial-and-error method of art has the richness of reality, but it is slow and does not lend itself to teaching. The system of abstracting from experience is faster and more teachable, but it is not applicable when the problems to be met are quite new, and planning cannot be extrapolated from the past. The new science-based mode, with its breadth of vision *and* its danger of oversimplification, offers the only hope for success. Let us look at it more closely.

Science-based management technology
combines statistical decision making . . .

The 20-year period following World War II witnessed a flowering of management technology. There were two primary stimuli. One came from the wartime development of a technology of complex decision-making called "operations research." Powerful analytic techniques developed for the planning of military operations supported a cadre of technologists who sought to apply their new skills to peacetime uses. The second stimulus came from a pressure from within business firms for better efficiency in meeting the economic needs of the times.

The resulting techniques were given the somewhat misleading name of management "science." It was not a science because it produced very few general theoretic insights either into behavior of firms or into management. For its so-called "scientific" foundation, management science used the basic hypotheses of profit-maximizing behavior advanced by Adam Smith back in 1776. To this, modern mathematics was added, particularly the new linear programming theory, probability statistics, and (to a much lesser extent) another new branch of mathematics known as game theory.[13]

This combination of disciplines was applied to a set of managerial problems which appeared accurately defined by these techniques. By and large this turned out to be a group of middle-management problems concerned with the movement and transformation of physical resources: inventory control, production scheduling, machine loading, goods distribution, and the selection of capital investment projects.

Toward the end of the 1960's, a welcome convergence began to take place between management scientists in academia and managers in industry. In its early development, the power of the scientific method to solve all managerial problems appeared unchallengeable. Management scientists felt that, given access to data and real operations, they could not only eventually solve all important problems, but also replace the manager-decision-maker in the process.[14] Naturally enough, this led to a conflict between managers and management scientists, the former being distrustful and apprehensive of the excessive claims, the latter perceiving the manager as myopic, unsophisticated, and unprepared to move with the times. Years of shared experience now appear to have led to a mutual appreciation of the role of management science in complex top management problem-solving as an important but auxiliary addition to the still important art of the manager.

. . . and application of behavioral science to complex organizational problems.

A second major postwar trend was in the application of psychology and sociology to the problems of complex organizations. More diffuse than management science, these applications have been somewhat vaguely titled "behavioral science." This trend is a curious combination of a search for broad scientific understanding and experience-based technology.

While management science continued to rely on the profit maximization hypotheses of Adam Smith, behavioral science has sought to build a new theoretical understanding of organizational behavior. While management science dealt with the effective performance of physical profit-producing tasks, behavioral science has focused on human behavior, usually to the exclusion of concerns with task-effectiveness.

At the individual level, theorists have dealt with such issues as personality, change, learning, motivation, attitudes, and leadership; at the group level with norms, interaction patterns, group conflict, problem solving, and leadership; at the organizational level with communication between groups, intergroup conflict, organization structure, and the effects of participation on performance.[15]

An early and unique contribution to an understanding of organizational behavior was made by Chester Barnard. In *The Functions of the Executive,* published in 1938,[16] he laid much of the groundwork for the modern-day sociology of organizations as well as for the emerging general systems theory. He described the organization as "a system of consciously coordinated activities," and dealt with the relationship between the individual and the organization, the limits of decision-making, acceptance of authority, the overlapping of work groups, and the role of the informal organization.

Barnard's work has been followed by many distinguished researchers. To date, however, few of the results have been redefined for science-based technology. Most of them are couched in a specialized language of sociology (and not of management), on levels of abstraction which make it difficult to translate them into practical prescriptive models of behavior.

Much more influential has been a branch of behavioral science, called humanistic psychology, which takes the view that an individual's effectiveness within an organization is highly dependent on his self-awareness of his potentialities and limitations and on his ability to understand and relate to other humans. A large number of experiential behavior-modification techniques have been developed, the best known of which are T-groups (for individual self-actualization) and organizational development (for group building). The trouble is that humanistic psychology lacks both explanatory and predictive powers, and it offers no consistent theoretical explanations.

Nonetheless, the behavior-modification technology found easier acceptance in American industry than did management science. With its emphasis on "practical outcomes" through relatively simple and readily understood steps, the technology was congenial to the pragmatic tradition of American management. It appealed to the gregarious character of American social culture. Nor did it pose a threat of management obsolescence. On the contrary, it promised full development of the individual's potential and enhancement of his work and decision-making effectiveness. (The American experience is distinctive from the European, where for historical and cultural reasons behavior-modification technology was viewed with distrust and suspicion.)

Behavior modification is modified—and married to problem solving.

Very recently, however, the popularity of the behavior-modification idea is beginning to decline. One reason stems from the fact that behavior-modification techniques have been focused on enhancing human attitudes and skills for what we have earlier called the competitive behavior of organizations—on cooperation, popular leadership, and compliance with prevailing social norms. As the demand for an entrepreneurial manager develops, it becomes increasingly apparent that an individual with a different behavioral profile is needed: an innovator, willing risk-taker, charismatic leader, self-actualizer, a loner who has the psychological strength to promote unpopular causes and live without social acceptance and approval.

A more immediate reason is simply that while this kind of "organizational development," as it is called, improves communications and organizational atmosphere, it usually fails to produce significant improvements in task-performance effectiveness.

The answer is just beginning to emerge. It appears to lie in a marriage of the behavior-modification technology with the branch of management science technology which concerned itself with techniques for rational (cognitive) problem solving.[17] The combination of the two holds the promise of a new behavior-modification technology that sets for its goal the development of integrated social-cognitive skills which will greatly enhance the decision making and problem-solving behavior of managers.[18]

PROSPECTS FOR THE FUTURE

As discussed in earlier sections, the advent of the Post-Industrial Era is characterized by the increasing interdependence of economic, psychological, social, cultural, and political variables. If management technology is to be responsive, a strong thrust toward a multidisciplinary approach is essential.

In the perspective of the preceding pages, it is apparent that both experiential and science-based management technology have lagged, rather than led, the priorities of management. They have helped managers solve their old problems better and more efficiently, but have not helped them to anticipate and prepare for new ones.

Such a lag is implicit in the nature of experientially-based technology, but is not necessary for the science-based. The lag of the latter has largely been due to the misplaced priorities of technologists, who, by and large, have sought a match between their scientific tools and existing problems, rather than seek out the important problems and develop appropriate tools. Put in somewhat exaggerated form, science-based technologists have been offering "solutions in search of problems."

The accelerating pace of change makes one fact quite clear: instead of lagging managers in the perception of problems, technologists must take the lead in anticipating them far enough in advance to develop solutions while the problems are still there to be solved.

Unfortunately, the economic success of the Mass-Production Era has produced self-satisfaction and euphoria among managers. The brilliant, if local, accomplishments of management technology have reinforced the scientist's conviction in the ultimate power of his method and have set up a powerful tendency to continue applying well-tested technologies, instead of seeking new ones. The bulk of the educational system today is focused on producing technology and training managers in the Mass-Production mold. There are stirrings of change, but how long it will take to move into the anticipatory and highly revelant mode of the Post-Industrial Era remains a major question.

Management in Higher Education

Peter Drucker has predicted that the Post-Industrial Era will cause the emergence of a society of knowledge workers. Daniel Bell contends that the university has replaced the business firm by becoming "the primary institution of the new society." Fritz Machlup reports that the production, distribution, and consumption of knowledge in America accounts for 30 per cent of the GNP. In addition, the production of knowledge alone is growing at twice the rate of the rest of the economy. The "industry" of higher education consists of 2,200 institutions with an annual revenue of $10 billion.

Faced with this new centrality, the institution of higher learning (IHL) is being forced to redefine its traditional role in society. For the past 200 years, universities and colleges have operated as closed systems, preserving a high degree of internal stability and deliberate *irrelevance* to the current problems of the environment. Frederick Rudolph, in his detailed history of American colleges and universities, referred to this policy as one of "drift, reluctant accommodation, belated recognition that while no one was looking, change had, in fact, taken place."

The recent tremendous growth and expansion in resource commitments to higher education, however, has created intense pressures for responsiveness to social problems. IHL's are being asked to perform their traditional functions more efficiently than before, to perform them for unprecedented numbers, and to accept new functions for which they have never been responsible (see Boyer, p. 150).

Yet traditional academic organizations have discovered that their capacities to respond to these environmental demands are inadequate. Years of incremental response have built up what sometimes appears as insurmountable inertia. Traditional decentralization of strategic decision-making authority has left chief administrators with little scope of influence for restructuring the institution and making it capable of effective response to change. This section will explore the reasons for this situation and discuss the managerial challenges which it poses for IHL's.

Management in IHL's has traditionally lagged both business and government.

In the past, both internal and external stability generated little survival pressure on the IHL. The need for management was minimal. As a result, there evolved a decentralized decision-making structure that was slow-moving and economically inefficient.

In the early organizational form, there was no separation of administrative functions from teaching functions. Whatever managing needed to be done was performed by members of the faculty. (When today many high-level administrators still teach.)

This organizational form was viable because of the simplicity of internal structure and low environmental survival pressure. The costs of maintaining academic organizations was a small proportion of GNP, and the sources of income were easily accessible. Great fortunes were being amassed, and universities and colleges became the recipients of large philanthropic donations. The value of higher education was unquestioned by society, so there was little or no attempt to subject the expenditure of funds to a market test. Within the organization, uncomplicated course schedules and small student bodies imposed minimal demands on management to be responsive to the needs.

In the final quarter of the nineteenth century, specialized administrative roles developed to handle increasing enrollments and the complexities of expanding curricula. Student personnel officers became responsible for the form and quality of student life; registrars began to cope with the massive paperwork which the adoption of the elective system imposed on the organization; and bursars became increasingly concerned with matching the organization's resources with its financial obligations. The attitude that the administration's role was to perform secondary service activity, rather than to give primary intellectual guidance, remained a basic characteristic of IHL's until the second half of this decade. Bureaucratic structure continued to expand in order to deal with nonacademic, administrative routine, but neither the nature of the adaptive response nor the role and the quality of management changed. Today, however, IHL's are being subjected to increasing societal and market pressures, which demand not only great improvements in economic efficiency but also major strategic adaptations as preconditions to survival.

Student disorders are symptoms of institutional
failure to keep up with the times.

The Free Speech movement at the University of California Berkeley campus in 1964 was the first indication that the cumulative pressures of external environment, coupled with the inability of the internal mechanisms to manage change, had produced a systems failure. Administrators began to ask difficult questions which they had long avoided. And the answers revealed that the students were not the cause of institutional disorder, but only a symptom of institutional malaise which had accumulated over many years. Academic organizations which had grown into widely decentralized, multi-constituency settings left little scope for the managerial influence that could lead them in adapting and responding to the pressures of the changing times.

It is ironic that some of the most prophetic insights into the problems of the university were offered by an administrator who would bear the brunt of the first student disorder. Clark Kerr, then Chancellor of the University of California, delivered a series of lectures in 1963 that was later published under the title, *The Uses of the University*. In these lectures he discussed some of the threats that could confront IHL's in the near future. Others followed, and so the early 1960's became a time of self-analysis and reflection, and the latter half of that decade became the period of trial and experimentation.

What did the administrators discover during this period of self-analysis? Basically they realized that IHL's had been overtaken by changes in the environments which they had neither perceived nor adapted to. Enrollments had skyrocketed. In the last decade, the number of students attending IHL's doubled, going from 3.5 million to over 7 million.

The IHL—a huge knowledge factory without
appropriate management technology.

The university was no longer chiefly responsible for providing knowledge in bucolic surroundings, but became huge knowledge factories with staggering budgets and monumental managerial inefficiencies (see Boyer's comments, p. 152).

Private universities encountered a widening gap between costs and available funds, and state universities were confronted with increasing budgetary pressures from legislatures. Available Federal support began to fall behind the demand for "soft-money" research programs, which had expanded rapidly in response to the needs of national priorities (defense, health, community needs), thus compounding the cost squeeze. Advanced management methods, such as program budgeting, seemed to be more useful for explaining causes of the ills than for finding cures. The complexity and inefficiency of growing operations, coupled with pressures for money-raising, increasingly absorbed the administrator's time. He ceased teaching and active research, thus becoming cut off from the faculty community.

His power for strategic decisions had also become severely limited. By their personal contacts in Washington, individual faculty members were able to attract hundreds of thousands of Federal dollars and thus commit the university to major strategic thrusts. Tenure protected the individual faculty member from administrative influence on the direction of his research and teaching. Thus, the power for determining the strategic thrusts of the university passed largely into faculty hands. A typical faculty's conception of its relationship to administration is that of a power conflict between bureaucracy and academic freedom. Attempts by the administration to influence academic affairs are regarded as an infringement on the prerogatives of the faculty.

Because of his primarily nonacademic pursuits, the administrator no longer had the time to spend with students and was, therefore, surprised and stunned when their discontent boiled over into confrontation. He had little power to respond on basic issues. Even if he had the power, he did not have the training. He was an "instant dean" or "instant president" or "instant department manager," often plucked from nonmanagerial, academic pursuits and plunged into complexities of administration that would frustrate the most highly trained manager.

*ILH response to crisis: train the manager,
use management technology.*

One important response is the growing concern with the training of educational administrators—in effect, management training. For example, both the University of California at Berkeley and the University of Michigan have centers for administrative research in IHL. Other universities have begun to sponsor workshops and seminars for college administrators. The American Council of Education has developed an internship program in which administrators with less than five years of experience spend nine months as participant-observers under the tutelage of a chief administrator on a campus other than his own. Most of the programs, developed with funds from the major foundations, have directed themselves to the present problems of in-service administrators. There is a parallel and equally urgent need to establish training programs for pre-service administrators before they are subjected to increasingly severe pressure which they will encounter on-line.

Within IHL's there is also a trend toward adoption of management technology from business and government. The increasing demand for accountability from state legislatures, the Federal Government, and the tax -paying public have necessitated more accurate record keeping. The program-planning-budgeting system (PPBS), instead of traditional line-item budgeting, is increasingly being used to satisfy both the public's need to know and the administrator's need for facts and figures for short- and long-term policy decisions. Computer simulation models have been an important development in planning for IHL's. An example of these models in CAMPUS (Comprehensive Analytical Methods for the Planning in University Systems), designed at the University of Toronto. The system simulates the interrelationship of major activities, considers a large number of variables, and then projects resource requirements based on the decision input of the programmer.

The proliferation of computers, EDP, systems analysis, PPBS, etc., have produced differing reactions. Many administrators suffer from "overkill" because of the towering amounts of data that these techniques are able to produce, and have questioned the need for such techniques. Very little attempt has been made to utilize these techniques for more than the clerical duties which they perform on most campuses. The trend is to accept them more for their vogue than for an insightful understanding of the sophisticated potential they have for providing relevant, vital information to high-level decision makers. Some administrators, like some of their counterparts in business management, are wary of allowing computers to do more than clerical bookkeeping and accounting for fear of the depersonalization of management.

Missing: entrepreneurial concern with the thrusts and nature of the IHL . . .

A survey of these responses leaves a strong impression that the predominant concern is with internal problems: accountability, cost controls, increase in operating efficiency, better resource allocation among existing programs, even divestment of some marginal academic and research programs. The management of these problems is within the power of IHL administrators, and the mass-production management technology offers many of the necessary tools.

What is missing is an address to the entrepreneurial questions about the thrust and nature of the university. Concern with the changed society and the university's role in that change is submerged in the reassertion of time-tested generalities—i.e., that the role of the university is to provide an environment in which each individual can satisfy his learning needs and find self-awareness, or that the role is to generate new knowledge. The crunching strategic questions that have caused riot and bloodshed on many campuses are avoided: *what* needs, *what* kind of self-awareness, *what* knowledge—knowledge to destroy the universe, to get to the moon, or to restore ecological balance? It has yet to be shown that the typical multi-constituency university of today has the abilities to overcome its collective inertia in coping with these questions.

. . . with one exception: the new and growing,
the democratic, community college.

Significantly, the new strategies are being developed, not in established four-year institutions, but in community colleges. Community colleges are extensions of the junior colleges which underwent an identity crisis in the late 1950's. Until that time, junior colleges tried to prepare those whose academic credentials were not sufficient for entry into a four-year institution with two years of college level experience. After 1955, however, community colleges began to look at what they could do best which four-year institutions couldn't do, and they began to concentrate on these areas.

Personal counseling and vocational courses became their main concern. The community college looked toward the community in which it was located and away from the four-year institutions which it had been trying to emulate. Courses for senior citizens, for secretaries on lunch break, and for high school drop-outs were organized. By widely enlarging entrance requirements and tailoring the curriculum to the needs of the community residents, the community college has become the most truly democratic of institutions of higher learning in America. As a result these colleges have been able to attract more and more qualified teachers and to upgrade the academic level of their traditional curriculum offerings.

Still bigger challenges face the beleaguered IHL in the future.

Beyond today's strategic challenges lie new ones in the future. The most obvious will be growth in enrollment, which will continue to increase at the same phenomenal rate of the past decade. University campuses will double and triple in size until they are forced to decentralize their facilities and give rise to Clark Kerr's "multiversity."

Rapid growth accentuates the already pressing problem of financing. Where will the dollars come from to support expanding facilities, new programs, and scientific installations? A report funded by the Carnegie Commission on Higher Education has observed that philanthropic and individual giving has decreased in the past decade. Larger foundations are allocating a higher proportion of their grants to social-need programs and cutting back on their gifts to IHL's. In addition, public reaction to campus disturbances has reflected itself in a legislative reluctance to increase educational budgets. Even without the reaction, the sheer growth and size of IHL's demands create pressures to contain them. While growth has been rapid, productivity increases in the education sector have been less than in any other sector of the economy. This fact, combined with a period of rising costs, means that the products of the educational system are becoming increasingly more expensive relative to other economic goods and services.

One possible answer lies in the capital-labor substitution made possible by advances in educational technology. The widespread use of educational television networks, the increased use of programmed teaching devices, and greater inter-institutional sharing of costly facilities should make higher education more capital-intensive.

However, IHL's still rely heavily on governmental support. The crucial question is the nature of the relationship between the IHL and the Federal Government. It is obvious that the Federal Government is the only institution available which has the necessary resources to maintain the current rate of expansion. An increased reliance on Federal funds has potential dangers for recipient academic establishments. To what degree can the national government heavily contribute without beginning to influence administrative decisions and thus subtly violating the cherished—and no doubt valuable—independence of IHL's?

Accompanying growth will be radically new products in education. Another Carnegie Commission report on higher education concluded that an increase in post-high school institutions below the college and university level will better serve educational needs than immediate accession to the university or four-year college. It should be made easy for an individual to drop out of the traditional four-year bachelor degree, as well as to return to it. Fast-paced technological society requires a shift of emphasis to continuing education from the present bachelor-master degrees. The latter should not be regarded as terminal points in individual personal learning careers, but only as milestones.

Will the present type of IHL fade gracefully
—or ungracefully—into obsolescence?

As noted, the administrative practice of colleges and universities has lagged far behind its business counterpart.

A benign environment, a peculiar institutional framework, and the nature of its technology, all combined to make the university a multi-constituency institution with widely decentralized strategic decisions and weak central administrations. The nature of the administrator's function was not conducive to the development of competent professional administrative cadres, similar to those in business management. The university evolved into what was, perhaps most successfully, an *un*managed cohesive and productive social organization. In this, it gained maximum freedom for the participating professional, at the cost of financial inefficiency and the inability for entrepreneurial response to social needs.

Much of management technology now available in the business sector can, and is, being applied to the university. It is, nevertheless, largely what we called mass-production technology, capable (within the peculiar institutional limits of the university) of improving efficiency and visibility of resource utilization, but inadequate to enable entrepreneurial response. Since the inefficiencies are so great and financial crises so pressing, there is a serious danger that preoccupation with financial efficiency will obscure the basic survival challenges which confront the university.

To address these challenges, the university needs to develop managerial capabilities that are not yet available in anyone's inventory of managerial technology. The central problem is not in educating entrepreneurial efficiency-minded managers, although these are needed. The problem is in restructuring the internal social fabric in ways that will enable the university to respond in nonincremental fashion to the discontinuities in the environment. It is not clear whether the solution will be found early enough to prevent the university as we know it today from being destroyed by violent confrontations, or whether the university will gracefully fade into obsolescence to be replaced by new and vital institutions.

Business vs. Nonprofit Organizations

Whenever an organization becomes so large and complex that voluntary cooperation and coordination among its members can no longer produce coherent and socially useful action, a need arises for an internal group devoted to the guidance and control of common behavior. In the business firm, this group is called management; in nonprofit organizations, administration. Over the years, each has created its separate art, technology, jargon, professional societies, and professional schools.

For reasons which have been explored in earlier sections, management has developed an image of the more professional, successful, sophisticated, and adventurous activity. Administration, on the other hand, has frequently been associated with routine, waste, inefficiency, and lack of responsiveness to its clients. Managers have had the status of respected, socially valuable entrepreneurs; administrators, that of wasteful unavoidable bureaucrats. Even as management is losing its "social centrality," there is an increasing demand for the application of "sound business principles" to straighten out "the mess in Washington," or in the ghetto, or in the city.

Business-management techniques have been advocated as the cure for the troubles of the government, hospitals, universities, and, more recently, the church. In some instances, such as in the application of PPBS to universities, the results are marginal; in application of the same technique to NASA's "race to the moon," the outcome has been spectacular, if not necessarily cost-effective. It is, therefore, not clear that indiscriminate transplantation of business management to other institutions will resolve or even address their important problems. An understanding is needed of the limits of its applicability.

In recent years, this understanding has become increasingly imperative. As society asks the nonprofit sector to address social problems in new and novel ways, nonprofit organizations increasingly need to exhibit entrepreneurial behavior not commonly found in administered bureaucracies. As an increasing fraction of social resources is diverted to "administered" institutions, effective application and efficient utilization of these resources become critical to national welfare. The peacetime cost-effectiveness of George Washington's army had minimal impact on the state of the Union. But today's $70-billion-a-year military-industrial establishment competes for resources with attempts to eradicate poverty, educational development, and improvement in the quality of the environment.

Is business management technology applicable
to other social institutions?

The purpose of the remainder of this chapter is to comment on the applicability of business management practice and technology to other social institutions. We shall look first at the comparative behavior of different organizations, and then at the commonalities and the differences of their managerial problems.

The business firm can be thought of as a member of a class of *purposive* social organizations, all of whom share these characteristics:

1. They deliver to society identifiable goods and/or services. They are rewarded for these in the form of sale price, university tuition, hospital charges, municipal water bill payment, and so on.

2. The goods and services are the result of an internal resource conversion process: "raw materials" are taken in (untutored student, sick patient); "value is added" to them by internal activities; and the final product is returned to society.

3. Because of their continuing need to replenish consumed resources, all purposive organizations need a consistently positive difference (called "profit" in the business firm) between costs incurred and the rewards received from the environment. If the difference remains negative for an appreciable period of time, the organization withers and dies.

The very fact that all members of a purposive organization (whether business or nonprofit) engage in activities directed toward a common output suggests that they pursue common objectives. The differences among organizations, however, are very significant.

In the *business firm,* the objectives are readily identifiable because they form the core of a common performance discipline. The focus is on the *outcome* of the activities, whether it be growth, profit, or market share. The performance against these objectives is measurable in quantitative terms and is usually measured through periodic reviews. New proposals for products, markets, or organizational changes, though not as easily measurable, are weighed in terms of their potential contribution to the objectives. A series of objective-setting techniques such as budgeting, management by objectives, and long-range planning is used in many firms. There are, of course, differences among firms in the extent to which they use the quantitative discipline of outcomes to run the business. Generally, firms that use it extensively are the more aggressive and successful ones.

The *nonprofit organization* resembles a less-aggressive business firm in its failure to use objectives as a management tool. The common agreement of the participants is not on common objectives but on the common *process* (e.g., curing patients, educating students, pursuing research excellence). Because nonprofit organizations are process-oriented, and because they lack quantitative measurements and techniques for evaluating outcomes, the performance discipline is usually lax and much less rigorous than in the business firm. This provides latitude for individuals to pursue their individual objectives simultaneously (though not always in accord) with those of the organization.

A case in point: the difficulty of applying advanced budgeting techniques.

Enhancement of the effectiveness of resource allocation, as well as of performance efficiency through the quantitative discipline of objectives, has been the principal aim of PPBS (see Carey on use of PPBS, p. 78). It is not necessary to resolve the parentage of PPBS (whether it was brought by Mr. McNamara from Ford Motor Company or by Mr. Hitch from the RAND Corporation) to recognize that the application of PPBS tries to put nonprofit organizations on a "business-like basis." The failures and frustrations of PPBS in the government has been used to suggest that the nature of governmental activity does not lend itself to performance discipline. The extraordinarily disciplined performance of NASA in its rush to the moon, as well as a number of other special projects, suggests, on the other hand, that at least some parts of governmental activity do lend themselves to effective goal-focused management.

Perhaps, also, the the failures should not be charged to PPBS but to the fact that the technique was planted into unprepared ground, which lacked quantitative information, skilled analysis, necessary authority structure, appropriate motivation systems—all of which made PPBS akin to a foreign transplant which was bound to be resisted by the recipient body.[19]

Particularly revealing is the recent, hardly successful, rush to apply advanced budgeting techniques to university management. It isn't that the university doesn't badly need fiscal discipline; but putting expenditures in order, when the income sources are threatened and the product is becoming obsolete, will neither remove the threat nor rejuvenate the product. It will merely slow down progress on the road to bankruptcy. In a firm whose product line is obsolete, if a choice has to be made (and it usually doesn't have to be) between controlling expenses and devoting energies to development of new products and markets, the decision would be clearly in favor of the latter. By contrast, universities today are spending much more energy on endowment management and budget cutting than they are on revitalizing their role in society.

This is not an altogether deliberate misplacement of priorities. Good and tested budgetary management techniques are still scarce and poorly understood. Furthermore, entrepreneurial behavior implies major and discontinuous change in the over-all direction of an organization. This behavior is difficult enough in strongly purposive organizations where management can exercise strong guiding authority. It becomes very difficult in settings such as the university where entrepreneurial decision authority on major academic thrusts is widely decentralized throughout the faculty.

Rather than interpret the emphasis on budgets as a deliberate misplacement of priorities by university management, the explanation may lie in the lack of skills and of techniques for leading a multi-constituency organization through a major strategic realignment with the environment. To preserve sanity, lacking the power to initiate the most essential action, individuals tend to turn to the next most feasible task.

One can visualize a spectrum of purposiveness, with the business firm and highly monolithic governmental organizations (such as the armed forces and NASA) at one end, and with multi-objective, "multi-constituency" organizations (such as churches and universities) at the other. In principle, the performance discipline of quantified management by objectives is applicable across the spectrum, but one would expect application to be easier at the "uni-constituency" end.

*The business firm and the nonprofit
organization must learn from each other.*

One can also visualize another spectrum along which purposive organizations can be arranged—a scale of environmental pressure. The business firm would tend toward one extreme, subjected to maximum pressure because of its primary dependence on market linkage and the higher intensity of pressure which that transmits, while nonprofit organizations would typically be under lower pressure to behave efficiently and to respond to environmental changes (with some notable exceptions, namely, NASA and the Post Office, which today are under greater societal pressure than many business firms).

Also, the question of cross-applicability of managerial capabilities is related to the organization's position on the spectrum. For example, a nonprofit organization that finds itself at the high-pressure end can use a high degree of business-like competence in both competitive and entrepreneurial management; but such competence would represent "overkill" in an organization whose environment permits steady unturbulent growth. The possibility of "underkill" is more real and potentially dangerous.

One danger is that well-developed and proven mass-production technology for handling marketing linkages may be inapplicable in an organization which needs to cope with its societal linkages. Thus, for example, techniques for influencing consumers through mass media have limited applicability in influencing budgetary decisions of the U.S. Government. Another danger is that, even when market linkages are at stake, competitive management may be applied in place of appropriate entrepreneurial techniques.

As we turn to the future, there is, on the one hand, a strong trend toward "publicness of private decision," as a result of increasing pressures on the firm through its societal linkages, and, on the other hand, a trend toward increased "privateness of public decision," as a result of pressures for entrepreneurial responses and for efficiency. As private organizations increasingly have to meet the societal test, public organizations will have to learn to meet the market test. The firm will increasingly have to cope with societal linkages; and nonprofit organizations, with market linkages. Thus, both will increasingly need to share the emerging Post-Industrial management abilities we described in earlier sections.

MANAGEMENT: THE COUNTERINERTIAL FORCE

Counterposed to the environmental pressure is an inertial tendency within the organization. It expresses itself in a resistance to change, a tendency to minimize response to the environmental pressures. Inertia is observable in all complex organizations, both profit and nonprofit. It is minimal in the birth stages when an organization is striving to establish and secure its linkages with the environment; it increases with age and maturity. It is more commonly observed in large organizations, but also appears in small mature organizations.

Its chief manifestations are a tendency toward routine, stable, or predictable behavior and the relaxation of internal performance discipline. A consequence is a low level of resource-conversion efficiency, such as is found in a business monopoly, a government department, or a university. There is also a tendency to stabilize interactions with the environment, to reduce environmental uncertainty, and to turn inward the focus of organizational attention. When this phenomenon occurs, individuals typically turn to the pursuit of personal goals, which often results in internal struggles and maneuvers for possession of critical resources, power, and prestige. Thus, a bureaucracy, which appears apathetic and change-resistant to its outside customers, may be a seething political cauldron within.

Because the business firm is under greater pressure and is forced to remain more active, its inertial tendency is less evident than in nonprofit organizations. One has only to observe mature entrenched monopolies, or firms in stable, slow-growing industries, however, to be convinced that nonprofit organizations do not have a monopoly on inertia. In fact, organizations show such a spread of differences in the degree of inertia and response to environment, both in the business sector and in the nonprofit sector, that there must be a very strong variable factor.

This variable is an internal *counter*inertial force called management (or administration). Management can affect organizational behavior in several different ways. At a minimum level, by increasing organizational awareness of the environment, it can control the "crisis gap" and enhance the probability of survival. Beyond that, it can increase the efficiency of internal operations, improve competitive behavior in the marketplace, and enhance the growth potential through new linkages with the marketplace. This role is accomplished through easily identifiable activities: setting of goals, anticipating changes in the environment, determining directions for organizational action, providing leadership, coordination, and assessment of action in pursuit of goals.

Key factors: (1) the applicability of
managers' skills to the particular culture . . .

There is a widely held view that the over-all quality of management is determined primarily by the quality of the managers. This view was valid in the
days when firms were small and simple. Today in large and complex organizations, good managers are still critical but are only one of the factors determining
the over-all quality. Of equal importance are the structure and process within
which managers work. The total organizational capability is a complex vector
of a number of different components, any one of which may be the weak link
in the chain. Thus, for example, outstandingly qualified managers would produce
bad decisions if given incorrect information by the system; they would produce
uninspired decisions if the reward system failed to motivate them.

Another view which is widely held, "a manager, is a manager, is a manager,"
shows that his skills are generic and applicable across industries and institutions.
A good business manager should be a brilliant success as a university president,
a hospital administrator, or a head of a government department. In Table 1
(p. 36), we saw that the requirements for managers' skills, as well as the
total managerial capability, change drastically from the environment of the
Mass-Production Era to the Post-Industrial Era. Dramatic failures of attempts to
transpose, without modification, American managerial culture to other lands,
support this point. So do case studies of mergers and acquisitions where the
managerial capability of the parent could not be applied successfully to the
acquired firm.

Thus, in addition to quality, the success of a managerial capability depends
on its applicability to the particular culture, technology, and problems and
challenges confronting an organization.

. . . and (2) match between managers' motivations
and the organization's reward system.

Within the over-all managerial capabilities, a critical contributor to success
is the match between personal motivation of the managers and the organizational
reward system. Since the economists have constructed the model of the profit-
maximizing manager, the perception by outside observers has largely been that
managers seek primarily money, prestige and power. The formal reward systems
of the Mass-Production Era were largely focused on these managerial aspirations.

Practicing managers, however, have long understood, and academic ones have
recently discovered, that additional and sometimes more powerful motivators
are a creative urge, a desire to make a difference, an excitement of risk-taking,
and the satisfaction of freedom to make choices and to act. As pointed out
earlier, the primary economic drives of managers are becoming saturated in the

age of affluence. New reward systems are becoming increasingly responsive to "higher" human aspirations. These freedoms have been greater in private than in many public organizations because of the traditionally larger degree of entrepreneurial freedom and turbulent environmental activity experienced by the firm.

A majority of governmental managers, on the other hand, have found themselves in strategically stable environments and in institutions with degrees of entrepreneurial freedom severely circumscribed by higher-level policy makers. The policy makers, while enjoying the power of decision, were frequently frustrated by remoteness from the "doing level" and an inability to control performance and take credit for results. Thus, both the doers and the policy makers have been denied the creative satisfaction of being "one's own boss."

It is only in rare project-oriented activities, such as NASA or the Manhattan Project, that entrepreneurial freedom and performance control have been combined in one organization. More typically, nonprofit sector managers enjoy this freedom only during the startup phases of new organizations.[20] Once the organization reaches maturity, opportunities for the satisfaction of creative drive become severely limited.

Paradox: increasing need for change, but increasing difficulty in effecting change.

As discussed previously, one of the characteristics of the multi-constituency organization is a relatively great importance of the internally granted authority, as compared with that which is externally conferred. In this lies one of the major paradoxes of the Post-Industrial Era. As the firm confronts new challenges, it must intensify its entrepreneurial involvement with the environment. This involvement requires a major counteraction of organizational inertia. But the basis of managerial authority is shifting from delegation from without to the internal "consent of the managed," thus increasing the inertia. The paradox, then, is that as the firm develops increasing needs for major changes, it will face increasing difficulties in overcoming resistance to these changes. The same paradox is already present in many bureaucratic nonprofit organizations confronted with new environmental entrepreneurial challenges.

In this connection, the convergence of problems and challenges among private, public, and voluntary organizations that we have observed throughout this discussion of purposive organizations may turn out to be a very favorable development—the convergence toward emphasis on entrepreneurial cost-effective behavior, on the one hand, and to more participative organizations, on the other. The hope is that all these types of organization will become increasingly alike, and will therefore be able to share and mutually reinforce emerging Post-Industrial managerial capabilities.

Management in the Future

We have been looking at the effects of society's transition to a new era. Such transitions seem to occur when familiar value systems lose their validity and different new ones emerge in their place. Typically, the social infrastructure that evolved and adapted in response to the old challenges is not able to respond to new ones, short of drastic structural changes and dislocations. Thus, the transition is an "age of discontinuity" during which the environmental stimuli and the social infrastructure are realigned.[21] The realignment is never peaceful, always turbulent, sometimes violent. Traditional organizations decline, or are destroyed, and new ones emerge in their place.

A managerial perspective on the current age of discontinuity shows three major stimulus-response conflicts which define the work of managers in the coming years:

1. *Conflict between the rate of environmental change and the speed of organizational response.* While the rate of change is increasing, size, complexity, and geographic dispersion have been reducing the responsiveness.

2. *Conflict between the discontinuity of change and increasing organizational inertia.* While the environment increasingly poses discontinuous challenges, the new basis of participation and reduction of managerial authority are increasing inertia and reducing the capability for drastic realignment of organizational dynamics.

3. *Conflict between innovation and strategic steady-state.* Successful exploitation of environment requires a pattern of organizational capabilities and a managerial culture which is significantly different from the needs of entrepreneurial innovative behavior. The Mass-Production Era perfected management of exploitative behavior. The Post-Industrial Era requires, not only a shift of focus to entrepreneurial behavior, but also a successful accommodation of both within a single organization.

In the business firm, in the institutions of higher learning, and in purposive organizations generally, the quality of management has been related to the quality of individuals that the respective institutions were able to attract. The business firm in the United States has been in a fortunate position as the central and most prestigious social institution. As a result, it has benefited from managerial talent that made the firm of the Mass-Production Era into an outstanding success. The sister purposive institutions offered neither the challenge nor the prestige of business. As a result, with brilliant exceptions, they had not had the benefit of outstanding managerial leadership.

The decline of social centrality of the firm in the Post-Industrial Era has started a "new ball game." We can increasingly expect the best young talent of the nation to turn its attention to managerial challenges of nonprofit institutions. The ability of the talented managers to influence their chosen organizations, however, will be limited by the freedoms for managerial action. These freedoms will be circumscribed, in part, by the historical development of the organizations, and, in part, by the environmental demands on them.

Historically, management of the firm enjoyed great freedoms of choice of the manner in which it related to the environment. The price of freedom was an almost total dependence for survival on the market forces. The sister institutions were both less free and less pressed by the environment, and, therefore, offered more limited opportunities for managerial leadership.

We must not let past successes blind us to future problems.

As the Post-Industrial Era progresses, past managerial successes in conquering challenges of the Mass-Production Era become a deterrent rather than a stimulus to progress. Developed nations, other than the United States, not having the benefit of our success (the French, the Russians, the Japanese), have less inertia born of past successes to contend with. If they are clear-minded enough to correlate our managerial hegemony to a past era, the chances will be good that they will focus their development on the new priorities and surge ahead of the United States. Perhaps the best act of self-serving chauvinism for the United States would be to initiate a massive managerial Marshall Plan—to inundate our friends and foes alike with boatloads of our mass-production managerial know-how while we focus development on management for the Post-Industrial Era.

If we were to do so, however, one major barrier, a major discontinuity in managerial know-how, would have to be crossed. Everytihng we said in this chapter about past managerial successes applies to *purposive* organizations. These are organizations which are *single-constituent* in nature: their participants subscribe (by volition, coercion, or seduction) to a common set of organizational goals. But our analysis has repeatedly suggested that society's trend is toward *multi-constituency* organizations in which the common intersection of individual and group objectives is diminishing. While multi-constituency organizations are well recognized in descriptive theories, practical approaches to managing them are almost totally lacking.

The most common approach is to reduce a multi-constituency situation to a single-constituency equivalent—i.e., to require diverse factions to agree on a common set of goals. But the experience of many community-action programs shows that this aproach leads to conservative, incremental, nonimaginative solutions that are unresponsive to demands of society. Hence, if social progress is not to be arrested and delayed by common denominator solutions, management art and technology will have to break out of its current uni-constituency perspective and move toward the much more difficult and challenging multi-constituency framework.

As society moves into the Post-Industrial Era, it brings with it the very impressive and successful management technology of the earlier era. Much of this

will remain applicable as we carry our problems from one era into the next. But
the past successes can obscure our vision of new problems, can invite us to rest
on our laurels and make us blind to the urgent needs for new technology. The
major practical and conceptual problems of management in the Post-Industrial
society—little understood, much less formulated—must be the target of our
efforts in the future.

Notes

1. Servan-Schreiber, *The American Challenge* (New York: Atheneum, 1968).
2. A. D. Chandler, Jr., *Strategy and Structure* (Cambridge: MIT Press, 1962).
3. John K. Galbraith, *The New Industrial State* (Boston: Houghton Mifflin, 1971).
4. H. I. Ansoff and R. G. Brandenburg, "A Language for Organizational Design," in E. Jantsch, ed., *Perspectives of Planning,* Proceedings of OECD Working Symposium on Long Range Planning, Bellagio, Italy, October–November 1968.
5. H. I. Ansoff, "The Evolution of Corporate Planning," SRI Long Range Planning Service, September 1967.
6. H. I. Ansoff, "Managerial Problem Solving," in John Blood, Jr., ed., *Management Science in Planning and Control,* Technical Association of Pulp and Paper Industry. Special Association Publication No. 5 (1969).
7. See *Business Week* articles on General Motors Fordtown Plant, March 4, 1972, pp. 69–70; March 25, 1972, pp. 46–49; also Judson Gooding, "The Accelerated Generation Moves into Management," *Fortune,* March 1971, pp. 101–104.
8. Hubert Kay, "Harnessing the R & D Monster," *Fortune,* January 1965, p. 160.
9. Alfred P. Sloan, Jr., *My Years with General Motors* (New York: Doubleday, 1963).
10. H. I. Ansoff and R. G. Brandenburg, "The General Manager of the Future," *California Management Reviews,* Spring 1969.
11. H. I. Ansoff, "The Innovative Firm," *Enterprise: Journal of the PE Consulting Group* (London), July 1967.
12. Ansoff and Brandenburg, "General Manager of the Future," op. cit.
13. *Ibid.*
14. Stafford Beer, *Decision and Control* (New York: John Wiley, 1966).
15. H. J. Leavitt, *Managerial Psychology* (Chicago: University of Chicago Press, 1964).
16. Chester I. Barnard, *The Functions of the Executive* (Cambridge: Harvard University Press, 1938).
17. See Ansoff, "Managerial Problem Solving," op. cit., and H. A. Simon, *The New Science of Management Decision* (New York: Harper & Row, 1960).
18. Andre Delbecq, "Management of Decision-Making within the Firm," *Academy of Management Journal,* December 1967.
19. Allen Schick, "Systems Politics and Systems Budgeting," *Public Administration Review,* March/April 1969.
20. J. G. March and H. A. Simon, *Organizations* (New York: John Wiley, 1958).
21. Peter F. Drucker, *The Age of Discontinuity* (New York: Harper & Row, 1969).

Contributors

Helpful comments and inputs from the following members of the author's panel are gratefully acknowledged (the author, however, assumes full responsibility for choice of content and interpretation):

General A. J. Goodpaster, Supreme Commander Europe, SHAPE
Ulric Haynes, Jr., Senior Vice President, Spencer Stuart & Associates
Saadia M. Schorr, Manager International Planning, General Electric Co.

The author wishes to acknowledge important contributions by James Lowenthal, who aided in planning the paper and coauthored the portion on higher education; by Robert Schmid, who collaborated on material relating to management technology; and by Larry Kugelman.

New Perspectives on Governance

THE managing of governments everywhere and in every time is concerned with *the usages of politics and power*. They are constants, while technique varies. To perceive public management as administrative technology is to miss the essence, because this does not have much bearing on the spirit or quality of the governing process. As for the content of public management, if in this era of consumerism we were required to label it, we could quantify its ingredients fairly as 60 per cent policy (what to do, and why), 30 per cent execution (how and through what mechanisms to do it), and 10 per cent administration (support and facilitation). These proportions are not likely to change much.

Political governance fascinates philosophers, idealists, opportunists, and optimists. As a category of management it is part profession, part sport, part addiction, and part crusade. It has a property of adhesiveness: it is very hard to let go once one has grasped it. For all that, it is a kind of management unlike any other for the reason that performance criteria are troublesome to define. The incentives are subjective, the rewards few; and the punishments hardly ever fit the crime. It is navigation through the tricky tides of shifting values and ethics, and often quickly fleeting opportunities—the work of a variety of men with differing abilities and objectives. A man can be broken by it, or lifted above what he might otherwise be.

A paper such as this can only be a meditation on how the future of governance could turn out. We simply don't know. On the one hand, there are trends that persuade me that we are in transition to a vastly more difficult set of arrangements brought on by new forces, values, and externalities—that, to put it at its essence, the old rules of ordered governance are gone for good, replaced by dynamics that are likely to bring about turbulence as the normal condition of governance. This would write period to the age of stability in the relationships of government with parts of the society in whose name it is supposed to act. On the other hand, it can turn out that this is wrong—that, in the end, we will run the film backward and stop it at the point where we find something more to our liking.

There is only one possible position from which to analyze management in government, and it is on one's knees.

The demands facing governance in this
half century are new and formidable.

The eventual test of the managerial process in governance is its ability to satisfy—that is to say, its capacity to cope with the expectations, stresses, and perceptions of its tangled constituency. Its role is not merely to mind the store, nor to provide an institutional priesthood, but to *comprehend the potential* of the society and, thus comprehending, to construct and execute strategies which realize that potential within limits and safeguards.

With these assertions, which have been time-tested far beyond the point of being mere assumptions, the managerial demands facing governance in the United States in the remaining decades of the century are formidable, matching in scale the towering dimensions of power, abundance, and influence that constitute both our achievement and our vulnerability. (For some of the problems of affluence, see Ansoff, p. 32.) If government, in this context, turns out to be seriously flawed, the probability is high that the wrong uses of power will threaten all the propositions on which the system stands.

In groping to understand the meanings of the managerial transition, one can be certain only of the pervasiveness of uncertainty. But if one is stayed by that affliction, one will not think at all. It is not prophecy that concerns us here, but rather the play of light and shadow on governance in the afternoon of an exhausted century.

The Rise of Shared Governance

In the next two decades, the hitherto accepted distinctions between political governance and the governed will be less apparent. As much as from anything else, this will come from an awareness of these disconcerting realities: (1) that the hierarchical tradition as an organizing principle has feet of clay; (2) that governments can make apocalyptic miscalculations whose consequences are paid for by the entire society; and (3) that concurrent evaluation, assessment, and interposition by quasi-public groups and institutions are necessary elements of democratic governance.

What this comes to is the adjustment of American politics to the principle of shared governance. It will no longer be taken for granted that governments are licensed to act in the stead of the governed and at low risk of interference. The opposite expectation will prevail: that public consent is not to be presumed but to be sought. Election to office will not be a blanket license to govern, but an indicator of *conditional* confidence.

The people are acquiring a new power and a sense of how to use it.

If it is objected that this premise has always been implicit in representative government, the difference is that it is now becoming enforceable. The people as a whole are acquiring a new power of information resources and a sense of how to use them. Moreover, the melting down of long-cherished secrecy barriers surrounding the processes of policy planning can only strengthen the accountability of decision makers and enhance the penalties for official manipulation and cover-up.

Driven into the open, public men will have to heed the rule of the late Mayor Curley: "Do unto others what they would do to you if they got the chance, only do it first." They will apply that advice by employing the disclosure as a disarming tactic to build constituency support, thereby raising to a higher form the rudimentary techniques of the "background briefing."

A formidable influence for shared governance is to be found in the rise of organizations for social criticism, policy analysis, environmental conservation, ombudsmanship, and citizen advocacy. Rich in analytic capacity of new masses of information about the functioning of society and ingenious in employing legal, interventionist, and attention-getting tools, these organizations already command large audiences and lead new and motivated constituencies. Public managers cannot ignore them, and politicians play to them.

It is no exaggeration to say that such organizations increasingly supply a flow of thought, motivation, and perspective both to the political opposition and to factions within the controlling political party, thereby achieving leverage on policy outcomes. The Kennedy, Johnson, and Nixon administrations have all found it to their advantage to look to "task forces" of informed outsiders in shaping policy initiatives across the spectrum of national issues, and the "blue-ribbon commission" goes back even farther as a way to dredge for ideas.

All this makes for a sharing of power and the blurring of distinctions between political governance and the governed. Herbert Gans, writing in the *New York Times* of the "American Malaise," has put it very well: "Matters previously decided by fiat, consensus, or by the application of traditional values now have to be negotiated, and in many ways, America has become a negotiating society."

Information technology will energize
power-sharing within our democratic system.

But perhaps the most significant development likely to soften these distinctions lies in the advancing information technology.

The technical capability to process enormous masses of general and particular information, disseminate it, and obtain rapid feedback can only serve to arm the general public, groups, and individuals to influence public management. Until now, government's power has been partly a function of its advantage in this technology. Neither critics nor advocates have had the same advantage. Even Congress (possibly because of institutional fears and inefficiencies) has been left far behind business management in capabilities for assembling and analyzing data and information.

In the coming decades, technology will put enough information, and the facilities to use it, at the disposal of individuals and groups to equalize the cross-fire between political governance and the governed. Public opinion, whether in the large or managed by surrogate institutions and organizations, will have the means—if it elects to use them—to influence, enrich, and modify public policy choices. This same capability will make it feasible for independent policy analysis groups to mount a continuous watch on the performance of public managers, holding them to account in a style not possible before.

It seems clear that information technology does have these capabilities to energize power-sharing within democratic systems and to transfer power to the society. The danger—and a serious one—is that the rise of information-based elites and structures can introduce a new and overvalued currency into the trading market of political management. Information technology can become the new faith of an advanced and hyperactive society that is too ready to grasp at "integrated" technological mythologies which seem to promise a "zero defects" public policy system.

Coupling the capabilities for acquiring data and analysis to the new itch for the immediate resolution of policy problems, and recognizing the trend to pressure decision makers into responding within short reaction times, there is no assurance that information technology will produce consistently better outcomes. But it can be argued, and strongly, that the right use of information and analysis can lengthen and deepen policy perspectives and guide managers to systematic choices and social investments instead of the lunges and failures that pass for problem resolution in these times.

Public management, to survive, must forge new mechanisms, new institutions.

The combined effects of these influences will be substantial.

For each of the three elements of management—policy, execution, and administration—there will inevitably be a certain decrease of flexibility and a heightened pressure for decisions, implementation, and disclosure. Lead times will be shortened, as will reaction times, and unless anticipatory policy research in both the executive branch and in Congress is far better than we see it today, outcomes will suffer. The analytic base for deciding problems of choice will be more sophisticated, as will be the base for opposition and criticism. The traffic of negotiated policies will be more congested with structured interventions and coalition strategies; and the central role of managers will be keyed to balancing target priorities with counterproposals emerging out of power-sharing arrangements.

If public management is not to be brought to its knees by incessant and intransigent policy struggles, it must, in Curley's words, "do it first" and do it better with mechanisms and institutions for the synthesis of social trends and alternative goals. The designing and shaping of these institutions with features of openness, self-destruct mechanisms, independence, and accountability is the highest priority business facing the new governance.

Expanded Scope of Government Action

In his 1971 State of the Union address, President Nixon declared that "people everywhere are simply fed up with government at all levels." That remark sums up one of the dilemmas of political governance. Most Americans indeed are at or near the limits of patience with government's disabilities. They cannot fathom its objectives, accept its word, or see where it is taking them. The crisis of confidence in government's performance is not only felt by "people everywhere," but is a deep malaise of public managers themselves.

Paradox: The public mistrusts government, yet wants it to do more.

Paradoxically, despite low confidence in the purposes and performance of governments, the public will go on demanding that governments enlarge their spheres of action. They will look to governments for protection, incomes, jobs, housing, health care, education, technological innovation, economic growth, peace and security, price stability, recreation, and services of infinite variety. They will expect governments to anticipate problems and apply corrections, and to manage the social order by allocating benefits and satisfactions evenly.

As the nation's aggregate influence and affluence grow, and economic poverty disappears, the inequities and inequalities in the distribution of income, power, and wealth will become both more visible and less acceptable, and governments will be expected to correct for the distortions through targeted tax policies, subsidies, transfer payments, and other administered strategies for profit-sharing of the nation's earnings and assets. Moreover, there will be a growing awareness of the factor of scale in problem solving, an appreciation of the inoperability of fragmented tactics by jousting groups.

How much can government do, and do effectively . . .

The managerial problem (and one shared by legislators) will be to make some hard choices as to how much government can do, and do effectively. This is certainly not a new question. It is a more urgent one. There is no way that government can pile on an infinitely growing pyramid of roles and responsibilities without coming to a breaking point.

The likelihood is that the roles of the national government will partially revert to what they were at the start of the century: raising money, managing foreign relations and trade, providing for the national security, and administering a limited number of civil and criminal laws of nationwide applicability.

Beyond this, we should expect the central government to be even more deeply engaged in the more equitable sharing of wealth and productivity. In addition, we can expect to find it administering public-owned common industries such as telecommunications, energy, and transportation, as well as maintaining public corporations to intervene in industry groupings which fail to meet productivity and innovation targets in an economy committed to full employment with price stability. Finally, the national government in all likelihood will be the focus in a network of what Alan Pifer calls "quasi-nongovernmental institutions" for national and regional policy research.

. . . and what will it no longer be able to do?

To accommodate rising demands, government will be obliged to shed unmanageable operational activities and bureaucracies—to lighten its own bulk. It will have to get out of the grocery business, the bakery business, the hospital business, the banking business, the insurance business, the transportation business, the radio and broadcasting business, and the rest of the enterprises that it has accumulated mindlessly. This is of a piece with the current yearning to spin off baffling human and physical resources development responsibilities to state and local governments through decentralization and revenue sharing. By any name, it amounts to off-loading peripheral, as well as contentious, functions which are making a shambles of public management and satisfying not even the benefiting constituencies.

The tactics of divestiture will vary. Contracting for technical services, production of large-scale public works systems, research and development, and management services will be carried on freely. New institutional devices will be invented as service and delivery agencies outside the direct management of governments, and funded circuitously. Regional consortiums of governments will proliferate on a wall-to-wall basis to deal with planning, development, resource management, priority setting, regulation, and the achievement of economies of scale in public administration.

An index of the dimension of American government in the next two and a half decades can be conjectured from projections of taxing and expenditure levels:

1. Assuming that by the end of that period the gross national product will be around $3 trillion, and interpreting the intensity of demands for enlarged governmental effort, it is not unreasonable to estimate that not less than 40 per cent—and up to one half—of the GNP will be committed to public purposes or strongly influenced through aggregate expenditures of governments, contingent liabilities, subsidies, and credit guaranties.

2. More of the taxing system will be unitary, administered nationally, and backed up by social performance accounts. And much of it will be programmed on the basis of national and regional priorities.

3. Public debt will dwarf anything now perceived, with the Federal public debt in the range of $1 trillion and, to cite Murray Weidenbaum's estimates, new state and local government debt increasing by $50 billion a year by 1980.

As Weidenbaum puts it, "Increasing portions of available investment funds are being preempted by government credit agencies and are not available to truly private borrowers. Let us face it, this means an increasing socialization of our capital markets, which are such a basic element in the strength and durability of a private enterprise system." [1]

The pursuit of liberty is yielding to the worship of accountability.

Judged by scale alone, and disregarding the risks to a balance of public, private, and individual roles and incentives, this forecast begins to illuminate the dimensions of public management. It does not seem to disturb the universal serenity regarding priorities and alternatives.

To no avail, the 1973 Budget Message of the President warns that the budget is so overcommitted relative to revenues that by 1976 the foreseeable "budget margin" is a wafer-thin $5 billion. The Council of Economic Advisers' projection of the composition of GNP for the same five-year period shows that 98 per cent of anticipated GNP is already preempted by claims of both the public and private sectors. In reality, given the laws of political behavior, neither margin will exist when 1976 arrives.

One would think that a society so disaffected by existing priorities and performance, and seeing a growth of $500 billion in national wealth by the end of the decade, would turn its energies to the questions of how best to apply that growth in resources to overtaking the nation's potential—but not so. The social costs in the 1980's and 1990's of retrieving the remains of that potential are unpleasant to think about.

With people so paradoxically fed up with government and compulsively demanding more—one is forced to wonder what political ideology *will* hold sway during the onrushing decades. One edges to the belief that the ruling passion will not be the pursuit of liberty but the worship of accountability, in a system where government is extending its arc of influence constantly, but with its actions and motives ritually monitored and recorded.

If so, this takes us very near the rejection of the market system of pluralistic choices and toward the inevitability of macropolicies engineered through a collective but answerable instrumentality. This is what scale and its associated galaxies of management "systems" can achieve with encouragement or enough indifference.

Accountability, if it is without soul and spirit, may be the final, terrible joke. We have had a taste of this in the outcry over "wasting" money on underdeveloped countries and domestic social problems, while almost no accountability was being exercised over far worse waste in defense and subsidy programs.

Discontinuity: Defense Against Power

The idea of structured discontinuity as a societal defense against technocratic, administered governance has begun to be respectable. As used here, "discontinuity" means those arrangements that are meant to bring governance up short, to intervene in the political or managerial process for the purpose of altering directions, assumptions, and outcomes. (For discontinuity as a force in business management, see Ansoff, p. 34.)

In a sense, it goes against the grain to doubt the values of stability and regularity in the administration of government. Every right-minded bureaucrat prays to his ikon that his day may not be plundered by the unexpected crisis or the unwanted distraction. (When a Baptist convention, not long ago, asked for a meeting with the Bureau of the Budget at which the roles of that arcane organization would be explained, word came back that it was out of the question since it might set a precedent. Presumably, Catholics or Seventh Day Adventists might come around next.)

In the same vein, the whole thrust of managerial planning, forecasting, and goal setting is to reduce uncertainty, put first things first, anticipate contingencies, and grasp for order. All rational systems strive for these benefits. This chapter is itself a tract for reason and choice in ordering public affairs.

Yet if managing the uses of power and resources implies straight-line decision processes in the hands of small and unseen elites, society may have to invent an array of circuit breakers to ensure sensitivity and accountability.

Discontinuity is constitutionally respectable. The founding fathers openly built trapdoors and potholes into American governance. Robert Lovett once described this as the "foul-up factor." If that expression seems inelegant, let us speak more grandly of positive discontinuity. Either way, it is the same thing: the intentional curbing of power. In the constitutional sense it takes the form of representative government, separation of powers, federalism, and checks and balances.

For two centuries, more or less, we have gloried in these safeguards as long as they were confined to the area of mischief called politics. Business management, on the other hand, is supposed to salute the values of efficiency and execution, and we get very upset over the problems of "getting from here to there." Impedances are resented, unless they are thought up by the system itself. Even so, planned discontinuity plays a role sometimes. A favorite beatitude of the analytic decision maker calls for "keeping one's options open," for example. While this sometimes merely means stalling for time, more often it is a tactic to keep both friends and foes off balance and using the discontinuity to advantage in preparing to come in for the kill.

Society can defend itself by diversifying the "foul-up" factor.

In governance, the uses of discontinuity are on the side of enforcing sensitivity and accountability. As the public management system acquires bulk, technology, sophistication, and leverage, and as it systematically deals with problems of scale, it seems clear that society must defend itself by diversifying the "foul-up" factor. People will not have it otherwise.

When an eastern state was formulating a thoroughly enlightened public law providing government with a strong handle on the siting of nuclear power plants, the ecology advocates withdrew their support for the legislation because, on reflection, they felt that continued confusion suited their purposes better. They reasoned that their impact on final outcomes, in particular situations, would be stronger through opportunistic interventions and guerilla tactics than if they accepted structured participative roles under a steady-state environmental management process.

Another instructive lesson is found in the current mechanics of Congress. In 1960, Sam Rayburn, Speaker of the House, broke the authority of the Rules Committee by enlarging its membership and deploying power to a variety of legislative committees—a strategy of discontinuity. But in February 1972, when the legislative committee handling the bill to break the West Coast dock strike dragged its feet, the supposedly toothless Rules Committee suddenly preempted the bill and brought it to the floor for passage, thereby demonstrating that uses of discontinuity cut two ways.

Among many forms, the voluntary social-issue organization will be powerful.

In the up-tight governance that is headed our way, managed discontinuity can take many forms. Regional clusters of governments can be put together to set decentralized goals and priorities, and to wield an aggregate voting power in the Federal legislature. There can be a systematic "hiving off" of elements of public management into the "quasi-nongovernmental institutions" as contractors and grantees entrusted with the delivery of services and governed by user groups.

Still another form of discontinuity will be found increasingly in the array of voluntary organizations concerned with social criticism and issue forcing (see Smith-Dixon, p. 202). Broadly based, and financed through self-taxation of their members, these organizations have the corrective characteristics found in the roles of Common Cause and the National Urban Coalition. A number of them are likely to achieve enough political leverage to send members to the Congress and to demand representation in high positions in the executive structure of government. At the least, they will be in a position to influence the issues and outcomes of races for the House and Senate as well as gubernatorial and mayoralty elections.

In a very real sense, these organizations can evolve into something like a new level of legislative power on top of our traditional bicameral structure—an extraconstitutional species of tricameralism with functions recognizable in the late Nicholas Golovin's ideal of a "third branch" of governance focused on evaluation and assessment. Fortified by access to advanced information technology, and staffed to provide their constituencies with a steady flow of analysis and commentary on public issues, they are likely to be in a strong position to invoke discontinuity tactics.

*But what about the accountability of
organizations using discontinuity?*

With all this, there arises the question of the accountability of such organizations. It is very probable that a love-hate relationship could develop between them and the system of political governance—the specter of McCarthyism revisited—as the organizations grow to resemble subgovernments with large advocacy roles, and draw funds from government grants as well as from their adherents (funds that might otherwise go into the coffers of political parties and candidates). These organizations cannot expect immunity to retaliation, and the penalties can be swift and telling, as the foundations discovered in the 1960's.

Subject to such slings and arrows, however, these organizations have a major part to play in exercising discontinuity functions in the public interest. But, hopefully, it will be institutionalized for constructive purposes.

In the absence of institutions for the management of discontinuity, political governance could generate an excess of alienation which it could cope with only through coercive means. That is no small danger. Nothing is going to alter the proclivity of dense and crowded governance to accumulate a stock of errors, nurse them to the point of infection, and waste time defending itself against deserved criticism. Discontinuity, whether it takes the form of "throwing the rascals out" or a reasoned, structured institutional form of interventions and social criticism, will be society's best defense for that syndrome.

Discontinuity for its own sake and without a comprehension of its own power and limitations might go so far as to make inoperable the processes of political governance and bring us close to a no-decision society.

Venting Mechanisms for Managing Pressure

The scale, intensity, and mass of the system of governance in the last decades of the century, augmented by a social criticism industry geared up for practised discontinuities, will task public management to innovate new kinds of process arrangements. In particular, there will be a need for venting mechanisms to manage pressures rising to overheat the system—mechanisms with a potential for channeling the pressures toward citizen and group satisfactions.

To some extent, government has already flirted with ideas of this kind, though for other reasons. The governmental stimulus for voluntary action is a manifestation of government's attempt to regenerate personal identity through the involvement of individuals in value-oriented social services—a kind of market approach in which shares of public responsibility are distributed over the counter.

Voluntarism: the antithesis of the passive,
stupefied, potentially enraged public.

Voluntarism is a growing amateur industry induced both by ethical dilemmas and by the sense that society is consuming itself rather than renewing its basic strengths. It is a decidedly effective representation of a venting process that is made to order for the needs of governance. It is equally and fortunately a partial strategy for contrasting the values on both sides of the choice between coercive or managed public action and the open market for the circulation of social capital. And it is the antithesis of the passive, stupefied, and potentially enraged public that awakens to the discovery that it has been the victim of the Murphy game. Voluntarism has a high potential for depressurizing an overdeveloped and fed-up society. Tomorrow's governance is likely to make the most of it.

The statutory ombudsman: a resident whistle-blower empowered to intervene.

But venting will not be confined to voluntarism. Statutory ombudsmen will come to be stationed in growing numbers at the intersections of governance with citizens, to seek corrections to the misuse of power. This comes close to a referee process, a form of relief through administrative equity. As a venting device, it works to reduce the accumulation of felt injustices. As with other types of built-in discontinuities it acts as a circuit breaker, propagating the idea that the system is permeable and anxious to do the right thing. Compared with other strategies for discontinuity, ombudsmanship is internalized within the house of government, whereas the others are external and threatening. That is no small difference.

Governments are grudgingly prepared to set up ombudsmen on terms that are limited to putting things right when individuals or groups have legitimate complaints. But this is a long way from inviting a public-interest advocate to take a seat at the policy table.

Governments will be slow to escalate the ombudsman's role to that of a resident whistle-blower empowered to intervene or to inform the public of mischief being hatched. The mind boggles at the thought of injecting such a process into the doings of the National Security Council or the Office of Management and Budget. But it is not so unreasonable to think of an ombudsman in the role of a referee within the Corps of Engineers or the Federal Highway Administration to champion alternatives compatible with environmental goals. Nor will it be long until a "consumer" agency is created with powers of intervention in policy-making and regulatory matters.

One can visualize more extensive and legalistic forms of venting arrangements, some already showing on the horizon. Class action suits on behalf of groups thought to be injured by explicit decisions or general policies are finding their way to the courts, and class action law appears destined to develop within limits.

Over time, special courts may be needed to apply the law of class actions as this remedy becomes a primary strategy for public interest organizations.

Beyond class action, there is the possibility that government will be obliged to create arbitration machinery to deal with management malpractice claims brought against public officials. If insurance is now being written to protect physicians, architects, and other professionals against such claims, it is only a question of time until the concept of managerial liability is accepted as a device to bring the ethic of accountability down to ground level.

The range of managerial malpractice can be quite broad: the failure to budget enough to fund a legislative authorization; gilding bad news in a report to the nation; failure to reject a construction project in an earthquake zone; failure to enforce nondiscrimination provisions in government contracting; continued development of a military aircraft when overruns have canceled out the incremental or remaining costs and benefits; failure to correct defects in governmental installations which result in stream pollution; or unreasonable use of force in suppressing civil disobedience.

Renegade venting could burn out the linings of governance.

This notion of "venting" must be structured in some way, or it will occur in its own state of nature. If public management ignores the need for it, we are likely to find that a renegade form of venting will literally burn out the linings of governance through defiance and denigration of authority. To confuse the matter further, this process will have its own ethical justification, its own political morality.

Already the patterns are being seen as young bureaucrats crowd meetings of professional societies to debate the limits and meanings of risk-taking and the ethical issues of organization loyalty. It is taking form through wildcat groupings of agency professionals bent on levying criticism at their policy chiefs. It is seen in the frequency of "leaks" of privileged documents, and in intimations of the legitimacy of infiltration into organizations for the purpose of obtaining and disclosing proprietary information.

These bureaucratic "partisans" are waging a war of information from a sense of rage and a conviction that they are on the side of the angels, as they sometimes may be. But the trouble with such forms of commando tactics is that they can bring governance to a state in which there is no trust, and sickness spreads throughout the system, playing neatly into the hands of demagogues bent on witch hunts and coercion.

The importance of structuring mechanisms for venting is linked with the issue of how far governance can take a nation when confidence in its efficacy is low. The indications of 1971 of a public confidence rating of only 26 per cent in government's ability to perform suggests that the supreme management problem is to build and sustain a base of support without which governance is merely futile overhead.

The Potentials of Information Technology

The management of political power in the next decades will be affected strongly by the new information technology—its ability to acquire, store, process, transmit, and utilize data and knowledge. Max Ways, in his introduction to THE CONFERENCE BOARD's 1972 report on information technology, terms these capabilities "a new resource of strategic and international importance."

Management information systems are spreading like prairie fire through corporate, financial, manufacturing, service, and governmental institutions to meet needs for productivity, inventory control, financial accounting, forecasting, and policy analysis. Coupled with operations research and systems analysis, these capabilities constitute a whole new armory of managerial power. To imagine that traditional mechanics for conducting political governance will somehow be unaffected by all this is to carry optimism—or is it pessimism?—too far.

Information technology may be an exciting new resource . . .

Impulse, hunch, intuition, knowledge of political feasibility, and "feel"—the primary enzymes that influence public decision making—cannot help but be overtaken by these developments. We are leaving the age of sail in our political navigation. Choices rather than impulses will take us wherever we are going. But a distinction must be registered here. The point is not that information technology will *resolve* these choices, but only that it will clarify them and make it possible to perceive their risks, benefits, and costs with more knowledge and certainty. The choice itself will remain value-related, as it should.

The new technology is not going to eliminate the right to be wrong, but it will circumscribe it. Though far from completely cured, we will be less prone to take altruistic plunges into open-ended wars on poverty or foreign aid without first testing strategies and tactics. Social investment, in short, will come to be seen as not so very different from private investment, in the sense of calling for clear objectives, awareness of opportunity costs, and risk analysis. It will represent the expectation of social returns over time rather than quick profit taking.

This is a portrait, not of an insensitive, computer-ridden process, but of a society that implements its values within a more rational frame of thought.

. . . but communications alone are unlikely to make the good society.

When Max Ways eulogizes the new technology as an important and exciting "resource," one is moved to enter a reservation. Too much of what passes for communications is too ephemeral to be counted as a resource. Gross communications can be seen as a social cost rather than a gain, when one looks closely at the product of information technology. Far too much of the output depreciates to zero value upon exposure.

In the government sector alone the volume of waste information is stupefying. In thousands of political jurisdictions each year, armies of public employees go through the motions of preparing and submitting "plans" of every description—comprehensive, functional, multistate, metropolitan, etc.—which pile up either unread or unbelieved. Tens of thousands of pages, charts, graphs, forecasts, and analyses are produced at great cost, as part of the alleged management process, to be looked at (maybe) but seldom studied. Government files are filled with thousands of consultant studies, with additional thousands of pages, unimplemented and unused. Copying machines proliferate millions of pages of information that have a half-life of minutes. The burn bags daily immolate untold quantities of moribund "information."

In the same vein, the world of commerce is no better. It would be stretching the truth to dignify as a "resource" the pandemonium of messages that emanate from our new technology. James Dickey has told of a survey aimed at measuring the count of advertising images that the average American is exposed to in a single day, and the number turned out to be 50,000. To term this undifferentiated swirl of communications a "resource" is too much. The very word is an economizing one that implies conservation of a trust. It is the opposite of a technological tyranny that is destructive of the thought and perspective which humanizes and deepens man and his environment.

A rich possibility: a new system of national social accounts.

If the "resource" potential of information technology is not to be measured in the capacity to generate output per se, we must find it elsewhere. One contribution it can make is in helping us to know who we are and what it is that we are about. This is not a bad thing for a society that means well and has some awareness of its power and its contradictions. We do need to know who we are, and who our neighbor is, and the Constitution made provision for this. Computers do not alter the validity of gathering facts about ourselves and our condition. If we govern without knowledge we are likely to govern very badly, a lesson it has taken some trouble to learn.

In the governance of the coming years, the likelihood is that the same information technology and related skills that provided the concepts and systems for the national income accounts will create a new system of social accounts designed to track and measure changes in the nation's social product. (For use of information technology in the voluntary sector see Smith-Dixon p. 215.)

We have begun to experiment with the formulation of social indicators but not yet to use them as explicit tools for deciding priorities. For a society becoming less sure that greatness is measured by GNP, or the size and power of its defense structure, or the proportion of college-age youth receiving the blessings of higher education, or the annual increase in car sales, a system of social accounts is inevitable.

Even as cost of living changes are now plotted and read as avidly as football scores, government in the near future will have the information and concepts to report shifts in basic social indicators—rates of family formation and breakup, urban-rural population movements, utilization of leisure and recreation, creativity in the arts and humanities, scientific discovery, the decencies of aging and dying, access to health care, economic justice for ethnic minorities, and wider choices of food, jobs, and housing.

All this assumes that the society will care about these matters, and that the dominant values will match these implied objectives. We cannot be sure of that, but the assumptions of this chapter lie in that direction. Seen in this light, information technology does deserve the accolade of a "resource."

Whether information technology is used
wisely by public management or not . . .

The responsibility of public managers will be to view the social accounts, together with concurrent information sets, as perspectives from which to choose policy options. Information technology need not dictate the choices, but it certainly will affect them. Social accounts tend to sharpen and clarify gaps and needs, quantify the unfinished business, and say something about the effectiveness of existing programs in relation to these needs. Information technology then sets about sorting out alternatives through the methods of policy analysis.

But this exercise, no matter how necessary and valuable, can often be thrown completely off track by overemphasis on costs and benefits. Moreover, what is missing in this scenario is the foul-up factor, the political judgment or imperative which overrides and overrules straightline analysis. In the writer's three years of experience with the planning-programming-budgeting system (PPBS) and its pandemic output of information and alleged "analysis," he would have been hard put to identify half a dozen decisions that bore even a shaky relation to PPBS. (For more on PPBS, see Ansoff p. 55.) Moreover, the resistance to program analysis by appointed and elected officials of government was deep, enduring, and in a way deserved.

Knowledge can be a threat to political action as well as an aid in rational policy making. This truth is unlikely to be exorcised by new developments in information technology, although the riverboat gambler approach to policy making probably has seen its best days.

. . . there is little doubt it will both spread and concentrate power.

Whatever else can be said of information technology, there is little doubt that it will serve to both spread and concentrate power. Because information can lead to knowledge, hence to power, the avarice of parties, groups, and opinion sectors for information is likely to equal their grasp for cash and visibility. And the universality of telecommunications, including the affliction of talk shows and "nonstop radio news," means that the supply of information must expand to fill the capacity of the delivery system, if only for economic reasons. The politics of telecommunications has already forced parties and candidates to develop the fine art of position papers, depriving them of the flexibility to shift around from one audience to the next.

At the same time, specialized information and the skills needed to process it tend to generate elites and to concentrate knowledge in small groups. When program budgeting was decreed for the civil agencies of the Federal Government, its theologians were few and elitist, and they set about training disciples who regarded the unlettered as barbarians. The hierarchy of think tanks and foundations in too many instances display an arrogance of intellectualism based on a command of analytic technique. Leon Kass has warned, in the field of biomedical science, of the risk in oligopoly of extraordinary knowledge by a handful of men.

The danger is more than academic that, given shortening reaction times, pressures for fast corrections, and a societal compulsion for the resolution of disagreeable problems, policy management may exceed the capacity both for execution and for the digestion of feedback. For all the copious circulation of information, little of it may be hard currency.

NEW MODES OF DECISION MAKING

If public management is to avoid the splintering of power and opinion to the point where governance of any kind is frustrated, some new forms of planning and decision-making will be needed. Governance may find itself entering into coalitions for policy studies aimed at shared or pooled analysis, with enough lead time to produce agreements on choices and strategies.

Public decision making will involve
multi-participants and multi-constituencies.

Decision by panel can become a primary managerial technique, a more advanced version of the existing task force system, and one one that fuses policy, execution, and user inputs for decision-making. If this does emerge as an element in managing a more complex governing process, it will put a heavy strain on transitional adjustments. It will call particularly for new ways of blending policy makers, planners, specialists, and group representatives in associative processes to confront the meanings of information and the dilemmas they pose.

At the same time, it will create a need for a new kind of public executive, coached to manage multiparticipant decision analysis with all of the difficulties of balancing data with value considerations—a combined convener, referee, synthesizer, and manager. This is not too far from being a definition of the roles of the Presidential staff system in the next stage of governance, when the office itself will become less of a party prize and more of a prime mover of goals and priorities.

The complexity of managing in the new style will be deepened by the emergence of new constituencies and the displacement of older ones. As the power of familiar constituencies is reduced over time, government will find that it must deal with unstructured but potent constituencies that are new: consumers, internationalists, isolationists, ideologues, ethnics, populists, centrists, voluntarists, and humanists. (Ansoff makes the point that all management, within business, government, or nonprofit institutions, will have to be oriented to multi-constituencies, see p. 61.) These will not necessarily be distinct or countable constituencies, which is where the managerial problem lies. They will shade into one another, holding multiple memberships as their objectives merge. They will be hard to predict, sometimes difficult to locate, and transitional.

Precarious balance: between the negotiating society and the adversary society.

In this predicament, public management faces a hard task. It will have to experiment with ways to cope with fluid constituencies. It will find it necessary to communicate on multiple frequencies and evolve networks of consent. Otherwise political governance may be at a standstill. Enough stability must be secured to keep governance moving—a kinetic stability edged forward by workable syntheses of opinion. Thus, we will be balanced precariously between the negotiating society and the adversary society.

What this implies, in an era when problems of choice will be scaled well beyond today's bargaining ranges, is precisely this capability in governance to reach these syntheses—and that is taking a deep breath, indeed. We have not yet seen the transition in these terms, and we are not using our lead time well. We are congenitally conservative in staying with forms that are familiar and confirmed by usage. American government is built close to the ground, and its habit is to address the need for change in modest ways—reorganization shuffles, decentralization programs, and small reforms in technique.

Progress will be in the hands of a minority with special expertise.

What, then, can we hope for from political institutions in the way of action to improve readiness? The answer has to be that progress will be spotty and slow. This puts the trigger for change in the hands of those whose concern for effective governance is high but who are outside the political institutions. Industry associations, labor organizations, centers for political action and policy analysis, coalitions of concerned citizens, and intermediary institutions will have to serve as sources for criticism, pressure, and advocacy.

With them we can hope for a variety of men whose actions, essays, and commentaries can shape thought and action on governance. When Don Michael (*The Unprepared Society*) ponders the role of education in providing a generation of leaders and citizens better able to cope, he is seeking "an approach to educating a special cadre of intellectually and emotionally highly skilled people who thereby will possess necessary if not sufficient resources to apply more wisely what we know to the long-range planning of our society."

While one may hesitate over the elitist implications of this cadre, one has to agree that higher education could, if it would, train an enriched managerial class for business, government, think tanks, the professions, and advocacy organizations. It is even possible that it might deliver them to the user groups in time to catch up with the changes of the next two decades.

But it is not likely that formal education will be capable of such a tour de force save for the very few who land in the right environment at the right time with the "right" motivation. More likely, in this writer's judgment, is the partial achievement of Michael's objective through a pass-through to user groups of very skilled and value-oriented people who have passed their apprenticeships in institutes and centers of policy analysis, research, and advocacy.

Unusual balancing abilities are needed
to bridge the changeover period.

The transition from "now" to "then" must go through trying stages. In some ways, we can visualize the longer range future better then we can figure out how to get there. If we take our usual route we will back into the future, our attention riveted on the fascinations of change while the meanings go unheeded and uncomprehended.

Government at all levels is congested with dilemmas of policy, execution, direction, and performance. Its margins of power and leadership in a divided society are narrow, and its options are constrained—or so it appears to think, perhaps wrongly. The hope for the transition years lies in widening these margins by the force of ideas, mainly through the leverage of knowledge and a lively awareness of its uses. And this means facing the contentious business of goals, objectives, and choices. There is no other way to influence future outcomes, and no other place to start from in reshaping management.

Reliance on negotiating means alone is good enough for incremental decision-making. It is far short of enough to enable governance to operate in the mixing-bowl world of policy making by groups, dispersed accountability, and lively discontinuity. Not only negotiating skills, but a high order of balancing abilities, are needed to bridge the changeover period. We may not know how to do it, but we can understand the necessity to try.

DIFFERENT PUBLIC MANPOWER ARRANGEMENTS

If public managers are to tackle the agenda that seems to be in the cards, different public manpower arrangements are needed.

Two pervasive features are visible in public service systems today: (1) continuity and (2) a relatively risk-free environment. Neither is especially good for lively governance. Discontinuities are as much needed in staffing arrangements as they are in governance as a whole. But in present systems the incentives and rewards favor the worker who keeps a low profile. Those who step out of the line of march are either administratively executed for the good example it gives, transferred to one of the wastelands that every bureaucracy maintains, or in rare cases appreciated and taken under the protection of a policy level patron. It is sad to watch a victim age and hang on while lesser men move past him. All governments have these tragic heroes.

We need a new kind of public manager, endowed with new abilities . . .

This is the age of governance now in the making. As external social criticism continues to mass, abetted and armed with the powers of information and communication, and as techniques for venting become refined, the value of the resident hairshirt will grow. His perceptions of reality and value conflicts will be welcome inputs to policy analysis. He may be the best available policy mediator to interface with the new constituencies. Such people have their uses, though government at present is blind to them. They provide the taste of discontinuity that one day will make a meal.

The values of improvisation and risk also must be higher in the new governance. Governments are burdened with the cult of guidelines and rules, and fascinated with review mechanisms, all supposedly in deference to safeguards. But as hierarchical patterns are broken down by the no-care necessity to divest indigestible functions, the roles of judgment and discretion will be larger factors in policy execution. If governance in a crowded environment ruled by uncertainties is to be at all workable, the breed of the risk-taker can do much to save it.

The new public management will have to stress innovation and improvisation just as heavily as the intellectual skills of policy research and analysis. If the graduate schools of business and public management serve up administrative technology at the expense of policy dynamics and managerial risk-taking and improvisation, we are not going to get very far, and it just may turn out that the most valuable managers will come instead from the sciences, arts, and humanities.

. . . and unimpeded by many of the old rigidities and prohibitions.

Looking ahead, the rigidities of civil service systems will be a barrier to the best use of public manpower. Locking people into indentured merit systems from which they can escape only by paying a stiff economic price has no future as a management practice. Governments are likely to come, in the near future, to the system pioneered by Sargent Shriver's Peace Corps—namely the "five-year flush"—which ensures a steady rollover of staff. Men and women will come to public service without expectations of secure tenure, through the arrangement of work contracts—an idea surfaced by the Nixon administration for the higher education of the career service and still being fought to a standstill by employee organizations for all the wrong reasons.

The provisions of the Hatch Act, the public service equivalent of Prohibition, will not for long continue to disqualify public employees from political involvement. Similarly, as workers become more militant and move freely from one level of government to another, a sizable number of administrative and statutory *do not*'s will fall of their own weight, among them some no longer pertinent concepts about conflict of interest.

Government will have to start planning for its manpower needs . . .

Manpower planning for the changing public service has never been a conspicuous feature of American government at any level. Brewster Denny can shock us by pointing out that only 700 public affairs students are graduating each year in the United States. That is an index of how little we care.

Manpower management indeed has approached the disaster level, with extremes of hiring followed by conscience-stricken economy drives, employment ceilings, and prideful and well-publicized orders from above to freeze employment. Meanwhile, from other platforms, hands are wrung over the decline in public service morale, loyalty, and productivity. Such contrariness is the stuff that chases good public administrators out of the system, as Adlai Stevenson put it, to "sit on the sidelines for a while, with a glass of wine, and watch the people dance."

Constructive planning for public manpower needs consists of more than estimating the number of spaces in different occupational categories. It will have to recognize the new dynamics of political governance and be prepared openly for the same manpower being sought out by business, centers of policy analysis, and advocacy groups. Nor can individual governments plan separately.

What is really needed, as a beginning, is a royal commission to investigate the parameters of the *nation's* public service needs in the near and more distant future, and put its mind to the idea of a national public service system based on shared standards of employment, separation, promotion, fringe benefits, development and mobility opportunities, and pay. Such a system could readily have variety as to modes of entry, tenure arrangements, portable pension rights, and incentives and rewards. It could provide for the reciprocal crediting of service in government, business, education, and quasi-governmental organizations concerned with voluntary action and policy research.

It is hardly arguable that governance in the United States is not the monopoly of political institutions and that it will be progressively less so. Planning for manpower needs and the uses of human resources for governance, on a new scale and with drastically new alternatives, has to start very soon, or it will be too late.

. . . and when it starts, it will have to be without constraints.

It is all very well, even necessary, to put stress on intelligence, ability to cope with complex variables, talent to handle policy analysis, and skill in balancing choices and alternatives. These go with decision making under pressure. But they are not all of it. Arrogance of intellect and reason may make for toughness of mind yet be corrosive of human relations, which is where the soul and spirit of governance is found. Cold logic, disciplined analysis, a passion for quantification, the information imperative—all this advanced weaponry of modern management, if it is not tempered with sensitivity for the condition of man and his struggle for meanings, can lead to the brutalization of governance.

What will count most in the making of public service manpower is the capacity for perspectives, the ability to see crisis and change as crossing-points in the human journey. If we come through the struggle of the new governance, it is likely to be because of compassion, grace, and laughter, and the awareness— in Stephen Bailey's term—that we have not made the good society but have caught an unforgettable glimpse of it.

STATE–LOCAL LAG

Managerial change in governance has large implications for the whole government system—state and local as well as Federal.

State and local governments today are badly bruised by the outfall of burgeoning population, the welfare society, outmoded political machinery, institutional lag, and fiscal disarray. Not much is going right for them. Relative to effective problem-solving, goal setting, and delivery of services, they face dismaying barriers.

State and local governments do have some assets to their credit . . .

Certain factors are on their side: they have an edge in accountability; they breed out political leadership; and they offer an alternative to the excessive centralization of decision making and execution. The critical questions concern *capabilities* and *scale,* and even on these two counts they can show some accomplishments.

As to the former, strong governors and mayors seem able to accomplish more than the built-in resistances would seem to allow. A few state governments have made striking progress in managerial reforms, notably in budgeting, evaluation, and forecasting. Some have been remarkably innovative in developing systems strategies for housing, health care, and transportation. The majority have adapted some kind of management information system, though with mixed results. A few are establishing centers of policy analysis.

As to the latter, all states are participants in a range of interstate compacts, consortia, or regional federations designed to achieve scale in problem resolution and policy execution. Urban governments, with Federal incentives, have formed multijurisdictional councils of governments on the metropolitan scale to formulate common objectives and strategies, again with mixed results. A few major cities have reached out for systems analysis and policy research support from captive think tanks or consulting organizations. Collective bargaining in state and local governments is a general, if nerve-racking, reality.

. . . but they also have even stronger deficits (and challenges).

The over-all profile of federalism is shakey, however. Federal Government initiatives tend to preempt state and local choices and resources. Partly because of Federal controls and standards, state government organization is balkanized. The revenue base of states and cities is constricted, and many governments are at the fiscal peril point. Rigid civil service regimes, like the spoils systems they replaced, result in uninspired "people systems" and alarming lags in productivity. Few state and local governments have consistent depth in planning, systematic analysis, technical innovation, or professional back-stopping for governors, legislators, mayors, or city councils.

It is this set of structures that is preparing to receive large transfers of fiscal and functional responsibility from an overloaded and exhausted national government within the present decade. In the next two decades, the demands addressed to state and local governments will rise at a geometric rate. Unready and unequipped, they face a real likelihood of immobilization.

This is one nightmare that must be headed off. The Nixon administration's strategy is to work on it from the top down by transferring large parcels of responsibility and modest amounts of resources, thereby exerting a demand-pull upon state and local governments on top of a poor infrastructure. It is doubtful that this is the way to go at it.

The first priority: to bring order to the confused management structure.

There are over 80,000 units of state and local government. This tangle must be thinned out and rationalized. The welter of states, counties, cities, municipalities, townships, regions, special districts, and miscellaneous clutter serves only to produce a web of redundancy.

To be sure, there are barriers to this housecleaning, some of them involving legal and contractual obligations, others linked to fears of annexation and cultural change. It may be necessary, for example, to amend state constitutions to extend full faith and credit to special bonds and other obligations of the jurisdictions that would be phased out. Jobholders may have to be assimilated by the larger units of government. And the sheer wear and tear of reorganization will be hard to live with and see through. Absent powerful rewards and incentives for change, the struggle to restructure state and local governments is sure to be slow and frustrating. But it is the first priority.

The next need: to improve executive and legislative operations.

This is only incidentally a question of reorganization of departments for more effective command, control, and execution, although this is not to be ignored. But the real target is the upgrading and enrichment of policy planning, analytic, and resource management capabilities at the level of chief executives. In large states and cities, a deputy governor or deputy mayor—in some cases more than one such official—is desperately needed. Program managers to knit together various state and local agencies wll be needed as problem solving takes on systems characteristics. Multiyear budgeting, program scheduling, and forecasting will have to be adopted in most units of government.

The predicament of the legislative bodies has a tendency to be overlooked, but it is crucial. With rising demands and expectations, and with the increasingly technical content of legislation, part-time, underpaid, and understaffed legislatures are losing the battle to make policy grounded in knowledge. Outgunned and outstaffed, and with only the rudiments of legislative research bureaus in most instances, the position of the legislatures is serious. To go into the coming decades without major corrections of these problems of state and local governments is asking for trouble.

Another area of distress: manpower for state and local government.

Most public service systems are built on the lingering fear of the spoils system, and state and local civil service commissions in many cases are so swamped with the administration of merit systems, grievance procedures, and appeals, that they have no time, and in some cases not much energy, for manpower planning and management. These are managerial functions which do not belong with regulatory bodies. Moreover, in many public-employee systems the rule of veterans' preference has the predictable result of waving off the best available job candidates.

In few jurisdictions is there a workable system for projecting future manpower needs, either quantitatively or qualitatively, and even less capability for follow-through when such requirements are perceived. Little sophistication exists in recruiting methods that would cause gifted and motivated young people to opt for careers in state and local service, and very little of the excitement and variety of public service is communicated through outreach to the schools. Unless these problems are faced, state and local governments have no chance to get even a minimum share of manpower from the national pool in the 1970's, with grim consequences for the decades to follow.

If these problems of infrastructure can be taken on, the groundwork can be laid for hiving off Federal responsibilities and resources. But it will not do to simply fire off a gun and declare that henceforth education, law enforcement, community development, manpower training, and transportation have been handed like prizes to state and local governments. Before these prodigious assignments, with shared revenues, are dumped on these governments, a two-year period of preparation should be provided with the aim of developing goals, priorities, and strategies for implementation. If the transition is unplanned, pressure politics and business-as-usual will move in. The prospects for revenue sharing afford a unique chance to begin the corrections that must be made now rather than later.

The most striking and hopeful
managerial innovation lies in regional governance.

A pragmatic though limited movement toward regional systems can already be detected. Legislation now before the Congress would carry it much farther. The New England, Southern, and Western governors to some extent work as blocs. The Council of State Governments has regionalized its liaison services to states. River basin and air quality regions have existed for some time, with multistate participation. The Appalachian Regional Commission has been an effort at developing goals, priorities, and delivery systems for a thirteen-state area. The five Regional Action Planning Commissions have been less successful but are accepted elements in American political geography. And the Federal Government has recently adopted ten regions for policy coordination and cooperation with state and local governments.

In the up-tight and congested governance ahead, regional systems can emerge to compensate for the inefficiencies of scale and resources in state government. Moreover, they will give reality to the ethic of "power to people" because the regional form—backstopped with institutional resources—can make it possible to aggregate needs, objectives, and resources and to assemble delivery systems that can be managed within a policy and financial synthesis.

It is no fantasy to suggest, as Charles Schultze indeed has, that within this decade a start can be made toward regional inputs to the formulation of the Federal budget and to matching these inputs with planned resource outlays by state and local governments. The assumption, to be sure, is that the states' capabilities for analytic programming and budgeting, along with information processing, will mature fast enough to make all this more than a glorified poker game. As the regional consortia develop, they will have the potential for designing and using social indicators, transferring public technology, and evaluating the effectiveness of social investments.

When these possibilities are considered, the outlook for management at the state and local level becomes brighter. Regionalism will not diminish state government. It can be the answer to sustaining it under pressure. But regional forms will not come easily, nor soon. Conservatism will fight the regional idea, unable to see that it is only another route to saving the same values of diversity and decentralized political self-governance.

The American Presidency

The American Presidency has come through the strains of the past decade buffeted and scarred. In its depleted state, through no fault of its present incumbent, the office is experiencing a crisis of loss-of-confidence. The notion is beginning to get around that all governance does not emanate from that epicenter, nor that it is to be followed in all things.

The revolt from authority has touched the Presidency, though not for the first time. When the people again feel the need for a shepherd, they will return.

Meanwhile, as best it can, the Presidency must do a job of work. The responsibilities of the office, whatever the condition of its prestige, continue to cumulate. Managerial decisions grow more complex, the choices and margins narrower, the scales larger, and the risks and uncertainties more tormenting. Social criticism is relentless and focused with intensity through the goodness of telecommunications. Small advances require disproportionate negotiating effort. Reaction times shrink; assessments are swift. Externalities can be counted on to upset plans, and the foul-up factor is hyperactive. These are some of the realities of a President's managerial lot, and there is no sign that they will diminish.

The years ahead are sure to test the Presidency in acute ways.

Information technology will in some degree give a President better tools with which to work. It will read public opinion more accurately, predict economic shifts with longer lead time, deepen the quality of policy analysis, monitor the causes and trends of social change, and shave the grosser uncertainties.

But at the same time it will create a problem of information overload, make small and large decisions more complex, amplify and accelerate noise levels, and arm social critics and opponents to the point where they can force a President's options. The development of discontinuity tactics, along with proliferation of venting mechanisms, will harass and constrain the office and complicate policy execution even as they help to sustain democratic processes and enforce accountability.

Inevitably, the Presidency will be obliged to develop a more extensive managerial staff system. Cabinet officers will combine the roles of managerial executive and policy advocate. Building on the models of the National Security Council and the Domestic Council, the Presidency will evolve a diversified policy-planning system with functional components, a network management system for policy implementation, and a strong evaluation capability. These, together with fortified components for budgeting, management, economic planning, information processing, and communication with new types of constituencies, will comprise the critical elements of the staff system.

The issue is whether all this machinery will add only weight rather than light and ventilation. There is a danger that it can suffocate the humanism that has always managed to break through and identify the office with man's predicament. The staff system will be the natural enemy of intuition and policy improvisation, of risk taking, but the society's defense is that it chooses a President in an electoral process rather than through a search committee. Intuition, while a suspect ally of rational decision-making, is still a property of political action and, in the end, is likely to have the last word.

The external role of the Presidency will grow in importance.

In the new setting of governance, the measure of the office will be its effectiveness in balancing mixed coalitions of opinion, criticism, and advocacy, and arriving at workable syntheses. The White House of the future will be no place for a recluse. In Holmes' terms, it will be the focus of passion and action.

It will no longer do to say that a certain person "holds" the office, as though it were fragile and breakable if handled roughly. It was not meant to be held, but to be hurled to heights where it can be seen and followed. That is the nature of the office, and the dimension of its managerial opportunity.

If government's first responsibility is, in fact, to *comprehend the potential of the society,* that opportunity is primarily Presidential. Whether men equal to the job are given the chance to try will depend on how the party system performs in producing them, and on the perceptions of an electorate that will have no excuse for misjudging its man. The man, in turn, will not be checked in the use of his powers if he uses them as he should. In the words of Clinton Rossiter, "If he cannot sense the possible, he will exhaust himself in attempting the impossible."

WILL WE WIN THE ORDEAL OF CHANGE?

The ordeal of change that is ahead for the management of governance would be serious enough for a country confident of its values and goals. It will be doubly painful for us because until now things have always gone well. We have had a long winning streak in the affairs that mattered. Governance could muddle through and count on the easy nature of the national character, the force of its idealism, and the nation's wealth.

Now anxiety has displaced idealism, and the moral set of assumptions that constituted government's brief is no longer so explicit.

Lippmann senses a quantitative difference in performance: "The American political experience has never experienced a time when it had to govern so many people, be governed by so many voters, govern for so many purposes." With this there is also the qualitative difference—the anxiety to apply corrections and to find the right uses of power and abundance. The combination serves to define the ordeal of change, and to locate its primary trigger.

In addition, externalities will have their effect on political governance and the management of change. Among them, first importance goes to the altered calculus of American power in world affairs—the diminution of political and military leverage, and the rise of combination economies to constrain our bargaining position in world markets. It will not come easily to run second or third in trade, in technological achievement, and in productivity, nor to be forced into hard terms of monetary exchange. We simply will no longer hold all the high cards, though we will hold enough if we play them soon enough—in rebuilding our ocean industry, in stimulating technological innovation, and in creating incentives for productivity.

In effecting change in public management, drift is worse than failure.

There is another trigger that will influence change in the management of governance. It is the trigger of failures.

To the extent that governance is tardy in recognizing and anticipating contingencies, or clumsy in addressing its internal deficiencies, correction will be forced upon it:

Overregulation, based on past economic legends, will lead to deregulation.

The failure of cities will force an urban growth policy.

Bankrupt and overmortgaged state and local governments will set the stage for alteration in federalism.

Inability to manage abundance will bring about the realignment of goals and priorities.

The failure of the party system to produce better than mediocre men will open up new options for the electorate and for advocacy groups.

Evidence of the erosion of the national character will at last force changes in the educational system, away from drills and calisthenics and toward the study of man and ethical choices.

But failure is not always disaster. Since much of human history, not excluding our own, is the chronology of the creation of higher orders of qualitative performance built on the rejection of failing systems, it means only that man and society can learn something from experience. If this is to be one of the routes to the ordeal of change, we can bear with it.

What we can least afford is drift, the political laziness of closing our eyes to the quantum problems of choice that will come with deterministic certainty. These choices, in large part, will be value-heavy and therefore critical.

A small glimpse of what they will be like has been described in *Science* by Leon Kass, in the context of approaching capabilities of biomedical technology for genetic manipulation and "cloning" (the capacity to reproduce oneself exactly through genetic engineering). As Kass puts it, until now traditional influences or interventions on man have been transmitted by speech or symbolic deeds, recognizing man as the animal who lives by speech and understands the meanings of action, and these influences are therefore reversible. But, he points out, the emerging biomedical engineering operates by circumventing the human context of speech and meaning, bypasses choice, and modifies the human material; and these changes may not be reversible. His warning opens a window on our future.

Such a technological assault on values, mores, and ethics can tear apart the social system in the absence of a political governance capable of judging and moderating the rate at which society can absorb value crises, and sensitive to the outer boundaries of human and ethical tolerances. It is with relation to these intensities of judgment and value analysis that governance in the coming decades will meet its most exquisite tests, and for which the time that remains for the transitional society should be used well.

Efficiency criteria will carry governance only part of the way.

The ordeal of change for governance is only in part a question of efficiency criteria and managerial corrections. It is fundamentally a crisis of values and perspectives on the goals and uses of power relative to the human condition. The crucial perspectives lie in the understanding of the meaning of man's long journey through light and dark to where he has at last come.

Notes

1. Murray Weidenbaum, "Financing Investment in the 1970's," presentation to the First Annual Business Financing Conference, co-sponsored by *Business Week* and *Corporate Financing,* New York City, December 15, 1971.

Contributors

Helpful comments and inputs from the following members of the author's panel are gratefully acknowledged (the author, however, assumes full responsibility for choice of content and interpretation):

HON. JACK M. CAMPBELL, Olmstead & Cohen, formerly Governor of New Mexico

EMILIO DADDARIO, Senior Vice President, Gulf & Western Precision Engineers Co.

MARSHALL E. DIMOCK, formerly Visiting Professor of Government, University of Texas at Austin

ROGER W. JONES, Consultant, Executive Office of the President, Washington

MURRAY L. WEIDENBAUM, Professor, Department of Economics, Washington University

ROBERT WOOD, President, University of Massachusetts

Four

MARVIN BOWER and
C. LEE WALTON, JR.

Gearing a Business to the Future

WE will be tomorrow what we are becoming today." This approach to judging an *individual's* future performance by his past achievements is based on the notion that an individual is not likely to change his characteristics or capabilities. Our experience shows that many business firms have the same incapacity to change. People get grooved in conducting the same old business in the same old way, so the future course of the enterprise is very much an unfolding of the present.

It is not necessary, however, that a business firm be in the future what it is becoming today. The people making up any business are responsive to decisions and leadership in changing the goals, objectives, organization structure, policies, programs, and style of managing the enterprise. Even the key people can be changed by decisions to reshuffle insiders or introduce outsiders. But without leaders who have the will and the wisdom to effect internal change, a business firm, like an individual, will in the future be just what it is becoming today, except that it will be pummeled by external forces with which it is ill-prepared to cope.

An Action-Oriented Approach

The business decision maker is currently being inundated with words about change and what it means to the future of every business. Futurists are busy predicting what will happen between now and the year 2000 and beyond.

In this report, we have tried to stand back from that torrent of words and sort out—for the top managements of business firms—what they might actually do in coping with change. We have developed an approach that they might use; and we have avoided going into detail on advanced techniques of analysis and decision making.

We offer no panaceas, short cuts, or easy answers. Success in dealing with change, we believe, requires properly timed but often fairly obvious decisions, followed by effective management action in carrying them out. Thus we describe what we believe is a useful, effective, and specific way of going about the important task of keeping a business in step with the forces at work in the evolving future, and we have drawn on the ways in which leading businesses are coping and might cope with these and similar forces.

93

The need for a business to cope with change is painfully obvious. The rhetoric about the extent and speed of change is made real by recent developments; imposition of controls on prices, wages, and profits; an overhaul of the international monetary system; and legislation requiring major expenditures for an improved environment. Business is currently faced with an unusual number of concurrent forces having long-term impacts, and technological developments are speeding up the rate of change.

If a business is to operate successfully, the top management must, of course, identify the external forces affecting it and keep the business geared to the favorable forces while countering the negative ones. In other words, success in coping with change requires correct responses to relevant forces.

The only effective response that any executive can make to any force is to make and carry out a decision. An oral wringing of hands may relieve tension and bring some self-satisfaction, but it is not an *effective* response. The decision may be to take action or not to act at all. And, of course, if—through neglect or lack of will—no conscious decision is made, it will nevertheless amount to a decision to maintain the status quo or to let the force operate without response. Naturally, if the conscious decision calls for action, the executive must exercise the will, authority, and leadership to carry it out.

This report discusses the principal types of forces that we and those interviewed foresee as requiring decisions and actions in the two decades. We believe, however, that it is more important to develop an approach to identifying and responding to the specific forces affecting the particular business (whatever those forces may be) than it is to develop responses to any general force that we discuss. Thus we are concerned chiefly with decisions and actions which the top-management executives of an individual firm can take now to prepare for *whatever* the future may hold for their particular enterprise.

All management decisions are rooted in the present.

All decisions are inherently present or current decisions. Even the development of a long-range plan is a *now* or current decision, based on present facts, present forecasts, present assumptions, and present evaluations of future possibilities and probabilities. The plan itself is not a forecast because the firm will try to implement the plan, or (in apt biblical terms) make it "come to pass." In fact, the people who make the plan should feel committed to making it come to pass.

Thus keeping a business geared to the future must initially be concerned with strategic decision making. We prefer the term "strategic" to "long-range" planning (or decision making) because the term "strategic" focuses thinking and decision making on substance and not time. For example, although a strategic plan is designed to help the business cope with the future, it will often include present action, such as selling off a business which is unprofitable or has poor prospects. Finally, broad use of the term "strategic" will help train people at all levels to think in strategic terms—and hence to recognize and evaluate forces affecting the business in fundamental ways.

In making plans come to pass, there will usually need to be a series of new, current decisions that hopefully will help achieve the objectives of the original plan (or decision). If that proves impossible, it will then be necessary to make a decision to scrap the original plan, set new objectives, and develop a new plan, i.e., make a series of new decisions.

Thus dealing with the future calls for an almost continuous flow of *present* decisions as the outlook is assessed and re-assessed in the light of new forces. Many such decisions will have an influence throughout the business; and some may commit resources with considerable finality. Some decisions may foreclose the making of others. So part of the skill in coping with change is to keep the options open as long as that can soundly be done.

Forecasts are useful as stimulants to thought, not as guides to action.

Much of the current thought about the future is concerned with trying to forecast what will happen in the next couple of decades. Such thinking is interesting, challenging, and stimulating. This speculation has real value in keeping managers alert to change, but since these forecasts lack the necessary "nowness," they have limited current operational (decision-making) value.

A forecast of future change is of limited value to the decision maker unless it is reliable and also includes a forecasted timetable of when it will become operative. Without the timetable the forecast merely keeps him alert that it will happen "sometime"; he cannot make sound decisions until he knows "when" the force will have impact. So a forecast has two risk elements—not just *whether,* but also *when.*

For example, nearly 30 years ago it was firmly forecast that atomic sterilization would soon revolutionize food canning, and that atomic power would soon replace other fuels for producing electricity. Atomic canning is still in the laboratory stage. Atomic power has moved ahead but it is well off its projected time schedule. Any management that had made significant decisions based on either forecast would have committed serious and costly errors.

Based on his own recollection of how far off the mark forecasts prove to be, the observant executive knows that a forecast, except for a very short period ahead, forms a shaky platform on which to base decisions. Thus coping with the forces for change requires decision making under conditions of uncertainty, because the future must always remain uncertain.

The best approach is to screen the possibilities in terms of probabilities . . .

We believe the best approach for coping with the future is to (1) evaluate the possibilities as they appear on the basis of today's most reliable information, (2) select several of the most attractive *probabilities,* and (3) from these choose the one most likely *probability*. This approach results not in a forecast of what will happen, but rather in an *assumption* of what is *most likely* to happen. With the risk analysis techniques, even the probabilities can be quantified judgmentally.

An advanced form of this general approach is dealt with in "Century of Mismatch" by Simon Ramo, vice chairman of the board, TRW, Inc.,[1] including a discussion on "the techniques of anticipation." Although he is concerned chiefly with making technological decisions, Dr. Ramo believes that by the systematic use of an orderly technique, a company can get an early warning of change—and can plan, prepare, and take timely action to attain its objectives.

Although, he says, it is an over-simplification of the technique, he recommends these six key steps for coping with technological change:

1. List the major technological changes that can be anticipated.
2. Order the list by relative importance; reorder the list as to probability of occurrence; then reorder it again as to time of occurrence if the events do occur.
3. For those listed events which have a strong enough combination of importance and probability, try to describe the potential impact on society.
4. For each such event, separate possible consequences into "good" and "bad."
5. Analyze and plan how to maximize the benefits and minimize the dislocations.
6. Organize to implement this plan.

. . . and to use sequential planning for flexibility—to keep the options open.

Closely related to this technique is sequential planning: making a plan to extend to a particular point in time or program, and then devising a new plan, depending on conditions at that time. This is a way of keeping the options open.

Fortunately, change is never as rapid as the current change rhetoric implies. Rapid is a relevant term. In addition to the natural fascination of human beings with the status quo, there are forces for stabilization as well as forces for change. The stabilization forces slow down the rate of change. Atomic sterilization of food, for example, cannot proceed until a whole host of technical, health, legal, political, and prejudice problems have been solved.

Often, there is sufficient early warning to enable an alert management to make the necessary decisions before the opportunity for sound decision is foreclosed. There were early warnings, for example, of the oncoming storm over pollution of air and water; and the probable demand for highway safety was clearly indicated by shocking articles about death on the highway which were given wide circulation well over a decade ago. That warning about possible impact of major forces is usually ample in time is demonstrated by our study. We find wide and general agreement on the forces with which business must cope in the next couple of decades.

The possibility for early detection of relevant forces, however, should not lead to a casual approach, because there is competitive advantage in what Alfred

Marshall called "the momentum of an early start." Yet as a matter of fact, the present approach of most companies is too casual. Our interviews show that many top-managements are doing too little to cope with even *current* forces of which they are fully aware.

Once management has recognized the realities of response (the need for "now" decisions, the limited reliability of forecasts, the likelihood of early warnings, and so on), and has determined the best probability for capitalizing on or coping with the forces most likely to affect the business significantly, it must carry out the decision through action. And this requires will, authority, and leadership.

It also requires that management keep alert to the possible need to start the process all over again as assumptions are proved to be inaccurate or new forces are detected. The need for internal change—or at least for consideration of internal change—will be continuous as one externl force after another develops an actual or potential impact on the business. Hence the firm should be organized and managed in the most flexible manner possible, so as to facilitate effective decisions in responding to the forces for change.

Most U..S. business managers already recognize that there are powerful economic, social, and political forces that will have major future impacts on their firms. About that they have little question. But they do have questions like these:

What specific forces will affect my particular business?

What will be the nature and consequences of the impact on my business?

What will be the timing of the impact?

What, if anything, can I do to deflect or modify the impact of the force?

What can I do to prepare for the impact?

Forces with Significant Impact

It is obviously impossible to answer such specific questions as those listed previously. What we have done is to suggest an approach to the task of (1) detecting and assessing the specific developing forces that will affect the particular business, and (2) determining how best to make the decisions and take the actions that will enable them to capitalize on the favorable forces and counter the negative ones.

As a basis for defining this approach as specifically as possible, we have selected carefully and discuss briefly nine major economic, political, and social forces that are now foreseen as likely to affect most business firms significantly during the next 20 years.

Even after some 50 interviews with prominent business executives, and after extensive study of the works of the "futurists" and reports of the Presidential and other commissions, we have not turned up a modern-day Jules Verne. (Certainly neither of the authors lays claim to a capacity to foresee the future, either.) With minimal exceptions, all the ideas we gathered as to what may happen between now and the years 1985 to 2000 appear to be essentially projections or extrapolations of present forces or the effect of recent technological innovations.

It follows that most of the forces we selected for discussion will be known to the sophisticated executive. Indeed, in view of the time required for any force to impact, most of these factors are, to some degree, being felt now. In any event, we believe that these nine form a solid basis for developing an approach which any company can adapt for dealing with changes of any kind:

1. Broad and urgent demand for improving the quality of the environment
2. Serious drain on the nation's natural resources
3. Further expansion of consumerism
4. Changing social attitudes and values
5. Growing involvement of government in business decision-making
6. Growing sense of social responsibility in business decision-makers
7. Continuing increases in foreign competition
8. Continued growth of the multinational (or international) corporation
9. Increasing tempo and impact of technology

We do not go beyond these nine forces; collectively they represent substantive and diverse impacts on business, more than sufficient as a basis for illustrating our suggested approach. Thus, we omit discussion of possible explosive changes in the biomedical field, the outlook for the general level of business and further potential revisions in the international monetary system, war (a powerful force in itself and an accentuator of other forces), and information technology (The Conference Board has already dealt with this subject),[2] all of which—and many more—can have significant effects on society generally and on business in particular.

Our analysis points up clearly why ours is indeed a technological society. It is difficult to identify any major force that either is not a direct result of technology or has not been indirectly influenced by it. The atom bomb, jet travel, instant communications (telephone, radio, TV), the pill, and the automobile are obvious examples of major technological causes or influencers of major forces with which society and business must cope.

Environmental demands, already strong, are destined to continue unabated.

The public outcry for an improved environment brands this as a powerful force which will undoubtedly continue unabated into the distant future. The pervasiveness of environmental problems among businesses is perhaps obvious. It is significant to note, however, that a *Wall Street Journal* survey [3] of executives associated with some 1,100 industrial companies showed that well over half were concerned with both air and water pollution; 48 per cent with solid waste disposal; 36 per cent with the noise level; and 18 per cent with visual deterioration;

and a significant proportion with all these types of pollution. Even among some 500 nonindustrial companies the results were not fundamentally different, except that waste disposal and visual deterioration were problems to a higher proportion of the companies, and air, water, and "silence pollution" to a smaller proportion. Among the industries most affected are automotive, electric power, pulp and paper, steel, petroleum refining, and aluminum and copper smelting and refining; but many others will also feel substantial effects.

Environmental improvement is, of course, a worldwide demand. The European Common Market, the Council of Europe, the World Health Organization, and the Organization for Economic Co-operation and Development, among other international organizations, are concerned with coordinating programs and the development of standards. So international corporations must deal with this force in every country, but undoubtedly in different ways in each. And the United Nations Conference on the Human Environment (June 1972 at Stockholm) made it quite clear that pollution is an international problem that must be solved internationally.

The magnitude of environmental problems is also shown by the *Wall Street Journal* Survey. Of some 1,300 respondents from industrial companies, 30 per cent said that it would take from 5 to 20 years for their industry to reach a level of nonpollution and environment protection that they consider desirable; and 9 per cent thought it would be more than 20 years or "never" before that level was reached.[4]

The costs to industry of meeting even the present pollution control standards defined by law are estimated at $22.8 billion by McGraw-Hill, Inc., with the petroleum industry cost at $2.7 billion, paper about $2 billion, steel $1.78 billion.[5]

As an individual company example, Texaco, Inc.,[6] the third largest oil company (in April 1972), announced plans to spend $150 million on new facilities at four refineries to permit the company to reduce lead additives in its gasolines; this is believed to be the largest program of its kind in the industry.

Thus it seems clear that most industrial companies—in fact, most businesses of any kind—will need to cope with this force continuously over the next 20 years. This means that most businesses must continue to make tough environmental decisions into the distant future.

Depletion of natural resource is serious—but how serious is only now beginning to be realized.

We selected this force for discussion because it contrasts with the environmental force. Environmental problems are here and broadly recognized by the public. On the other hand, serious depletion (and alleged exhaustion) of some of our natural resources is a force with an impact that is only beginning to be felt or even broadly recognized.

Nevertheless, this force has been discussed actively since 1952, when *Resources for Freedom,* the report of the President's Materials Policy Commission (the

Paley Commission), was published. This was followed in 1963 by the monumental study, *Resources in America's future,*[7] which concluded that while there is unlikely to be "any general running out of resources in this country during the remainder of the century"; there is, however, "great likelihood of severe problems of shortage . . . ; and deficiencies either of quantity and quality . . . will also occur in some instances." More recently, "the energy crisis" has become a problem of real concern; and the President, in April 1972, said: ". . . all the evidence now shows that we are going to have a major energy crisis in this country in the 1980's." [8]

One authority at the 1972 White House Conference on the Industrial World Ahead stated that "assuming a fairly high level of economic activity, the 1990 GNP will be more than twice that of 1970" [9] and that this would produce the following estimate of requirements of raw materials for 1990, compared with 1970: nuclear energy, 100 times; aluminum and electricity, about $2\frac{1}{2}$ times; copper, iron, lead, zinc, petroleum natural gas, and lumber, about double.

Of course, forecasts of the requirements for raw materials are subject to all the deficiencies of any forecast. Also, increasing prices will tend to restrict consumption; and the impact of higher prices is virtually at hand. Further, there will be decreases in demand due to technological changes that permit substitution.

Nevertheless, in making decisions on natural resource uses, the business executive has an opportunity to serve his nation as well as his enterprise by making decisions and technological studies that will help the conservation of natural resources. Especially should he use technology to find substitutes for those that are becoming scarce; and rising prices will provide an economic incentive for doing so.

The problem of natural gas shortages in the United States illustrates all of these considerations. The shortage of natural gas reserves is widely recognized in industry, and is being brought home to the consumer. Higher prices are resulting. And technology is providing the means for importing liquefied natural gas at low temperatures; but, of course, the imported gas will be higher priced and less dependable in terms of delivery to the United States.

Therefore, industries using natural gas are experiencing the impact of this force right now, and must make decisions for coping with it.

Consumerism has exploded—in intensity, in scope, and in public pressure.

So intense is the force of consumerism that it can be counted on to operate as a major influence as far ahead as can be foreseen. The consumer movement can perhaps best be described as the gap between what consumers expect business to deliver and what consumers perceive that business is actually delivering. Narrowly defined, "the consumer movement wants safe, reliable products and services that perform as advertised and that are repaired or remedied promptly when they fail. In addition, the activists say, consumers want more detailed information about goods and services to enable intelligent comparison before a purchase is made." [10]

The consumer movement is strong enough to support a number of consumer advocates like Ralph Nader, who can easily get hearings before governmental bodies and extensive publicity in the press and on television. Their capacity to bring public pressure to bear on business firms has been amply demonstrated, and business and governmental response to the movement has been substantial.

In June 1971, the White House Office for Consumer Affairs reported that it was "receiving complaints numbering 2,500 per month compared with 1,500 per month a year earlier." The Federal Trade Commission has responded to the movement by ordering manufacturers in automobile, television, electric shaver, air conditioning, and toothpaste industries to provide documentation to support selected "concrete" claims for their products.[11] Consumer advocate demands for greater automobile safety have been so widely publicized as to need only mention here.

There has been a rash of statutes enacted in state legislatures designed to help protect consumers, including requirements that high schools provide consumer education courses.[12] The National Conference of Commissioners on Uniform State Laws has mounted a nationwide drive to enact a uniform consumer credit code. One count showed that there are no fewer than 2,000 agencies to which the consumer can turn for help, from the local levels of government up through at least 35 Federal agencies and including the services established by individual companies or industry associations and consumer groups.

Not surprisingly, the strength of the consumer movement—with the attention it is receiving in the newspaper, magazine, and broadcasting media—is creating an increasingly negative attitude toward "big business." A social research public-opinion survey in 1971 found that 60 per cent of the people it polled in the Chicago area thought that "big business forgets the public welfare"; that figure compares with 40 per cent in 1964.[13]

Consumer advocates are also capitalizing on the strength of the consumer movement to mount a campaign to seek popular support for antitrust action to break up the largest corporations.[13]

The virility of the consumer movement has been increasing so sharply for a decade that it is surely a force with which business must cope for the next 20 years. In fact, the antitrust enforcement tangent shows the fissionable character of the movement. This increases the likelihood that the movement could easily break out into new forms as more consumer advocates and consumer groups recognize the power of grass roots protest when organized to achieve social goals.

Social attitudes are changing rapidly,
but the effects are still not clear.

There is wide current discussion about our society being "in crisis." For example, the preamble to the report on the White House Conference on Youth, 1971, declares: "We are in the midst of a political, social and cultural revolution." [14] Pointed to as evidence of crisis are the confrontation and violence on the campus and in the streets. There is a growing exercise of power through public protest, including some in stockholder meeting rooms. Churches and universities are using the power of their shareholder proxies in an effort to bring about changes in corporate action related to social goals.

There is discussion of the lowered motivational value of the work ethic. And it is claimed that the interest in acquiring material wealth is being eroded by a growing interest in the quality of life.

Whether these discussions and developments do or do not reflect a "crisis," they do indicate changes in social attitudes and values that the business decision-maker should try to identify, evaluate, and respond to in keeping his firm geared to the future. For the attitudes and values of customers, factory and office workers, managers at all levels, stockholders and the general public are all important to the business firm.

In 1969, *The Economist,* that astute London observer of life in the United States, put it this way:

The United States in this last third of the twentieth century is the place where man's long economic problem is ending, but where his social problems still gape. On any rational view, the enormous fact of that approach to economic consummation should rivet all attention. It is also certainly the most momentous news story so far in the history of the world. But people in the United States are at present wracked by the stretching to snapping point of too many of their temporary social tensions, so that this society which represents man's greatest secular achievement sometimes seems to be on the edge of a national nervous breakdown.[15]

In 1972, Dr. Daniel Yankelovich, professor of psychology at New York University, head of an attitude research firm bearing his name, made this observation:

The student revolution is also exerting an impact on work within the corporate framework. In exchange for loyalty and hard work, students want more than just a job, more than just money, more than just security. They want work that provides them with an opportunity for self-expression, a sense of challenge, a chance to give service, the right to do a whole job and not just part of one, involvement in the decision-making process, true identification with their employers and co-workers, and a chance to contribute to society.

It would be one thing if these desires were confined to college students. But they aren't. We see them arising in many negative forms within the present work population: in the angry, sometimes unreasonable demands of union workers; in widespread withdrawal of interest in work, as evidenced in higher turnover and absenteeism rates, cheating, shrinkage and the like; and in a kind of *managerial obsolescence* whose primary cause is a sense of being excluded, a feeling of meaninglessness, and a disaffection with work and career, and whose primary symptom is lack of motivation.* Nowhere is this disaffection more pronounced than on production lines, where workers often do only one simple operation.

To put the whole matter another way, there is an economic and a psychological

* What is probably meant by "lack of motivation" is a lack of organizationally acceptable motivation. Even the hippie is motivated.

aspect to productivity. And for too long companies have concentrated on the economic side, almost to the total exclusion of the psychological side. Pressure from
students will cause some redress in this imbalance in the years ahead.[16]

But while there is general agreement on the *fact* of social change, there is very
little agreement on the probable *effects* of social change during the next 20 years.
Indeed, we can find very little hard, objective evidence on how social change is
affecting business firms even currently. For example, there was considerable
speculation in the press about social causes for the strike at the highly automated
General Motors plant at Lordstown, Ohio, whereas close observers of the situation regard it as a typical management-labor dispute.

Professor Paul A. Samuelson of the Massachusetts Institute of Technology
states that his studies fail to indicate that changing attitudes among the young
have yet had any influence on cutting output. He said, "The fact that we're all
preoccupied with it doesn't mean that there's anything to be preoccupied with." [17]
We do not mean to indicate that changes in social attitudes and values will not—
or even are not—having substantial effects. It is simply that these changes are
difficult to assess, and their consequences even more difficult to measure; but
this presents an opportunity for the progressively managed business.

There is much more agreement on the causes of current social change. These
include rapid communication through the mass media; progress up the five-level
hierarchy of basic human needs, with self-fulfillment at the top having been
reached; the rising level of education; and disappointment with the performance
of our basic institutions such as government, the corporation, the university, and
the church. (See the results of the Yankelovich survey cited in Boettinger, p. 10.)

The difficulties of making reliable forecasts in any field, as discussed earlier,
are compounded in the field of social change. Even measuring the impact of
changes that are operating currently is challenging even those best qualified.
Moreover, the current racial tensions and deeply held attitudes concerning the
Vietnam war have made objective assessment of the extent and consequences of
social changes a difficult problem.

Yet social changes of major force are operating now and, clearly, will operate
over the next 20 years. Top-management executives must learn to cope effectively
with such intangible changes, whatever their nature and intensity. That is why
we selected this broad group of social forces as possibly representative of other
intangible forces with which top-management executives should be prepared to
deal.

*Government involvement in business decision-
making is entering many new fields.*

The growing involvement of government at all levels in business decision-
making is so obvious a force as merely to require mention in order to establish
its current heavy impact and probable increasing impact on business over the
next 20 years. Clearly, the American people want more benefits from govern-

ment and more regulation by government; and the two major political parties are busy outpromising each other in order to capitalize on this voter desire. Also, there are areas, such as international business, where business needs, and indeed seeks, government help.

Transportation, power, insurance, and other regulated industries have long ago adjusted their decision-making to government regulation. Regulation in the brokerage, underwriting, and investment fields is still growing as the Securities and Exchange Commission extends its jurisdiction; and the SEC is expanding its requirements on companies with publicly listed and held securities.

The National Labor Relations Board has long involved itself in decisions affecting employees; and in recent years various Federal and state agencies have implemented laws to prohibit employee discrimination.

The consumerism movement has stimulated increased governmental involvement in the decision making of a broad range of companies. The Federal Trade Commission has expanded its regulation of advertising, even to the point of requiring the advertiser to run subsequent ads to correct earlier statements which lacked factual support. And the Food and Drug Administration has acted to prohibit and regulate food and drug products considered harmful to health. More detailed labeling of product contents and stickers showing the prices of automobiles are now matters of regulation.

Massive Federal and state regulation reflects the acute public interest in an improved environment.

Antitrust action has been vigorously pursued, and the guidelines from recent court decisions are not easy to apply even in such a frequent decision as an acquisition.

Perhaps most dramatic of all has been the regulation of wages, prices, and profits under the New Economic Policy. Acceptance and support of this policy by the public and by business leaders does not suggest an early end to this type of government involvement in business decision-making.

So as far ahead as the mind can project, the executives of business firms must learn how to deal with an increasing degree of government involvement in their decisions—or, perhaps better, actually work *with* government on matters of mutual concern (e.g., as noted later, remaining competitive overseas).

Business decision-makers are increasingly
accepting their social responsibilities.

The classical and strongly held view of the typical business decision-maker was, until a couple of decades ago, that the basic objectives of a business is to earn maximum profits. This is still the view of some decision makers. But by the beginning of the 1950's this view was beginning to change as an increasing number of executives began to accept the social responsibilities of business. (While we are here talking primarily about *domestic* social responsibilities, our experience has shown that the concepts of "optimizing" rather than maximizing profits in a manner of "enlightened self-interest" has been practiced for decades by the multinational corporations in respect of their social responsibilities to the host country in which they operate.)

During the past decade, acceptance of social responsibilities gathered increasing momentum, until today it is held sufficiently broadly that we decided to treat it as a significant and representative force—and one likely to operate with substantial and perhaps increasing impact during the next 20 years.

There are two strong reasons for this shift in viewpoint: (1) Many business decision-makers, as citizens, have decided they will manage their enterprises so as to help solve some of the social problems of the nation, some of which are laid at the doorstep of business. (2) Competitive forces require that the leaders who hold any significant viewpoint be followed by others. Thus a management which is regarded as enlightened and/or progressive is likely to attract customers from companies that do not enjoy such a reputation. That is probably even more true in the case of job applicants at all levels, because they are likely to inquire about management attitudes when they have choices among jobs.

In any event, in June 1971, the Research and Policy Committee of the Committee for Economic Development (CED) published a national policy statement entitled, "Social Responsibilities of Business Corporations." [18] This statement constitutes a milestone in executive thought, because the majority of the 200 CED trustees are leaders of many of the country's largest corporations, the balance being leading educators and other professional men. The tone of that policy statement is indicated by the following excerpts:

> Experience with governmental and social constraints indicates that the corporation's self-interest is best served by a sensitivity to social concerns and a willingness, within competitive limits, to take needed action ahead of a confrontation.[19]

> The doctrine of enlightened self-interest is also based on the proposition that if business does not accept a fair measure of responsibility for social improvement, the interests of the corporation may actually be jeopardized. Insensitivity to changing demands of society sooner or later results in public pressures for governmental intervention and regulation to require business to do what it was reluctant or unable to do voluntarily.[20]

> And we have suggested that responsible management must have the vision and exert the leadership to develop a broader social role for the corporation if business is to continue to receive public confidence and support.

> We believe business will respond constructively to this new challenge, as it has to many others in the past, and that it will contribute significantly to the common task of greatly improving the quality of life in the United States.[21]

There are, of course, in addition, numerous examples which could be cited of companies which have already undertaken major, forward-looking programs. The policy statement cited above and reflecting the viewpoint of an organization composed principally of business leaders, indicates that there is an increasing trend toward a progressive approach in business decision-making. There is every reason to believe that this trend will continue to grow at an accelerating pace in the future.

This is not to say, however, that the businessmen of the CED, or businessmen generally, do not recognize the importance of profits to every business and to the nation. Businessmen recognize that without satisfactory profits they cannot accumulate or raise the capital needed to make capital investments for increased productivity and for growth needed to produce new jobs. And, more than many others, businessmen know that without the wealth that corporations produce the government will not have the resources to pay for the social benefits that voters want.

Foreign competition, despite higher labor costs, will continue to increase.

Foreign competition as a present and future force affecting American business has been widely discussed elsewhere; we deal with it here only as a basis for suggesting later what the executives of the individual firm can do to cope with it.

The situation is well set forth in the summary of a report on the international economic situation, dated December 29, 1971, prepared for the President, the Cabinet, and members of Congress by Peter G. Peterson, then Assistant to the President for International Economic Affairs, and subsequently Secretary of Commerce.[22] Mr. Peterson writes:

> The central fact of the past 25 years had been the conviction—ours as much as that of other countries—that the United States was dominant, both in size and competitiveness, in the international economy and that the practices, institutions and rules governing the international trade and payments were structured to fit that fact. We as a nation and the world as a whole were too slow to realize that basic structural and competitive changes were occurring; as a result, international policies and practices were too slow in responding.
>
> Some of the changes . . . relate to the increasing competitiveness of various economies—notably those of the European Community and Japan—and their role in world trade and finance which grew while ours declined.
>
> We see that, while the American economy has remained basically strong during this process, our international competitive position has been weakening for a variety of reasons; changes in international trading practices and patterns; developing inequities in both agricultural trade and the proliferation of preferential arrangements for industrial products; basic changes in the United States economy, and a monetary system whose lack of flexibility resulted in intolerable burdens being thrust upon the United States as we continued to meet our international economic and security obligations.
>
> These problems were brought to a head as a result of inadequate increases in productivity, excessive domestic inflation over the last half of the sixties, a breakdown in the classic international monetary and domestic adjustment mechanism—and, of course, massive short-term capital flows.

This analysis shows that responsibility for improving U.S. competitiveness rests both with government and with business. Just before the Peterson report was prepared, the country's competitive position was improved by revaluing the dollar and realigning it downward against other currencies in the international monetary agreement of December 18, 1971 (the Smithsonian Agreement). But currency changes produce results slowly, and our negative balances of trade and payments still continue as serious problems.

The Peterson report gives the following data on export growth in manufactures for selected countries, expressed in per cent of increase during the period 1960–70:

West Germany	200
Italy	310
Japan	400
United Kingdom	91
United States	110
France	165

The cost of producing goods in the United States relative to other countries is, of course, an important element in determining the flow of trade. A study by the Department of Labor shows that in the United States employee compensation amounted to 68 per cent of "gross product originating" in manufacturing in 1969, with the proportion in other industrial countries ranging from about 50 to 70 per cent.[23] This study analyzed relative output per man-hour and hourly compensation in the 10 other industrial countries, and reached these conclusions:

1. Unit labor costs in manufacturing—virtually stable in the United States during the first half of the 1960s—increased rapidly between 1965 and 1970. This trend contrasts sharply with the experience of most industrial nations.

2. In 1970, however, unit labor costs in most of the European countries accelerated sharply, and the rates of increase in Belgium, Germany, Italy, Sweden, and the U.K. surpassed the U.S. rate of increase.

There is some reason to believe, therefore, that as compensation rates for labor in other countries rise more rapidly than those in the United States, the labor cost differential, which currently favors competing nations, will be lessened. Also, the currency realignment should provide a further improvement in the U.S. competitive position. On the other hand, there is an offsetting trend within the United States—i.e., pay for time not worked, such as longer vacations and added holidays.

The United States in September 1972 consummated important trade agreements with the USSR and the PRC. Indications are that more agreements with Socialist countries may be on the drawing board.

No business can count permanently on solving its foreign competitive problems through tariffs or quotas. As a nation, we are firmly committed to freedom in international trade. As the President said, in September 1971, in his address to Congress in support of his economic plan, "We cannot remain a great nation if we build a permanent wall of tariffs and quotas around the United States and let the rest of the world pass us by." [25]

Looking forward from 1972, even to the end of the century, international competition holds the probability of being one of the principal forces with which most manufacturing firms must continue to cope. And business and government *working together* must keep the United States as an effective competitor in a struggle that promises to become increasingly severe. The President summarized the situation well in his address in June 1972 to the joint session of Congress, at which he reported on the summit meeting in Moscow from which he had just returned:

And in this period we must keep our economy vigorous and competitive, if the opening for greater East-West trade is to mean anything at all and if we do not wish to be shouldered aside in world markets by the growing potential of the economies of Japan, Western Europe, the Soviet Union, the People's Republic of China.

For America to continue its role of helping to build a more peaceful world we must keep America No. 1 economically in the world.[25]

*Multinational companies face rising pressure
from foreign economic rationalism.*

By whatever name, the international, transnational, or multinational company is not a new development. Well before World War II, the operations of companies in the extractive industries (from oil and minerals to rubber and bananas) spanned many countries. So did a number of manufacturing corporations—Coca Cola, Heinz, Woolworth, Ford, and Singer—whose names had become international household names by the time World War II paralyzed overseas trade and investment.

But following World War II, a virtual explosion of multinational activity occurred. One reason for the great growth in corporate direct investment abroad, mainly by American companies, was the upsurge in demand for goods and services created by the need for reconstructing the war-ranged economies of Europe. Another reason was the competitive edge enjoyed by most large U.S. firms through their superior technology and management know-how. Still other reasons were the lower labor costs prevailing in most overseas economies relative to the United States, and actual or feared tariff barriers to the entry of goods exported from the home plants of American companies—especially in Common Market countries.

All of these factors, aided and abetted by the rapid advances in transportation and communications of the last 20 years, combined to propel the number of foreign subsidiaries of leading U.S. corporations from 2,300 in 1950 to more than 8,000 in 1970.[26]

Most of this foreign direct investment took the form of establishing wholly owned subsidiaries or acquiring controlling interests in existing local enterprises. Both were typically in high-growth industries where the American comparative advantage—in manufacturing technology, marketing, and new product development—tended to be greatest.

But not all foreign investment decisions were soundly based. Observation of many of the leading multinational corporations indicates that not infrequently these decisions were more emotional than rational; and many, in hindsight, have proved to be expensive mistakes. During the 1960's, particularly, many large and otherwise well-managed corporations made acquisitions, especially in Europe, because it was fashionable—the "in" thing to do. It was something of an acquisition race to "beat the other fellow to it." Also, acquisitions helped to increase stock values, permitted top management executives to feel proud among their corporate counterparts, and provided interesting travel opportunities (at least initially). As a result, the "morning after" for many competitors in the overseas investment and acquisition race finds them owning subsidiaries that fit no corporate strategy, provide an inadequate return on investment, and require uneconomic expenditures of top-management time.

The pressures on management to think globally in formulating and implementing corporate strategy include the progressive integration of the world economy, the opportunity to supplement maturing markets at home with growing markets abroad, and the need to compete for new sources of raw materials and to take advantage of lower costs overseas for other production inputs. This strategy has to take into account sharp shifts in the attitudes and actions of host-country governments. As Professor Raymond Vernon writes:

> Time after time, the Mexicans have pinched and prodded one foreign-owned enterprise or another into selling off portions of its interests to local businessmen. The Chileans have chewed up Anaconda and Kennecott; the Peruvians have swallowed International Petroleum. To cap the climax, the Andean Subregional Group has emblazoned the principle of foreign fade-out and local takeover in the clauses of an international treaty.[27]

Such concern about the growth of foreign direct investment, though most widespread in the Third World, is by no means limited to these countries. Canada, Australia, and less conspicuously the European Common Market countries have passed or are contemplating measures to restrict or slow down the expansion of foreign-owned or foreign-controlled investment. Thus, the greatest challenge facing the managements of multinational corporations—and those that are considering overseas investment—will be to resolve the conflicting forces of growing trade internationalization and rising economic nationalism. This will call for new forms of overseas resource commitments that are responsive to the interests and attitudes of host countries and that at the same time serve the needs of the multinational corporation.[28]

*Technology is under attack from social
criticism here and competition abroad.*

In his State of the Union message in January 1972, President Nixon said:

As we work to build a more productive, more competitive, more prosperous America, we will do well to remember the keys to our progress in the past. There have been many, including the competitive nature of our free-enterprise system; the energy of our working men and women; and the abundant gifts of nature. One other quality which has always been a key to progress is our special bent for technology—our singular ability to harness the discoveries of science in the service of man.

Secretary General Thant of the United Nations in his final annual report said: "Scientific and technological advance is the most important single factor in bringing about changes not only in the lives of the peoples, but also in the balance of power in the world." [29]

Yet technology is being viewed with suspicion—not by business decision-makers but by thought-leaders in other fields. There is a large and growing body of thought that calls into question technology's impact on human values. The extreme of this view is found in the school of thought that advocates zero population growth in order to reduce substantially the negative impacts of technology on the quality of life.

Thus the great force of technology, which has done so much for mankind, comes into conflict with changing attitudes and values—the force discussed earlier. And the business decision-maker is caught in the crossfire of that conflict, as is well known to those who seek to build nuclear power plants whose purpose is to serve people better.

Resolution of this conflict is being found by balanced and thoughtful leaders in the social sciences. An academic psychologist puts it this way: "The question, therefore, is not whether man can master technology: the question is whether man . . . can master himself. This is the technological imperative; this is the humanistic imperative." [30] As he stands in the crossfire, the business decision maker has a major role to play in dealing with both imperatives. This will require tempering his entrepreneurial drive with his social responsibility. Indeed, enlightened self-interest demands that the business decision-maker find the correct balance.

Technology must be looked to, however, for improvements to make our business firms more competitive. Clement E. Sutton, Jr., vice president and group executive of General Electric Co., said in a speech:

For the U.S. to increase its productivity rapidly enough to offset the recent rounds of wage increases, we estimate that industry will have to double or even triple its investment in automation. What this all adds up to is that American industry is in serious trouble—both at home and in the international marketplace—and we must make dramatic improvements in productivity through automation if we expect to remain competitive and profitable.

There is widespread concern that other industrial nations are overtaking U.S. technological leadership at a pace which threatens the country's competitive viability.

Yet data from the National Science Foundation, which has analyzed R&D spending patterns since 1953, shows a declining trend in the ratio of these expenditures to GNP. The peak was 3 per cent in 1964; but after a slightly lower three-year plateau, the percentage declined each year from 1967 to an estimated 2.6 per cent in 1971. These data also show that in recent years basic research has accounted for 14 per cent of total R&D outlays, applied research for about 22 per cent, and development approximately 64 per cent.

In 1969, the latest year for which data are available, R&D spending totalled $26.2 billion. The Federal Government was the primary *source* of R&D funds (the largest amount being for basic research), while industry was the primary *performer* of research (the largest amount being for development).[31]

The Federal support for R&D has naturally flowed to national defense industries, with aircraft and missiles receiving the largest amount ($5.2 billion); electrical equipment and communications next ($4.3 billion); followed by chemicals, machinery, and motor vehicles and other transportation equipment in that order at less than $2.0 billion each.

Here, then, is a force which clearly receives its major thrust from government; and the Administration is committed to increasing that thrust. In fact, if this country is to reestablish clear-cut technological superiority, Federal support may have to extend beyond the conventional R&D expenditures to include tooling-up, start-up of manufacture, and even marketing. This was the conclusion of a major study by the Commerce Department, "Technological Innovation: Its environment and Management, 1967," which involved a panel of executives associated with U.S. electronic, transport, communications, chemical, and photographic firms. These executives concluded that "research, advanced development or basic invention" accounts for less than 10 per cent of total cost.

But after analyzing the proposed new initiatives of government, Karl G. Harr, Jr., president of the Aerospace Industries Association, states:

But will these steps be enough? I think not, unless two other elements are present. First we must obviously have the same kind of dedication from industry that has brought us to our present pre-eminence in high-technology development—and we must have it applied with renewed vigor to the new world in which we now find ourselves.

Second, we must have an entirely new approach by labor to the world we now live in. Labor has an enormous stake in finding the right answer. Because not only are we already exporting our precious technological superiority but, in the absence of effective initiatives here at home, we are on the verge of exporting jobs by the hundreds of thousands. Today we are losing the race—and losing it badly. If we wish to escape the ultimate consequences—a drastically reduced standard of living—we have little time indeed in which to reverse our course.[32]

Thus decision makers in at least every manufacturing business will have to cope with technology as a force; and nearly every business offers some potential for the application of technology. While these will be specific decisions affecting particular businesses, nevertheless decision makers will also need to consider the larger national issues involved. Especially will they need to weigh the contribution of technology to the competitive position of the particular enterprise against any detriment to human values that may result.

COPING WITH FORCES

Coping with forces such as these will involve changes—perhaps almost continuous change—in a company's strategy, structure, policies, and management style; and in the two sections that follow we suggest what some of those changes might be. As mentioned earlier, we believe that the forces discussed here are sufficiently representative so that, by preparing to cope with these particular forces, a company will be well equipped to cope with just about any forces that may develop.

In suggesting an approach that is applicable to any company, we face limitations which should be clearly recognized. Naturally, many of our proposals will be "old hat" to top-management executives of well-managed companies; in fact, we know from our own experience that most of our proposals are being successfully employed in one or more highly successful businesses.

The value of most business decisions to a particular enterprise grows largely out of their suitability, fit, timing, and, especially, the effectiveness of their execution. Indeed, it is no exaggeration to state that most business success results from fairly obvious but well-timed decisions which are skillfully executed.

Let us illustrate. Two of the ways we believe that a business can cope effectively with several of the forces we have discussed is to develop better programs for external communictaions and government relations. Neither activity is new; but we believe that currently they take on new significance, need new emphases, and require better execution.

Therefore, we now move from discussion of representative individual forces to current decisions and actions that the top management of a company might consider for improving its strategy, structure, and management style so as to put it in a better position to capitalize on the favorable forces affecting it and to counter the unfavorable ones.

Strategy and Structure

Responses to many of the forces discussed in the preceding section will require changes in company strategy, in organization structure, and in management style. Since structure should be designed to carry out strategy [33] and since strategy and structure are closely intertwined—we deal with them together in this section, leaving management style for the next and final section.

The CEO must be strongly involved—and strongly supported.

The speed of change—which is being accelerated by technology—has added to the workload of the Chief Executive Officer (CEO). As the executive responsible for keeping the business adjusted to the external forces for change, he must devote more of his personal time to seeing that responses in increasing numbers are developed and put into effect.

There are some who advocate that the CEO spend a major proportion of his time on the future, but this is unrealistic. We believe, however, that the CEO must be oriented to the future at all times. We feel that he should avoid preoccupation with comparative quarter-to-quarter performance, and concentrate his attention on short-term activities that have *future impact,* such as elimination of unhealthy segments, strengthening of weak functions, and, of course, making present decisions on how to cope with the forces of change.

In very large corporations, the top office of the CEO can be a team, but with one member of the team the designated chief executive. Thus the General Electric "corporate executive office" has a chairman and/or president, and three (sometimes four) vice chairmen, who provide points of contact for divisional group executives and staff departments; but all members of the team work closely together. TRW has an executive office consisting of the chairman, vice chairman, and president; the vice chairman is responsible for long-range plans, and the president for operations.

If the business is a sizable industrial concern (with, say, a $75 million sales volume),[34] the CEO will need suitable programs and special executive assistance to cope with major forces such as the nine we covered. The particular apparatus we suggest can be scaled down for smaller concerns, but the activities indicated should at least be provided for:

1. An effective strategic planning program and support staff
2. A full-time environmental protection executive and necessary support staff
3. A strong research and development department at corporate and divisional levels, with R&D activities closely tied to strategy and adequately financed (Establishment of an atmosphere that encourages innovation is a matter of management style, and is discussed in the next chapter.)
4. An effective external affairs function to handle external communications, governmental affairs, and public affairs
5. A personnel function headed by a progressive executive of stature, who is committed to and qualified for helping line managers develop human effectiveness under present and future conditions, including removal of the constraints to effective performance and personal development
6. A full-time organization planning executive, and possibly a small staff to

provide for the frequent structural adjustments needed to cope with external forces.

We will now discuss these six elements.

STRATEGIC PLANNING

Management fashions, like women's fashions, ultimately become so popular that they reach the fad stage, usually accompanied by gimmicks and often even acquiring some mystique. That has been the case with "long-range" planning, a more popular term than "strategic" planning for the same management process.

In the initial fad stage, long-range planning frequently focuses on endless projections of historical sales and profit data for unrealistically long periods ahead. Since such an approach gives the illusion but not the actuality of coping with change, it can be dangerous. A strategic plan is not a forecast. It is a set of current decisions about future forces designed to be carried out; and those who prepare the plan (the line organization) are committed to making it "come to pass."

Thus, strategic planning is a creative decision-making activity, not a procedural, report-producing one. (Often the most powerful strategy can be expressed in a page or two.) The quality of strategic decision making, therefore, depends on the creative abilities of those who make the decisions:

1. Perceptivity in detecting external forces in the environment, including competitive forces.
2. Analytical skill in diagnosing opportunities, challenging current assumptions, and weighing the impact of external and competitive forces.
3. Conceptual skill in formulating strategies, policies, and programs to capitalize on opportunities and to counter negative forces.
4. Skill in allocating resources of all types for implementing strategies. It also requires that the responsible executives have the will, authority, skill, and leadership necessary to carry out the plan (decisions).

These elementary features of strategic planning are frequently disregarded, because too often planning is treated as something apart from the realities of current decision making—as a staff responsibility, not as a basic part of the job of the line organization.

Strategic planning is a total approach: It includes goals, objects, strategies.

Strategic planning is a concept that comes from military science. The military approach to strategy happens to fit well with the approach to coping with military change that we recommend. The dictionary defines "strategy" as "the science and art of employing the political, economic, psychological, and military forces of a nation . . . to afford the maximum support to adopted policies in peace or war." [35] As in military science, strategic planning in business is a total approach—a set of guidelines for thought and action by everyone. Continuing the military approach:

1. The *goal* should be to win the war in such a manner as also to win the peace.
2. *Objectives* are subgoals designed to help achieve the primary goal—major campaigns for particular accomplishments that lead to achieving the goal.[36]
3. *Strategies* are plans, courses of action, or ways for achieving goals and objectives. These plans must be specific in order to provide a basis for allocating resources and taking action.

This kind of approach to strategy—when applied to a business—will also help make executives at all levels sensitive to keeping the business responsive to external change. Such a sensitivity can be not only a valuable resource in keeping executives looking outward but also a unifying force through the development of a greater commonality of purpose.

*The goals of a business reflect achievements
to be sought over the long term . . .*

The goal of a business firm defines the kind or type of business in which the firm wishes to engage, the character of the business (whether a leader in innovation, a volume operator, etc.), its growth objectives, the values of the management, and any other target which it will seek to achieve over the long term.

Goals are usually expressed in idealistic and motivational terms that reflect far-off attainments. T. Vincent Learson, then chairman of International Business Machines Corporation, says: "Our goal is simply stated. We want to be the best service organization in the world." [37] Xerox puts it this way:

> The basic purpose of Xerox Corporation is to find the best means to bring greater order and discipline to information. Thus our fundamental thrust, our common denominator, has evolved toward establishing leadership in what we call "the architecture of information." [38]

All goals need not be lofty and searching. Donaldson, Lufkin and Jenrette, Inc., a successful investment firm, has for years included among its half-dozen goals the statement, "To have fun."

Time spent by line executives in formulating goals is useful because it forces creative thought on fundamental aspects of each business which the firm conducts and on the external forces affecting them. Opportunities in new fields may be disclosed and limited opportunities in old fields may lead to divestments. Continued over a long enough period, collective thinking can help key executives to expand their conceptual thinking, i.e., the capability of translating particular external events into strategic plans or into policies or programs.

. . . whereas objectives are subgoals specifying
desired accomplishments for shorter time periods . . .

Objectives are usually focused on achievements to be attained during shorter time-periods. Objectives should be stated in specific and realistic terms that permit measurement of progress and meaningful performance evaluation. For example, a 10 per cent increase in share-of-market should include the period over which the increase is to be obtained, the amount of added expense to be incurred, and the rate of profit to be expected during and after the period of special effort.

Objectives should be internally consistent. Too often companies select a series of financial targets that are in conflict with each other, i.e., they establish targets for sales, earnings, return on investment, dividend policy, etc., without clearly recognizing that a decision on any one of these objectives constrains the range of choice on all others. The same consistency check must be rigorously applied to non-financial targets, e.g., when the manufacturing division sets quality leadership as a target, and the marketing group sets a volume/price leadership goal, and the finance department is seeking to reduce external funding requirements, then problems of inconsistent objectives are likely to arise.

Finally, objectives should respond to external forces. It is surprising how many institutions identify emerging threats and/or opportunities, but then fail to convert them into action-inducing objectives for their executive group. For example, many companies clearly sensed the growing pressures for environmental quality that were described earlier. Yet how many converted these forces into meaningful targets for their managers—targets that had the full force of the company's reward system behind them? Too many simply gave lip service to these forces and continued to set goals for, and evaluate performance on, purely internally oriented profit measures. Now, outsiders are setting the environmental quality objectives; the companies have lost control.

. . . and strategies spell out the action steps needed to attain the objectives.

Strategies, like objectives, must also stand the test of consistency and relevance to external forces. Here the critical ingredient is tough-minded, analytical problem solving—as far away as possible from "blue skying" and academic truisms. The task is to turn objectives like "We need to respond more effectively to international competition and to rising consumerism" into specific action steps. This means outlining a series of decisions that have to be made *beginning now* in order to successfully implement the objective.

There is no single or simple approach that can be prescribed for developing strategies. They must emerge from a deep understanding of the present and future profit economics of the industry, the competitive position of the company, the unique external forces impinging on the industry and company, and the specific goals and objectives the company has established.

For example, the General Electric Company has recently been awarded a unique contract to help the State of Connecticut deal with the problem of solid waste removal. On the surface, this appears to be an unusual example of fine strategic planning—identifying an environmental trend, converting it into an opportunity based on a clear understanding of the company's unique resources, and then developing a decision-oriented program for action. There was no textbook approach for GE to follow in developing this opportunity. It clearly required extensive inputs of creative but analytical based thinking.

Since all we can suggest is an approach, we offer the following as the critical factors for developing the strategy of a manufacturing business (or, by adaption, to a service type business)—using "business" in the sense of a product/marketing group that makes up a strategic business unit—frequently a manageable profit center:

1. *Product performance*—suitability to the task, effectiveness, quality, durability, style, costs, etc.
2. *Service*—availability, effectiveness, reliability, costs, etc.
3. *Company and product image*—confidence in the company for producing products of quality, reliability, value, etc.; image of the product itself for quality, reliability, as a status symbol, value, etc.
4. *Price/value*—a derivative of how the other critical factors blend to provide competitive strength. (For example, without competitive strength from a combination of product performance, service, or company/product image, customer value must depend on lower price.)

While strategic planning is a line responsibility, with the CEO being finally responsible for strategy, the CEO of the company—and probably of each major division—should be provided with some staff support to assist him in these three activities. For example, in Mobil Oil Corporation the Long-Range Analysis and Strategy Group has responsibility "to project and comprehend technological, social, economic, governmental, and population factors that may affect Mobil's business as much as 30 years ahead." [39]

ENVIRONMENTAL ORGANIZATION

Even without environmental legislation and legal standards, any management can safely assume that it is a fact that society is showing its unwillingness to assume many of the "spill-over" costs of corporate action—i.e., damage to the environment or to people resulting from decisions made in the corporation's interests. This low tolerance for spill-over costs must simply be factored into the corporation's decision-making process.

Problems of the environment are relatively so new for some businesses and so extensive for others, however, that many companies need to establish a department or senior position with functional authority to see that environmental requirements are met. A number of leading companies have done this—e.g., General Motors, Republic Steel, and Texaco. In GM there is a vice president in charge of the "environmental activities staff," which has major units for automotive safety engineering, automotive emission control, product assurance, experimental safety vehicle, plant and environmental engineering, and vehicle noise control.

The environmental affairs executive should determine (1) what the environmental requirements actually are; (2) what corporate decisions are affected by environmental factors and how they should be modified; (3) what opportunities, if any, environmental factors may present; and (4) what socially responsible action can be taken to get sound legislation passed and sound regulations established and properly administered (in collaboration with the external affairs executive). Here again new political initiatives will be needed to ensure—in a responsible manner—that legislative and administrative actions will soundly meet the interests of the public and the concerned businesses.

Coping with environmental demands will be expensive and often aggravating, but the force is a powerful one, and the best tactics of the business community would seem to be to join forces with government to achieve sound results rather than simply fighting the imposition of new requirements. This approach includes an effort to get legislation and regulations based on realistic and non-emotional assessment of the facts. (Needless to say, a progressive, factual, and socially responsible approach by business will gain credibility and will facilitate real and effective cooperation in the best interests of all constituencies.)

But once the environmental requirements have been finally determined, they simply become facts to be taken into account in making decisions. Hence, no future decisions which concerns the environment can be safely made without assuming that the public will no longer accept significant corporate spill-over costs; i.e., no corporation can expect the public to accept significant air, water, thermal, or silence pollution.

This will typically mean substantial changes in manufacturing processes, plant design, products, and packaging. Costly though these changes may be, industry has dealt with more serious problems in the past.

RESEARCH AND DEVELOPMENT

Basic and applied science and product development (collectively called "R&D") will continue to be one of the prime stimulators of change, because one scientific advance often begets many others. Consequently, changes occur at an accelerating rate. For example, the invention of the electric light bulb called for a whole system of instruments for producing and distributing electricity; and this system resulted in the invention and development of an infinite number of other devices utilizing electricity. Similarly, the atuomobile has had a "Roman candle" effect as it sprayed change, not only over our own economy, but over the entire world.

These and other technological developments have contributed to the current environmental problems, but over the balance of the century technology must also provide most of the solutions to these problems. Indeed, these solutions are creating new product opportunities for many companies.

Also, R&D will have to play an important role in increasing productivity to meet our standard-of-living expectation levels, to provide jobs for oncoming generations, and to rebuild a favorable balance in international trade. Finally, R&D must play the primary role in developing substitutes for our raw material resources that are or will be in short supply. For these reasons, it becomes the responsibility of each individual business to increase the effectiveness and funding of its own R&D effort.

Needed: a tough-minded attitude and considerable support from government.

In general, both industry and government must take a more tough minded attitude toward R&D, and must find ways to obtain more output for the effort and dollars expended.

Industry cannot do it alone. The magnitude of the responsibility of R&D for solving so many of the nation's problems is greater than the corporations of the country can collectively assume. This is leading—and will probably continue to lead—to greater R&D cooperation between business and government over the next two decades.

This cooperation is taking, and should take, these forms:

1. As indicated earlier, government regulations must provide the direction for solving environmental problems, because no company alone can afford competitively to assume the cost burdens of technological solutions unless other companies in the industry are required to assume the same burden. Industry needs to provide more leadership in aiding the development of regulations so that government will not impose unrealistic and unworkable standards.

2. Even greater governmental subsidies will be required to finance large-scale basic and even applied scientific research, so as to enable industry to solve national problems and to compete with companies in other countries where, as in Japan, government provides technological direction and support for business in the national interest.

3. The government will need to strike a proper balance between regulation to protect the public and a degree of regulation that stifles the motivation to innovate. Recent dramatic examples are found in the food and drug fields, where efforts to protect the public have also added significantly to the costs of developing and introducing products such as pharmaceuticals. The time for proving a new product to the point of approval has been doubled and tripled. Thus political and social constraints have been added to the normal technological difficulties of product discovery, innovation, and development.

Top management involvement in R&D becomes more and more important.

As these broad and underlying forces are taking shape and gathering momentum, the individual business needs to face the realities, as well as the difficulties and opportunities, of capitalizing on R&D. Here are some observations and insights for top-management consideration:

1. The expenditures made and/or required are often so substantial that they affect the survival and growth of the whole business. Thus, in one company recently, the board of directors itself was asked to decide whether to shift the product mechanism from electromechanical to electronic.

2. The product life-cycle is shortening, which increases the burden on R&D. Recent examples are found in computers and calculators, where a new generation now appears about every four years. Already some of the calculator business that had been captured recently by the Japanese is being regained in the United States, through the development of sufficiently superior technology to compete with the lower level of Japanese wages.

3. Top management must learn to use, and not to worship, technology. A business can no longer afford the luxury of top management's setting up a "science center," spending a substantial sum on its construction and staffing, and then washing its hands of any responsibility for its effective utilization. One management that spent $20 million on such a symbol of R&D effort found after a few years that nothing useful was coming from the facility.

4. Technology and creativity must be *managed* so as to achieve specific objectives. Creativity, of course, depends on people and their leadership, but their accomplishments can be monitored in terms of expenditures and time.

This has been proven by a few companies that get the most for their R&D money on a scheduled basis. In these companies, R&D people are given specific objectives to be reached and are asked to present programs for achieving these objectives, accompanied by budgeted amounts and scheduled time. If the budget and schedule are satisfactory to top management, they are approved and R&D personnel are expected to deliver accordingly. If the project schedule and budget are not satisfactory, R&D people are expected to develop a new project program. If approved project budgets and schedules are too frequently not met, then new R&D leadership must be provided. This type of tough-minded top management involvement can be developed without top management trying to become "super scientists."

5. In the final analysis, innovation and research are creative activities, and so must depend on the creativity of the people involved. Therefore, R&D leadership must know how to select, train, direct, and motivate creative people. The hard truth is that more effort and more money will not improve R&D results without effective leadership.

6. In view of the complex network of social, political, legal, and economic factors that are constraints on innovation and the end-products of R&D, technology alone cannot do the job. Therefore, a company needs to provide organizationally the means for coping with these constraints on successful innovation and R&D output.

This concept—relatively little explored to date and with no big success stories to fuel its acceptance—will unquestionably be difficult to translate into an effective operating function. But the first step is to recognize the reality of these constraints so they can at least be considered in budgeting R&D and in setting a timetable for results.

In this brief report, there is not much more that we can say regarding R&D except to emphasize the important of R&D effort to the nation and to the individual company and to suggest an emphasis on top management involvement to provide better leadership in defining and requiring expected results.

EXTERNAL AFFAIRS FUNCTION

Coping with the forces for change will, in our opinion, require every sizable company to have an External Affairs Department at the corporate level, headed by a competent executive of stature who enjoys the confidence of the CEO. This department would replace any present public relations and governmental relations departments.

This new department would be responsible for external communications, governmental affairs, and public affairs. We believe that the term "relations," frequently used in this context, has unfortunate connotations in overemphasizing the company's self-interest in its relationship with government and the public. Although every business should, of course, seek to serve its own interests, the approach of the external affairs department should reflect the statesmanlike attitudes of the socially responsible corporation, by advocating only positions that are in the public interest as well as the corporation's interest.

The public affairs department of the multinational corporation, for example, will be serving the public interest as well as its own interest in taking steps designed to explain the importance of international trade. In his Budapest speech, Senator Ribicoff said, "It is time to grasp the idea that the process of international trade increases productivity as surely as machinery and technology does." [40]

The forces for change are relentlessly
pushing business and government closer together . . .

The next 20 years will probably see coming to fruition some of the steps now being advocated, such as more government assistance for technology, mentioned earlier. It is the responsibility of the public affairs department to detect and analyze these forces, and to provide the initiatives to support the changes that are in the public interest and to disapprove those that are not.

The Federal Trade Commission reports that in 1968 the 200 largest manufacturers held about 60 per cent of the assets of all manufacturers (up from 45 per cent in 1947). Among the 200 largest industrial corporations in the *Fortune* 500 for 1971 were 18 with more than 100,000 employees, and the range was from 773,000 (General Motors) to a small number with fewer than 20,000 employees. The total employment of these 200 industrials was about 11 million. [41]

Certainly these 200, all of the large nonindustrial corporations, and many smaller corporations of all types are political institutions whose employees, stock-holders, and suppliers interests, as such, are vitally concerned with what the government is doing and might soundly do to help them cope with the forces for change.

An external affairs department whose purpose is to help formulate and execute government business programs is not the typical "Washington office," although that type of office may perform some of the functions of the proposed new office. The hallmark of the external affairs department should be its socially responsible, statesmanlike, posture in advocating positions and taking actions only of the kind that are in the interests of both business and the public, as likely to be judged by nonbusiness thought-leaders who are not antibusiness.

Given the confidence of this posture, the external affairs department can move aggressively and effectively ahead in the public arena, *provided,* of course, that it is in fact reflecting the policy and actions of the corporation it represents. As we study the forces for change, we believe that such actions by leading corporations are an important—indeed even essential—way to cope with the forces that lie ahead.

. . . and business should provide the leadership
for developing this with a partnership.

Since coping with the forces of the future will inevitably bring business and government closer together, the business community should take the lead rather than letting that leadership come from others. The fact remains that the business community will be judged by its products, service, advertisements, and other tangible manifestations, and not by its words. So no external affairs department can risk either words or actions that do not truly reflect the current and prospective actions of the company.

If this approach is effectively pursued by a few corporations whose leadership is recognized, it could even lead to reducing the "cold war" between government and business. If world political trends are substituting "economic war" for the "cold war," it is essential that U.S. government and business team up to protect the interests of the nation.

Some 82 million Americans are currently on corporate payrolls. There are about 37 million shareholders. And 7 million are dependent on corporate investments as pensioners and trust-beneficiaries. Hence, there must be a commonality of interest between business and the public which is greater than is currently recognized by the electorate.

Therefore, the business community has an opportunity as well as a responsibility to exercise more effective and more statesmanlike leadership in developing new relationships between government and business that can cope effectively with forces now foreseen and those that will develop as the world "economic war" heats up. Such leadership must come from corporate CEO's, but external affairs departments can help in formulating and executing programs. If the growing social responsibility of business executives is the force that it promises to be, it will have an impact in stimulating progressive business leaders to assume a new and/or larger role in advocating a more effective government-business partnership in the interests of the whole nation.

PERSONNEL FUNCTION

Changing social attitudes and values have an impact on the effectiveness, aspirations, and job satisfaction of every employee in every organization—from the lowest ranking clerical and plant jobs to the CEO. These changes impact directly on the organization's ability to attract, retain, and motivate employees. Hence, they can have a direct, though seldom measured, impact on the competitive position, growth, productivity, and profitability of the enterprise.

*The goals of the organization and the
goals of individuals must be compatible.*

Some time ago, psychologists and other students of management developed the thesis that work effectiveness at all levels is best achieved when the goals of the organization and of the individual are most compatible—i.e., "I'll walk hand in hand with the devil as long as he is going my way." This theory of compatible goal attainment has been put into operation in some highly successful companies. One of these is Texas Instruments, whose president, Mark Shepherd, Jr., writes: "The most important continuing challenge to industry in the years ahead will be to establish innovative programs that encourage the achievement of compatible employee and company goals." [42]

Changing social attitudes and values will have an impact on the employees' goals; goal change can lead to goal incompatibility, and thus to dysfunctional organizational conflict.

The role of the personnel function is to provide line management with the staff assistance required to: (1) identify, perhaps anticipate, changes in attitudes and values in the work force, or segments thereof; (2) measure the impact of these changes on organizational performance, in terms of productivity and profitability; and (3) design programs that will help ensure individual and organizational goal compatibility.

The compatibility of company and personal goals is so important that some companies have changed company goals in order to bring them into greater harmony with employee goals. An early example of this is found in the Procter and Gamble Company. Colonel Procter, a pioneer in advanced personnel thought, believed that steady employment was a desired goal of the employees. In 1923, the company established the policy of providing 48 standard work-weeks of employment for all employees with tenure of two years and more. In 1945, a subsequent CEO described how the company had to be changed basically in order to support this policy—and how profits were stepped up in the process. [43]

The so-called goal-oriented, involvement, or participative school of management [44] believes that the goals of the firm and the individual can be brought most closely together when individuals are involved in setting their own goals, are accountable for their own behavior, and share in the responsibilities and rewards for accomplishing organization goals. Mark Shepherd puts it this way:

Management's role in attracting, challenging, and retaining the members of the coming generations is as vital to an organization's success as any breakthrough in technology or newly designed production equipment.

The truly successful growth organization of the future will require a marriage of industry's richest assets—the capabilities of human beings and the efficiency of operational systems. As high-volume, repetitive, and rigidly paced manufacturing systems place unyielding demands on people, management must show the same dedication to improving job satisfaction that it has in the past to improving equipment design and satisfying people's pay requirements. [45]

We believe it is mandatory that organizations develop effective responses to changes in social attitudes and values. Few companies, however, are equipped to meet this challenge. Too many separate responsibilities for operations management from responsibilities for people management, leaving the latter too much to personnel specialists, and not requiring line managers to manage people and jobs so as to ensure the greatest mutual compatibility of objectives. Only when responsibility for meeting both personal and organizational goals is vested in the line can the enterprise hope to explore—and make—the necessary trade-offs in an optimal fashion. Otherwise, line managers will view their role in purely operational terms—i.e., to get the product down the assembly line in the fastest way, no matter how dull and boring the assembler's work becomes. If participative management is to be effective, the participation must be between the line manager and the individuals they lead. (The experience of Koch and French in Sweden likewise shows that the individuals being "led" also have a need to participate.)

The personnel function must be upgraded —must break from its traditional orientation.

Line management responsibility for both people and operations does not mean that the personnel function should be eliminated, or reduced in importance; quite the contrary. The role of the personnel function can and should take on increasing importance, but it must break from its traditional orientation. The role of the personnel manager is one of a professional advisor. He must pinpoint changes in attitudes and values. He must measure their impact on goal orientation and thus individual motivation. But, too often, personnel managers—and indeed line executives—assume that they know what the attitudes and values of their employees are. And should these assumptions prove incorrect, the rhetoric turns quickly to what they *should* be. It is understandable why personnel and operations plans go awry when they are based on faulty input assumptions.

Beyond just identifying and measuring changes in attitudes and values, the role of a professional personnel function is to establish the link between these factors and the hard measures of organizational performance. The fact that company loyalty may be eroding in younger employees takes on meaning only when it is linked to increased turnover, which in turn is correlated with decreased productivity and increased recruiting, orientation, and training costs. Changed social attitudes and values become new facts that must be dealt with in new ways to increase human effectiveness and satisfaction under new conditions. More companies need to dedicate their efforts just as fully to increasing human effectiveness as they do to improving marketing and productive effectiveness.

The most difficult function of the personnel department is to develop new approaches to matching personal and organization goals. Biographical data analysis has proved useful in reliably identifying individuals whose needs, values, and attitudes match or do not match job requirements. Performance reinforcement techniques have been developed to provide timely, unthreatening feedback on performance. Productivity bargaining and performance councils have enhanced collaborative efforts between unions and management. Job enlargement and job enrichment have reduced the monotony of many clerical and production jobs. And the 4-day week and flexible work hours have been developed to better meet employees' commuting and leisure needs.[46]

Most of these innovations have not achieved their full potential. The benefits are seldom quantified—either in terms of employee satisfaction or of organizational performance. As a result, line executives become skeptics, especially when the program is viewed as an end in itself, rather than a means to an end. Moreover, the innovations often are not extended to their logical conclusion in other parts of the organization, let alone other organizations. And when they are transplanted, it is seldom done with an eye to determining what conditions made the program effective in one place yet are nonexistent, or different, in the new organization.

With social values and attitudes changing at an accelerating pace, there is great need for further pioneering efforts in the personnel function. Although the hard sciences have been exploited extensively for research and production, few companies have made an adequate exploration of the possible usefulness of the behavioral sciences in improving human resource management. Admittedly, the latter is more difficult; indeed, many top management executives have difficulty in even understanding the behavioral scientists. Yet the responsibility for adequate exploration rests with the businessman, since he has the job to do.

If such a dynamic and difficult approach is to be employed under the functional direction of the personnel officer, he must have stature within the business and enjoy the confidence of the CEO. Such an executive can provide leadership in helping line managers to increase the work effectiveness and job satisfaction of their people. He can help them to adjust managing processes, job content, and work flow to changing social attitudes and values of people at all levels.

But the CEO must have the will to take this approach; and he must provide continuing leadership for it. He must also ensure that the company climate is one in which it can flourish. His will and leadership must rest on the conviction that line managers can contribute to the company's improved performance and profits through their dedication to continuing and productive actions to increase work effectiveness through job satisfaction. There must also be general conviction that this is a tough-minded as well as a warm-hearted approach—and that from the satisfactions of people with their jobs flow improved morale, greater productivity, improved competitive position, and larger profits.

ORGANIZATION PLANNING EXECUTIVE

A plan of organization defines the responsibilities and authorities of the positions that are established to carry on the activities of the organization, and the superior, subordinate, functional, and staff relationships of the people holding these positions. Since nearly every response to change will require changes in the types and number of activities carried on by the company, positions will need to be added, changed, or dropped; and organizational relationships among people holding the positions may need change as well.

It follows that an acceleration in the rate of change will result in an increasing need for reorganization. Reorganization is usually feared, because it means a disturbance of the status quo, a threat to people's vested interests in their jobs, and an upset to established and comfortable ways of doing things. For these reasons, needed reorganization is often deferred, with a resulting loss in effectiveness and an increase in costs.

A company should be prepared to reorganize whenever change dictates.

One of the country's largest, most successful and rapidly growing corporations reorganizes so frequently that "reorganization" is no longer an ugly word, and the process is accepted without either surprise or fear. Acceptance of reorganization as a normal operating process is a desirable attitude to cultivate in any business. This will be easier if the company has an atmosphere of confidence and mutual trust, which is an important feature of management style.

In any event, as the rapidity of change steps up, it may be wise to provide an organization planning executive; and, in a sizable company, he will need a small staff. This executive should not only be technically competent, but have imagination and the capacity to gain the confidence of people so they will 'level" with him about sensitive organizational problems. He should not stimulate organization change unnecessarily, but he should help line executives to keep the plan of organization in tune with changing activities.

But the organizational planning staff can do much more than just keep the structure "updated." Forces of the type we have discussed can be better dealt with if business firms can develop new organizational concepts and approaches.

The "invention" of the integrated business division as a profit center in the early 1920's is still serving business well as a means for decentralizing decision-making and fixing accountability for profits. More recently, the product manager and project manager concepts have made significant contributions to increased organizational effectiveness.

As businesses grow larger and more complex, however, new organizational concepts will be needed in order to respond effectively to the forces for change. Some of the activities required for effective responses to change can probably not be easily assigned to "profit centers." In fact, in large-scale enterprises there are already many activities for which effectiveness cannot be measured by profit alone. So new ways for fixing accountability must be found. This is particularly true for the large and complex national organization with its multiproduct and multidivisional makeup, especially when some divisions serve all others.

Finally, if the concept of substantially greater self-government for the individual is employed as a response to changing attitudes and values, this can have an important impact on organization structure. Thus, if self-government is real, there is less need for close supervision; and perhaps the hierarchical structure can be modified, especially when the information for decision making is more readily available through computers and telecommunications. For instance, if managers are really self-governing, a substantially larger number of them can report to a single superior.

The organizational planning executive should also experiment with the use of group effort in increasing productivity, possibly drawing on Japanese experience.

These hypotheses are mentioned merely to indicate that new organizational concepts and forms will undoubtedly be needed, or could be useful, in managing the new activities and managing processes required for effective responses to fundamental change. Therefore, the organizational planning staff can become a significant resource in coping with change. Also, the organization planning executive, whose duties require him to range broadly throughout the company, can make an important contribution to keeping the business flexible so it can "roll with the punches." And he can help in developing the style of management which is discussed in the final section of the chapter.

Before going on to discuss this important matter of management style, however, we want to look at the multinational as a prime example of the need for making decisions about strategy and structure.

MULTINATIONAL STRATEGY AND STRUCTURE

The significance of the multinational's role today was trenchantly outlined by Senator Abraham Ribicoff in a speech he made in Budapest during a visit to Rumania and Hungary in his capacity as chairman of the International Trade Subcommittee of the Senate Finance Committee, in June 1971. Here are some of his significant observations:

The activities of multinational corporations, and the increasing use of joint ventures and consortiums are crossing frontiers and erasing national boundaries more surely and swiftly than the passage of armies and the conclusion of peace treaties. . . .

Increasing technological, economic, and trade considerations are determining the nature of relations between nations. . . .

I am convinced that during the last quarter of this century, ecopolitics will replace geopolitics as the prime mover in the affairs of nations.[47]

At the same time that international trade barriers are breaking down, however, the new forces of economic nationalism noted earlier are gathering strength. It is clear, therefore, that formulation of strategy for a multinational corporation will require the development of a new competence in, and sensitivity to, international political developments.

*Economic battling on the international
arena calls for new initiatives . . .*

As the "cold war" with the Soviet bloc winds down, there are indications that an "economic war" is taking its place. It will be well for multinational strategists to remember that when Premier Khrushchev visited the United States some years ago, he boasted that the Soviets would ultimately "bury the West economically."

As trading increases with the U.S.S.R. and other socialist nations (including China), U.S. corporations will be dealing with governments or government instrumentalities, which may put them at a disadvantage. Even now, many U.S. corporations face difficult competition from Japanese corporations, which enjoy strong support from their government.

Hence as the internationalization of trade broadens, U.S. corporations may need new types of support from the U.S. Government. And certainly the interests of the whole nation will be better served if antagonisms between government and business can be replaced by cooperation. This will require the exercise of social responsibility by corporate management, accompanied by new corporate political initiatives.

. . . while at the same time labor puts business under increasing pressure.

Multinationals must also counter demands of organized labor that they be curbed in a number of basic ways, allegedly to prevent the transfer of jobs to other countries. The demands of organized labor for restrictive legislation is likely to continue into the distant future unless the public, Congress, and even labor leaders themselves can be convinced that the net effect of expanding international trade will be to increase opportunities for American works and benefit all citizens.

Bringing about broad public acceptance of this role for the multinational is a responsibility of the business community, which will require the exercise of political and informational initiative. If these initiatives are to have credibility, they must have objectivity and a genuine dedication to the public interest. Thus politics as well as ecopolitics will be critical elements in the success of national and multinational corporations; and here the CEO's strategy staff will need to assess political opportunities and threats.

The corporation will need to make important decisions about structure.

How will the multinational respond to these many new forces? Strategic planning of the kind we have discussed is even more essential for them; and that, in turn, will lead to decisions about structure.

Multinationals face basic structural problems as they expand to new countries and increase worldwide sales volume. The classic structural issue calls for determining (a) whether headquarters direction of subsidiaries in other countries shall be provided by an international division covering all countries; (b) whether there shall be groupings of subsidiaries by regions; or (c) whether there shall be worldwide product/market units coordinated by their respective parent company divisions. The best results seem to be obtained by the last of these alternatives, provided volume is large enough and other essential conditions are met; but, of course, provision must be made for coordination among all product/market units in the same country on such matters as relations with the government, labor, and the public.

Dealing with ecopolitics may require structural changes of other types too, including new departments. For example, one large multinational has its own "state department" under another name. This department is staffed chiefly with former government officials, whose responsibilities include the assessment of its subsidiaries' political risks—and opportunities—present and prospective.

And, here again, management style is crucial. In a study of the financial control of multinational operations undertaken for the Research Foundation of Financial Executives Institute, the researchers found that the difference between successful and unsuccessful operations lies, not in procedures or formal arrangements, "not in what you do, but the spirit in which you do it—a matter of style, really." [48]

Style of Management

Management style—which may be defined as "the way we run the business"— has received inadequate attention from top management as a means for improving company performance. As outsiders who get behind the scenes of many well-managed companies, we have observed the power of style as an unwritten law governing quite precisely how people shall make decisions and conduct themselves generally within the company.

Hence the style with which a business is managed can have specific value in coping with particular forces, and broad value in keeping executives sensitive to change. Therefore, we recommend that, in coping with change, top management give greater attention to developing the company's management style through attention to making managing methods work and to leadership example.

NATURE AND POWER OF STYLE

"The way we run the business" usually develops as a matter of practice and of following example, rather than through the conscious development of guidelines for decision making and personal conduct. Everyone down the line watches for "signals" from top-management executives as to how he should conduct himself; and these signals are not what the CEO and those reporting to him *say*, but what they *do*. In fact, written policies and organization plans can easily be nullified by failures of top-management executives to follow them, because the unwritten law of leadership action is more powerful than the written law of the leaders.

Style reflects the personal values of the leaders, as consciously and subconsciously disclosed by their actions. Over time, their actions and reactions crystallize into the unwritten law that governs people's conduct within the corporation.

Many of the factors influencing management style are dynamic and interactive; but collectively they combine to produce a well-defined "climate" within the organization. This climate has a continued and powerful influence on the attitudes and decisions—and on the actions, reactions, and interactions—of people at all levels. And an effective management style can help to ensure that external forces are detected and responses developed.

Therefore, one of the ways to cope with powerful forces is to *plan* the style of managing the business; write the style out and publish it (perhaps calling the brochure "management philosophy"); communicate it in every way possible; require that it be followed through discipline and example; and provide financial and nonfinancial incentives for following it. Above all, the top-management executives must be the stylesetters and style leaders. They must communicate it by their *actions* and by pointing out on-the-job how the actions of people square with or violate the company's management style or philosophy.

Discussion of just a few elements of style will illustrate how management style can help a business cope with particular forces for change, make it more flexible and responsive to change generally, and improve performance throughout the business.

1. Giving work more meaning
2. Fact-based decision making
3. Self-government for the individual
4. The role of profits
5. Climate that encourages productivity

6. Sensitivity to external forces

7. Staffing with "style conscious" executives

In discussing these elements, we point out a number of ways to develop and communicate the company's style of management.

GIVING WORK MORE MEANING

The people working in a business spend at least half of their waking hours in their particular business "community." The total enterprise is an over-all community, whether it is a multinational corporation or a small business operating at a single location, and a total company style will develop. For geographical, physical, or organizational reasons there will be communities within the larger community, such as an overseas subsidiary, a geographically separated division, a plant, or an office. Each of these subcommunities will probably have style characteristics of its own, reflecting the values and actions of its present and past leaders; but all will be influenced by style factors of the total enterprise.

The people coming to the business bring all of their individual attitudes and values developed in society generally, and take home their attitudes and values as shaped by their experience in their particular business community. The interaction between conditions in their business community and the society outside will determine their attitudes, values, and motivations.

Opportunity: to serve society's interests as well as the company's.

The corporation has an opportunity to influence the attitudes and values of its employees in ways which will improve their work performance, and, in addition, to provide a favorable climate for development of the attitudes and values they reflect in the home and in society generally.

The National Commission on Marijuana and Drug Abuse, as part of its work, conducted a seminar on "Central Influences on American Life." Participants in the seminar were 13 educational authorities and other thought leaders. Here are some excerpts from the report on the seminar:

One overriding influence in contemporary America is the declining capacity of our institutions to help the individual find his place in society. As one of the participants at the seminar observed:

"A society is stable, peaceful, happy, not when it has rid itself of the tensions—because you never get rid of the tensions, because people's drives will be satisfied in ways that clash and so on—but when a very high proportion of the people feel fulfillment of some sort within the context which the society normally provides. The long-term problem now for many, many people, not just young people, is that this condition is not met."

Many Americans, due to the nature of their jobs in an automated economic system, find little personal satisfaction in their work, and many are now searching for individual fulfillment through the use of free time. Where meaning is not found in either work or recreational pursuits, the outcome is likely to be boredom and rest-lessness. Whether generated by a search for individual fulfillment, group recreation or sheer boredom, the increased use of drugs, including marijuana, should come as no surprise.[49]

Corporations throughout the world have the same reasons for seeking to aid in the development of social attitudes and values of their employees. For example, Kazutaka Kikawada, chairman of the board of the Tokyo Electric Power Company, Inc., in a speech at the annual meeting of *Keizai Doyukai* (Japan Committee for Economic Development), of which he is chairman, had this to say:

I think that we in management must, through new development of management policies for human welfare, start in earnest to try to find a basic solution to the problem of modern man in the corporation, which, after all, is a part of society. Modern enterprises in themselves constitute communities. Their position now is such that they are going to have to become a nucleus for giving to community consciousness, which is so weak in Japan, especially in urban society, a concrete shape that is appropriate to the new age and its demands by pushing this corporate community further socially. In this sense I think it is necessary that managerial policies for human welfare be vigorously put into practice that will serve to build a new order . . . for qualitative fulfillment in human life, a place rich in humanism where one can achieve self-realization.[50]

Idealistic? Yes. Difficult? Certainly. Impossible? Not for a corporation whose CEO has the values, the will, and the leadership to put established principle into practice. Never has there been a time when the social forces to be coped with were stronger—or the needs of business and society greater. What, then, are the principles which, if put into practice, will enable people to find "meaning" in their work and get "self-realization" from it?

Needed: compatibility of goals, participation,
democracy, respect, informality, even humility.

We have discussed earlier two requirements for enabling people to get meaning from their work: (1) compatibility of company and individual goals, and (2) participation in establishing those goals and in the work and working conditions involved in achieving them. Further, many people are demonstrating that they do not want to work under authoritarian direction; and this is requiring changes in management style in many corporations. When goals and work are specified in an authoritarian manner, the individual not only gets less meaning from his work, but reacts to set his own goals that circumvent, violate, or change company goals.

When assignments are made, they should be tied to goals to give the individual the satisfaction of "how" the task or duty that is assigned helps to achieve the goals that, hopefully, he accepts. The story is told of the president of a refrigerator company who, while going through the plant, asked a worker who was crating the finished refrigerators what he was doing. The worker said, "I'm crating refrigerators." The president, "Oh no, you are protecting the refrigerator from getting damaged so it will arrive in good shape and satisfy the customer, on whom all our jobs depend."

Ideally, the work itself will be intrinsically interesting. Even monotonous and distasteful work will be more tolerable, however, when the individual recognizes that it leads to meaningful goals. Hence, goals which have maximum motivational value are (1) influenced by the individual, (2) visible, (3) desirable, (4) challenging, (5) attainable, and (6) lead to satisfaction of individuals' needs for growth, achievement, responsibility, recognition, affiliation, and security.[51]

Work will be more meaningful in a democratic, open, working atmosphere where mutual trust and respect prevail and corporate politics and personal backbiting are discouraged by everyone. Such an atmosphere is encouraged by managers and supervisors whose behavior reflects confidence in, and respect for, others. They share company information freely, help people under their supervision by involving them in solving problems.

Work will have more meaning—and people will be more productive—in an atmosphere where people treat each other with mutual respect and the informality of social peers. To achieve this, efforts should be made to eliminate hierarchical and status symbols insofar as possible. "Levels" should be minimized in dining room facilities and avoided in parking lots. The chairman of one of the largest and most profitable companies has no special place in the parking lot; and (unless he is entertaining visitors when he uses a private dining room) he carries his tray in the cafeteria line and sits at a table available to any employee.

In such an informal atmosphere, people address each other by their first names, and are free to dress as they wish. No effort is made to discourage grapevine communications. Flaunting of symbols of rank is avoided; and real, not feigned, humility is the normal attitude of everyone.

Superiors are expected, indeed required, to be fair in judging people; and their evaluations are based on performance. High standards of ethics are prescribed by the unwritten law of example by the leaders. People are not afraid of "getting out of line" or being unfairly criticized. Therefore, there is a real and substantial upwards communication, which can be particularly useful to top management in coping with change.

Management style in the U.S. multinational corporation has several other dimensions, especially since the cultures of the people in subsidiaries located in other countries will differ (often substantially) from the American culture. Nevertheless, the participative, open, management style usually provides a better foundation than the authoritarian style for developing effective and satisfying relations with people in other cultures.

Participative management as a feature of style cannot be developed easily or quickly. As we have mentioned, the CEO should be the stylesetter. But much progress can be made in developing participative management in a separate segment of a business if the top leader of that "community" becomes the style leader.

FACT-BASED DECISION MAKING

A high standard of fact-based decision making is an important feature of a management style that is well suited to coping with change. Of course, every company bases decisions on facts to a considerable degree—otherwise it would fail. Like so many other management concepts, however, the value of the fact-based approach depends on the degree, effectiveness, and consistency of its use. If there are frequent references to "who's right," that is an indication of a poor standard of fact-based decision making. In the company where fact-based decision making is a real part of its management style, the automatic approach is "what's right," not "who's right."

Only the most successful companies really use facts adequately.

Too often, decisions are based on "experience" and are impaired by fixed attitudes of senior executives toward particular issues. Such deficiencies in the decision-making process are particularly serious in a period of rapid change. It is then that fact-based decision making really pays off.

Three chief executives of General Motors Corporation have maintained publicly that fact-based decision making is one of the four major reasons for the success of GM. In testimony before the Senate subcommittee investigating dealer practices in the automobile industry, Harlow Curtice, then the president of GM, put it this way:

> Now we come to the second fundamental reason for the success of General Motors—our approach to problems. It is really an attitude of mind. It might be defined as bringing the research point of view to bear on all phases of the business. This involves, first, assembling all the facts, second, analysis of where the facts appear to point, and, third, *courage to follow the trail indicated even if it leads into unfamiliar and unexplored territory.* This point of view is never satisfied with things as they are. It assumes that everything and anything—whether it be product, process, method, procedure, or social or human relations—can be improved (emphasis supplied).

The factual approach to decision making cannot be legislated. It can only be built into a company through action over time in collecting and analyzing facts and then acting on the alternative that is best in the light of the facts. Ideally, the job of building the fact-based approach starts at the top. The higher the executive, the more powerful will his example be. But the head of any department or other organizational unit can build the factual approach into his unit. If he insists on facts and acts on facts, his subordinates will gladly do the same.

The fact-based approach has particular value in coping with the forces for change, for these reasons:

1. Any force ultimately becomes a "fact." (For example, environmental demands that have not yet been incorporated into legislative standards are, nevertheless, facts to be dealt with.) Top-management executives must be openminded

in viewing forces as facts. If some intangible force is incorrectly evaluated as not being significant, then that "fact" is not being faced.

2. Once a force and its potential impact can be factually established, alternate ways for dealing with the force can be developed and evaluated and a choice made of the most attractive probability among the alternatives. If the probable impacts of any of the forces likely to develop during the next couple of decades are simply treated as facts, the whole process of coping with change is made more manageable.

3. If the fact-based approach is part of the company's management style, it will make the enterprise more flexible and hence more responsive to change. Thus when the fact-based approach is employed, plans and decisions are readily changed as new forces (i.e., facts) come into play. This provides automatic justification for the executive who must change his position or prior decision; in truth, he *is* acting consistently, because, in making both the old and new decisions, he is simply guided by facts. In such a climate, readjustment to reality is continuous; and this is one of the central requirements for coping with change.

4. The fact-based feature of management style supports the participative management feature. Company-wide respect for facts facilitates objective evaluation and lowers the barriers between levels of authority. The factual approach leads to fairness and better relations among people, because discussion replaces argument, and personal differences and personality conflicts are minimized. When everyone feels that "we are in this together to find and face the facts, and to do whatever the facts dictate," the upward flow of communications is stimulated, and subordinates are encouraged to speak up with factually supported differences of opinion.

If top management should make a determined effort to incorporate the fact-based approach to decision making as a real and vital part of its management style, this will, of course, also lead to better decision making and improved performance generally.[52]

SELF-GOVERNMENT FOR THE INDIVIDUAL EMPLOYEE

The American dream of self-government for every citizen, reflected in the Constitution, is lost for eight hours a day when the individual works for a company where he has no say about what he does on his job. At the same time, if a company does pursue self-government for its employees as an ideal and makes it something of a reality, it can do much to cope with changing social attitudes and values. It will never be possible to achieve this ideal (nor would every individual want it). But if every management seeks to make self-government a definite element of its management style, progress can be made in the right direction.

Some of the ingredients for achieving this ideal have been discussed earlier—developing compatibility between company and individual goals, participative management, and the fact-based approach to decision making. Further steps toward the ideal of self-government can be taken through the development of other guidelines for individual effort, such as clearly stated major policies and well-defined organization structure. Also, the computer can provide the individual with the information that he needs for making decisions, thus freeing him further from the need for detailed instructions from his superior.

Even at the lowest level, self-government
is worth striving for.

With disappearing management prerogatives now a reality, the competent and informed individual expects to be freer to work on his own, even at the lowest level. If the company's management style is developed to achieve that objective, and there is a genuine participation of the people it will affect, self-government of the individual can be made sufficiently a reality to step up both employee satisfaction and performance. The dedication and effectiveness of people working in voluntary organizations to "put out" without compensation is an illustration of what can be accomplished under proper conditions for self-government.

A number of companies are working toward this goal. For example, the Chrysler Corporation is conducting an extensive experiment on the production line, as reported in a *New York Times* article of June 19, 1972:

The Chrysler Corporation is . . . trying to make work not simply a penalty a worker feels he has to pay to survive but something that provides satisfaction in itself.

For the last year and a half, workers in many of Chrysler's 32 plants have been meeting with their foremen, engineers and production managers to exchange ideas, solve problems and make suggestions about their jobs.

Some plants are experimenting with letting workers supervise their own assembly lines, letting them control the flow of material on the lines, and allowing them a choice of working on an assembly line or at tables where they can make whole components.

The program is still in its early stages. Its problems are complex, and any judgments would be premature.

Eugene A. Cafiero, group vice president of the Chrysler North American operations, said:

"We've changed more in the past year and a half than in the last 12 years. This company has been through a small revolution."

The company that can develop the reality of a significant degree of self-government for the individual will not only cope more effectively with changing attitudes and values and step up its productivity, but also attract a higher calibre of individual. And even a significant degree of success of a few companies in making self-government part of their management styles will stimulate others to try harder.

APPROACH TO PROFITS

In preparing a business firm to cope most effectively with the forces for change, we recommend that top management build into its management style an approach to profits that is not only long range in time focus but oriented to the discharge of its social responsibilities. Let us stress immediately, however, that in coping with change, we see no reason for a management to deemphasize profit as an *incentive*. In fact, the profit motive is one of the best incentives to keep business fully responsive to the forces for change.

Further, business must, of course, make a profit to stay in business. Indeed, the profit level must be high enough to provide—either from retained earnings or from bank borrowings and/or sale of securities—the funds for research and the capital required for the automation needed to increase productivity and meet competition. But meeting these very real requirements means that profit is better used as a measure of performance rather than solely as an objective.

We believe that the managers of any business will make better strategic decisions if profit is treated as a *reward* for serving users well—and relatively better than users are served by competitors. Thus profit becomes a yardstick for managerial effectiveness, e.g., offering products and services of such value to the user as to *entitle* the company to expanding volume and profits. In other words, in a competitive market economy, profits must be *earned*. They are a basic measure (but not the only measure) of the relative value of the company's contributions to the users, distributors, employees, shareholders, and the public.

Overemphasis on short-term profit increases is not a sound objective.

The beguiling notion that profit is the only objective of a business firm can be both dangerous and self-defeating. Especially is this likely to be the case if profit is regarded as a short-term objective. Indeed, if the short-term view of profits that prevailed generally in the 1960's were to prevail over the next couple of decades, most businesses could not cope effectively with basic forces of the type we are considering.

During the 1960's—and for many companies continuing to the present— many top managements set as an objective a regular growth in quarter-to-quarter profits calibrated to a specific compounded rate of annual profit growth, usually ranging from 10 to 20 per cent. This approach was also found to be the best way to achieve a high price/earnings ratio for the company's common stock.

Regular profit growth and a fully priced common stock are, of course, desirable for the business as well as for the stockholders. Indeed, the declining rate of profits for American business during the past decade is serious, not only for business but for the nation generally. But when there is too heavy an emphasis on short-term profits, then the basic health of the business can easily be sacrificed in the interests of top-management pride and higher short-term stock prices. This likelihood is increased by executive bonuses based on annual profits. Peter Mc-Colough, chairman and CEO of Xerox, puts it this way:

If we ran this business Wall Street's way, we'd run it into the ground. . . . We're in this business for a hell of a long time and we're not going to try to maximize earnings over the short run.[53]

If management style requires a focus on short-term profits, then needed but not urgent long-term expenditures can easily be deferred. The result can be an undermining of the basic health of the business, which means a lowering of long-term profits and stock prices. Since the steps for coping with the forces for change will usually involve long-term expenditures, a short-term profit emphasis can cause a management to overlook opportunities or leave the company vulnerable to external threats.

We recognize that the notion of treating profits as a reward for serving users well and not as an objective, may seem academic. We believe, however, that the distinction is real and useful, and that this approach to profits will help a management to cope more effectively with change and will also help to ensure better health for the business as measured by long-term profits.

Senior executives must recognize that their personal motivations are involved.

One subtle and little-discussed factor affecting the short-term profit viewpoint is the personal motivations of senior executives. The CEO will receive greater applause of stockholders, the press, security analysts, and his peers, if the profits of the enterprise expand regularly and at a uniform rate during his administration. Therefore, his pride provides strong motivation for concentrating on short-term profits. Indeed, this is the reason that quarter-to-quarter earnings comparisons became so popular a few years ago. Division managers are likely to be even more stimulated to showing short-term profit results, because their advancement and compensation are likely to be predicated largely on this factor.

The short-term profit pressures on these key executives can easily result in decisions that are detrimental to the long-term health of the business. This subtle factor has substantial significance in the decisions necessary for coping with the forces for change of the type we have been discussing. The CEO who is only a few years from retirement must wrestle with his conscience frequently in making major decisions that will enhance long-term, but reduce short-term, profits. In coping with change there is probably no better way to deal with this major influence than the exercise of conscience by the CEO and the division manager. They can live with themselves better by making the decisions and taking the risks that they know are sound for the long-term health of the enterprise.

It should help, however, if chief executives and division managers will bring this factor out into the open and discuss it candidly. If there is understanding and approval of their peers, the outcomes of wrestling with their consciences are likely to be more favorable to the long-term health of the enterprise. This approach can be extended to the board of directors. If the CEO makes it clear to his board that a sacrifice in short-term profits is likely to bring substantially greater long-term profits, then his directors can help him cope with the criticisms of lower short-term earnings that will come from stockholders, security analysts, and outsiders whose esteem he values.

Courage to make the "right" long-term decisions will be an important quality in senior executives who will guide their enterprises in coping with the forces for change during the next 20 years. And boards of directors will do well to probe for undersirable emphasis on short-term profits. Directors too must recognize that their pride favors the short term; and their consciences should trouble them unless they conquer the pride factor.

CLIMATE FOR PRODUCTIVITY

Today it is difficult to read an issue of a major newspaper or general magazine that does not in some way refer to the challenge of increasing the productivity of American industry. With both foreign competition and productivity increasing, the challenge to American business corporations is both obvious and serious. But increased productivity is important to all institutions, including governments, hospitals, schools, and universities. And it is the best answer to inflation.

In an excellent speech, "Productivity: Its Meaning for America," [54] Richard C. Gerstenberg, chairman of General Motors, found his definition of the word in a clause in GM's contract with United Automobile Workers, signed in 1950 but still in force: "[The Contract] further recognizes the principle that to produce more with the same amount of human effort is a sound economic and social objective." Mr. Gerstenberg goes on to say:

Productivity is not a matter of making employees work longer or harder. Increased productivity results mostly from sound planning, from wise investment, from new technology, from better techniques, from greater efficiency—in short, from the better exercise of the functions of management.

I regard productivity as a measure of management's efficiency, or lack of efficiency, in employing all the necessary resources—natural, human, and financial. . . . If America is to improve its productivity—and we must—then productivity must be everybody's job. . . . There is great room for significant increases in the productivity of management. . . . Management must take steps to increase its own creativity.

Greater productivity can be achieved if the CEO makes a constant demonstration of interest in productivity and effectively communicates a sense of purpose to achieve it all down the line. Thus, for example, Texas Instruments makes known to all employees the company goals, and actual results achieved, for (1) net sales per employee, (2) unit output per man-hour, (3) profits after taxes per employee, (4) assets per employee, and per cent of return on assets after taxes.

Communications such as these help to instill a sense of productivity achievement in *everyone,* and make productivity a real element in management style.

Other ways to improve productivity include
capital investment and innovations.

One of the most important ways to increase productivity, of course, is to increase the investment in machinery and other facilities so as to reduce unit output per man-hour. One company has announced to all personnel its goal of increasing assets per person from $12,000 to $15,000. This is part of its program to make productivity an element in its management style.

In a service company or other business with high labor intensity, it is even more important to make productivity an element of management style. Since automation is a less attractive possibility in such a company, the leadership and motivation of people is the primary means for increasing people effectiveness; and that is what management style is all about.

We believe that a spirit of innovation can also be made an element of management style. In fact, innovation is one way to increase productivity, so they are closely related. In a technological company, of course, the primary innovation is done through R&D; but innovation can take many other forms throughout the business. So innovation can be built into style in a manner similar to productivity.

SENSITIVITY TO EXTERNAL FORCES

The natural tendency of any executive group is to be concerned with day-to-day activities and internal problems. Sweeping external forces for change are read about, but usually their relevance is overlooked, and they are not translated into actions to seize opportunities and counter threats.

We have proposed earlier a staff for the CEO, with responsibilities for detecting relevant forces and suggesting responses to them, and that is indeed desirable. But the business firm will be much better equipped if sensitivity to external forces can also be made part of the company's management style. This means that *all* executives and managers are trained to keep alert to what is going on outside the business and what the firm ought to do about it. The executives who "think outward" will be best equipped to cope with the changes of the next 20 years.

The outward thinking executive will also be more openminded and, hence, a better executive and leader in other respects. He will also be more sensitive to people, because most forces are launched by people and all have an impact on people.

Such an attitude of mind cannot be decreed—it must be developed. Like all other aspects of management style, the best development process is example. If the CEO and other top-management executives demonstrate that they are outward thinkers and put a premium on sensitivity to outside forces, then others will follow.

There are specific steps, however, that top management can encourage to help executives and future executives develop this attitude of mind:

1. *Attending education programs at graduate business schools.* There is general agreement among those who attend such programs that one of the greatest benefits is gaining an awareness of new forces and an opening of the mind to new issues and values.
2. *Attending meetings that will develop a sensitivity to new forces.* These will ordinarily not be concerned with management techniques, but with nonbusiness forces that may affect business.
3. *Engaging in outside activities that require discussions with thought-leaders who are not in the business field.* These can be public service activities for universities, foreign affairs organizations, or any type of organization that will bring the executive in contact with those who are studying nonbusiness and business-related trends. The academic mind is a splendid tonic for the business mind—and vice versa.
4. *Making sure that some reading is done outside the business field.* Every force that came to our attention is thoroughly covered in books and articles that not only have value in themselves but make the mind more sensitive to other forces.

With knowledge such an important ingredient for improved business performance, the executive who is best equipped to help his company cope with change will need intellectual interests and should have some intellectual pursuits.

Much has been written about obsolescence of the business executive who gets out of date through changes in some discipline—e.g., chemistry or engineering—but there is a broader obsolescence that he must contend with, too. This is the obsolescence that comes through a hardening of his beliefs, attitudes, and values, which, in turn, results in a closing of the mind.

An executive with that kind of obsolescence is ill-equipped to detect external change, to evaluate its impact, or to bring about the internal changes needed to keep his business effectively geared to the future. An effective management will create an atmosphere that can help put off the obsolescence and stimulate renewal of mind and viewpoint.

This leads to the last aspect of our discussion of coping with change—how a business firm might go about staffing its top management posts with executives who have the other qualities needed to provide the leadership for coping with change.

STAFFING WITH "STYLE-CONSCIOUS" EXECUTIVES

Our study of the forces for change convinces us that individuals who serve as chief executives, top-management executives, and general managers of divisions and other business/product centers will be better equipped to cope with change if they have capacity to develop the style of management we have just described. In fact, many executives now occupying key positions such as these are poorly equipped to deal with the forces that lie ahead. Many of them will reach retirement age, however, before the full impact of many of these forces is felt by their particular companies.

We have indicated earlier most of the qualifications of executives who are most likely to be successful in coping with change; but we summarize below the principal qualifications that we believe are required (omitting discussion of basic qualifications for leaders which do not change over time, such as character, integrity, initiative, personal effectiveness, forcefulness, good judgment, and the like):

1. Capacity To Think Strategically. Most of the forces likely to affect the business enterprise during the foreseeable future will require strategic responses, and the executive who thinks in day-to-day operating terms is not likely either to recognize the need for strategic change or to have sufficient will to bring it about. This limitation is being illustrated currently by CEO's who are surprised by the impact of forces to which they were oblivious.

The conceptual thinker is an individual who, through reflective thinking, can form, from specific facts and developments, significant ideas which can be applied generally as guides to thought and action. The conceptual thinker grasps the meaning or significance of an idea, while the operating type of thinker merely has an apprehension of concrete particulars. Thus the conceptual thinker will keep alert to external developments and will have the reflective curiosity to evaluate their meaning or significance to his business. The strategic thinker is also more likely to have the vision and political sense that will be needed during the next 20 years.

2. Intellectual Qualities. Business is surely going to be affected during the next 20 years by many noneconomic forces, such as those we have discussed or indicated: ecopolitics, politics, psychology, sociology, and mathematics. With knowledge and competence gradually replacing management prerogatives derived from authority, the future leader will need some understanding of a variety of intellectual disciplines that were not required in earlier periods; and his intellectual interests will need to be sufficiently strong so that he will make the effort to keep up with nonbusiness forces.

3. Perceptivity of and Sensitivity to People. As indicated earlier, there will need to be fundamentally different approaches to conducting business operations in ways that will stimulate people to be effective through work that is more meaningful and more self-fulfilling. We have discussed participative management as one approach which shows promise. Leaders at all levels of the business will need to have a willingness to experiment with that and other new ways for managing and leading people.

4. An Open, Flexible, and Innovative Mind. Coping with external forces will, of course, require constant change. Leaders and key executives of the business firm should have a continuing dissatisfaction with the status quo and a desire for improvement that requires an open, flexible, and innovative mind.

5. Dedication to Facts. As we have tried to emphasize, the best approach to coping with future forces, whatever they may be, is to treat each of them as a fact to be recognized and factually dealt with. Therefore, the executive who instinctively makes fact-based decisions will be best equipped to cope with future forces. His orientation to facts will also make him more open- and flexible-minded, and will help to ensure that he makes better decisions of all types.

6. Idealism. The individual who is most likely to appreciate the feelings of others and the social responsibilities of his enterprise will be above-average in his idealism. This does not mean that he should not be tough-minded. Indeed, he might be described as a tough-minded idealist whose will to manage is so strong that he himself adheres to the elements of management style required for success and insists that others do so, too.

We believe that executives and corporate directors in a position to influence executive development will better prepare their enterprises to cope with future forces if they give careful attention to selecting, training, and advancing to leadership positions individuals who have the best possible balance of strengths in these six qualifications—along with the other fundamental qualities of executive leadership ability that are timeless in their importance. Indeed, if there is one single way that any corporation can be best prepared to cope with whatever forces develop over the next couple of decades, it would be for the directors of the corporation to make sure that the next CEO they elect has a good balance of strengths in these six qualifications.

This chapter has discussed some of the forces that many believe will exert powerful influences on the future of all institutions, and business in particular; it has emphasized that companies must respond by reaching suitable *now* decisions; and it has pointed out that enterprises need not be tomorrow what they are becoming today. As management gears itself for the Post-Industrial Age, it must adjust by making strategic moves to ensure that institutions will remain viable and useful to society in the years to come.

Notes

1. Simon Ramo, *Century of Mismatch* (New York: David McKay, 1970), chap. 2.
2. Conference Board, "Information Technology: Some Critical Implications for Decision Makers," 1972.
3. *Wall Street Journal,* "National Survey of Environmental Protection" con-

ducted by Erdos & Morgan, in two phases in 1970 and 1971. Report published in 1972. See p. 31.

4. *Wall Street Journal,* November 26, 1971.

5. *New York Times,* May 12, 1972.

6. *Wall Street Journal,* April 28, 1972.

7. Hans H. Lansberg, Leonard L. Fischman, and Joseph L. Fisher, *Resources in America's Future,* published for Resources for the Future by Johns Hopkins Press (Baltimore, 1963), pp. 4, 5.

8. Text of interview with President Nixon on April 30, 1972, at the ranch home of Secretary of the Treasury, John B. Connally, Jr., at Floresville, Texas, as reproduced in *U.S. News & World Report* of May 15, 1972.

9. "Resources for Business" by Joseph L. Fisher, President, Resources for the Future. Prepared for the White House Conference on the Industrial World Ahead, "A Look at Business in 1990" (Washington, D.C., February 7–9, 1972). See p. 3.

10. *Wall Street Journal,* June 21, 1971.

11. *New York Times,* December 23, 1971.

12. *New York Times,* December 6, 1970.

13. Bruce E. Thorpe, "Consumer Report/Campaign seeks popular support for anti-trust attack on giant corporations," *National Journal,* July 17, 1971.

14. "Youth's Agenda for the Seventies—Report on the White House Conference on Youth with a Summary of the Recommendations," by Wade Greene. Conference held at Estes Park, Colo., April 1971.

15. "The Neurotic Trillionaire: A Survey of Mr. Nixon's America." Special Report accompanying the May 10, 1969, issue of *The Economist.*

16. Dr. Daniel Yankelovich, "The Real Meaning of the Student Revolution," *Conference Board Record,* March 1972.

17. *Wall Street Journal,* May 24, 1972.

18. "Social Responsibilities of Business Corporations," Committee for Economic Development (New York, 1971).

19. *Ibid.,* p. 29.

20. *Ibid.,* p. 28.

21. *Ibid.,* p. 61.

22. *New York Times,* December 3, 1971.

23. *Monthly Labor Review,* U.S. Department of Commerce, August 1971. Article by Arthur Leef, Economist in Division of Foreign Labor Statistics and Trade, Bureau of Labor Statistics.

24. *New York Times,* September 10, 1971.

25. *New York Times,* June 2, 1971.

26. Review by Peter P. Gabriel of Professor Vernon's *Sovereignty at Bay* (footnote 27) and a reply by Professor Vernon in an article in *Fortune,* June 1972, p. 120.

27. Raymond Vernon, *Sovereignty at Bay: The Multinational Spread of U.S. Enterprises* (New York: Basic Books, 1971).

28. See a pamphlet published by The Foreign Policy Association, *Latin America Toward a New Nationalism,* by Ben S. Stephansky. It contains a list of reading references.

29. *New York Times,* September 20, 1971.

30. Melvin Kranzberg, "Technology and Human Values," *Virginia Quarterly Review*, vol. 40 (Autumn 1964), pp. 578–92.

31. For a useful analysis of these and other data, see "The Troubles of U.S. Technology," an article reporting on a study in *Morgan Guaranty Survey*, February 1972.

32. *Wall Street Journal*, January 13, 1972.

33. See *Strategy and Structure* by Alfred D. Chandler, Jr. This book—based on an intensive study of General Motors, Du Pont, Standard Oil of New Jersey, and Sears Roebuck—was first published by the M.I.T. Press in 1962. Now available in paperback (New York: Doubleday Anchor Books, 1966).

34. The sales for company #500 in the *Fortune* 500 industrials for 1971 is $176 million, while #1000 in the second 500 is $59 million.

35. *Webster's Seventh New Collegiate Dictionary*.

36. "Goal" and "objective" are often used in a reverse order—with objective being the ultimate end, and goal a milestone along the way. Indeed, one of the authors (Bower) used the latter meaning in his book, *The Will to Manage;* but he now feels that the original military meanings of the terms are preferable.

37. Included in a statement at annual meeting of IBM stockholders at Dallas, Texas, April 24, 1972.

38. "The Architecture of Information," speech by C. Peter McColough, President, Xerox Corporation, to New York Society of Security Analysts, March 3, 1970.

39. Mobil Oil Corporation Annual Report, 1968.

40. *Wall Street Journal*, September 2, 1971.

41. *Fortune*, May 1972.

42. From the Foreword to *Every Employee a Manager* by M. Scott Myers (New York: McGraw-Hill, 1970).

43. "Management's Responsibility Toward Stabilized Employment," speech by Richard R. Deupree at Conference on General Management, American Management Association, October 11, 1945.

44. One of the pioneers in participative management was the late Professor Douglas McGregor of M.I.T.

45. Myers, *Every Employee a Manager*, p. 150.

46. See *4 Days, 40 Hours: Reporting on Revolution in Work and Leisure* (Cambridge: Bursk and Poor Publishing, 1970).

47. *Wall Street Journal*, September 2, 1971.

48. Edward C. Bursk, John Dearden, David F. Hawkins, and Victor M. Longstreet, *Financial Control of Multinational Operations* (New York: Financial Executives Research Foundation, 1971), p. 100.

49. The report on this seminar is included in the report of the National Commission on Marijuana and Drug Abuse. Excerpts from the seminar report appear in the *Wall Street Journal*, April 4, 1972.

50. "Toward a Harmonious Society of Freedom & Order," address by Kazutaka Kikawada, chairman of board of Tokyo Electric Power Co. and chairman of Keizai Doyukai at the Annual Meeting of Keizai Doyukai, April 14, 1971.

51. See Myers, *Every Employee a Manager*, pp. 42–44 (reference 42 above).

52. For a more complete discussion of the fact-based approach see Marvin Bower, *The Will to Manage* (New York: McGraw-Hill, 1966), pp. 27–33.

53. *Wall Street Journal*, August 16, 1972.

54. From a speech before the American Newspaper Publishers Association, New York City, April 26, 1972. Printed in *Michigan Business Review,* July 1972.

Contributors

Helpful comments and inputs from the following members of the authors' panel are gratefully acknowledged (the authors, however, assume full responsibility for choice of content and interpretation):

HENRY BOETTINGER, Director of Planning, American Telephone and Telegraph Co.

PAUL KNAPLUND, Vice President, International Business Machines Corp.

JOHN MCKITTERICK, Vice President and Staff Executive, General Electric Company

SIMON RAMO, Vice Chairman of the Board, TRW Inc.

In preparing this paper, a number of top business leaders were interviewed to enlist their help in identifying the forces likely to influence business in the future and to consider how best to cope with these forces. A list of these contributors is appended.

ERNEST C. ARBUCKLE, Chairman of the Board, Wells Fargo Bank

NORMAN BARKER, JR., President, United California Bank

WILLIAM W. BOESCHENSTEIN, President, Owens-Corning Fiberglas Corporation

DONALD C. BURNHAM, Chairman, Westinghouse Electric Corporation

EDWARD W. CARTER, President, Broadway-Hale Stores, Inc.

WALKER L. CISLER, Chairman, The Detroit Edison Company

JOSEPH F. CULLMAN, III, Chairman, Philip Morris Incorporated

R. MORTON DARROW, Vice President, Planning and Analysis, The Prudential Insurance Company of America

REP. CHARLES C. DIGGS, JR., Representative from Michigan

GEORGE C. DILLON, President, Butler Mannufacturing Company

CARLES E. DUCOMMUN, President, Ducommun Incorporated

DR. ROGER O. EGEBERG, Special Assistant for Health Policy, Department of Health, Education and Welfare

SHERWOOD L. FAWCETT, President, Battelle Memorial Institute

KENNETH C. FOSTER, President, The Prudential Insurance Company of America

DR. NORMAN E. FRIEDMANN, President and Chairman, Computing & Software, Inc.

EDWARD GELSTHORPE, President, Hunt-Wesson Foods, Inc.

R. BURT GOOKIN, President, Heinz (H.J.) Company

KERMIT GORDON, President, Brookings Institution

PAUL A. GORMAN, Chairman of the Board, International Paper Company

DANIEL J. HAUGHTON, Chairman, Lockheed Aircraft Corporation

WALTER E. HOADLEY, Executive Vice President, Bank of America National Trust & Savings Association

EDWARD R. KANE, Vice President, du Pont (E.I.) de Nemours & Company

MRS. VIRGINIA H. KNAUER, Director, Office of Consumer Affairs, Executive Office of the President

ROBERT D. LILLEY, President, American Telephone & Telegraph Company

EDMUND W. LITTLEFIELD, Chairman of the Board, Utah International Inc.

J. PAUL LYET, II, President, Sperry Rand Corporation

PAUL W. MCCRACKEN, Chairman, President's Council of Economic Advisors (Now Professor, School of Business Administration, University of Michigan)

IAN K. MACGREGOR, Chairman, American Metal Climax, Incorporated

DONALD S. MACNAUGHTON, Chairman, The Prudential Insurance Company of America

MEYER MELNIKOFF, Senior Vice President, The Prudential Insurance Company of America

OTTO N. MILLER, Chairman of the Board, Standard Oil Company of California

G. WILLIAM MILLER, President, Textron Incorporated

JOHN A. MORGAN, Chairman, Butler Manufacturing Company

GENERAL LAURIS NORSTAD, Chairman of the Board, Owens-Corning Fiberglas Corporation

PETER G. PETERSON, Secretary of Commerce

CARL SCARBOROUGH, Vice President-Finance, Owens-Corning Fiberglas Corporation

HORACE A. SHEPARD, Chairman, TRW, Inc.

J. H. THOMAS, Vice Chairman, Owens-Corning Fiberglas Corporation

LYNN A. TOWNSEND, Chairman, Chrysler Corporation

C. WILLIAM VERITY, JR., President, Armco Steel Corporation

Dr. CHARLES E. WALKER, Deputy Secretary of the Treasury

HENRY A. WALKER, JR., President, Amfac, Inc.

GEORGE H. WEYERHAEUSER, President, Weyerhaeuser Company

RAYMOND E. WILKINS, Director of Corporate Research and Planning, The Firestone Tire & Rubber Company

ROGER C. WILKINS, Chairman, The Travelers Corporation

HAROLD M. WILLIAMS, Dean, Graduate School of Business Administration, University of California, Los Angeles

THORNTON A. WILSON, President, Boeing Company

ROBERT G. WINGERTER, President, Libbey-Owens-Ford Company

GENERAL RICHARD A. YUDKIN, Vice President, Public Affairs, Owens-Corning Fiberglas Corporation

Managing Tomorrow's Education

The Novelty of Management in Higher Education

THERE was a time—and not too long ago at that—when education would hardly have merited a chapter in a book looking at the changing world of management. The prevailing assumption was that the public school system operated in a kind of automatic, Newtonian fashion, practically without human intervention. As for the college or university, it was viewed as an intimate, cohesive, and autonomous community of scholars who collectively, amicably, and informally charted their own course, with the president and deans merely carrying out what Rousseau would have called the "general will" of the campus.[1]

Until recently, there was little interest in
the governance of educational institutions . . .

Reality never coincided with this image, but so self-contained was the world of education, and so tortoise-like the pace of change within that world, that the accepted view had a certain plausibility. Even the wheeling and dealing of aggressive academic chieftains in the late nineteenth century did not fundamentally alter the prevailing notions about educational governance. Such men found it expedient to pay lip service to Rousseauistic vision, and the actual methods by which they "led" their institutions remained correspondingly obscure.

The process by which even far-reaching decisions were arrived at was often shrouded in a fog of inspirational rhetoric. Any persistent interest in the actual distribution of power within an academic community was considered a breach of good taste. Except for occasional manuals on how to run a dining hall, solicit larger contributions, or (more recently) give student representatives a larger voice in policy decisions, the massive literature on American education includes astonishingly few works devoted to the subject of management.

. . . in part because of education's peripheral place in American life . . .

For all the powerful rhetoric of a Thomas Jefferson or a Horace Mann in praise of learning, the truth is that in the nineteenth century it was only the rare individual who attended school for more than a few years. As recently as 1940, the average American adult had completed only 8.6 years of formal education.

And the money spent on those who did attend school was niggardly at best. In terms of contemporary purchasing power, Americans of 50 years ago spent only 71 cents per day for the education of each public school pupil. Even 20 years ago, the figure was as low as $2.10; today it is over $5.00. In this era of multi-million dollar budgets, it is hard to realize how slender was the shoestring which sustained the colleges and universities of yesteryear. As recently as 1950, the average tuition at even the most prestigious private colleges was only about $600—a sum not appreciably higher than that of the Depression decade of the 1930's.

In 1950, the United States spent $9 billion on education—a scant 3.4 per cent of the Gross National Product, and only *one tenth* of the total expended in 1972.[2] And anyone who (like me) began his or her teaching career in those years can all too vividly recall the appallingly low salaries that were another indicator of the low esteem in which education was held.

. . . and in part because of its insulation from technological and social change.

In terms of structure as well as status, education long held a peculiar and anomalous position in America. Until very recently, our schools and colleges remained largely unaffected by the powerful social and technological forces that were reshaping our national life. While the village was being absorbed by suburbia, the independent businessman losing out to the chain store, the family farm giving way to vast agricultural enterprises, small religious sects merging to form large denominations, and the *laissez faire* state giving way to the welfare state— while all these centralizing and integrating forces were transforming American society in the years from the Civil War to World War II—education remained curiously unaffected.

The academic enterprise continued to be made up of thousands of small, autonomous units. Only 25 years ago, in 1947, there were about 92,000 separate school districts in the United States, each setting its own policy. Under heavy state pressure, this number declined by 1970 to about 19,000, but only about 6 per cent of these districts had enrollments of more than 6,000 students, while 60 per cent—some 14,000 districts—still enrolled fewer than 600 pupils.

A similar allegiance to rugged individualism long characterized higher education as well. Of the more than 2,500 colleges and universities in America in 1970, the great majority remained quite small. True, the average size of these institutions increased from about 600 students in 1920 to 3,100 in 1970, but this aggregate figure obscures the fact that there are still only 65 colleges and universities enrolling more than 20,000 students, while fully one quarter enroll fewer than 500 students, and nearly one half enroll fewer than 1,000.

Furthermore, most of our colleges and universities to this day continue to be completely autonomous in their management. Even many of the public higher education institutions established in the past quarter century were not integrated into a comprehensive network of state educational services, but functioned like their private counterparts in a relatively independent way. The nation's 380 Roman Catholic colleges also for the most part stand alone, uncoordinated by their diocesan bishops and not subject to the planning or economic scrutiny of any statewide or national Catholic educational organizations.

If modern management theory has developed, in part, in response to the emergence of large-scale and intricately linked social institutions, then the nation's educational enterprise has until very recently lacked the basic characteristics necessary to attract such theoretical attention. So long as public school education was simply taken for granted, so long as higher education was mainly a frill for relatively few young ladies and gentlemen of social standing, so long as education remained a fragmented undertaking affecting neither the lives nor the pocketbooks of most people very deeply, then the question of educational management was hardly one of urgent concern.

The Changing World of Education

But today all of this has changed. From all directions, educators face demands for better academic governance. Even within the schools and colleges, voices may be heard calling for firmer direction, more effective cost controls, sharper delineation of purpose, and more imaginative planning for the future.

What has occurred to alter the traditional public tolerance of education's casual attitude toward management? Why, at long last, are schools and colleges being subjected to standards of accountability that have long been applied to other institutions in our society?

Education finds itself involved in contemporary life—to its own dismay.

The answer, putting it in the baldest possible way, is that in the last 20 years the educational enterprise has moved from the periphery to the center of our national consciousness; and in the process some of our most fundamental assumptions and methods of operation have been shaken to the core.

It is by now almost hackneyed to point out that America has become a knowledge-oriented society. Nevertheless, some of the implications of that fundamental historical truth must be explored if we are to grasp what has happened in the world of education.

The "knowledge explosion" has changed curriculum and teaching patterns drastically.

Gathering momentum with World War II, the Cold War, and the Space Race, and the flow of federal research money that each brought in its wake, the knowledge explosion has dominated the consciousness of our generation. In 1948 (the year the transistor was invented), the annual *New York Times Index* ran to 1,211 pages; by 1970, the total had soared to 2,291 pages. *Dissertations in Progress, Scholarly Books in America, Paperbacks in Print,* scores of professional and technical journals—all have doubled, tripled, or quadrupled in size during this amazing era.

In the academic world, the ramifications of the knowledge explosion were felt at every level. Elementary school textbooks were rewritten to include anthropology, economics, set theory, algebra, and genetics. High school programs were revamped to accommodate sculpture, psychology, advanced chemistry, Asian and African history, statistics, comparative literature, electronics, music theory, and a host of other subjects traditionally reserved for the college years.

In the colleges and universities, Soviet and Asian studies, space science, urban sociology, computer theory and technology, population research, econometrics, polymer science, biochemistry, linguistics—these and many more unknown or arcane specialties burst into prominence. Like amoebae in a super-enriched culture, university faculties multiplied, subdivided, and regrouped in a fantastic array of departments, programs, and institutes.

More people are in schools, for longer and longer periods of time . . .

In the face of all this activity, many Americans quite naturally began to take a second look at what they regarded as the humdrum world of education; and most people concluded that what they had hitherto taken for granted was essential to their success, well-being, and happiness.

Parents began sending their children to school earlier and keeping them there longer. For example, two decades ago under 10 per cent of the children in the three-to-five age range attended nursery or pre-elementary classes. By 1970, 37.5 per cent of the eleven million youngsters in that age group were enrolled in pre-primary schools.[3]

At the other end of the public school ladder, the year 1970 found 90 per cent of all sixteen-year-olds in school—in contrast to about ten per cent in 1910! With the growth of nursery schools, a slight lengthening of the school year, and fewer absences because of illness, the average high school graduate of today has had the same number of hours of formal schooling, and reached the same academic level, as the college sophomore of a generation ago.

Nor has higher education remained immune to this national drive toward more schooling. Increasingly, a college education, at least through the junior college level, has come to be considered essential by most persons, just as the high school diploma was viewed as the necessary minimum a generation ago. From 1950 to 1972, enrollment in post-high school education went up from 2.1 million to 8.4 million—a growth of 400 per cent.

Gone are the days when the average youngster was taught to read, spell, write, and perform some simple arithmetical operations and was then pushed out into the world. With high school graduation rates approaching 90 per cent, and college enrollments far higher than before, growing numbers of people now spend close to one third of their entire lives attending school.

. . . with a corresponding rise in the money spent for education.

The financial evidence of the nation's heightened regard for education is as impressive as the enrollment statistics. From 1950 to 1970, while average earnings in the non-agricultural sector of the economy were rising by about 50 per cent, the salaries paid teachers and professors (in terms of actual purchasing power) shot up by about 200 per cent. Taxpayers also willingly footed the bill for a considerably reduced teacher-student ratio. In the 1960's alone, that ratio fell from twenty-six to one to twenty-two to one. Between 1950 and 1972, overall public school revenues jumped (again in terms of actual purchasing power) a whopping 405 per cent. In the same 22 year period, college and university revenues rose from $2.9 billion to $31 billion—an increase, even when adjusted for inflation, of almost 500 per cent.

At the same time the social, economic, ethnic mix has broadened . . .

Overwhelmed in the 1950's and the early 1960's by a massive surge of public interest and support, America's colleges and universities had simultaneously to adjust to dramatic changes in their student clientele. Historically, as we have seen, higher education in the United States was open primarily to members of the upper and middle classes. Conversely, children of the underprivileged, the minorities, and the immigrants were all too prominently represented among those who dropped out of school as soon as they could legally do so.

But all this was radically changed by the great educational expansion of the postwar years, coupled with the belated national commitment to equality symbolized by the Supreme Court's school desegregation decision of 1954. From 1966 to 1971, the number of black Americans in college rose by 80 per cent. Scholarship programs and the rapid growth of low tuition public higher education enabled millions of young people of working class families to attend college for the first time.

In the wake of this development, the homogeneous, upper middle-class tone of most campuses gave way to a varied, complex, and at times tension-filled reality which more closely mirrored that of American society itself. In ivy covered administration buildings across the country, presidents and deans suddenly found themselves grappling with issues more serious than panty raids, fraternity beer blasts, and interdepartmental rivalries.

New age groups as well as new racial and economic groups have introduced further diversity into the student population. The imperatives of the knowledge explosion have in recent years sent many skilled professionals back to the classroom for constant updating. Many women, newly conscious of their potential, began launching or resuming careers in middle life. With a shorter work week, the trend toward early retirement, and a steadily lengthening life span, the ranks of the leisured have grown by leaps and bounds.[4] All of these trends have converged to produce a pool of millions of Americans beyond the traditional college age who were nevertheless vitally interested in what the college or university has to offer. Between 1945 and 1970, the number of adults enrolled in some form of higher education increased fourfold, from 6 million to 24.3 million.[5]

*. . . and young people themselves have changed
physiologically and psychologically.*

Even among those young people who have traditionally gone to college, dramatic physiological and psychological changes have occurred. In the half century after 1920, the average age of the onset of puberty has dropped one and one-half years in the United States (from 15 to 13.5 for boys; from 13.5 to 12 for girls), with full height being attained nearly two years earlier.[6] Thanks to medical and nutritional advances, young people today are healthier, taller, heavier, and more vigorous than ever before in our history.

Psychologically and intellectually too, young people of today grow up to a different time clock. On standardized academic tests, they score significantly higher than did their parents' generation at the same age. Under the impact of television, travel, and greater freedom of discussion of once taboo topics, today's youth have an awareness of wars, poverty, social inequality, violence, politics, human psychology, and sexuality far beyond that possessed by their parents at the same stage of life. Inevitably, their moral and social attitudes are affected by this precocity. Not long ago, most students entered college certain of a sharp distinction between right and wrong, and accepting the authority of various moral arbiters within the school and beyond. Today, one encounters skepticism, even cynicism—as well as intense, if highly individualistic, idealism—among barely post-adolescent youngsters. This is the era of the "put on" and of "hanging loose"; but it is also a time of passionate commitment, religious questing, profound social concern, and renewed interest in long obscured cultural and ethical roots.[7]

Remember the blend of hedonism and puerility which the epithet "sophomoric" once evoked? Today's college sophomore is more than likely taking two stiff science courses so that he can spend his junior year abroad, doing volunteer work at a nearby center for the retarded, and—in spare moments—reading Marcuse and Anne Sexton, and seeing the films of Buñuel and Bergmann.

*The range of resources and techniques available
has also enlarged enormously . . .*

When my institution, the State University of New York, was founded in 1948, television, computers, microfilm, commercial jets, transistors, cassettes, rapid copiers—all the sophisticated gadgetry we now take for granted—were either just beginning to make themselves felt or not yet available. Today, 25 years later, each of these developments has had a great impact on some aspect of the academic enterprise. Scholarly research, library techniques, the teaching of languages, economics, and science—all have been transformed by the new technology.

Advances in photography, transportation, sound engineering, and electronics have made possible more frequent professional meetings, international telephone seminars, the rapid diffusion of new findings, and short-term student research projects conducted many miles from campus. An entirely new level of mobility enables teachers and students alike to move with relative ease from one academic center to another. Quite obviously, the impact of all this on the traditional *modus operandi* of the average school or college has been immeasurable.

. . . while learning has spread beyond the individual campus or school.

One of the most striking and visible trends in education is the movement away from single institution training and toward interconnected educational networks involving many kinds of institutions. Our national preoccupation with learning has spilled over the traditional academic boundaries, and more and more instruction is taking place outside the schools and colleges. Public libraries and museums routinely offer courses, discussions, lectures, and practical training in the arts. Training programs have proliferated in the military and in industry. Informal study groups are coming together to explore their culture heritage, their environmental problems, their status in society, or other issues of immediate concern.

Thus, for many education is ceasing to be primarily a one-shot enterprise directed largely by the faculty and administration of a single school or college, and becoming instead a continuing, broad-scale experience shaped largely by the student himself.

Indeed, education today probably should be defined more broadly still. From the cradle on, children are bombarded with "educational" toys, games, and television programs. For many of today's youngsters, the first teacher they will remember will not be Mrs. Jones or Miss Brown, but television's Captain Kangaroo, Big Bird, and Easy Reader. Older children travel abroad and attend summer camps that teach music, art, drama, nature studies, or foreign languages. Executives drive to work to the sound of instructional tape cassettes before them on the front seat.

Education is called on to play a crucial part in achieving society's goals.

As education—or what passes for education—increasingly has come to seem the vehicle through which the American dream would at last be fully realized, our schools and colleges found themselves beset by demands that they tackle with both hands all the complex problems, inequities, and dilemmas of contemporary society. Culture center . . . social service agency . . . weapon against discrimination and social injustice . . . seedbed of political change . . . repository of tradition . . . bridge over the generation gap . . . source of knowledge that could take men to the moon . . . quell urban riots . . . purify the environment . . . end all war—the American university has been called upon to perform all of these functions and more.

President James Perkins of Cornell outlined the nature of the problem in 1966 when he suggested that American higher education should add "public service" to its traditional research and teaching functions.[8] A year later, and more grandiloquently, sociologist Daniel Bell reinforced the point about education's new place in the social order:

> If the business firm was the key institution of the past hundred years, because of its role in organizing production for the mass creation of products, the university will become the central institution of the next hundred years because of its role as the new source of innovation and knowledge.[9]

Like so many Walter Mittys who had long been left to their dreams of grandeur, American educators of the 1950's and 1960's awoke, blinked, shook themselves, and discovered to their amazement that they had been selected as the impresarios of a vast circus whose great shows and colorful midway they had hitherto watched rather longingly from the bleachers.

The Response: A Mixed Record

What does Walter Mitty do when his dreams come true? How have our schools and colleges responded to the massive and unprecedented forces of change of the past generation?

In some respects, education has responded to the challenge very well indeed . . .

Faculty salaries have risen from sadly inadequate to at least respectable. In terms of curricular innovation, heroic efforts have been made to keep abreast of the knowledge explosion. Modern equipment has been acquired, libraries expanded, and massive building programs undertaken. The physical growth of our educational plant during the past quarter century surpasses that of the preceding two centuries; it is estimated that the United States now has a larger capital investment in its schools than it does in its factories. During the 1950's and the 1960's, new campuses—especially to house community colleges—sprang up at a rate of one every ten days.

. . . but it is still held back by convention, caution, inertia.

But there are less tangible yardsticks by which education's response to change must be measured. For all the physical growth and higher salaries, has education, in any fundamental way, come to terms with the strikingly new situation it faces? The answer must be heavily qualified. Remarkable strides have been made, to be sure, but the restraining forces of convention, caution, and inertia remain very powerful.

In one area after another, American education has responded only hesitantly to new conditions. For example, the rapid growth of instructional ventures outside the formal academic framework has raised profound questions about what precisely should go on *inside* the schools, and has suggested the necessity of forging new linkages between our schools and colleges and the proliferating educational programs of corporations, unions, museums, and hospitals.

Such a move toward multi-institutional educational structures has broad implications for educational management and governance. How are such networks of learning to be managed? Can they be managed? Despite the urgency of such questions, education's managers and professionals have been agonizingly slow in overcoming the traditional insularity and automatic suspicion of any educational efforts which seem to challenge the credentials-conscious academic world.

Example: Education is still far short of meeting adults' growing demands.

Or, to take another example, at a time when more and more adults are demonstrating their interest in further academic training, our colleges have remained oriented toward the on-campus, full-time instruction of that small slice of the population deemed to be of "college age." Moreover, with the needs of the rapidly swelling ranks of the retired becoming a matter of national concern, education has only begun to confront the educational dimensions of this challenge.

Simple institutional self-interest should suggest the importance of responding to the educational needs of the larger adult population because the demographic handwriting on the wall makes clear that the college-age pool will be shrinking in the years ahead. In the past two decades, as the population bulge generated by the post-World War II baby boom moved toward our campuses, we urgently threw up new dormitories to accommodate it. But the United States birthrate has been declining since 1957 and it is now approaching the level necessary for zero population growth. The problem of underutilization of facilities, already a real one on many campuses, may well become more severe in the years ahead.

Yet surprisingly little is being done to retool for adult education. True, some urban universities have long offered so-called extension courses at night for adults; and some graduate schools, especially in business, medicine, and engineering, have moved imaginatively with specific professional groups. But overall, it remains difficult for the average working adult or retiree, even the most highly motivated, to break into the routine of the average college, with its prerequisites, credit-hour and residency requirements, and its bankers' hours of classroom instruction. Accustomed to dealing with the young and relatively privileged, education has not fully recognized that in the future its concern must be the continual, maximum intellectual development of the nation's total human resources and not just the training of the young.

*There are no lines of communication among
the levels of the educational establishment.*

In early America, the academic process was rather loose in its flow of students
and in its organizational arrangements. But by the twentieth century that process
had solidified into a set of granite-like chunks: a year of kindergarten, eight years
of elementary school; four years of secondary school; four years of college; with
graduate school stretching on beyond. Educators subsequently tinkered with the
time-blocs and introduced new layers—junior high school and junior college—
but the basic structure remains intact, and the lack of communication among
the various levels is almost total. Frequently status-conscious to a fault, many
college teachers and administrators find it somehow demeaning to approach their
opposite numbers at the high school level, with whom they should have so much
in common.

As a consequence, American education continues to resemble a giant club
sandwich, with each layer preoccupied with its own requirements, budgetary
needs, and administrative structures. Practically the only people concerned with
the *entire* educational process, from nursery school to Ph.D., are the students.

Is it surprising that many young people find the last years of high school and
the first years of college boring and repetitive, or that graduate students find
themselves simply rehashing material already covered in college? Clearly, a
reassessment of the overall educational sequence is urgently needed. Yet it is
not occurring.

Nor, to cite a final instance, has education begun to come to terms with the
technological developments of the past two decades which have revolutionized
the movement of people, information, and ideas. As long ago as 1959 the
noted academic administrator Henry M. Wriston observed that the traditional
fact-oriented college lecture was "obsolete," calling it the world's "slowest and
least effective mode for the transmission of knowledge." [10] Wriston's judgment
has been amply confirmed in the intervening years, and yet the old satirical
definition of the college lecture as a means whereby information is transmitted
from the notebook of the teacher to the notebook of the student without passing
through the head of either remains all too apt.

In the absence of overall institutional leadership in assessing the implications
of the new technology, the academic world has become polarized between the
traditionalists who deplore any technological intrusion into the learning process,
and the uncritical enthusiasts who see each shiny new gadget as the greatest boon
to teaching since the Socratic method.

Education is undergoing the turbulence of an "Industrial Revolution."

Thus, for all its growth and changes of the past two decades, American education remains in a stage of serious institutional lag, with its traditional assumptions and modes of operation ill-suited to the new and as yet not fully defined

social role toward which it is moving. Within our schools and colleges, the lag has led to bewilderment and turbulence. Principals, presidents, provosts, and deans have recently come and gone almost on a revolving door basis. Experimental programs and new administrative formats have sometimes been pushed through in an almost desperate "try anything" mood.

Perhaps the best analogy to the changes which education is undergoing today, and the social consequences of those changes, is the period of the Industrial Revolution. Then, too, vast new social and economic patterns were superimposing themselves upon traditional cultures which found them confusing and at times profoundly threatening. Tumult and bloodshed often accompanied the birth pangs of the modern industrial state and the social transformations it brought in its wake. The changing role of education is, in some ways, similarly disruptive of the *status quo*, and it should not surprise us that the process has involved antagonisms, confusion, and sometimes a threatening sense of lost moorings.

This discontent and uncertainty has not been confined to educators; it characterizes the mood of society generally. And just as attitudes toward industrialization fluctuated wildly 100 or 150 years ago, so public attitudes toward education today oscillate between euphoria and hostility. The 1950's and early 1960's were years of exaggerated hope, of an almost religious faith in the power of education to lead us to finer, juster, and more humane civilization. When we became belatedly conscious of the continuing strain of racism in our national life, it was equality in the schools that became the focus of our concern. In the war on poverty and the quest for economic growth,[11] a broadening of educational opportunity was given top priority. During the Kennedy years, intellectuals in Washington enjoyed a prestige they had not felt since Woodrow Wilson's day.

But then, in the late 1960's, the pendulum swung again.

Public confidence in, and support for, the schools has become eroded.

This reaction had a number of reasons. Campus turmoil made clear that academia was not immune to the tensions and conflicts abroad in society as a whole. The economic recession of 1969–71, leaving numerous college graduates and even Ph.D.'s out of work, further jolted the public's worship of the college degree. The involvement of some intellectuals in unsuccessful or unpopular foreign adventures—the Bay of Pigs, Vietnam—gave rise to sober thoughts about the varied uses to which a trained brain could be put.

A rash of articles and books denounced the schools and colleges as ineffective, irrelevant, or meretricious in their social effect. A book with the provocative title *Deschooling Society* [12] became a minor best seller. Scholarly research began to document what sober common sense should have suggested all along: education was not an automatic guarantor of either individual success or social progress.

By the early 1970's the public's attitude toward schools and colleges had grown chary. Sources of additional funding began to dry up. Bitter budget fights tore many school districts. Several colleges were forced to close their doors. Others, including a few major universities, faced the grim prospect of bankruptcy. In place of euphoria and growth, one found among many educators and faculty a mounting sense of crisis, retrenchment, and malaise.

This is not to suggest that the present financial crisis in education is wholly the result of a capricious shift in the public mood. The crisis also has deep roots in objective reality. Educational costs have risen at a staggering rate. Higher salaries, lower teacher-student ratios, expensive new equipment, higher maintenance costs, expanded student services (counseling, placement, child care, recreation) and massive construction programs all have contributed to the monumental budget requests against which taxpayers and legislators are now so vociferously in reaction.

The soaring cost trend was somewhat obscured so long as public support kept pace. But today, while costs continue to climb, the money is not being made available with the same uncritical largesse. The result is a budgetary crunch of major proportions.

But, at least, educational management is now getting serious attention.

Education, that bright but somnolent enterprise, has moved with dizzying speed from the fringes to the core of contemporary life. The old hermetic world of education has been transformed into one which penetrates society at countless points and, in a complex symbiosis, is in turn penetrated by society. What campus has remained untouched by computers, drugs, the Vietnam War, the sexual revolution, women's liberation, environmental concerns, the growing self-consciousness of racial and ethnic minorities, and our national love-hate attitudes toward the welfare state and modern technology?

As a result of all this, the long inattention to problems of educational management has ended. Education is simply too central and too touchy a matter to be trusted to a policy of benign bumble and drift. The current demands for more effective cost controls and planning, while they usually have their immediate source in the budget crisis, reflect a larger concern over the nature and quality of management procedures at all levels of education. The easy assumption that a school or a college is simply a big happy family which can easily run its own show without much attention from the real world—or much effect *upon* the real world—is simply no longer tenable. A central challenge confronting education in the seventies is the challenge of management. And it is one whose dimensions education has hardly begun to explore.

The Traditional Polarities

To understand the uncertainty and confusion which surround this subject, one must recognize the force of certain deeply entrenched—and mutually contradictory—notions. Traditionally, education's approach to academic management has vacillated uneasily between two ideological poles, the *hierarchical* and the *collegial*, with primary and secondary schools tending toward the former, colleges and universities toward the latter.

The hierarchical model is derived from the world of corporate business and ultimately, perhaps, from the father-dominated family. The collegial model looks to town meeting democracy, the congregational strain in Protestantism, and certain professional societies and craft guilds. If we move beyond the beliefs described early in this chapter and begin to probe the reality of academic management, we find that both models have had an important influence.

On the one hand, the hierarchical model has often been dominant in practice . . .

We have always admired and somewhat idealized the strong academic leaders whose vision, vigor, and dedication lifted their institutions to new heights of academic glory or financial stability. Academia has generally, if reluctantly, accepted Alexander Hamilton's maxim: "Energy in the executive is the leading element in the definition of good government." The maxim has not been without empirical support. Several studies have shown a close correlation between the progress of a school or college and the strong leadership of specific principals, headmasters, or presidents.

Before the days of Charles W. Eliot and Nicholas Murray Butler, Harvard and Columbia were both provincial and stagnating institutions. Between 1870 and 1930, many of today's leading academic institutions were either created or remade by vigorous, visionary, and (sometimes) ruthless administrative heads— "captains of erudition" Thorstein Veblen called them—aided by small cadres of loyal lieutenants. (The first university dean appeared in 1870, the first vice president in 1889, and—portentous event—the first business manager in 1906.)

Further in the background, but essential to the hierarchical structure, have been the boards of trustees. Most such boards are, by charter or statute, legally accountable for the total conduct and operations of their specific institution. Indeed, until the 1920's they often vigorously exercised that power in some places, dismissing almost at will presidents, deans, and even individual professors. More recently, however, while the legal power of the trustees remains, their actual exercise of that power has sharply declined. This curious situation— great legal power coupled with minimal operational use of that power—has produced a mild identity crisis among some trustees. It is, to say the least, unsettling to find oneself labelled (usually with equal inaccuracy) both a "tyrant" and a "pawn."

Confronted by such alarming ambiguities, and naturally apprehensive about who is actually exercising the power legally invested in them, numerous trustees tend toward the hierarchical, or strong executive, concept of academic management. A president may prove to be autocratic and not entirely competent, but at least he is visible above the swirling confusion.

. . . while, on the other hand, the collegial model still has strong support.

The collegial ideal has always retained its appeal and attracted its eloquent spokesmen. A university, these advocates contend, should not be structured like General Motors, but as a community of peers guided by the collective wisdom, foresight, and fiscal sagacity of the group as a whole.

This collegial view has won an enlarging number of adherents during the 20th Century as the various scholarly professions attained full maturity and confidence—a development kicked off in 1915 when John Dewey and others formed the American Association of University Professors and cast in bronze the principle of academic tenure. On many campuses, academic departments have assumed much of the administrative initiative, sometimes—not unlike the great feudal baronies of medieval days—acting quite independently of the over-all institutional aims formulated by the trustees, the president, and the deans.[13]

Observing this development, some faculty members concluded that it was the teachers themselves—joined perhaps by key supporting staff such as librarians, registrars, and technicians—who should control the destinies of their respective institutions. The idea is certainly a plausible one, although (as one educational historian has pointed out) it does imply a syndicalist rather than a democratic approach to academic governance. Under such a principle, notes education historian W. H. Cowley, "military men would completely control national defense establishments . . . , clergymen would have exclusive dominion over the churches, and civil servants would be unrestrained in the management of civil governments."[14] The complexities of the collegial version of governance were further underscored in the past decade when *students* began to point out that they too were of the academic community, and to demand a greater voice, and even a considerable measure of power, in academic policy making.

Attempts to bridge the gap lead to stalemate, lack of control, ineffectiveness.

The clash of these varying visions of academic leadership has produced a near stalemate on some campuses. On others, it has led to a kind of *de facto* division of powers, with the departments controlling day-to-day academic affairs while the presidents and their staffs deal with financial problems and a wide variety of housekeeping chores, ranging from scholarship disbursements to parking lot allocations. The major drawback of this arrangement is that neither side trusts the other to oversee the *whole* of an institution's operations or to plan its future course. "The universities and the departments within them are out of control," concluded a 1970 educational study.[15] "At many universities, no one is in charge," agree the authors of a 1971 article on academic management.[16]

It is true that for decades the wide gap between the two contending principles of academic management was bridged fairly successfully by the pragmatic device of recruiting top administrators from the ranks of the leading faculty. Naturally, such scholar-administrators have been sensitive to the feelings of their erstwhile faculty colleagues; some, indeed—at least in the early years of their tenure—have been eloquent defenders of the collegial principle. Through this strategy, which carefully limited top administrative positions in education to "safe" individuals, the necessity of a measure of central power was recognized, but the principle of collegiality was also acknowledged.

Thus the usual route to a college presidency or similar university position has included several years of teaching, scholarly research, and leadership of an academic department. So well established has this pattern become that the academic administrator who did not follow it, like former President Herman Wells of Indiana University, who came out of business, was looked upon as something of a maverick.

There is mounting evidence, however, that this ingenious method of glossing over fundamentally different notions about academic governance may be reaching the end of its effectiveness. For a variety of reasons, fewer and fewer of the more able faculty members are willing to make the shift into administration. In part, this represents simple good sense. While only one college president, to my knowledge, actually died of a heart attack during a student sit-in, the overall wear and tear on the typical academic administrator of today is not such as to send life insurance actuaries dancing in the streets.

Teachers, not just administrators, are under terrific pressures.

It is upon teachers that the trauma of the educational unheavals of recent years, and the strains of conflicting demands placed upon the schools, have fallen most heavily.

There was a time when a teacher was primarily expected to do just that—teach. At the more prestigious institutions he was also expected to achieve a measure of professional recognition; at the smaller, to help in the moral supervision of his young charges. In either case, the expectations were fairly simple and clear-cut. Today, by contrast, while the pressures to produce in the traditional ways have not diminished, the faculty member is also exhorted to involve himself intimately in the far more complex social role the university is gradually assuming.

While teachers have not generally reacted with overt hostility to these exhortations, their response has been tempered by what they perceive as a potential threat to their own chosen role and life-style. For while most intellectuals and academics are as eager as anyone else to feel that what they are doing is "meaningful" and "relevant," they also tend to be independent and somewhat anti-institutionalist by temper, suspicious of controls, restraints, or commitments which might imply a surrender of autonomy, individual judgment, and critical distance.

Yet as education has moved to the center of our knowledge-oriented society, educators have had to confront the fact that they are part of a complex organizational network which in one way or another involves every major institution of our society. The resulting dilemma has been a painful one: how is the academic intellectual to influence his generation without losing his independence of mind, and maneuver in a thicket of bureaucratic procedures, organizational constraints, and divided loyalties?

The dilemma has a stark economic dimension was well. For while the university has been moving toward an enlarged social role, the rewards—tenure, promotion, money—still tend to go to those who shine in research and publications.[17] Deep down, this is what many colleges and universities (especially at the departmental level, where crucial personnel decisions are usually made) still want: the reflected glory that comes with attracting and holding academic superstars.

Teachers have responded in varying ways to these pressures. Some, sympathetically recognizing the turbulent and difficult transitions their institutions were undergoing, have given of themselves unstintingly to help chart education's future course. Others have removed themselves from academic life, concluding that a more effective social role lay outside the campus hedges. John Gardner, Daniel Patrick Moynihan, Henry Kissinger—these are some of the many names that come to mind.

*Most teachers have turned inward rather
than outward in response to pressures.*

Teachers tend to give their deepest professional loyalty to professional colleagues rather than to the institution as a whole. This process has been reinforced by the mobility of modern life. Few teachers today remain at one or even two institutions for their entire professional lives, and it is not surprising that their strongest ties should be with their fellow historians, biologists, or physicists rather than with the particular school at which they momentarily find themselves. The proliferation of government and foundation grants has served to weaken institutional ties further. Deriving a significant portion of their income from outside sources, many of the more prominent academics function essentially as scholars-in-residence rather than as full-flegded, involved members of a particular college community.

The sheer size and physical dispersion of the modern college and university have also been instrumental in reducing the attachment the average faculty member feels for his or her institution. At many large schools and universities, few teachers or professors know intimately more than a handful of their faculty colleagues. At a small college or school, the 20 or 30 faculty members might form a genuine community; but this is far less likely at an institution where the faculty numbers in the hundreds. Physically, the modern university may cover several square miles, with research stations and study centers scattered throughout the world. Increasingly, faculty members are no longer even in close geographic proximity, not to speak of intellectual or social proximity.

A final, and quite specific, development affecting faculty attitudes toward their institutions is the remarkable growth of the two-year community colleges. (The number of such schools grew from 525 in 1952 to 934 in 1972; at present they enroll 30 per cent of all college students in the United States, and it is estimated that by the end of the decade this figure will rise to 50 per cent.) The community college teacher has often come to his or her post by a different route from the faculty members at the four-year college or university, and exhibits a correspondingly different set of professional attitudes. More are drawn from the "outside world"—business, industry, and some of the professions—and are less deeply committed to the venerable collegial model of academic management.

The rapid spread of trade unionism contradicts the collegial ideal . . .

A variety of forces, then, have combined to weaken the individual faculty member's sense of identification with, and loyalty to, the institution where he or she teaches. It is no coincidence that the recent years have seen the rapid spread of trade unionism among both public school teachers and college professors. For this development not only reflects a natural desire to protect the gains of the recent past in salaries and working conditions; it is also a protective response to institutional changes which many academics find deeply unsettling.

The collegial model assumed, with great validity on some campuses, that the faculty was a participant in the policy-making process. Although the precise distribution of power within the college or university may have been rather hazy, most people recognized that a significant share of it lay with the faculty. But now that the labor-management analogy has been frankly introduced into the academic world, isn't it possible that its logical corollary—policy decisions and long-range planning completely in the hands of "management" with faculty "labor" relegated to the role of bargaining over wages and working conditions —could also gain general acceptance? In any event, the collegial ideal can hardly be defended with quite the same clarity by a teaching staff or faculty that has chosen the trade union option.

With fewer and fewer academics—particularly those with the prestige of a national scholarly reputation—willing these days to make the shift into administration, the customary method by which the collegial and the hierarchical traditions were bridged has become far less viable. More broadly still, the loosening of institutional bonds and loyalties has undermined the entire rationale upon which the collegial view of academic governance has been built.

. . . but the resurgence of one-man rule is no longer a possibility.

This is not to suggest that we are therefore about to witness a resurgence of one-man rule such as that personified by William Rainey Harper of the University of Chicago or the incredible Eliphalet Nott, who endowed Union College with $600,000 of his own money in 1804 and dominated it as president for the next sixty-two years.[18] If nothing else, the professional maturity, pride, and independence of today's teachers and scholars—not to mention the antiauthoritarian sentiments of students—make any such development unthinkable.

Even in business, the day of the hunch-playing corporation boss and the buccaneering financier is drawing to a close. Indeed, a growing number of big corporations—Macy's General Electric, Borden's, Motorola, and others—have eliminated the concept of the top man entirely, relying instead on a "corporate executive office" made up of three to five individuals who share top management responsibilities [19] (see Bower and Walton, p. 93).

But even were it possible internally, the return of the old style "captain of erudition" would be a disaster in terms of education's larger role. Today's academic leader must be able to deal not only with the usual quartet of faculty, students, alumni, and legislators, but with many other constituencies as well: regional interests, Federal government agencies, community spokesmen, ethnic or minority group leaders, trade union officials, angry taxpayers, the media, environmentalists, feminists, international agencies, and emissaries from the counter culture. The task of communicating with such an array of groups requires skills of a more subtle and complex variety than those usually possessed by the academic martinet, no matter how nobly motivated or how revered on campus. At a time when education is establishing new kinds of institutional ties at all levels of society, the academic managers must have a keen political sense and an intimate knowledge of the multifarious enterprises and structures of modern life, many of which may be very far indeed from the confines of his or her particular institution.

What education needs is a fresh approach transcending these old polarities. In short, neither the collegial model, the hierarchical model, nor the uneasy compromise between the two which did service in the past are any longer of much use in the quest for a pattern of academic governance equal to the demands of the present.

As a matter of fact, the outlines of a new approach to educational management have already begun to take shape amidst the confusions of recent years.

The Managerial Revolution in Education

While the forces of change whipped up by the knowledge explosion and exacerbated by the tensions between differing management concepts were threatening to ravage the world of education like a Kansas twister, a quiet managerial revolution was also beginning to make itself felt.[20] Hardly a coordinated or highly self-conscious effort, this revolution began simply as a series of pragmatic, defensive steps aimed at holding the educational enterprise together and responding in some fashion to unprecedented challenges.

The first stage: gradual expansion and rearrangement of the school's administration.

For many schools and colleges this began during the great growth years of the 1950's. It was in that period that a few academic presidents began to recruit vice presidents for planning to help cope with explosive enrollment pressures and physical expansion needs. Then came financial vice presidents, who (unlike the traditional business managers or bursars) concerned themselves with long-range financial planning, fund drives, and, in a few enlightened cases, cost-benefit analyses. And because the rapid changes in the schools and colleges were often deeply upsetting to alumni and local communities, some presidents brought in vice presidents of communication (or information, or public affairs) to facilitate the flow of information and criticism between the campuses and their growing number of constituencies.

Thus the presidents, in response to urgent pressures, began to put together a new kind of managerial group. And, in a break with the traditional dependence on the faculty exclusively for managerial talent, many of these new administrators came from the worlds of business, finance, journalism, or government.

The second stage: self-examination and research, made possible by the computer.

Stage II of this managerial revolution can be dated quite precisely: 1953, the year computers were commercially introduced. The academic world was quick to adopt this innovation to speed the collection, storage, and dispersal of all kinds of data such as tuition payments, expenditures, grades, library records, registration figures. Incredible as it now seems, most colleges and universities well into the 1950's still used—as some still do—small armies of retired women, graduate students, faculty wives, and local unemployed to enter grades on student transcripts by hand and keep pencil count of course enrollments. Now, for the first time, academic administrators had available reliable and rapidly obtainable information about their own operations.

The computer on campus quickly became a symbol, however, for those who were convinced that the university was becoming a soulless and impersonal machine. The hostility and suspicion were intensified because in many schools, as in many businesses, computers were introduced clumsily and without adequate preparation. Rarely was it pointed out, for example, how many tiring, mindless, and eye-wearying hours of human labor had formerly been expended in performing the statistical labors the computer could handle in a fraction of the time.

Spurred by the rise of executive cabinets and computerized data flow, universities began tentatively to look at themselves in a more comprehensive way, to keep more fully abreast of new trends in education, and to play with possible models for the future. On campus after campus, offices of institutional research began to appear. In 1955, only ten colleges and universities had such centers; by 1964 the number had grown to 115, by 1970 to over 300. Though faculty and students usually had access also to such research facilities, it was primarily the administrators, desperately trying to cope with rapid changes and mounting costs, who turned to them for self-studies and long-range projections. Most academics, concluded a 1967 study, "know more about everything else than they know about themselves and their habitat." [21] The burgeoning offices of institutional research were one attempt to remedy that serious educational blind spot.

At last, colleges, universities, and some larger schools had the staff and the facilities to begin to pose hard questions about their overall effectiveness and their long-range priorities. If an institutional research study revealed, for example, that 33 per cent of the school's classes enrolled fewer than eight students, the question arose: Is this academically desirable, or merely inefficient? How important are small classes? What do we know about the effectiveness of small versus large classes? If the planning office assembled data demonstrating that opportunities for non-campus learning were multiplying, and that cassettes, television, and film were attracting increasing attention as teaching supplements, other fundamental queries demanded attention. Have we fully explored the implications and the potential of such unorthodox approaches to education? Is the traditional requirement of 120 hours of classroom instruction for a baccalaureate degree any longer defensible?

And so the managerial revolution in education gained momentum.

While it is true enough, as has been pointed out, that this development involved "a greatly enhanced potential for administrative dominance," [22] it is equally true that it has never been rooted in any bureaucratic lust for power. It was an emergency response to powerful new demands on the schools and colleges coming largely from outside constituencies.

Some of these broad demands have already been noted; others were even more specific and more immediate. The Federal government required a central accounting of all publicly-funded faculty research. Student activists demanded data on the nature and extent of the institution's corporate investments and each faculty member's involvement in military and governmental research. Mayors and governors wanted to know what the colleges and universities in their territory were doing to focus on community problems and upgrade human resources. Minority leaders and government officials requested statistical evidence of nondiscrimination in employment and in admissions policies, and they demanded affirmative action by central management to balance off inequities of the past. Alumni leaders and state budget officials requested detailed breakdowns of current spending. Feminists, backed up by Department of Health, Education and Welfare lawyers, sent college officials scurrying to the records to examine sex ratios and salary differentials in staff and faculty.

What all this added up to was a new emphasis on accountability.

What the new demands made urgently clear was the need for a central management that could collect and disseminate information on each campus, analyze and defend (or criticize) current policies, and organize decision-making in a coherent way. Old patterns of informal, catch-as-catch-can academic governance had become obsolete. A quiet managerial revolution had begun.

The Future of Education Management

So much for the past; what of the future? The task now is to understand the nature of this revolution, to build management structures adequate to education's new role, and to pinpoint possible dangers in the transformations that are overtaking the world of academic governance.

The challenge, of course, is a complex and interconnected one, but for purposes of analysis, we may identify five points of special focus.

THE PROBLEM OF ATTITUDE

If education is even to begin devising management structures and techniques adequate to its needs, the first requirement is a fundamental change in attitude. This may sound commonplace, but it is basic. It means recognizing that today's radically different social context is not some temporary aberration, but the emerging shape of the future. Education needs to analyze calmly the new reality, and to design new structures appropriate for it.

The need: to come to terms with change, not fight it, not surrender to it.

The tendency all too often is to repudiate history, to lash out at the propellants of change, and to idealize an imagined past. The persistent Jeffersonian dream of the small-scale, pastoral, independent life has its educational counterpart in nostalgia for the undisturbed, isolated, and homogenous little college. Though such institutions happily still exist, and must endure, today's broader educational thrust is in quite a different direction, and schools and colleges must come to terms with it.

The contrary tendency, however, is simply to embrace contemporary trends with open arms and closed eyes, to "get with it." Proponents of this view (much smaller in number) urge that education simply swim with the tide, discarding all traditions which impede the drift toward an unknown but undoubtedly glorious tomorrow.

Both extremes only serve to obscure the responsible and involved role that education must play. The burning need is for an attitude among those in educational institutions which neither denies nor surrenders to the new reality, but which understands its force, ponders its meaning, and then helps chart a fresh course accordingly.

THE PROFILE OF LEADERSHIP

If the first step in revamping academic management is attitudinal, the second is one of recruiting men and women whose personality and talents are fitted to the changed demands of educational leadership.

The new leader will be astute, energetic, sensitive, tough, flexible . . .

In 1920, it was said by some that Warren Harding's greatest political asset was that he *looked* so much like a president. In education, too, institutions have often selected top management persons with attractive style but questionable abilities. In the future, the quiet, scholarly, pipe-smoking manner, the benevolently autocratic mien, or the well-publicized record will not be enough. The new imperatives of educational management will increasingly require men and women who are intellectually acute, poltically adept, financially astute, and organizationally sophisticated. They will need to be audacious and ready to accept the responsibility of reshaping education's structures in fundamental ways. And they will need to be tough enough, persuasive enough, and sensitive enough to achieve that goal despite the congenital nay-sayers and the uncritical enthusiasts.

The academic administrator of the future should also be a person with plenty of raw energy to meet the mounting physical demands of unrelenting pressure, yet a reflective person who can throw a saddle of rational perspective over his own—and others'—instincts and changing emotions. He will need a "Geiger counter" quickness about locating points of agreement and a talent for converting his findings into a cheerful consensus. He should have a low (but humane) tolerance for ineffective performance but a high boiling point. He needs the sureness of himself and of education's highest ideals that can furnish courage during wild moments, yet enough self-criticism to permit a sense of humor amidst life's assaults and banana-peel flops.

Above all, perhaps, educational managers of tomorrow must be persons who can live comfortably with ambiguity and a certain amount of disorder. The complexity of modern life makes uncertainty the norm, and the accelerating rate of change does not permit feelings of *stasis* and the comfortable order that derives from stopping history to build neat balances. Nothing but trouble lies in wait for the president, provost, or principal who insists on spelling out authority with clean precision or who tries to establish the exact divisions of power among all the constituencies within his or her domain. More than in other institutions, power in an academic institution is a fluid and elusive thing. The person who tries to fix it, free of all ambiguity and shiftings, will find it slipping away like sand in the face of storms and driving tides.

. . . but, above all, he must accept the obligation of leadership.

Paradoxically, despite all these ambiguities, the educational leader of tomorrow must unflinchingly accept the obligation to *lead,* in the broadest sense of the word. He or she must be able to savor the excitement, and endure the disappointments, of grappling imaginatively with large questions of long-range goals and new directions, rather than just with the concrete demands and the direct playback of day-to-day management. The serious lack of attention to the educational enterprise as a whole—both as it is and as it might be—has been the most crippling inadequacy of academic institutions in the past. Correcting that failure should be the central priority of the next generation of educational leaders.

Finally, the decision to become head of a particular school, college, or university will become less and less akin in its finality to taking religious vows. The world of education has become increasingly interconnected and a far greater mobility among administrators is inevitable. Educators should not regret this change. While the old-time headmasters or presidents who dominated their institutions for 20 or 30 years before passing from the scene may have set a splendid example of loyalty and dedication, their protracted tenures in office frequently proved deadening to both their own vitality and vision and to their institution's initiatives and boldness.

The emerging pattern of thoughtful mobility in top administrative positions is salutary. New leadership frequently means new vigor and new perspective.

RESTRUCTURING THE STAFF

Even with the most forward-looking of attitudes and highest of aptitudes, no educational leader can be much stronger than the staff structure of which he or she is a part. It is precisely here that the inadequacies of educational management are exerting their greatest drag. While much of the writings of school and college leaders and faculty has heralded the new era of rapid change in which we live, the alignments of staff at most educational institutions is much as it was 50 years ago.

Historically, the administrative structure of the typical school or college was geared to manage a slowly changing *status quo.* (Most business firms were no different.) In choosing his chief lieutenants, the principal or president surveyed his academic operation as it was presently functioning and selected men to supervise each of what he regarded as the main categories of operation: academic affairs, finances, student affairs, physical plant, public relations.

The presumption was that each institution was basically organized already in a satisfactory way and that the main duty of management was to make each of the discrete parts move forward gradually and gracefully—on the present course. The machinery was there; management's role was to keep it well oiled and running efficiently. That the machinery itself might be outworn or inadequate for the new conditions was seldom, if ever, questioned. In a phrase made popular some years ago, it was an in-basket-out-basket approach to management.

This traditional design will no longer suffice. The more intricate intertwining of functions and the pace of intellectual and technological change now require a structure that will allow the entire institution and its operations to keep renewing itself. In essence, education has been confronted with a new definition of efficiency. No longer does efficiency lie in the smooth purring of the parts but rather in the relationship of the whole enterprise to the needs of people and society at any point in time. A beautifully maintained steam locomotive is no longer a high form of effectiveness in an age of metroliners and jet airplanes.

The administrative staff will shift their main focus from operations to development.

Rather than perpetuating the established ways, tomorrow's administrative structure will have as its primary function to keep the whole operation abreast or ahead of change. This will entail three major tasks: the setting of priorities, the development of policy, and the evaluation of the overall enterprise. In this framework the day-to-day details will be kept in perspective. Rather than viewing the daily operations as the dominating priority, with planning, policy, and evaluation as neglected appendages, the ongoing operational activities will be viewed as that part of management responsive to these other three facets.

In short, educational management of the future must be structured to chart the swiftly moving course of intellectual and aesthetic work and of society, to set priorities and devise policies to keep abreast of the shifting course, and to evaluate the appropriateness and success of the policies formulated and directions taken. Darwinian adaptation rather than Henry Ford mechanics will be the model. The management of rapid and basic change requires a different structure from the management of simple expansion. None of this is entirely new to educational circles where change is the master word in academic prose and rhetoric. But the time has come to enact specific management reforms that translate the rhetoric into reality.

Just as today's top educational leadership positions need to be filled by a somewhat different type of incumbent, so will the new staff structures require men and women gifted with a new kind of imaginative versatility. How shall such persons be identified and recruited?

In his intriguing book *Space-Age Management*, James E. Webb, the director of NASA from 1961 to 1968, tells how he organized the flight to the moon.

In the first place, he discarded all *a priori* notions about who should do what, or to which professions he should turn, whether to business executives, generals, academics, engineers, or lawyers.

Next, since he didn't know who could best lead this unprecedented enterprise, Webb developed an imaginative new management strategy he calls "upward pressure." He kept assigning to all sorts of people tasks that were slightly beyond and outside their normal experience and demonstrated competence. Some failed, some succeeded. Those who failed were reassigned to tasks equal to their abilities; those who succeeded were given even greater assignments, still further beyond their known skills. Again, some delivered, some didn't.

Traffic jams occurred, and egos were wounded, but, concludes Webb, "these are not too high prices to pay for the continued development of strengths, for removal of weakness, and for identifying executives of the highest quality." [23]

And the United States did get to the moon—ahead of schedule.

Needed: an Apollo program to get American education to the moon.

The parallel is hardly exact but, in a sense, education too needs an overhaul and redesign of such magnitude and such unprecedented character that the lunar undertaking seems a comparable analogy. I suspect that the key educational manager will introduce something akin to what Webb tried in an intensive search for, and development of, talent fitted to help manage education's "Project Apollo." It should be unnecessary to add by now that such a search must take no account of race, background, or sex; it may be less obvious that the quest should be pursued with equal vigor among persons both inside and outside the academy, paying little attention to whether an excellent prospect happens to have behind his name a Ph.D., M.D., M.B.A., or no initials at all.

Faculty, alumni, taxpayers, indeed everyone interested in education, must realize the urgency of locating and elevating such men and women to education's staffs if schools and universities are to remain healthy and responsive. Managerial stalemate in an era of rapid change is tantamount to institutional suicide.

DIFFUSION OF ADMINISTRATIVE AUTHORITY

While the higher levels of academic administration will concern themselves increasingly with long-range planning, operational priorities and evaluation, more and more operational authority will be delegated to "middle managers." Business corporations have moved in this direction in recent years, and in a sense college deans have acted in this capacity for decades. But the complexity and dispersion of the modern campus, the build up of pressures on top management, and the emergence of sizable academic networks like the State University of New York and the University of California suggest a further spread of middle management authority in the future.

Middle managers will play an increasingly important and different role . . .

The middle manager—at once leader, peer, and subordinate—is in a touchy and difficult position. It is he who must convert broad goals and objectives into operating procedures, strategies, assignments, and timetables. Although on the flow charts he is simply a division head, it is on his desk that the buck in fact frequently stops.[24]

Here education can profit by studying the experience of other institutions, for *all* authority in the contemporary world is becoming more akin to that of the middle managers. Indeed, the very notions of autonomy, final authority, and ultimate power are being challenged.

We now live in a world of mutuality and interdependence, in which individual initiatives have complex repercussions. What the medical profession and the large corporation do affects education, politics, and international relations. And what education does, or fails to do, affects the economy, public health, the military, community well-being, and foreign understanding. Socially speaking, we are all part of the same eco-system today. The university president, dean, or department head, or the school principal who moans about the erosion of his autonomy and authority will in the future be counted a person who has not understood the complex interplay of power and responsibility in our time.

In a sense, we have all become middle managers, carrying responsibilities greater than our authority. We shall all have to learn the middle-management lesson: how to exercise a limited and ambiguous degree of autonomy within a pattern of growing complexity and constraint.

The movement of society toward professionalism, with the emergence of a new class of free-wheeling, somewhat independent specialists with few organizational attachments, has important implications for educational management. So does the general shift from a predominantly unskilled, blue-collar work force to a predominately skilled, white-collar work force. Both of these interconnected developments mean a decline in "hard" management, with its specific assignments, tight controls, and close surveillance. Instead, the academic managers of the future, without abandoning their broad perspective or the ultimate responsibility for their institutions, will have to lead primarily by formulating goals cogently and persuasively and by relying upon middle managers, who, while retaining a high degree of flexibility, will move their organizations toward those goals.

Fortunately, in moving toward this new design, educational institutions in one respect have an edge. For years, college and university administrators have been dealing with multiple constituencies (students, faculty, alumni, government) and with "employees" who were not simply wage workers but relatively mobile and independent professionals. Thus education not only may draw upon the experiences of other institutions in society, but it may also be in a position to make some practical and theoretical contributions as all of society's institutions grapple with the management challenges of the future.

. . . and there will be much greater use of ad hoc task forces.

Along with an enlarged role for middle managers, the educational management of the future will increasingly depend on temporary, *ad hoc* "kleenex" task
forces. Rather than build up bloated full-time support staffs, the astute administrators of the future will bring together teachers, students, administrators, and
outside experts to tackle specific problems and then return them to their normal
duties when the special assignment is completed. The management prerogatives
of such task forces will be at once broad, shared, and temporary.[25] While the
temporary groups will bring concentrated energy and authority to bear on
particular problems, their ephemeral character will be less likely to raise old-style
bureaucratic fears and abrasiveness. These fluid alliances will also permit a wider
participation in the management process while preserving the clarity and ultimate
responsibility of a central leadership structure.

Such an approach is not, of course, without problems of its own. There is the
risk, for example, that the instant experts on such task forces will hastily pro-
pose solutions without adequately grasping the full complexity or total context of
the problem they are studying. Here the NASA experience might come into play.
The men and women called upon for such assignments will tend to be those who
seem particularly adept at concentrated, short-term analysis and handling of a
problem. Further, the freshness of such assembled talent should add great daring
and vitality to management, since unlike the entrenched bureaucracy, the kleenex-
type task forces will have no solid positions to maintain or ongoing enterprises
to protect.

ESTABLISHING LIMITATIONS AND BOUNDARIES

But even with the appropriate attitudes, recruitment procedures, and managerial techniques, tomorrow's educational leadership could fail resoundingly
if it did not recognize the need for—and help to devise—clear-cut checks and
restraints on its own power.

Educational managers must be both more forceful and more accountable.

In theory the very complexity of modern life imposes restraints; but, in the
real life of a campus, such theoretical assurances are not enough. In the future,
a far more precise and explicit delineation of the power and responsibilities of
each of the various components in the educational structure will be necessary.
The university must accept the fact that it is, in a way, a political community.

This assertion does not spring merely from an abstract belief in the relevance
of democratic theory to the school or college life. My concern is quite practical,
for only in a climate of trust can bold and effective leadership flower. No matter
how brilliant the ideas of an administrator, they will prove to be will-o'-the-wisps
if they are not undergirded by the political and moral support of the faculty,

the students, and the other constituencies for which the enterprise is maintained.

What educational institutions of the future need, in sum, is a new climate which permits the management to lead more forcefully than before while at the same time operating within more definite arrangements for prior consultation and accountability than before.

Educational managers should have fixed
terms of office with periodic review.

To further the development of this new climate, educational management should logically address itself to its own tenure. In point of fact, the length of service in top management positions has been growing steadily shorter. In 1960, the average college president had served for eleven years; by 1970, the average had dropped to seven years. But the academic equivalent of "dictatorship tempered by assassination" cannot be trusted to guarantee the necessary rotation in office. What is needed is the establishment of fixed terms of office for the top management positions in education, with a periodic opportunity for the constituent groups within the institution to indicate their wishes formally as to the administrator's continued tenure.

The precise length of such a term of office is, of course, a matter of discussion. It must be long enough for the incumbent to find his bearings, demonstrate his style, and begin to achieve results. But it must be short enough to provide for a change before incompetence turns into disaster. President Kingman Brewster of Yale has suggested seven years as about right; I myself would incline toward a somewhat shorter term—six, or even five years, with the possibility of a one-time renewal of the mandate at the end of the term.

Whatever the details, a movement toward specific terms of office for education's top management seems both desirable and inevitable. If academic management is to become, as it must, more vigorous and innovative, then compensating safeguards against excessive central power and incipient academic Napoleons must be devised. Education is one of the few enterprises—some religious institutions are another—where central management is not called to account or reviewed on any systematic, regular basis.

So long as trustees selected "safe" consensus-sure presidents, so long as the pace of academic change was not so swift, and so long as the need to redesign education was not so urgent, this anomaly could be tolerated. But as education recruits more enterprising and creative management, arrangements whereby the quality and new directions of that management can be periodically evaluated become imperative. And the constituencies that participate in such an evaluative process must reflect the fact that the individual school or college is no longer an island, distinct unto itself, but merely one segment in a complex and interconnected social enterprise.

What education needs is an arrangement which gives the top administrators some assurance that they will have a reasonable period of time to move their institutions forward, and a counterbalancing assurance among all the constituencies directly affected by these initiatives that they will have an opportunity to assess and judge the quality of their leadership, and either endorse it or replace it.

Improvement of education's management may be society's most vital task.

The problems and challenges of academic management and governance have not traditionally been such as to attract either serious intellectual attention or passionate emotional involvement. Yet it is in just this overlooked arena that some of the most far-reaching decisions of the next few decades will be made.

In a knowledge-based society, where the capital for growth is increasingly to be found in the heads and hearts of individuals, education becomes the critical enterprise. Thus it is no overstatement to suggest that the improvement of education's management, and the redesign of education itself, may well be the most vital task we face as we move toward the twenty-first century.

Notes

1. See, for example, Paul Goodman, *The Community of Scholars* (New York Random House, 1962).

2. *Digest of Educational Statistics, 1970* (Washington: Department of Health, Education, and Welfare, Office of Education, 1970). Many of the educational statistics in this chapter are derived from the same source.

3. U.S. Department of Health, Education, and Welfare, news release, October 10, 1971.

4. On the shrinking work week, from 43.4 hours in 1945 to 37.5 in 1968, see Juanita Kreps, *Lifetime Allocation of Work and Leisure* (Washington, D.C.: Dept. of HEW, 1968), p. 36.

5. Wilber J. Cohen, "Education and Learning," in *Educational Investment in an Urban Society,* ed. Melvin Levin and Alan Shank (New York: Teachers College Press, 1970), p. 357.

6. J. M. Tanner, "Sequence, Tempo, and Individual Variation in the Growth and Development of Boys and Girls Aged Twelve to Sixteen," *Daedalus,* vol. 100 (Fall 1971), pp. 907–930.

7. William G. Perry, Jr., *Forms of Intellectual and Ethical Development in the College Years* (New York: Holt, Rinehart & Winston, 1970).

8. James A. Perkins, *The University in Transition* (Princeton: Princeton University Press, 1966).

9. Daniel Bell, "Notes on the Post-Industrial Society," *Public Interest,* No. 6 (Winter 1967), p. 30. See also Peter Drucker, *The Age of Discontinuity* (New York: Harper & Row, 1969).

10. Henry M. Wriston, *Academic Procession: Reflections of a College President* (New York: Columbia University Press, 1959), p. 131.

11. See, for example, Theodore W. Schultz, *The Economic Value of Education* (New York: Columbia University Press, 1963), and Gary S. Becker, *Human Capital* (New York: National Bureau of Economic Research, 1964).

12. Ivan Illich, *Deschooling Society* (New York: Harper & Row, 1971).

13. John J. Corson, *The Governance of Colleges and Universities* (New York: McGraw-Hill, 1960). "[Academic] departments have the power to initiate most actions that affect the basic function of the institution" (p. 92).

14. W. H. Cowley, "Some Myths About Professors, Presidents, and Trustees," *Teachers College Record,* vol. 64 (November 1962), p. 164.

15. Paul Dressel, F. Craig Johnson, and Philip Marcuse, *The Confidence Crisis: An Analysis of University Departments* (San Francisco: Jossey-Bass, 1970), p. 232.

16. Earl Bolton and Fredric Genck, "Universities and Management," *Journal of Higher Education,* vol. 42 (April 1971), p. 281.

17. Christopher Jencks and David Riesman, *The Academic Revolution* (New York: Doubleday, 1968); Neal Gross, "Organizational Lag in American Universities," *Harvard Educational Review,* vol. 33 (Winter 1963), pp. 58–73.

18. Frederick Rudolph, *The American College and University* (New York: Alfred A. Knopf, 1962), p. 171.

19. *Wall Street Journal,* July 7, 1972, p. 26. See also H. Igor Ansoff and Richard G. Brandenburg, "The General Manager of the Future," *California Management Review,* vol. 9 (Spring 1969), p. 65.

20. Francis Rourke and Glenn Brooks, *The Managerial Revolution in Higher Education* (Baltimore: Johns Hopkins Press, 1966).

21. Nicholas Demerath, Richard Stephens, and R. Robb Taylor, *Power, Presidents, and Professors* (New York: Basic Books, 1967), p. 8. On the growth of offices of institutional research, see Paul L. Dressel and Sally B. Pratt, *The World of Higher Education* (San Francisco: Jossey-Bass, 1971).

22. Rourke and Brooks, *Managerial Revolution,* p. 118.

23. James E. Webb, *Space Age Management* (New York: McGraw-Hill, 1969).

24. Hugo Uyterhoeven, "General Managers in the Middle," *Harvard Business Review,* vol. 50 (March–April 1972), pp. 75–85.

25. Warren Bennis and Philip Slater, *The Temporary Society* (New York: Harper & Row, 1968).

Contributors

Helpful comments and inputs from the following members of the author's panel are gratefully acknowledged (the author, however, assumes full responsibility for choice of content and interpretation):

ROGER HEYNS, President, American Council on Education

MARTIN TROW, Professor, University of California, Berkeley

Intersects:
The Peculiar Organizations

IN the twentieth century many societies have witnessed the development of "peculiar" organizations which did not fall into any of the well-recognized categories. They are not quite government, although they are usually the result of some kind of government action. They are not quite business, although they perform many business functions. They are not quite educational or charitable organizations either, though they may also perform some of these functions. They frequently occupy "cracks" or interstices in the organizational structure of society. They have been named "intersects" because they have some qualities of more than one conventional type of organization.

Considering their relative newness, intersects are surprisingly prevalent and important in today's social scene. Yet little attention, and even less research, has been focused on them to date. We need some idea of what has brought them into being, and some appreciation of the role they are now playing, if we are to assess their own style of management and their impact on management style in other types of organization.

Are they a temporary phenomenon due to decline; have they reached a plateau; or will they continue to grow and, perhaps, displace more conventional organizations? It is hard to tell. But, in any event, they would appear to be a manifestation of a dynamic social ecology, where new ideas and new structures come into being to meet new needs, and where, for reasons allied with the social and political structure, other forms are not acceptable.

The Peculiarity of Intersects

But, despite the neatness of their name tag, intersects do not form a homogeneous or well-defined class of organizations. If we are looking for "peculiar" organizations, we shall find that almost all organizations are peculiar in some degree or another. It is an instructive exercise, for instance, to try to nominate a "typical" business or government office. There are very few organizations today which exist in a pure market environment or a pure governmental environment. If we nominate some organizations as more peculiar than the rest, it is by no means clear that they form a homogeneous class, but then there is no homogeneous class of business or government organizations, either.

There are good reasons for these difficulties of definition. In the world of biological organizations, it is fairly easy to define species because of the universality of the property of genetic reproduction. This gives the taxonomists in biology a great advantage. In social systems there are certain parallels to genetic reproduction, in the sense that ideas and images of the future constitute the "genes" of all organizations. Nevertheless, organizations do not reproduce by bisexual methods, but have, as it were, a very large number of sexes, and any particular social organization is generated by the interaction of large numbers of others. We cannot therefore rely on a genetic test to define a social species; and as there are no other good tests, either, social species are inevitably vague in definition. The devision of the set of all organizations into subsets of any kind is inevitably somewhat arbitrary. A subset that we define for one purpose may not be meaningful for another.

Intersects are midway on various spectrums
—public/private, operating/regulatory, etc.

Nevertheless the set of all social organizations is not a heap of sand; it has pattern and structure. Organizations can be ranked along a good many dimensions. Many of these dimensions constitute a fairly continuous spectrum without clear dividing lines.

It is interesting to specify some of the dimensions along which the intersect organizations might lie. First there is the public/private dimension, where I suspect we would put intersects in the middle but toward the public end. Then there is the profit/nonprofit dimension, which has an increasingly large middle (what I have called the "not for very profit" organizations). This is almost the same as the market/nonmarket dimension, a measure of which would be the proportion of the total revenue of an organization derived from sales and the proportion derived from grants or gifts. Intersects, again, would be somewhere in the middle of this spectrum.

Another possible dimension is the operating/regulating spectrum. Here the measure could well be the proportion of output which consists of goods or personal services, by contrast with information. The output of regulating organizations consists of information transmitted to the parties that constitute the environment of the organization. Here again, intersect organizations may be found toward the middle of this scale, although more in the direction of regulation rather than operation. Another possible scale would be the coercive/noncoercive continuum, with coercive organizations invoking the police power when they are legitimate (or unofficial sanctions when they are illegitimate, like the Mafia), and noncoercive organizations on the whole utilizing the market environment for their survival. Here again, intersects may well occupy a middle role.

What seems to emerge from this analysis, is that the more peculiar an organization, the more in the middle range it seems likely to be. While, at first glance, this may seem odd, there may be a good reason for it.

*Intersects may serve as buffers and mediators
between conflicting organizations . . .*

Intersect organizations may serve as "buffers," rather like a buffer state. They may be set up to separate two organizations that otherwise might be in unbearable conflict. They may be set up also to negotiate and mediate, connect and interpret, between two or more other organizations. Example: the Denver Regional Transit District, which brings together city and state planners as well as private land developers in an attempt to coordinate land use. The term "intersect" is particularly appropriate for organizations of this kind, because they do in fact occupy the intersection of two sets; i.e., they belong in some sense to two groups of organizations, or fill odd-shaped spaces between the organizations.*

Not all intersect organizations, however, perform a mediating role. Interstices may develop between organizations which are not very much in conflict, but between which there is an odd-shaped piece of social space, which does not quite fit the conventional patterns. In this role they are, indeed, the "dough between the cookie cutters."

* A note on the mediating role of intersects by the Associate Project Director, Theodore A. Smith.

The choice of an organization to perform certain tasks is conditioned by social and political ideas of what constitute legitimate functions of conventional institutions. This doctrine varies with time and with the locality. While, for example, it may not be considered legitimate for government to operate an industry in the United States, there is no objection in Sweden.

The choice is also influenced by inherent operational constraints associated with organizations. Business must earn a profit. Government must be subject to electoral control—it should be possible "to vote the rascals out."

When the environment changes, it may no longer be possible for an organization to perform its functions satisfactorily without conflict with its basic constraints. Thus, privately operated municipal bus lines have become unprofitable and, so, inappropriate for business to operate. Government control of both U.S. and British Postal Services suffered from political constraints which grew to be intolerable.

Responsibility for each service could have been transferred to another conventional structure (i.e., government to run buses, and business the post office), but this would violate the functional legitimacy. The easier course was to employ another organizational form more free of constraints—an intersect.

Thus intersects can be a moderating influence on ideas of organizational legitimacy— a buffer, for example, between legitimacy ideals of socialism and capitalism. They are characterized by a form and structure relatively free of inherent constraints, and less subject to traditional notions of legitimacy in behavior.

There is a certain tendency of hierarchical organizations to be "round," the hierarchical layers being concentric circles or spheres. If in certain parts of the organization the hierarchical chain is longer, this part is perceived as something of an excrescence and may be spun off or withdrawn. Smaller organizations often can survive in the interstices or larger ones even if they are round. We see, for instance, the survival of the corner grocery in the face of the supermarkets, and the survival of many small plants in industries dominated by large firms. If there are striking diseconomies of small scale, however, this process of creating smaller "round" organizations cannot go on for very long, and there will still be odd-shaped spaces which will be filled by organizations of a peculiar, perhaps non-hierarchical, kind.

There are a good many intersects indeed which have a fairly standard hierarchical pattern, like the Port of New York Authority or the TVA, and these may, in a sense, be an accident of history, in the sense that the space that they occupy could just as well have been occupied with other forms of organization. When we get to the "compacts," however, we will see organizations that are distinctively interstitial, and these are not only the most prevalent, but also the most likely to present interesting problems of management.

Birth and Death of Intersects

The dimensions listed above all concern what might be called the "life," that is, the ongoing operations of the organizations. For a more complete understanding, we must turn to their time patterns, and especially to their birth and death as well as their life—birth of course being their origin, and death their dissolution.

If we are looking at the total set of organizations in an ecological system, the forces underlying their birth and death are particularly important. Obviously, organizations that cannot come into existence are not of much interest to us. Those which are in existence may be there more because of certain peculiarities connected with their origin than they are because they have survival value, either for themselves or for the total system. The death of organizations, again, is of particular importance from the point of view of the organizational ecosystem.

Birth: by budding, by compact, or by entrepreneurship—but especially by compact.

Organizations, unlike biological individuals, can come into being by a great variety of operations.

There is one process that corresponds somewhat to asexual reproduction in biology, which might be called "budding." A church forms a college to educate its people and propagate its doctrines; a corporation may form a subsidiary as a separate corporation; a country may establish a colony, as Britain did in the

American colonies. This operation is frequently associated with something I would call the "Pinocchio Principle." Somebody sets up what is supposed to be a puppet and it starts to walk. The church-founded college starts to behave like a college and eventually it breaks its church connection. The subsidiary takes off on its own and may buy itself back from the mother company and become independent. The colony may have a revolution and become another nation.

Another method of organization formation is the compact. This may take place either between individuals, as on the Mayflower, or between organizations. The prerequisite here seems to be a "group" either of people or of organizations, the individual members of which are brought into contact, often by somewhat extraneous forces, and then find that the interaction among them requires regulation, so they set up an organization to regulate it. An example is the Delaware River Basin compact for regulating use of common sources of water shared by three states.

Regulatory compacts often follow the "Pinocchio Principle."

Some compacts are mainly regulatory organizations; some start out as regulatory, but, again following the Pinocchio Principle, take on a great deal of operational function, and become relatively independent of their sponsors. Others are operational from the beginning, like the Bay Area Rapid Transit Authority.

A third method of formation of organizations is entrepreneurship. An individual, or perhaps a small group of individuals in close contact, conceives some image of the future, in which an organization comes into being through the activity of the entrepreneur himself. He communicates with his environment, he obtains support funds, he hires people, and so on; and an organization is the result. Henry Ford and the Ford Motor Company is, of course, a famous example. Even here the Pinocchio Principle may be observed. Once the organization gets underway, the original founder may be squeezed out, as in the case of Mr. Sears and Mr. Roebuck; other more managerial rather than entrepreneurial types may take over; the purposes of the organization may change under pressures of its environment, and so on.

One may venture the generalization that intersect organizations are seldom formed by budding, are most usually formed by compacts, and are occasionally formed by entrepreneurship. It is not surprising that an intersection organization can be formed by a compact among the parties or sets of which it is an intersection. A group of people or organizations perceive, as it were, some kind of niche or gap between them, and compact to form an organization to fill it.

Even in the formation of compacts, entrepreneurship is an important element. Organizations are not created merely because there is need for them or because there is a niche they might occupy. Unless there is some kind of driving force, some person who perceives a need and has a vision of the organization to come, even compacts that are useful to all the parties may not take place.

We often hear "it would be nice if somebody did something," and then nobody does it. There is a principle of nucleation involved in the formation of any organization; i.e., the system has to generate enough energy or information structure to get it over a threshold. These threshold phenomena are important in all systems; they are particularly important in the social system. Thus, a business faces growing multiconstituency responsibilities, as Ansoff and Drucker envisage; the need for mediation between the public and private sectors may build up enough pressure to generate a new set of intersector organizations—or, of course, either business or government may move to act within the scope of its own present structure. Only time will tell.

There seems to be no general theory of niches, either in biology or in the social sciences, or even in language (which can almost be defined as a set of verbal niches created by the occupants of other niches). In the evolutionary process, however, it is clear that some structures of niches are more probable than others and tend constantly to reappear. We have, for instance, the fascinating story of the oceanic islands, like Mauritius, New Zealand, or Hawaii, which were inaccessible to the mammals but accessible to the birds. In these islands, before man introduced mammals, birds had developed to occupy all the principal mammalian niches, to the extent indeed that in some of them there were even rabbit-like birds that lived in burrows, birds that had lost all power of flight, and so on.

We have already seen that the size and shape of organizations may create interstitial niches. A new successful mutation, whether in biology or the social system, creates niches for itself and also in the process often creates niches for other species, both for old ones and for potential new mutations. Evolution eliminates enormous numbers of species; it has already eliminated more than are now extant. But most of the older types of species survive; thus, evolution did not displace the amoebae or the invertebrata. So the end result is an increase in the total variety and complexity of the ecosystem, and we may be tending in that direction with organizations.

An important source of new structures is
dissatisfaction with old structures . . .

Dissatisfaction can create a shrinkage of old organizations, at least a relative shrinkage, and this may provide opportunities for new forms which it is contemplated would create less dissatisfaction.

A particularly important aspect of the problem here is a mysterious rise and fall of legitimacy or credibility. If we have a rise in something here which is neither government nor business, this may, partly at any rate, be because of a decline in the legitimacy of both government and business. There exists a certain "plague on both your houses" feeling when it comes to the niche the intersect is to fill. The public sector is seen as too bureaucratic and inefficient, and the private sector as too selfish and irresponsible. Hence, there is a yearning for something which combines (1) the supposed responsibility of the public sector for the total society, and (2) the efficiency and pragmatism of the private sector. The result seems to be a demand for a kind of private-enterprise socialism.

Mere dissatisfaction, of course, does not necessarily imply a solution. It is just as easy to fall between two stools as it is to stand on them, and it is quite conceivable to combine the worst of two systems rather than the best. Thus, Amtrak may well turn out to be a failure, in contrast, say, to NASA or TVA.

The dissatisfaction-demand for organizations often depends on the way in which "problems" are visualized. An organization is often set up to solve a perceived problem, but the perception of the problem may not have very much to do with any underlying reality.

A very good example of supply creating its own demand in the field of organization was the setting up of the Social Security Administration in 1930's. There was apparently very little popular demand for social security in the United States before the Great Depression. Indeed, the American Federation of Labor was passing resolutions condemning it as late as 1929. The social security system on the whole was a product of a group of socially concerned intellectuals, many of them students of John R. Commons at the University of Wisconsin, who felt that the absence of a social security system was a serious defect in the American polity and set themselves out to remedy this defect. Once Social Security was created, of course, it became popular, and no government could now be elected in the United States on a program for doing away with it.

The TVA can be considered in somewhat the same light. It can almost be regarded indeed as an exercise in liberal northern imperialism, designed to improve and to bring into the modern world the technologically backward areas of the Southern Appalachians. Here again, once it was set up, it became popular and has survived, although its enemies in state politics and among public utilities have prevented any extension of this form of organization to other river valleys—for example, the Missouri Valley Authority proposal, which was a failure. That the TVA could be established in a politically weak part of the country is an exercise in what might almost be called "virtuous colonialism." Its counterpart could not be established in those parts of the country which were politically more dominant, such as the Middle West and the Eastern states.

The Bureau of Reclamation is an interesting example of an organization which was born partly in response to an intellectual movement—what might almost be called the "first conservation movement"—of the 1900's, and was an expression of a liberal, almost socialist, at least "Populist," ideal in its inception, as reflected in its dislike of interest and in the 160-acre limitation on the size of the farms that it serviced. As an ongoing organization, it acquired a good deal of political power and know-how in the arts of marketing in the Congressional budget system, and there is considerable feeling abroad now that, its original mission having been accomplished, it is going on to projects of continuing declining social value. Here it looks as if the demand that was created by a certain supply of ideas and ideology has persisted after the original need has been met, out of sheer inertia.

. . . reflecting a need for more independence, less accountability.

A general principle which undoubtedly lies behind the formation of intersect organizations is that of a demand for decentralization and for independence in operation of operating agencies. A good many organizations as diverse as General Electric and the Soviet Union have run into cycles of centralization, decentralization, and recentralization. I am tempted to call this the "GIGOTOSOF" syndrome, which stands for "the grass is greener on the other side of the fence." There may be problems that are virtually insoluble which give rise to cycles of this kind. Any existing situation is regarded as unsatisfactory. Dissatisfaction leads to pressure for change, and there is change. The pressure for adaptation leads to a new pattern. The new pattern, however, also proves unsatisfactory and creates pressures for change—frequently back into the old pattern.

This is of course, the thesis that every revolution is only a half revolution. A full revolution brings you back to where you were before, from the Czar to Stalin, or from Louis XVI to Napoleon, or from the last Chinese emperors to Mao Tse-Tung. Like many things which are profoundly true, this is only a half-truth. The cycle never comes back to just where it was before. Hopefully, we learn and reach a higher level; despairingly, we unlearn, and reach a lower one.

But we cannot escape the fundamental process by which dissatisfaction leads to change. It is important to ask, in the case of all our intersects: What particular dissatisfaction led to this particular change? An even more ticklish question is why a particular dissatisfaction leads to a particular change, for often the change does not cure the dissatisfaction and often seems strangely unrelated to it.

One dissatisfaction which can easily lead to the setting up of intersects is dissatisfaction with bureaucracy, gigantism, scales of organization that are too large for either efficiency or humanity. Out of these dissatisfactions arises a demand for smaller and more independent organizations that will not have to refer everything back to some large and anonymous central authority, and hence can be free to experiment, in forms of internal organization, in products, in markets, and so on.

The "GIGOTOSOF" syndrome can
lead to the "King Lear" syndrome.

Decentralization, however, often results in a lack of accountability. The principle that "the more independence, the less accountability," and "the more accountability, the less independence," has often been remarked by political scientists. (In fact, as noted earlier, part of the reason for an intersect may be that it needs to be less accountable to achieve its purpose.) But this can lead, in turn, to what we would call the "King Lear" syndrome; the king divides his kingdom and lives to regret it. Power which has become a burden is sloughed off to decentralized and independent agencies, but then these begin to compete with what remains of the central authority, and there is often an attempt, sometimes successful, to draw back the loose reins into the hands of the centralized authority once again.

Insofar as the intersects have arisen mainly by some kind of devolution of government authority, as in the postal esablishment, the decentralization-independence motivation can be seen to be strong. Thus, public dissatisfactions with the Post Office—an institution that found itself almost incapable of adapting to the increased scale of complexity of the modern world—took the form of identifying political control and patronage as the main source of the evil, and hence led to the creation of a more independent organization with a more professional staff. (But again, this does not mean that the new organization will succeed; that depends on whether the new *management* will be equal to the task.)

In the case of Comsat, we have something that looks rather different—a desire to provide a vehicle for many diverse organizations, to work together in a complex situation without creating a monopoly, and in this sense represents prevention of centralization, rather than desire for decentralization. Comsat is particularly interesting here because the alternatives seem almost too large and cumbersome to bear thinking about. Comsat indeed is a good example of a "buffer" organization, occupying a certain social space betwen 82 nations, A.T.&T., I.T.&T., and all their prospective customers.

Death: unfortunately social organizations have no self-destruct provisions.

The demand for organizations includes not only a demand for their birth, but also a demand, which unfortunately seems to be less effective, for their death.

In the world of organizations, it nearly always seems to be easier to create a new organization than to get rid of an old one—unlike the biological world. This is in part because of the different genetic structure. In the biological world, all phenotypes are self-destruct machines, in the sense that their genetic code contains in it instructions for aging and death, at least for an increase in the probability of death with aging after a certain point. But social organizations rarely contain self-destruct apparatus in their genetic codes or constitutions. There are occasional foundations, like the Rosenwald Fund, which are created with the specific provision in their constitution for their dissolution, but neither business nor government organizations usually have any plan for aging, and regard survival as their objective.

Almost the only social system which has formalized apparatus for the death of organizations that have served their term is capitalism, with its law of bankruptcy. Indeed, one could argue that it was precisely the institution of bankruptcy which gave such vitality and expansive power to capitalism. By contrast, it is virtually impossible to get rid of any political organization once it has been set up—even organizations as obsolete as the American county and township. The bankruptcy of the national state is achieved only as the result of a process of appalling disorder and cost, namely a war of conquest.

It may well be that part of the demand for intersects arises out of our failure to get rid of old organizations that are no longer performing a useful function rather than any desperate need for new organizations. Amtrak certainly is the ghost of the bankrupt Penn Central and of other railroads that perhaps should have gone the same way but did not. This is a problem, however of great difficulty, and I have no great optimism about its solution. The lust for life even in organizations is very strong. It is even becoming an increasing problem for persons, as we find that the medical profession is increasingly devoting its expensive energies towards keeping alive people who, though it seems harsh to say it, would be better off dead. One wonders if the financial intravenous feeding that seems necessary for Amtrak does not have a parallel in our best hospitals.

Management of Intersects

Life interposes itself between birth and death for organizations as well as for persons. In the case of an organization, where birth is usually the result of conscious decisions, the image of its future life and activity is an important element in the motivation leading towards birth, and the realized pattern of its life and activity is the major factor leading to survival or to death. The life of organizations, however, is encompassed very largely in management, as indeed it also is for the person. Management is the process of making decisions, that is, choosing activities in the light of some of the images of the future which are associated with them. Management is choice, both in the life of the person and in the life of the organization.

Is management in intersects different from management in other organizations?

It is an important question, therefore, whether the skills and patterns of management are essentially different in intersect organizations from what they are in business, government, or other more conventional forms.

The truth in this regard, as is so frequently the case, seems to lie between the two extreme positions: (1) Management is management whatever the organization to be managed; i.e., its principles are much the same whether in business, in government, in education, or in intersects; hence it is a waste of time to try to find any very special principles of management, no matter how peculiar the organization. (2) Intersects are peculiar, so their management problems must be peculiar too; hence we should expect to find somewhat different personality types and considerably different operational principles in intersects from what we find in other organizations.

I must confess that my prejudices would incline me closer to the first view than the second. But the fact is that the study has thrown up some interesting problems which suggest that the spectrum of management skills and problems is wider than is usually recognized in the conventional works on the subject, and intersects may contribute some significant variations of their own.

Let us first look at those problems of management, life, and ongoing activity of organizations which are likely to be common to all.

*For all organizations, management is
decision making in the light of the future . . .*

The first proposition is that the main activity of management is decision, and the "life of an organization" consists largely of a decision tree—i.e., a decision, its consequences, a further decision, its consequences, and so on.

The second proportion is that the agenda of decisions—i.e., the set of alternatives among which choice has to be made—consists of alternative images of the future, each begun by an act which is under the power of the decision-maker. It is the key to the precariousness of the human condition that all decisions are about the future but all experience is in the past. The link between experience of the past and the image of the future is knowledge—that is, the perception of patterns of order and regularity in the past which enables us to project these patterns into the future. Thus, I decide to turn left in front of an oncoming car because my perceptions give me knowledge of its velocity and distance, and that knowledge enables me to project that it will not hit me if I turn in front of it.

There are many ways by which images of the future are derived. We may get them from simple projection of trends, as in the above example, or in the prediction of eclipses and the movement of the heavenly bodies. We may get them from having observed time patterns in the past, which we now perceive beginning in the present or the near past. Thus, we have a great deal of confidence that a kitten, if it survives, will grow up into a cat, not into a dog.

This is the phenomenon which the biologists have called the "creode"—the pattern of development from the origin of an organism. In social systems this takes the form of drama. We come into a playhouse and witness the first act of Hamlet; we have a great deal of confidence that we are about to witness the other acts; and if we have seen Hamlet before, we have some idea of what is to come. A great deal of management, likewise, involves the recollection of past drama and the projection of the future in the light of witnessing the first act, where the social learning process is a crucial factor.

A critical question is whether the structure of organizations and the interaction of persons permits a social learning process—enables the decision-maker to learn from his past mistakes, and so improve his images of the future as he acquires new skills.

It is one of the dangers of hierarchy that it insulates its higher members from the learning process, simply because of the status relationship involved. If a superior is to learn, he has usually to be corrected by a subordinate, but the hierarchical relationship often prohibits this. In extreme cases, top management, whether of a large corporation or of a government, can become almost completely insulated from reality, simply because it has control over its own information system. This is what I have described as "organizational schizophrenia," as indeed it has many parallels with schizophrenia in the person.

There are several defenses against this condition. One is the setting up of informal lines of communication—in the men's room, or on the golf course. Another is the development of "staff" communication which bypasses the hierarchy. Another is the employment of outside auditors or management consultants, who are not dependent on the favors of a single employer. Another is the encouragement of an element of randomness in promotion, especially to the higher echelons. Where these safeguards are not operative, there is a strong tendency for organizations to deteriorate and the larger the organization, the more rapid and disastrous the deterioration can be.

. . . and the value system stems largely from the manager's reference group.

A decision involves not merely having a set of images of the future. It involves also being able to order these according to some value system, at least in a cardinal ordering, so that we can pick out which is "best." Every decision, almost by definition, consists of doing what is thought best at the time, out of all the apprehended alternatives.

The values or preference functions by which the alternative images of the future are ranked in order of value depend not just on the manager's self-image of his role but also on the values of his "reference group"—the values of the people that his role obligates him to please. There may be some, usually not very important circumstances, in which decisions can be made according to some "objective function"; that is, a number can be assigned to each of the alternatives, measuring, say, their profitability, and the best alternative is then the one with the highest number attached to it. But the higher the level of management, the less likely are decisions to be of this mechanical, quantitative character, and the more likely are they to be qualitative judgments.

All valuation processes, however, involve taking a large number of considerations and weighing them according to some pattern, which often is almost unconscious. These value patterns are again learned and can change over time, as communications and experiences, failures and successes, modify the image of the decision-maker as to what is valuable and what is not. This is a process which is mysterious and little understood. Nevertheless, we cannot assume that values are either given or fixed, even though they may be fairly stable over short periods.

This is why the reference group of the decision-maker is such an important aspect in the formation of values. In the case of a manager, this may consist of his board of directors; it may also, however, consist of his staff and employees, particularly those with whom he comes into immediate contact. It may consist of labor union leaders, environmental leaders, political leaders—all those, indeed, who he is aware may criticize him. More remotely, it may consist of magazines, inputs of information from various authoritative sources, and so on.

But there is a significant difference among reference groups . . .

The processes of formation of the values of the manager from his experiences with reference groups may not differ very much from case to case, but there are major differences among different organizations in their different reference groups. Almost all intersects operate under the aegis of a board, a commission, or a council appointed by the founding organization or organizations. Since most intersects operate in the public sector, the board has authority to perform regulatory, operational or mediating functions within specified limits, often with power equivalent to that of government. The board is apt to have a considerable degree of independence—both due to "Pinocchio" development and to the fact that intersects are often relatively free of constraints. From a practical standpoint therefore, intersects tend to be less accountable than direct governmental agencies.

The management of intersects, like the management of other institutions, varies particularly with size and complexity. Small organizations may differ considerably among themselves. The problems of management of large organizations, however, are all somewhat alike, and are very different from those of the management of small organizations. The main difference lies in the degree of formality and complexity of the information system. The manager of a small organization can be in personal touch with most of the members of his reference group; the management of a large organization has to rely on elaborate processes of information processing through the hierarchy and may indeed have to be more concerned with the information processing than with the information itself.

Thus, the management problems of a large intersect organization like the Port Authority [of N.Y./N.J.] are not likely to be enormously different from those facing the management of a similar sized corporation. But it has no stockholders; and the value system—the criteria by which its performance is judged—is more than economic. In some sense, the Authority is more open to public criticism when, for instance, it builds the World Trade Center than when, shall we say, the Chase Manhattan Bank builds a similar building on Wall Street; yet the Authority appears to be less responsive to its reference group (the public) than a direct government agency would be.

. . . and this does make management different in many interesects.

Where we do seem to find the special problem of management of intersects most clearly is in the relatively small organizations that occupy specifically intersectoral roles, such as those created by interstate compacts, where the reference groups often include industrial groups and citizens' groups as well as the political organizations, and where the function of the organization has strong elements of mediation among conflicting interests, and of communication among groups that otherwise would not be in communication at all. While none of these is large compared with a typical business corporation (or even a university), there are many of them, and in total they bulk large.

In these types of organizations the precepts of standard management science, or even management wisdom, have only limited application, and the style of management seems to approximate more clearly that of the counselor than that of the bureaucrat or corporate executive. At this level it is quite possible that a genuinely "intersect-management" type is beginning to emerge, combining some of the virtues of the politician, the counselor, and the businessman. (See also Drucker on intersect management, p. 266.) How to train these people outside the hard school of life may become a very interesting problem for that sector of the academic community which is in the management training business.

Evaluation of Intersects

The evaluation of any form of social organization is one of the most important, and yet one of the most difficult, tasks of social thinking. I say "social thinking" quite deliberately, rather than social science, because although the social sciences can make important contributions to this task, it must be conceived as a task of the whole social learning process, and it is something which is continually going on in the whole society. The prophet, the preacher, the politician, the journalist, even the novelist and the artist, all make their contribution towards the vast social learning process which goes on through communications of all kinds—teaching, lecturing, writing, editorializing, electing, defeating, voting, protesting, practicing civil disobedience, and even indulging in violence.

These are the processes by which legitimacy is won and lost, and this is the battleground on which the survival of any particular form of organization is determined.

The criterion is social welfare, but how do we measure it?

Insofar as this brief paper can be concerned with such a vast problem, it has to be at the level of the contribution of social science and social philosophy.

Thus, economics has developed the concept of a social welfare function, which measures the result of many variables; it goes up when enough of the right kind of variables get better, and down when the poorer elements prevail. What makes the problem of evaluation so difficult is that the various elements in the welfare function are interrelated, so that when one goes up, another usually goes down. Furthermore, and particularly important, some are "goods" and some are "bads."

Almost every human activity produces both goods and bads, and whether the activity itself is justified depends on whether the goods outweigh the bads. Thus, if an organization increases the GNP, which is good up to a point, but increases pollution, which is bad, or if it diminishes conflicts, which is good, but makes income more unequal, which may be good or bad depending on where one puts the optimum, how are we to add all these up in a final evaluation? Quantitatively the task is clearly absurd. Nevertheless, we have to make qualitative judgments about these things all the time, and these judgments will either be better informed or worse informed according to the amount and quality of the analysis that we have done.

We must look to the divergence between
personal and social value systems . . .

We may well despair of finding an exact formula for the general welfare function, but we can perhaps identify certain problems and things to look for which will better inform our judgments. Thus, one thing we are looking for, as we have noted earlier, is whether the organization of society facilitates or hinders the social learning process by which images of the future become more realistic.

Another, very crucial, question is whether the personal value system with which every decision-maker operates diverges from some social value system, according to which the choices made by him are ordered by the general welfare function rather than by his private welfare function. This divergence depends partly, at any rate, on the distribution and objects of benevolence and malevolence—values that are derived from perceptions of the welfare of others. (If my valuation of an alternative is raised when I perceive or believe that this alternative will raise your welfare, I am benevolent. If it is lower under these circumstances, I am malevolent.)

When we distinguish social values from private values we are simply postulating an optimum distribution of benevolence-malevolence. The situation grows more complicated, however, when the dynamic interaction of benevolences and malevolences is taken into account. It is possible at least to postulate the existence of an optimum preference function for each individual faced with a number of alternatives, from the point of view of some larger aggregate, frequently defined as a nation, although logically it is hard to prevent an extension of this aggregate to the whole human race.

The question then becomes: What social processes, organizations, and structures diminish the divergence between the personal value systems, according to which decisions are actually made, and the optimum value systems, which we postulate as socially desirable? Adam Smith's "invisible hand" operates when actual personal choices are in fact the optimum social choices in all cases. Perhaps we should take a more modest view of the invisible hand and settle for a system in which divergences between personal choices and optimum choices tend to diminish through the operation of social processes.

. . . recognizing that suboptimization may
illuminate less than ideal goals.

The problem presents itself as suboptimization, which can be defined crudely as finding the best way of doing something which should not be done at all or, a little more accurately, choosing the best among a number of alternatives by a personal value ordering which is not identical to some postulated ideal value ordering. The classical example of this is the production manager who said that all he wanted to do was to reduce costs, until it was pointed out that the way to do this was to shut down the operation and so reduce the cost of operation to zero.

A major source of suboptimization is misleading indicators—i.e., things that are in the information system which can become objects of policy, either to maximize, to minimize, or to hold them at some level which is regarded as optimal, but which lead to the neglect of other variables which ought to be put into the evaluation function.

We find innumerable examples of this in political life. Parity in agricultural policy is a famous example; there is no law of justice whatever that says that the terms of trade of agriculture should be stable, which is what the parity formula implied. National security is another example, for the search for maximum security is almost always self-defeating, especially in a world of sovereign states.

Virtually the only formal solution to the problem of suboptimization is the economists's model of perfect competition—unrealistic, limited, and inadequate as it is. This unfortunate fact has moved the management science practitioners toward trying to simulate decision-making under perfect competition within the organization. There is a good deal to be said, of course, for the proposition that hierarchies corrupt and that this corruption is proportional to the rigidity and to the size of the hierarchy. It does not necssarily follow, however, that we can always do things better by substituting market interactions, whether real or simulated, for hierarchical control.

How, for instance, do we set up specialized organizations to do something which it is in the social interest that they should do badly? Organizations set up to do something always want to do it well, at least according to suboptimal criteria. The business of sending people to hell has been conducted with gross inefficiency over the centuries, and this inefficiency is most praiseworthy. The business of socializing people into society, through the family, the schools, and the churches, has likewise been done with moderate inefficiency. This inefficiency is the only thing which has allowed progress of any kind, for an efficient society would simply replicate itself every generation, and there would be no possibilities for development.

In any organization and in any society there is an optimum degree of disorder and disorganization. I have argued indeed that the reason why the breakthrough into science came in Europe but not in China, where one would have expected it, is that Chinese society was too well ordered, with not enough separation into independent political units. Europe evidently had the optimum degree of disorder, and science was the result.

The issues which have been raised above are very large and unanswerable. This is, however, the framework within which any evaluation of the development of any special type of organization such as the intersect has to be conducted.

Intersects may or may not perform functions
that other organizations can't . . .

The first question to ask perhaps is: Are there any alternative forms of organization which could perform the functions of the intersect organization in a more traditional, conventional way? One can't answer anything more positive than "maybe" or "maybe not"—and both answers are probably right, depending, of course, on the organization itself. Consider:

Is the organization of the Tennessee River for public purposes much better or worse than that of the Wisconsin River, developed in a very different way? It is not easy to say.

If we had not had the Small Business Administration, would small businesses decline more than they have done? Again, it is hard to say. And if in fact they have declined, would society be any worse off? This is still harder to say.

If rural credit had been left to the private banking system, would farmers have been much worse off, or would society have been much worse off? As a matter of fact we do not know.

One can go down the whole list and come up with equally inconclusive evaluations.

. . . as illustrated by the Federal Reserve System,
still debatable after 50 years.

The evaluative problem is illustrated acutely in the case of the earliest and still perhaps the largest of all the intersects—the Federal Reserve System. We have not tried to examine it in this study, for it would require a massive study in itself. Nevertheless, it fulfills all the requirements for an intersect: it was instigated by government, it has strong government connections and control, yet it is officially a part-private organization, and it interacts very powerfully with the private sector of the economy.

Economists still, even today after over 50 years of operation of the System, are sharply divided about its evaluation. It has been enormously successful in the sense that it has survived, it is almost universally regarded as legitimate, and there are virtually no plans afoot for changing it organizationally in any essential degree. Nevertheless, if one were to do a cost-benefit analysis of it from the point of view of the total society, I am not at all sure how the results would come out. It has given the United States, of course, a unified monetary system, and has prevented any real regional monetary autonomy. It has certainly not been successful in alleviating business cycles, and it was undoubtedly a major factor in deepening the Great Depression. Its policies have often been arbitrary and very hard to explain on any rational grounds.

The critical question is: Would its policies have been any better if it had been a completely governmentally owned and controlled central bank? It is hard indeed to visualize that they would have been very different, for they would have been made by much the same set of people. It is hard to see that the reference groups of the Federal Reserve Board, the managers of the separate Federal Reserve banks, would have been very different if the central banking system had been completely nationalized. What mistakes it may have made emerged out of the banking subculture within which almost any institution of this kind has to exist. It is hard to see that a change in the form of organization would have changed this subculture more than superficially.

The question might be raised, of course, as to whether we would be better off without *any* central bank—as to whether the old national banking system with all its defects would not have served us better. The question is not absurd even though the consensus of economists seems to be that central banking is an absolute necessity in the modern world.

This example suggests, as the whole study suggests, that intersects intersect largely on the side of government rather than on that of private business. The alternative to an intersect is rarely a purely private organization; rather it is likely to be a purely governmental organization.

Intersects may reallocate resources toward
activities deemed socially beneficial.

A still more difficult aspect of the evaluation of intersects is in the whole impact of these organizations on what I have called the "grants economy," both explicit and implicit.* That is, what redistributions of income and of net worth take place as a result of the formation of the intersects?

Almost all intersect organizations involve some kind of government subsidy or grant, whether of money or of privilege. As noted earlier, one possible spectrum along which the intersect quality might be measured is that of the proportions of the total gross receipts of an organization which are derived from the market (i.e., through sale of goods and services), on the one hand, or from grants (i.e., one-way transfers), on the other.

Grants have essentially two purposes, which can easily be contradictory: (1) the redistribution of income or economic welfare, in which it is generally assumed that the poorer the person, the better is the case for a grant *to* him; and the richer the person, the better the case for a grant *from* him; and (2) the reallocation of resources toward activity which is believed to be socially beneficial, and which would not be supported by the market. Negative grants, such as

---

* Dr. James Morgan estimates that in the United States in 1969, grants or one-way transfers amounted to $71 billion from government sources. Private charity, including foundation grants, furnished about $20 billion.

taxes, can likewise be used to discourage activity which is believed undesirable, such as pollution.

One general reason for shifting the distribution of resources by grants is that certain uses are thought to be intrinsically more valuable socially than others, such as the opera. We may feel that having an opera gives tone to a society, so that even if we wouldn't be seen dead seeing one, we are still prepared to subsidize it.

Another reason is that there are what the economist calls "externalities"—i.e., joint production of other goods and bads, which can neither be paid for nor penalized through the market mechanism. This is closely related with a third reason: that without a grants economy there would not be adequate provision of public goods, or penalization of public bads.

How far the intersects fulfill these complex criteria is a question far beyond the scope of this study, or perhaps of any study, but it is a reasonable guess that they go far enough to make many of them a social plus.

All institutions must be judged by their long-run positive payoffs . . .

While these evaluative questions almost of necessity have to be left vague, they are not for that reason any less real. The survival of any institution depends ultimately on whether those who run it and those who are affected by it consider it legitimate. I have argued, indeed, that the dynamics of legitimacy is perhaps the most important single factor in the over-all dynamics of society, although it is in itself a dynamic which is hard to penetrate and is frequently subject to unforeseen changes. Legitimacy bears a loose long-run relationship to over-all evaluations. Institutions which lose value—i.e., which are no longer regarded as having positive payoffs—in the long-run tend to lose legitimacy.

In the short-run a reverse process may be at work, which I have described elsewhere as the "sacrifice trap," in which negative payoffs, or sacrifices, produce legitimacy since they are involved with the identity of the sacrificer. People may sacrifice a little for the TVA, but no one is going to sacrific very much for Amtrak or for Comstat, and not much more for the many smaller intersects. The national state still retains a great deal of sacrifice-originating legitimacy, and insofar as the intersects are creatures of the national state, the legitimacy of the national state extends toward them; and, in this sense, their legitimacy may stand or fall with the legitimacy of the national state itself. Even though the legitimacy of the national state has been in decline, perhaps because of the excessive sacrifices which it has demanded, it would be very surprising if it collapses within the time span of which we are thinking.

. . . and on this score most present-day intersects appear to be viable.

It is to the positive payoffs, therefore, that we must look for the most part in estimating the future legitimacy—and longevity—of the intersects. Amtrak certainly looks vulnerable on this score; if passenger service on the railroads continues to deteriorate, Amtrak could well fold. (Whether the passenger train will go the way of the stagecoach is another question, however; the service may be deemed to be too important for that, and another organization—intersect or otherwise—may then be formed to fulfill the function.)

A single example of this kind, however, would not upset the general validity of the intersect principle.

The question of the viability of any—and every—intersect is related both to the legitimacy of the function performed and to the competence of the organization performing it (though, in default of either, death may be slow in coming). As stated earlier, questions can be raised as to the social value of some of the services undertaken by intersects, but it would appear that generally they are useful and some seem to be essential. Also, a fair number appear to be well managed; but here the real question is whether, well managed or not by conventional standards, a given intersect succeeds in performing its assigned function better than another form of organization would.

The Future of Intersects

To a rather high degree, intersects are employed because of the inherent constraints on more conventional organizations. If, therefore, the constraints are altered, conventional government or industry might well be able to perform their tasks. However, it seems unlikely that major changes will occur rapidly, and so, intersects may be with us for a long time. Whether or not they represent a "wave of the future" is, however, another matter.

Intersects are not likely to become the
dominant form, but will continue to be useful.

Those predictions are by no means easy to make. Adam Smith, for instance, thought that the corporation did not have much future; that it would expand into a very limited niche, generally in the public works type of industry; that its internal disadvantages were so great that it would never replace the unincorporated business or the family firm. The nineteenth century certainly proved Adam Smith to have been wrong in this prediction, although the "organizational revolution," which event eventually established the corporation as the dominant organizational form in economic life, was something that Adam Smith himself could not reasonably have predicted.

At the same time, other forms of organization, like labor unions, do seem to have expanded into relatively limited niches in society, and do not show many signs of expanding further, and certainly show no signs of becoming the dominant form of organization, even in the labor market.

At the moment I must confess that I feel about the intersects very much what

Adam Smith felt about the corporation, that it is a useful form of organization in the limited field, but that it is unlikely to become the prevailing form in society. If anything indeed I would rather expect the GIGOTOSOF principle to come into play, and to find a reaction away from the intersects toward more direct governmental organization and operation of this type of agency. If I am wrong about the prediction, at least I will have been in good company.

There will be some exciting new niches for the intersects to fill.

I do not mean to say that intersects will not continue to multiply. In our dynamic social ecosystem, new intersects will be born to fill new, or newly perceived, niches. But, by the same dynamism, there will also be some deaths; and this, I am convinced, will keep intersects from ever swamping other forms of organization.

The question is: To what extent will births outnumber deaths? And this depends on where new niches will develop. As an exercise in attempting to define the potential niche of the intersect organization, one might try to write down the rough specifications of as many potential intersect organizations as one could think of which might come into being in the next 30 years. Although it is difficult to think of many, some of those that do come to mind are rather exciting:

Radio and television is a possible candidate. We have, after all, the BBC in England, which is a typical intersect, but there does not seem to be strong pressure for more public broadcasting than we already have in this country, though one could be wrong about this.

Education is a field which perceives itself to be in crisis, and in which, therefore, the development of intersects would not be surprising. Any movement toward a voucher plan for subsidizing the student rather than the schools might produce a wide variety of public, private, and intersect organizational experiments in education which are now suppressed because of the nature of the grants system in education.

The police are another area where there is a certain sense of crisis, where intersect organizations are by no means inconceivable, occupying perhaps a middle ground between Pinkerton and the city police.

The crisis in parochial schools might even produce an intersect in church-state relationships, in spite of the long tradition against it.

Even when we extend this list as far as we can, however, the intersect still looks unlikely to threaten the great governmental and private organizations of our society. Intersects are for interstices, and while I suppose we could move toward a society in which everything is interstitial, as I think the extreme participatory democrats and would-be anarchists would rather like to see, I suspect that this will not happen, and that the solid conventional business and government bodies will stay around.

The ultimate future of intersects depends
on the dynamics of our social ecosystem.

At the same time, though, the interstices between business and government may widen, and new interstices appear. I do expect intersects to continue to play an important and useful role. Whether that role becomes even more important in the future depends largely on the dynamics of our social ecosystem. So I would like to close with this list of questions, for the reader to answer for himself and thus form his own idea of the future of intersects.

Questions

1. Are there likely to be ever-widening areas of "social space" which intersects will fill in future years, or will conventional institutions adapt to fill the gaps? For example, will intersects continue to supply some of the needs for regional governance and for operation of public services?
2. Are intersects which function in the public area as responsive to the public constituency as they should be?
3. What are the criteria for judging the success or failure of intersect organizations—considering the varied nature of purpose and structure?
4. Since intersects—both domestic and international—appear to be less subject to constraints than their institutional parents, are there likely to arise any demands for regulation or control over present practices?
5. As government assumes greater responsibilities for formulating public choices, will it "bud-off" some of the functions to intersects, so that they will assume a larger proportion of responsibility in the public area?
6. Is the creation of international intersect structures, such as those dealing with scientific, educational, or ecological matters, likely to provide a pathway leading toward world government?
7. If intersects functioning in the public area continue to increase in number, will there be a tendency to form systems of intersects with like interests which may assume growing influences not provided for by any one intersect or by present concepts of national government? (The Education Commission of the States, might be an example of an intersect network.)

Contributors

Helpful comments and inputs from the following members of the author's panel are gratefully acknowledged (the author, however, assumes full responsibility for choice of content and interpretation):

EMILE BENOIT, Professor, Graduate School of Business, Columbia University

JAY FORRESTER, Professor of Management, Alfred P. Sloan School of Management, Massachusetts Institute of Technology

JAMES WEBB, Formerly Director of NASA

Douglas N. Ross conducted an empirical study of intersect organizations in association with the author. He is now a Senior Economist with The Conference Board.

Seven

DAVID HORTON SMITH
with JOHN DIXON

The Voluntary Society

EVEN responsible dissent may not be a welcome element on every occasion, but . . . it is absolutely essential to progress. Without the change bred by honest and enlightened dissent, man is bound to die in mind, spirit, and body. It is his unique ability to be dissatisfied that imbues him with the dedication and drive required for the enlightenment of all great works."

These are not the words of some firebrand revolutionary, but part of a speech delivered by David Rockefeller to the commencement exercise for Choate School in June 1967. We could have used a similar quote from any of dozens of other luminaries, yet coming from Mr. Rockefeller these words seem especially relevant to this discussion and the larger endeavor of which it forms a part.

For this chapter is concerned with the voluntary sector, and most of the dissent, both responsible and irresponsible, that arises in society comes from that sector. So do many other important things.

In our view "voluntary action" and "voluntarism" do *not* refer just to the "do-gooders"; the voluntary sector is much more encompassing. We include the Black Panthers, the Yippies, Nader's Raiders, Cesar Chavez' United Farm Workers, Martin Luther King's SCLC, Women's Lib and many other types of issue and cause-oriented voluntary groups or movements, as well as the more traditional social-service oriented voluntary groups.

We also include as voluntary groups scientific societies; trade unions and professional associations; churches, religious sects and religious voluntary groups; leisure, recreational, artistic, and social voluntary groups; and fund-raising, charitable, and philanthropic voluntary organizations.[1]

Our specific focus, of course, is the *management* of voluntary group. We interpret the term "management" in a very broad sense to include all aspects and levels of governance—policy making, administration, and operation. (We prefer the term "governance" to the term "management," in fact, since the former has a broader, more participative connotation than the latter. One of the major problems of the voluntary sector may indeed be too much "management" by the leaders/executives of business and government, coupled with too little effective, participative governance under the guidance of voluntary organization leaders.)

And we are concerned both with how voluntary groups are managed *internally* by their own leaders, staff, and members and with how they are managed *externally* by their environment (business and government organizations). We hope to provide the interested reader with a better understanding of the role of the independent voluntary sector in society as a whole, and also the optimal roles of voluntary organization leaders within the voluntary sector. The two are inextricably linked, and failure to understand the former leads to inadequacies in the latter.

The prime characteristic of "voluntarism"
is that goals are noneconomic, even idealistic.

We consider voluntary action to be behavior that is primarily motivated by some sort of desire for psychic benefits or approaching some kind of ideal or set of higher values, by commitment to some larger and often "public interest" goal. Individual voluntary action, in this sense, is very often that which gives personal meaning to life. It is that which one freely chooses to do either for enjoyment in the short term and/or from commitment to some long term goal.

There *may* be situations where voluntary action is remunerated, and voluntary institutions *may* have economic objectives. When this is the case, however, the economic aspect is different from the economic aspects of true business corporations. *At the individual level,* voluntary action is usually distinguished by the fact that the individual performing it is not fully remunerated at the market value for the services rendered. For instance a volunteer may be paid absolutely nothing for some quite valuable services rendered, or a VISTA or Peace Corps volunteer may be paid only a fraction of the true worth of his or her services.

It is also true that in foundations, fund-raising organizations, and large national voluntary organizations, there are generally staff members and administrators who *are* paid the full market value of their services, and hence are not volunteers or even quasi-volunteers in the economic sense. Nevertheless, even these people are parts of the voluntary sector and may be engaging in voluntary action if their primary commitment is to the goals and values for which their institutions stand rather than to the money that they might be receiving for their services.

The State of the Voluntary Sector [2]

As a result of our thinking, discussion, and consultation with major figures in the voluntary sector both in the United States and abroad, and a careful reading of much of the literature dealing with voluntary organizations and voluntary institutions in society, we have come to several major conclusions about the state of the voluntary sector and the problems of governance in voluntary groups both today and in the coming two or three decades. We here present these major conclusions in a straight-forward way without a great deal of elaboration or discussion.

VOLUNTARY SECTOR'S IDENTITY AND ROLES

First of all, it is important to realize that voluntary action and voluntary organizations have played a major role in the key historical changes of human society over the past several thousand years.

For example, nearly all major revolutions have been instigated and initiated by voluntary groups of one kind or another. All the great religions and political movements started as voluntary organizations, often very small informal groups led by a single charismatic leader. Major changes in the conduct of human affairs, such as the decline and abolition of slavery in most countries, have come about as a result of ideological changes that were fostered and promoted by voluntary groups of one kind or another.

Voluntary action and voluntary organizations have played a major role in history in preserving values, ways of life, ideas, beliefs, artifacts, and other productions of the mind, heart, and hand of man from earlier times so that this great variety of human culture is not lost to future generations.

For example, there are in the United States numerous local historical societies that specialize in preserving the history of particular towns and areas; there are nonprofit organizations that run local museums and historical sites; and there are a number of voluntary organizations whose primary function is to preserve the values of cultures that no longer have any great power or importance in American society, but that nevertheless represented a way of life of a significant number of human beings at one point in time (for instance American Indian groups or immigrant associations in the United States).

Western European and American legal and political traditions support the rights of free association, assembly, dissent, and collective non-violent action of various kinds.

This right of association, assembly and dissent is conceived to be a very fundamental one, as indicated by its inclusion in the First Amendment of the Bill of Rights of the American Constitution.[3] The application of this right of free association to an ever larger set of types of voluntary activity generally takes time, but it does occur. For example, at one time, trade unions or labor unions were considered to be conspiracies in restraint of trade, although eventually the right of employees to organize and bargain collectively with their employers was recognized in the law.

In terms of the political theory of pluralist democracy, voluntary organizations play an important part in relating citizen interests to governmental decision-making.

The voluntary sector, therefore, is an important countervailing influence in a variety of ways to the kinds of decision-making processes that take place within government in various agencies and at various territorial levels.

In fact, a vigorous and free independent voluntary sector may be viewed as the hallmark of a free society, while one of the first acts of most dictatorships is to engage in repression of voluntary associations that are not under government control and to attempt to take over whatever voluntary associations might serve the purposes of the dictatorship. For example, in Nazi Germany,[4] one of the first actions of the Nazi party as they worked their way into greater and greater power was to take over the various voluntary associations, right down to the grass-roots level, and to install party control or else to eliminate, sometimes outright and sometimes through consolidation, the various voluntary associations that did exist.

The independent voluntary sector is based on a grants economy—i.e., an economy whose money, goods or services are given without equivalent monetary value being received in return.

The grants that provide basic support to the independent voluntary sector are made, for the most part, without expectation of economic gain, in contrast to the grants economy of the government sector, which is involuntary (i.e., taxes); while the business sector, on the other hand, is based on a market economy. Understanding that the *grants economy* is different from the *market economy* is crucial to understanding the nature of the independent voluntary sector and the financing and funding of voluntary organizations.

The independent voluntary sector presents both the image and the reality of the good life to large numbers of individuals in society.

For example, religious and other voluntary kinds of organizations have long tried to serve as the conscience of the business and government sectors. It is voluntary institutions that have provided the "play element" in human societies for thousands of years, wherever that play element has been collectively organized; and it is voluntary organizations that in large part provide sociability and enjoyment of various kinds of artistic performances.

The independent voluntary sector is the prototyping testbed of new social forms and ways of organizing to do things in society.

Nearly every function currently performed by governments at various levels was once a new idea, an experiment of some voluntary institution—this is true of education, welfare, care for the aged, Medicare, etc. In fact, in early American society, there were voluntary associations even for the building of roads and the performing of other kinds of public works, so that even as obvious a thing that government might do as taking care of public works was once done by voluntary associations in this very country of ours.

And the interesting thing is that voluntary associations in various ancient societies, such as ancient India, performed precisely these same kinds of functions. Voluntarism was *not* born in America.[5] *Everywhere* voluntary action has played *the* key role in social innovation.

Noneconomic, nongovernmental decision-making is and should be very distinct from the process of decision-making used in business and government; voluntary group decision-making is more broadly participative, while business, government, and many peripheral nonprofit organizations tend to be much more hierarchical and non-participative in their decision-making.

The leaders/administrators of voluntary organizations need to be even more independent in their thinking, values, goal-setting and planning rather than being derivative of other institutions in the economic or governmental sectors. Unlike the government and business sectors, voluntary organizations can and should seek to set their goals and to perform their long-range planning in an atmosphere of experimentation and inclusiveness in terms of values and ideals, whereas the government and business sectors are much more limited in the range of possibilities and values that they can encompass in their planning and goal-setting.

FUTURE TRENDS IN VOLUNTARISM

Many new forms of action and organization have arisen in the voluntary sector in the past two decades and promise to become even more widely used and important in coming decades. By this we mean that the times are changing as much for voluntary organizations as they are for business, governmental, and other kinds of organizations.

One manifestation of new forms of voluntary action in future decades probably will be the more rapid turnover in voluntary group memberships and more rapid changes in the membership composition of established voluntary groups as a result of the increased mobility of the population and more frequent changes in the goals of voluntary groups, shifting coalitions and mergers among groups, and a general sense of "temporariness" in social identities and affiliations. The voluntary activity of individuals will thus become much more spasmodic, cyclical, and variable than at present.

At the organizational level, we expect there will be correspondingly great increases in the more temporary, *ad hoc,* short-term, and problem-focused voluntary groups that will form, be active, and quickly disband as the need or problem they addressed is dealt with or recedes in importance. (As it is today, there are too many deadwood organizations that have outlived their usefulness and thus represent a waste of human and other resources.)

A major part of the thrust toward more *ad hoc* voluntary groups will continue to come from the young. One very important aspect of the so-called "Generation Gap" is the marked decline among young people of respect for organizations *per se*. Youth are very often uninterested in "taking hold of" and participating in traditional membership structure voluntary organizations. They feel less need of organizational continuity for its own sake. Yet they are quick to mobilize resources when necessary to respond in a complex way to crises or new problems. Thus, the old "vertebrate" model of a voluntary organization may be on the way out, to be replaced by a "crustacean" model—where an old shell (organizational structure) is shed when it has served its purpose, and the living body (volunteers) can adjust to growth and new circumstances.

The independent voluntary sector may well expect to drain off from other sectors of the society an increasing proportion of the highest quality minds, both idealistic young people and experienced and practical managers/administrators, as voluntary action professionals.

For instance, we expect to find an increasing number of mid-career dropouts from among the top ranks of business and government executives, as people who have made it in the establishment world of big business and big government opt out for a kind of activity that allows them to make a greater contribution to the general human welfare and the sum total of human happiness. In some cases it may be the very bigness itself of big business and big government that is the disturbing quality to a number of highly qualified and high-quality business and governmental executives and administrators.

As a consequence of increased professionalization, the next few decades will also see a large increase in the degree and rapidity of "rotation of leadership" among voluntary groups. As voluntary organization/nongovernmental organization administration becomes more "professionalized" and established as a recognized, high-level specialty of its own, these leaders will feel increasingly free to move among positions in different voluntary organizations, in much the way that there is often high mobility among business executives, government officials, teachers, etc. There will even be national executive placement and recruitment firms that specialize in voluntary action professionals.

The role and impact of the independent voluntary sector are likely to increase in importance in the coming decades, as our society moves further toward a leisure and issue-minded society and a post-industrial service economy. At the same time, the independent voluntary sector will command an increasing share of both the time and the commitment of the general population.

For example, as people have more leisure, they will have more time to devote to voluntary action of various kinds. As our society begins to emphasize more and more service occupations of one kind or another, there will be an increasing emphasis on voluntary action, which is essentially a kind of service, although usually an unpaid one. As we become more and more a post-industrial society, the production and consumption of goods will take a position of declining relative importance to the production and consumption of well-being, so to speak. The quality of life will increasingly become uppermost as a consideration at all levels of society, and voluntary organizations will continue to take a lead in this realm.

The nature and composition of the voluntary sector will change, perhaps markedly, in coming decades.

Issue-oriented and advocacy groups will continue to come to the fore and intensify their demands for justice, equality of opportunity, power, ecological balance, etc. There will be a declining emphasis on some kinds of traditional service-oriented voluntarism as more of these tasks and goals are taken on by business and government. But new kinds of social service voluntarism are likely to continue emerging as fast as traditional roles decline. For instance, there has been a fantastic growth (i.e., from zero to 250,000+) in college student off-campus volunteer service programs,[6] in volunteers in the courts and probation system, and in volunteers in education (from Head Start pre-schools to high school teacher aides) over the past several years.

One of the most important areas of future expansion of service-oriented voluntarism will probably be in "self-help" voluntarism. The patronizing type of "social service to the unfortunate" voluntarism will increasingly, though gradually, lose out to groups of people with problems who want to help themselves. The great success of Alcoholics Anonymous, for example, has stimulated the growth of Neurotics Anonymous, Suicides Anonymous, etc. Other self-help groups of people with problems (e.g., the handicapped, the divorced or widowed) will also continue to increase markedly in size and scope.

There will be a relative decline in essentially "social groups" like fraternal lodges, fraternities, sororities, and ethnic associations as cultural/class distinctions on which they are based change and lose much of their importance.[7] Most sociability in formal groups will take place in common *interest* groups, rather than common *background* groups.

There will be also an increasing importance of certain kinds of such voluntary action (art, music, sports, hobby, and related groups) as a means of dealing with the anonymity and alienative pressures of modern society. Also, consummatory-expressive voluntarism will become more important as the more developed nations move toward leisure societies and away from a one-dimensional focus on GNP and internal economic growth as primary goals. There will be an increased emphasis on consummatory-expressive voluntary organizations as major mechanisms for enhancing the individual and collective quality of life.

Scientific societies will continue to increase in numbers in coming decades as a proliferation of such groups becomes increasingly necessary to cope with the information explosion, the rapid growth of science, and the increasing differentiation and specialization within the scientific communty.

Organized religions will in the coming years continue their slow but steady decline, although they will continue to constitute a very major portion of the voluntary sector in terms of both numbers and resources (e.g., charitable dollars). In 1971 the U.S. churches received about ⅓ of the roughly 21 billion charitable dollars given to voluntary groups and nonprofit organizations. In that same year they also claimed about 128 million official members (out of a population of 210+ million). We expect both figures will decline proportionately.

In line with our becoming ever more a service society and the increasing proportion of professionals in the labor force, professional associations will probably grow in proportionate strength in coming decades. Businessmen's groups will continue to flourish, but will become more socially responsible than at present.

The relative decline in industrial/manufacturing jobs will mean that the unions, by contrast, will have trouble holding their own, eventually declining somewhat in numbers, wealth, and power. Yet like the churches they will remain as a powerful periphery to the voluntary sector. They are too skilled in their tactics and strategy and too well organized and financed not to remain as a major force. Yet they no longer play the same *moral* role in the voluntary sector which they did 50–100 years ago, and it seems unlikely that they will be able to regain this. There are now new organizations to speak for the poor, the hungry, and the oppressed.

The independent voluntary sector already provides a great many specific benefits and services for society as a whole that go relatively unrecognized and are little understood. At the same time, the independent voluntary sector has a great potential, both for short and long term, for more and better contributions to the general welfare and the quality of life for all mankind.

We may expect future decades to see a greater *recognition* of these contributions of the independent voluntary sector and, at least in some degree, a greater *realization* of the potentials of this sector for contributing to human happiness.

Implications for Voluntary Sector Leaders

Now what do all of these conclusions mean for the leader of a voluntary organization or a voluntary program? Just what should he try to accomplish?

BUILD DISTINCTIVE STRENGTHS

Voluntary action and the independent voluntary sector are of such importance historically, and have such a solid legal base and political tradition to back them up, that members and leaders of the voluntary sector and voluntary organizations have no need to feel inferior.

The leaders and administrators of the voluntary sector should stand up for the importance, the potential, and the great past contributions that voluntary organizations and the voluntary sector have made to human society. Leaders of voluntary organizations should also be aware that there is every reason to believe that these contributions will increase in scope, in magnitude, and in importance in the coming years.

Thus, the first important implication of our study of management in the voluntary sector is more a matter of changing perceptions, changing consciousness, changing awareness and acting on the basis of this changed awareness, than of any specific set of techniques that need to be implemented, or programs of a specific sort. In fact, this may be the single most important implication of the entire study.

The leaders of voluntary organizations must be ever on the offensive in protecting the rights of free association, dissent, assembly, collective non-violent action, etc.

Specifically, the leaders of the voluntary sector must not only be ever on the alert for protecting the rights of their *own* organization to participate in the voluntary tradition, whether in service or in cause-oriented roles or in some other way, but also be quick and vigorous to protest any infringements of the rights to participate in voluntary action on the part of *other,* even opposing, organizations.

A concrete example of where voluntary organization leaders and administrators can be on the alert against infringements of the rights of free association, assembly, and dissent is, for example, the expansion of the Subversive Activities Control Board, the activities of the House Un-American Activities Committee, the so-called Attorney General's list and similar attempts to force registration and control on the voluntary sector of society without any evidence of clear and present danger to the principles of American society or the practices of American society.

We know from historical study of various societies, especially colonial societies, that the very act of instituting registration of all voluntary organizations is in fact a way of instituting control over them by the government. We have seen earlier that one of the major roles of the voluntary sector is precisely to experiment with what many would call "wild ideas," at the very least to experiment with new ways of doing things, new values, new approaches to human life and behavior. Therefore one may expect that along with registration will come *refusal* of registration to certain kinds of organizations. There will be organizations that, although having no apparent conflict with the goals of the nation or its constitutional principles, nevertheless will be denied registration simply because they are in some ways odd or different.

The leaders of the voluntary sector should be very wary of growing dependent to any significant degree on direct government grants, contracts, subsidies, and support.

This is admittedly a hard line to follow in these days when voluntary groups need so much money and government has so much money to play with. Nevertheless, to follow any other course is to undermine the very nature of the voluntary sector as an *independent* source of ideas and values in society.

Instead, leaders of the voluntary sector should seek ways for increasing their dependence on charitable grants and, perhaps more importantly, for increasing charitable grants as a proportion of the gross national product. In other words, the main limitation on the amount of money, time, goods and services available to the independent voluntary sector is simply the degree of commitment of our population (or that of any society) to the independent voluntary sector.

The key is to find the right goals, the right methods, the kinds of volunteer organizations and voluntary action that, to use common parlance, really turn people on.

The leaders of all kinds of voluntary action should take great pains to stress in their own organizations those activities that are most distinctive and unique, rather than emphasizing those types of activities and qualities that are duplicated in the government or business sectors.

Specifically, this means that voluntary organizations should emphasize their role in creating and attempting to implement images of the good life, utopias, and moral visions of a voluntary society—visions of what life could be if we all lived up to our greatest human potential. Whatever the pressures of expediency and circumstance may be, the leaders of the voluntary sector should pay special attention to the larger obligations of voluntary organizations in representing some higher set of values and acting in accord with them rather than bowing to kinds of economic or coercive values that business and government have to bow to very often (let's say, in the majority of cases).

A related implication is that leaders of the voluntary sector should play to the hilt their role as a prototyping testbed of new social forms. In this sense, the voluntary sector holds most of the *social risk capital* of society. It is the voluntary sector that is able to try out really new ideas, even "crazy" ideas—ideas that may or may not work out, where there is a great risk of failure in order to come up with those 2 or 3 or 50 or 100 out of the thousands that are tried which turn out successfully and which 50 years from now will be so commonplace that both business and government will think *they* invented them.

To give a very simple example, we could cite insurance. The insurance industry as part of the business sector, and the whole idea of public medical insurance and social security in the government sector, both grew out of several hundred years of development in the *voluntary sector*. Mutual aid societies and mutual benefit societies were the forerunners and prototypes. Then, eventually, when the idea had been tested and proved fruitful in the voluntary sector, the notion of personal life, health, and old age insurance were accepted and institutionalized on a massive scale by both the business and government sectors of society.

It is vitally important for the leaders of voluntary organizations to understand that they can—and must—embrace error more than any other sector of society.[8] And to this end they need to re-think and completely restructure their reward systems to enhance the probability that leaders and members will take risks in trying out new things and then learn from the trial and error that takes place. Today change is constant, and as other authors in this volume have observed, one of the chief responsibilities of the management of our major institutions today is to encourage them to function effectively within a state of controlled instability, where action and reaction, direction and the redirection, follow hard on the heels of each other. Institutions failing to do this will find themselves under increasingly prompt and severe scrutiny from those committed to their financial support, will eventually find themselves spun off harshly to the sidelines, and will, if they continue to function from the periphery, draw off precious resources which other institutions could use more effectively.

Much more than in the case of business and governmental decision-making, voluntary organization decision-making should hold true to the overriding values of an organization and the overriding purposes which it is attempting to achieve. This is accomplished in some sense by the leadership of voluntary organizations having an unusual singlemindedness. It means placing one or two particular values or purposes far above any other kinds of considerations and making decisions about how those values or purposes can best be implemented, given the existing present and probable future situations.[9]

Because voluntary organizations depend for motivation on the commitment of their members, the leaders of voluntary organizations must involve these members in a very real way in the planning and decision-making processes.

Government attempts in some small degree through the voting process to involve the citizenry in its decision-making processes. However, voting is an extremely "blunt instrument." Voting a particular candidate or slate of candidates in or out of office can only be done at lengthy intervals of from two to six years, and so the voting process cannot be very responsive to the fine grain of decision-making on the part of government agencies and officials.

In business corporations, of course, decision-making is even *less* responsive to the "membership" of the business organization (if the full range of employees are considered "members"), let alone to the best interests of consumers. However, this situation is gradually changing as consumers become more and more aware of their power over businesses, and more and more aware that each decision to purchase (or not purchase) something is in fact a vote for (or against) a particular product or a particular company.

Our main point, however, is that decision-making in the voluntary sector, in order to be effective and in order to involve members of a particular voluntary organization, has to go a great deal further than business or even government in involving constituencies and members in the actual decision-making process. The members of voluntary organizations need to feel that decisions that are made by their organizations are in some very real sense *theirs*.

Voluntary organization leaders and administrators need to work very much harder on the whole question of devising and implementing evaluation systems.

Voluntary organization leaders need, first of all, therefore, to understand what evaluation systems would be adequate for each level or kind of voluntary action. This will involve a certain amount of training or learning, whether done by one's self or through course-work, formal or informal. It will also involve developing a better infra-structure of consulting resources.

It is a curious fact that although the voluntary sector is indeed very excellent at trial-and-error, at trying out new ways of doing things and new ways of thinking, it is very *inadequate* on the self-evaluative side—i.e., making *use* of errors, discovering that errors have been made and doing something about them, or altering programs to become more effective (see Ansoff on the trial and error mode, p. 22). The business community knows when it has produced an Edsel because it simply does not sell, but voluntary organizations can go along producing the equivalent of an Edsel for decades.

One way that voluntary organization leaders can begin to emphasize evaluation more is to build it into the whole goal-setting and long-range planning process. Everytime a program is planned, the decision makers should ask at the same time "How can we evaluate progress toward this goal; how can we tell that we are getting somewhere with this program; how can we tell we are moving closer to the over-arching purpose that this program is intended to move toward?" And if they cannot come up with some measurable indicators of progress toward the higher level goal, then the program is itself probably not worth doing, however much it may be someone's pet activity or however traditional it may be in terms of the organization's customary way of doing things.

The fact that the compliance structure of voluntary organizations is fundamentally different from that of business or government makes it all the more important for them to have effective personnel policies and practices.

This means that voluntary organization leaders should know what is different and peculiar about their sector, and should adopt approaches that are designed especially to overcome those differences and try to turn them into strengths rather than weaknesses.

In the area of recruitment, for instance, voluntary organization should pay special attention to emphasizing values, ideals, and effectiveness. Because of differences in the motivational background of potential participants, appeals to a sense of moral obligation and goals can be expected to be much more persuasive than appeals to monetary rewards or possible legal compulsions. Voluntary organizations also must realize that because of their peculiar compliance structure, they need to place a great deal of emphasis on training and on the details of task or role allocation.

It is often the case in voluntary organizations that leaders feel that all you need is some people with a "good spirit" or commitment, and that nothing more is called for than simply putting them on the job—they can learn everything they need there. This may be the case in relatively simple kinds of situations, where all that is required is that one be a warm human being or a caring person, etc. But in more complex kinds of tasks that characterize the missions of the 1970's and 1980's, especially those that involve issue-oriented kinds of voluntary activity, substantial amounts of training will be needed to realize the required effectiveness.

Perhaps sets of voluntary organizations with similar training requirements might go together in supporting various general training programs or training institutes, then applying some finishing touches in terms of their own special organizational needs and technical skills.

In role allocating what should particularly be avoided is underemploying the volunteer. To put highly qualified volunteers in roles that do not make optimum use of their particular talents is to short-change them in their commitment to voluntary action. And of course it also short-changes the organization to have large numbers of volunteers who are not putting out their highest level of performance for its goals or purposes.

A further kind of concern that voluntary organization leaders have not given sufficient attention to is the whole question of *reward systems*. In *work* organizations, where people are basically *paid* for doing their job, reward systems are fairly straightforward and involve money, bonuses, well-furnished offices, company cars, etc. In voluntary and especially volunteer organizations, where money, objects, and perquisites of this sort are relatively de-emphasized or non-existent, other kinds of reward systems have to be devised.

Hence it is important to do some self-inquiry within the voluntary organization to get at the roots of why people really are interested in aiding a particular organization. In this way the leaders of the organization can devise a reward system that can begin to fit the motivations of its people.

The problem of the leadership is to determine ways of communicating a sense of effectiveness to the individual participants. It may be as simple a matter as explaining in depth at regular meetings or sessions (perhaps small group sessions or individual sessions) how the activity of a particular individual has contributed to some accomplishment of the organization.

A completely different kind of reward or set of rewards that voluntary organizations and leaders should pay substantial attention to is the whole matter of interpersonal or social rewards. Many people are engaging in voluntary organizations substantially because someone that they care about, or would like to have care about them, has asked them to do so. Therefore, the social aspect, the sense of friendship, companionship, and camaraderie, becomes very important, even in the most instrumental and cause-oriented voluntary organizations.

IMPROVE INFORMATION SYSTEMS

The independent voluntary sector has inadequate information systems; hence voluntary organization leaders should be working to improve the situations.

There are two levels where improvements can be made.

At the level of their own organization, these leaders should be thinking hard about kinds of information they need in order to enhance their own effectiveness. They should be thinking about how they can get information on impending legislation if they are issue-oriented organizations; or about how they can get information on the activities of business and government in a particular service area if they are service organizations. They should be considering where they can find help from resource organizations in accomplishing whatever their goals might be. They should be trying to find, or figure out how to find, consulting help or technical expertise that they need in order to structure or restructure their organization in an optimally effective way. And they should be doing all of these things in a continuous, long-term way, rather than doing it as a one-shot operation.

The second level of concern that voluntary organization leaders should have in the area of information should be to devise information systems, and in particular information analysis systems, that are adequate for meeting the needs of several similar organizations simultaneously. For example, environmental organizations could sponsor an information analysis center that would be primarily concerned with monitoring legislation, publications, research, and other activities relevant to their concerns. (In a few areas of voluntarism such centers already exist in some form, but are lacking in most other areas.)

The Center for a Voluntary Society has suggested in a recent paper [10] that a whole network of such information centers serving different content areas of voluntarism might be linked together. In addition, there might be one or more "generalist" kinds of information centers whose particular function would be to transfer information from one area of voluntarism to another, and to find out where there are gaps in the special-interest information centers (and, hopefully, do something about filling in these gaps). The Center for a Voluntary Society and the National Center for Voluntary Action, in collaboration, have indeed embarked on an informal joint venture to provide precisely such a generalist information system.

The voluntary sector needs a master data base on its own activity (as contrasted with a variety of other kinds of useful information); hence voluntary organization leaders should begin to work on this problem.

Here too there are two levels involved.

The first is again within the organization itself, where the leader can institute recordkeeping and self-study procedures that will make it possible to accumulate over time an adequate data base. This data base should include, at the very least, appropriate indicators of the amount of time, energy, and other resources devoted to the various major programs and components of an organization's activity, with repeated measurements over time—at the very least once a year but preferably oftener.

For example, if a voluntary organization that was providing transportation for the elderly were able to monitor regularly the effectiveness of its particular transportation network or system, it would soon find out how well it was working. Then appropriate adjustments could then be made in the organizational structure to deal with these findings.

At the second level, voluntary organizations need an information system that can be shared, as far as support and design are concerned, across a whole class of voluntary organizations or perhaps across the whole voluntary sector. We are speaking here of the need for generalized surveys made on some periodic basis of, for instance, the whole environmental movement or the whole consumer movement or the whole set of hospital volunteer programs of the United States.

The Center for a Voluntary Society and other groups and researchers have been trying for several years to interest various funding agencies (both government agencies and foundations) in supporting a National Baseline Survey of Voluntary Action which would, for all segments of the voluntary sector, attempt to provide a master overall data base. This proposed national baseline survey might be done annually, biennially, or perhaps every three years, and would consist of a nationwide survey of both individuals and organizations involved in the voluntary sector.

A related kind of general-level data base for the voluntary sector is the notion of comprehensive status reports on major segments or sectors of voluntarism. For instance, there has recently been a study of the environmental movement in this country, supported with EPA funds, which attempts for this particular portion of the voluntary sector to take stock of what it is doing, who is involved, why they are involved, what the problems are, and so on.[11]

The same kind of status report could be produced for each subsector of the larger independent voluntary sector. We suggest that the National Baseline Survey is more likely to eventuate if the subsector surveys have first been performed in several different areas and have been shown to have a substantial usefulness in improving the efficiency of the voluntary action there. In short, these subsector surveys could be a kind of "test marketing" of the larger Baseline Survey.

IMPROVE RESEARCH AND RESOURCE UTILIZATION

Voluntary organization leaders need to establish more and better contacts with the social science research community and especially with voluntary-action scholars.

There needs to be more of an awareness on the part of both scholars and leaders of voluntary organizations of each other's perspectives, needs, interests and activities. When a voluntary-action scholar knows *personally* several voluntary organization leaders, he is much more likely to become involve in *relevant* research on voluntary organizations. The recently formed association of Voluntary Action Scholars provides an opportunity for such linkage. The Association undertakes research on voluntary organizations and publishes the "Journal of Voluntary Action Research."

Another specific activity that voluntary organization leaders could engage in is to get to know some of the institutions, departments, research institutes, etc., in their vicinity that might be interested in doing revelant research and in providing free or even paid consultation. Still another possibility is to join with leaders of the voluntary-action scholarly community on some sort of joint applied research committee; this could provide a concrete on-going mechanism for relaying the research and scientific knowledge needs of voluntary organization leaders to the community of voluntary-action scholars.

Finally, voluntary organization leaders can attempt to keep up with the results of recent research in various ways, especially through the annual Voluntary Action Research series of volumes [12] and through various other publications.

Voluntary organization leaders need to pay careful and increasing attention to knowledge utilization and resource utilization systems in order to increase organizational effectiveness.

For instance, most voluntary organizations have inadequate accounting systems and inadequate public relations efforts. There are many of these kinds of inadequacies that could be dealt with by obtaining advice and consultation and help of various organizations, nonprofit and profit-making, that are established to provide precisely this kind of technical advice.

It is also possible that much better systems of *sharing* this kind of information among voluntary organizations themselves could be established than are now the case. The Center for a Voluntary Society is currently involved in producing a *Directory of Resource Organizations for the Voluntary Sector,* which will attempt to provide an across the board coverage of different kinds of resource organizations on a national basis. For instance, there will be information on how to get funding help, how to get legal help, how to get advertising and public relations help, how to obtain information or research help, etc. This kind of directory will be of substantial help, we believe, for the leaders of large national voluntary organizations and, to a lesser extent, for leaders of lower territorial-level voluntary groups.

However, there is still a need on a *regional* basis and on a *local* basis for voluntary organization leaders to spend a significant amount of time taking stock of what resources of various kinds are available to them in their own areas. Too many voluntary organizations and their leaders conceive of the resource base of their organization as consisting mainly of the membership, and perhaps even only a small active core of the membership.

In point of fact, given the compliance structure and the nature of voluntary organizations, the whole society, indeed the whole world, could be thought of as a resource base for any given voluntary organization if that organization can make its case clearly enough, strongly enough, and compellingly enough to the particular organizations or individuals whose help they would like or need. This puts voluntary organizations in a very distinctive and different kind of position from that in which most businesses and government find themselves.

COOPERATE WITH OTHER GROUPS AND SECTORS

The leaders/administrators of the voluntary sector should cooperate a great deal more among themselves for common ends.

Indeed, if the leaders of the voluntary sector do not increasingly cooperate, the general effectiveness of the voluntary sector in society may well decline over the coming decades, owing to the increasing complexity of the problems that confront our own and other societies. These problems are of such a magnitude that they cannot easily be solved by a single line of attack or devotion to a single problem or purpose.

A great deal more cooperation is also needed among voluntary agencies, government agencies, and business organizations in dealing with the various kinds of mutual problems and overlapping goals that they all have in certain areas. Nevertheless the most important place to start, it seems to us, is at the level of cooperation among voluntary organizations. To begin somewhere else is to ignore the fundamental differences that characterize business and government organizations and voluntary organizations—a real source of difficulty.

Therefore, voluntary organizations should first attempt to put their own house in order, and attempt to forge a workable coalition or cooperating network in a given voluntarism and/or geographical area. We have already mentioned a number of instances, such as information systems and data bases; these should only be the beginning.

But how does cooperation between voluntary organizations come about? There are basically eleven different steps which preferably should be performed in sequence, grouped into three major categories or phases (*formation, appraisal,* and *negotiation*), presented here in the form of questions (suggested by Gerald Klonglan; source: Note 14) that the organizations should ask themselves:

I. Formation
   1. What is the problem situation?
   2. What is the geographical area to be covered?
   3. Who are the relevant agencies or organizations to be involved in the coordination effort?

II. Appraisal
   4. What will the cooperation or potential cooperation mean to this particular organization?
   5. How much interorganizational commitment do we have?
   6. What is the legitimacy of other organizations in the area of interest?
   7. What are the cost/benefits of the proposed cooperation to *our* organization and to each *other* organization in the proposed cooperative effort?

III. Negotiation
   8. What are the specific impact goals and indicators of progress for the cooperating entity?
   9. What is our implementation plan?
   10. What will be the resource allocation—the actual commitment of money, staff, materials, and other resources to the coordination and implementation effort?
   11. Now, shall we make a final decision to go ahead?

The leaders of the voluntary sector must also work harder at developing effective, rational cooperation with organizations of the governmental and commercial sectors of society.

It must be said, in all fairness, that as things stand now, the organizations of the voluntary sector are better at cooperating with business and government organizations than at cooperating with other voluntary organizations. One of the reasons for this, perhaps, is that the government and business organizations involved in cooperative relationships with voluntary organizations are perceived as less threatening than other voluntary organizations would be.

Perhaps the best way for all three major sectors of society to pull together is for organizations representing them to attempt to bring to bear their own unique resources and approaches in a collaborative way on the various problems that face us as a society and as a world.

More concretely, a voluntary organization leader should first examine in detail what his or her own organization is attempting to do and where and for whom. Then careful attention should be given to precisely which commercial organizations and which governmental organizations of different kinds and levels are duplicating the effort. Once this kind of overlap or area of common interest has been defined, then the voluntary organization leader should approach the relevant commercial and governmental organization leaders and attempt to create some kind of working arrangement or areas of cooperation, perhaps even a division of labor.

The various steps for bringing about cooperation that were discussed earlier in respect to voluntary organizations apply here as well except that it may be more difficult to deal on an equal basis with either government or business leaders.

Voluntary organization leaders, however, can do a great deal to enable open, frank, and mutually respectful negotiations to take place. If leaders are aware of the resources they can offer in a given area of activity, this awareness will manifest itself in an appropriate manner of interpersonal relations and will in effect demand treatment of voluntary organizations as equals. Another thing that voluntary organization leaders can do is to engage in a substantial amount of educational activities for the relevant business and government organizational leaders prior to entering into negotiations with them.

An example of a problem area is the relationship between national voluntary organizations with some interest or involvement in overseas programs and the U.S. State Department. Thus, we find the State Department making unilateral decisions, and then leaving it to voluntary organizations to do the work. (It is the same situation with the United Nations.)

More recently some State Department people (especially in A.I.D. and the Educational and Cultural Affairs Section) have been showing a deeper understanding of the potential role of voluntary organizations.

UTILIZE NEW ORGANIZATIONAL FORMS

Since there are many new forms and types of voluntary organizations springing up with increasing frequency in the present and most probably in future decades, the leaders of voluntary organizations both need to recognize and to utilize these new forms of organizations.

The great danger here is that the leaders of established voluntary organizations will write off as unimportant, trivial or ephemeral certain new kinds of voluntary groups simply because their form of organization is not the traditional one. No greater mistake can be made. Over the past five to ten years, many new kinds of flexible, informal, "unbureaucratic" voluntary groups and movements have had a tremendous impact on our lives; the various student and youth movements are perhaps the best example.

To discount an organization, group, or movement simply because it does not have a regular dues-and-membership structure, a regular place of operation, or whatever, is to commit the "bureaucratic fallacy," as we may term it. The bureaucratic fallacy is the unwarranted assumption that, unless a group or set of people is a bureaucracy, it cannot function and be effective.

Instead, something more like a series of temporary task forces may be much more suited for dealing flexibly with the problems of a rapidly changing social environment. This kind of loose coalition or network of common resources formed, dissolved, and then reformed around some other goal at another point in time is precisely the style of organization that many groups have been using over the past several years with substantial effectiveness.

The possible forms of human organization are numerous—and all of them are imperfect. No one of them is sufficient for all kinds of purposes or goals, nor sufficient indefinitely in time. They range from the conventional membership, through mailing-list, demonstration, "be in," and mass meeting, to campaign, movement, and network.

The key question is: What is the most appropriate form or style of organization during a particular phase of organizational life?

We would venture the prediction that the coming decades will see a proportionate decline in the importance of conventional membership organizations (a decline which we can already see in terms of impact over the past decade) and a proportional increase in the importance of other forms of organizations for voluntary action, with an emphasis on the importance of different sorts of networks, often supported by the mass media.

Future decades are also likely to see new kinds of network styles of organizations developed as a result of technological advances. For instance, we may expect that the widespread use of video cassette tapes and the widespread existence of cable TV, and especially community controlled cable TV, will result in additional forms of voluntary action based on these kinds of technologies as they become more widespread.

THINK AND ACT TRANSNATIONALLY

The increasing trend toward transnationalism in voluntary action has a number of specific implications for the leaders/administrators of voluntary organizations.

Perhaps the most important point is that no longer can the leaders of national or even regional or state voluntary organizations and other kinds of voluntary groups in the United States operate as if there were no voluntary organizations and voluntary action outside the U.S. boundaries.

At the same time, leaders and administrators of U.S. voluntary groups will have to face up increasingly to the fact that there are numerous problems of all kinds outside the United States, that these problems are generally more severe than the ones in the United States, and that in many cases the solution of problems in other countries is as important as in the United States—perhaps, more important—and certainly related to the solution of problems in the United States.

The magnitude of the economic development problem and the modernization problem for the developing nations of the world is simply far too great to be handled by their own resources alone or by the relatively small amount of money available through the UN Development Program, or even through the governmental foreign aid activities of the more developed nations. Every contribution that can be made in an appropriate way through voluntary organizations and the voluntary sector of our society is going to be an investment not only in the future of the rest of the world but in our *own* future as well.

The world has experienced numerous revolutions in individual countries over the past hundred to two hundred years, usually with the overthrow of a powerful and wealthy traditional ruling elite by a set of revolutionaries, "representing the people"—initially organized as voluntary groups! Whatever one may feel about the outcome of these various revolutions, from the American to the Chinese, there is a lesson to be learned that has relevance for the whole world. If the gap between the elite nations and poor nations is not closed, and closed effectively, sometime in the next few decades, we may very well expect to see a bloody world revolution of these poor nations against the elite nations, comparable to the kinds of anti-colonial and anti-monarchical revolutions that have taken place within countries in the past 200 years or so.

However, voluntary organizations and leaders of the voluntary sector of this country cannot simply expect to apply successfully their own form of voluntary action without modification in developing countries. In many cases, if not in most, the activities of voluntary organizations from all developed or industrialized countries are perceived by many people in the less developed countries as a form of neo-colonialism, as indeed they often are. Too often, the voluntary worker from developed countries comes into a poor country as a "lady bountiful," duplicating overseas the same kind of now outmoded form of voluntary action that has been prevalent in the voluntary sector in England and America over the past century. Thus, American voluntary agencies must take into account the sense of pride and desire to develop their *own* competence that is present in people everywhere, especially in developing countries.

The notion of a *one-way* exchange of information, aid, training, technical assistance, and so forth, via voluntary organizations should also be examined carefully. There are many ways in which American voluntary organizations and their leaders can learn from what is going on in less developed countries or other countries abroad. This aspect of *two-way* exchange should be played up to make for a more equal relationship and hence a more satisfying one.

In particular, when volunteer programs are exported abroad, they should pay careful attention to developing the ability of lesser developed nations to become self-sufficient in various ways. It is thus much more useful in the long run to train foreign leaders in an underdeveloped country to take over, and then direct some kind of technical or service program themselves, than to go there and simply perform those services for the countries in question.

Another major fact of the world situation is that there is an increasing interconnectedness of all the countries in the world and of all the events that take place in the world. It is no longer possible on a large scale for major events in one country to be unconnected with events in another country. The proliferation of communication and transportation links among countries and cities of the world has seen to that.

The 1972 Stockholm Conference on the Human Environment, organized by the UN, is an example of the fact that there is an increasing awareness that the whole problem of the environment is not a problem of a single nation, but rather a multinational or world problem. A similar recognition of the existence of world problems has occurred in a number of other areas, most of which are related to by some segment of the voluntary sector in American society.

Parallel to the technical interconnectedness in terms of communication and transportation that exists in the world, there is also a kind of interconnectedness of values and ideologies that is increasing—precisely the kinds of values for which many organizations in the voluntary sector stand. These values generally transcend national boundaries and are pan-human values. The result is and will be that voluntary movements transcending national boundaries are becoming increasingly important.

Another kind of interconnectedness or interrelatedness at the international level that is very important for voluntary organization leaders is in the area of operational or structural problems. The same kinds of organizational problems are found in different countries. For instance, at the recent Milan conference [13] held by the Union of International Associations over 40 international voluntary organizations participated; and the problems that came out were very similar to the kinds of problems that emerged from a national conference on Voluntarism and American's Future held by the Center for a Voluntary Society in January of 1972.[14]

So there is much that can be done in the way of sharing of information, sharing of problems, and sharing of solutions to these problems. The publication of the Union of International Associations form a useful source of information on national coordinating and conceptual linking agencies.

For a fuller view of problems *and opportunities* in this area, the reader is referred to the monthly issues of *International Associations,* published by the Union of International Associations,[15] and to the forthcoming volume, *Voluntary Action Research: 1974,*[16] which will deal with transnational voluntary action and the research that has been done in regard to it.

IMPROVE GOVERNANCE QUALITY

Since the role and impact of the voluntary sector are likely to increase in the coming decades, the leaders and administrators of voluntary organizations must increase the quality of their management and governance to meet this challenge.

We have already suggested a number of areas where voluntary organization leaders and administrators could improve their approaches and techniques. In the present section we would simply like to highlight the importance for the voluntary sector and its leaders of understanding that there may be great increases in the sheer volume of time that people from the general population make available to voluntary action in all of its areas.

There is nothing clearer than that we are moving toward a leisure society and a service society, and this does not simply mean increases in *un*organzied individual leisure. It also means that there will be large increases in the amount of *organized* voluntary action as a means of absorbing and using creatively one's "leisure tmie." The voluntary sector will also have an increasing proportion of the *commitment* of the general population, and this can also be turned to the advantage of the voluntary sector by consciously planning, preparing for, and stimulating this increased commitment.

For instance, it is especially important for voluntary action leaders to be aware of the necessity of developing or affirming some higher-level ideals, values, or goals, other than sheer economic gain in the longer term or some other kind of self-serving end, since the various kinds of "other-oriented," society-serving and society-changing voluntary action seem to be the areas of greatest increase. The voluntary sector leaders have to learn better how to generate and sustain commitment.

That there is a great potential here is made clear by the fact that more and more of the highest quality minds and talented people are making careers in the voluntary sector. The voluntary sector is often, also, where people commit themselves *after* they have "made their mark" in business or government. Yet the leadership of the voluntary sector will be letting these people down unless it actively recruits them and actively absorbs them into its own leadership structure.

Given the substantial past, important present, and great future potentials of the voluntary sector, the leaders of voluntary organizations have great obligations resting on their shoulders—obligations to recognize their own responsibilities for self development.

Indeed, they may have a greater obligation than that resting on the shoulders of business and government leaders in the long term, although few see it this way at present. Business and government leaders certainly have greater official power and greater control over financial resources in the present, and hence great power to change the nature of society. Voluntary organization leaders, in contrast, have relatively moderate or little official or financial power at present—yet very great *potential* power and very great possibilities to affect the future.

But this kind of potential power of voluntary organizations and their leaders is one that can only be fulfilled if it is continually sought, preserved, and exercised by the leaders of voluntary organizations. It is not something that comes automatically. Hence the individual voluntary organization leader should become increasingly aware of and increasingly committed to the general role of the voluntary sector; should work hard to develop in himself a consciousness of his responsibility to improve his techniques of governance in the many ways that we have suggested in the preceding sections; and should do his best to communicate this sense of responsibility for improved leadership to other leaders in the voluntary sector.

In particular, there should be more emphasis on true professionalism and competence rather than on paid leaders or staff. The term "professional" actually should refer to the level of competence and not to the level of pay, if any. There can be paid staff and paid leaders in any organization who are by no means professional; and there can be voluntary leaders and staff who are very professional indeed. It is the latter who are important.

To this end, voluntary leaders should develop better professional associations for different subsectors of the voluntary sector and should work toward some kind of effective voluntary association of a professional sort encmpassing all leaders and administrators in the voluntary sector.

Not the least of the virtues of the kind of national professional association of voluntary organization leaders that we have suggested here would be its capacity and potential for fostering greater cooperation among voluntary organizations of various kinds. The periodic conventions of such an association would permit an opportunity for various groups to meet on a neutral ground, without any special commitments on the part of any parties involved, to work on possible collaborative arrangements, increase informal contacts, get new ideas about cooperation, search out new possibilities for colaborating groups, and so on.

Implications for Business and Government Leaders

Recognize the Voluntary Sector's Role. Business and government leaders should understand the changing nature of voluntary organizations and their future role in society. Because of the importance of freedom of assembly and dissent in the American and Western European tradition, business and government leaders should protect—and foster—voluntary action as a manifestation of that tradition. Business and government leaders should recognize that decision-making in the voluntary sector is inherently different from hierarchical decision-making; that it may involve trial and error; and that the experimental role of voluntary groups can be important in providing innovation in society.

Help the Voluntary Sector with Technical Problems. Business and government leaders can aid in sharing experiences in the use of information systems, in evaluating programs, and in other ways.

Relate to Transnational Voluntarism. Business and government can find ways to collaborate with voluntary groups engaged in international activities for their mutual benefit.

Invest in the Future. Business and government can aid in improving the quality of life by working with voluntary groups—perhaps learning from their experiments, as a "test-bed"—and by observing some of their best qualities and methods.

"To thine own self be true" is an even more important motto for voluntary groups and movements than it is for individuals. For when all groups as well as all people can be true to themselves and their highest, most creative sense of self-expression, understanding and respecting the equal rights of other persons and groups to their own self-expression, we will have arrived at a voluntary society. This is what we seek.

Notes

1. For more on distinctions between types of voluntary organizations, see David Horton Smith, "Types of Volunteers and Voluntarism," *Volunteer Administration,* vol. 6, No. 3 (June 1972).

2. Many of the trends described in this section were briefly described in "Future Trends in Voluntary Action," *International Associations* 24, No. 3 (1972). They were also discussed in more detail in "The Importance of Formal Voluntary Organizations for Society," *Sociology and Social Research,* July 1966.

3. See David Fellman, *The Constitutional Right of Association* (Chicago: University of Chicago Press, 1963).

4. See William Sheridan Allen, *The Nazi Seizure of Power* (Quadrangle Books, 1965).

5. See David Horton Smith, "Part One: Voluntary Action through Space and Time," *Voluntary Action Research 1973* (Boston: Lexington Books, D. C. Heath, 1973).

6. See Smith, *Voluntary Action Research 1973,* chapter by Virgil Peterson.

7. See Smith, *Voluntary Action Research 1973,* chapter by Alvin Schmidt and Nicholas Babchuk.

8. See "Information Technology: Some Critical Implications for Decision Makers," chapter by Donald Michael (Conference Board, 1972).

9. See Donald Michael, *The Unprepared Society* (New York: Basic Books, 1968).

10. David Horton Smith, "Information Systems for the Voluntary/NGO Non-Profit Sector: Volinflo and the Voluntarism Information Center Network," *International Associations,* vol. 25 (February 1973).

11. See Clem Zinger et al., "Profile of the Environmental Movement," Environmental Volunteers in America, Washington, D.C., Environmental Protection Agency Report, October 1972.

12. Voluntary Action Research series, Lexington Books, D. C. Heath, 1972, 1973. See also *The Journal of Voluntary Action Research; Volunteer Administration,* and *Journal of Volunteers with Delinquents.* The Association of Voluntary Action Scholars and the Journal of Voluntary Action Research are located at 1507 M Street NW, Washington, D.C.

13. Reports on the Conference can be found in *International Associations,* vol. 24 (1972).

14. Reports on the Conference can be found in *Voluntarism and America's Future* (Center for a Voluntary Society, 1972).

15. Located at 1, Rue aux Laines, 1000 Brussels, Belgium.

16. To be published early in 1974 by Lexington Books, D. C. Heath & Co.

Contributors

Helpful comments and inputs from the following members of the author's panel are gratefully acknowledged (the authors, however, accept full responsibility for choice of content and interpretation).

James Luther Adams, Professor, Andover Newton Theological School and Harvard University Divinity School

Jack T. Conway, President, Common Cause

Anthony J. N. Judge, Union of International Associations, Brussels

James Turner, Fensterwald and Ohlhausen, Washington

Cynthia Wedel, President, National Council of Churches

Andrew J. Young, Executive Vice President, Southern Christian Leadership Conference

Eight

Global Management

SINCE the end of World War II, the world has experienced a "management boom." Virtually the whole world has become management conscious. And the boom has had tremendous impacts on managements everywhere.

Now the boom is over. And now it is becoming clear that while management everywhere has emerged as a central and highly visible social function, it has not become "Americanized." Rather, the boom has tended to strengthen the distinct and different characteristics of managements outside of the United States and their embeddedness in their own national traditions, cultures, and values. Management, like world polity and world economy, has become "polycentric."

The most stringent requirements for management performance are ahead of us.

At the same time new management tasks and challenges have arisen which require concepts, policies, techniques far beyond the ideas on which the "management boom" was based and crying out for new approaches and new solutions. There is the multinational corporation. There is the urgent management need of the public-service institutions—hospital, universtiy, government agency. There is a new and pressing productivity challenge. There is the dilemma of management of knowledge and knowledge workers. There are the demands of the environment and of social responsibility together.

For the American manager all this means fundamental rethinking and readjustment. He will have to become as willing to learn from the management traditions of foreign countries as foreign managers were willing to learn from Americans these last 25 years—e.g., in the area of governmental relations, or in fitting personnel policies and employee benefits to the needs of specific groups within the enterprise. Particularly if he works in a multinational company—as more and more American managers are likely to do—he will have to learn to live and work with a variety of management patterns and management styles. And even if his business is purely domestic, he will have to accept the reality of a polycentric management world.

The preceding three paragraphs summarize roughly the order and the rationale of this chapter.

The Management Boom in Perspective

In the past 25 years management has been "discovered" as a central function of modern society, as a profession and as a discipline. In developed and developing countries, in the Free World and behind the Iron Curtain (though, so far, not behind the "Bamboo Curtain"), within and without business enterprise—everywhere there has been intense concern with management and organization, with managerial methods and technologies, with teaching and learning of management, and with the manager's social role and impact. The Japanese have called it "the management boom."

What started as an adoption of U.S. concepts and techniques . . .

It was a management boom largely "made in America." It was based heavily on the export and application of United States management concepts, management tools, management techniques, and management fads and follies. The world's leading businesses everywhere were made over and cast in the moulds of broad American concepts such as "decentralization." Management books by American authors became best-sellers in Great Britain, in Germany, in Japan—and also in Communist Czechoslovakia.

At the boom's height, in the mid-1960's, professors from American business schools were in demand throughout the world to lecture, to conduct seminars, and to aid in starting local management institutions. American consulting firms developed a worldwide practice. American public relations and advertising organizations conducted meetings, prepared market plans, and advised their clients about the new management mystique. The large American auditing firms went "multinational."

Writers in Europe, such as Servan-Schreiber, whetted the appetite of business men to know more about this marvelous development, and in Japan management became the national pastime. Even in the Soviet Unoin where the role of management is a corrosive political problem, two new, lavishly financed, so-called management schools were established and top people from Russian industry were sent there in droves. In many ways, management during these years was the "counterculture," unacceptable to much of the prevailing orthodoxy—hailed as the battering ram against rigid class structures; as the symbol of a social order based on performance rather than on rank, wealth, or birth; and as the "wonder drug" to cure economic stagnation and to produce economic and social development.

. . . has now broadened, changed, and been replaced by new challenges.

It is now becoming apparent that America has no monopoly on management or in the world economy. Europe has regained confidence that it can compete successfully in the modern world. Japan has emerged as a superior industrial nation with its own management structure and its own basic management concepts. Management has become polycentric rather than as many believed, in these last 25 years, an "American invention." In short, the boom is over. And, by the same token, the time for management performance has come.

But, along with the boom, the belief in management as the "wonder drug" has faded. It is clear by now that management is not "*the* answer." It is even more apparent that we do not have "all the answers" for management itself. The management boom was largely based on the knowledge and experience that had been amassed in the 25 years—if not the 50 years—before World War II. Now we need new knowledge to meet a host of new challenges.

It is time, therefore, to take stock and to appraise the impacts of the boom, the wellsprings from which the new concepts flowed, and their effects throughout the world.

How did the boom unfold? Through
production, human relations, marketing . . .

We in this country became management-conscious as a result of the production achievements of World War II. It was only natural, therefore, that the "management boom" started out with production management. "Scientific management," i.e., the purposeful and systematic study of manual work (see Ansoff, p. 28), had of course been around a long time; the very name was coined in 1911—by no less distinguished a "public relations man" than Mr. Justice Brandeis. But World War II showed that production and productivity in manufacturing industry depended on a great deal more than engineering individual jobs—on factory layout and organization; on the structure of foremanship and on training; on the management of the flow of materials and parts; on process and cost control, on information, and many more—in short, on production management.

But almost simultaneously we also became aware of the fact that production is people. The idea of universal human needs, of emotional and psychic satisfaction in addition to economic rewards, and of the people within an enterprise as a resource, began to gain acceptance in America along with other management concepts.

Cost accounting goes back to the 1920's or further. But it is doubtful that many American businesses—even substantial ones—had much by way of cost information or cost management before World War II. The balance sheet rather than the income statement was the basic control tool and the focus of managerial attention. World War II, with government contracts demanding detailed cost information, changed this.

A little later American management discovered marketing. The concept of marketing as a major element in management represented a departure from the production-oriented ideas of past years in manufacturing companies. Marketing became respectable. And, in the early 1950's "information" and "planning" came in as general concerns.

. . . and, most important of all, discovery
of management as a distinct function.

But beyond any one aspect or function of management, the big step forward was what one might well call "the discovery of management." In those immediate postwar years we became aware of the fact that management is not something that "just grows"; it needs to be designed, thought through, structured, organized. We came to realize that "management" is not just a term to denote rank; it is a crucial and distinct function.

Within a few short years management structure and organization were "in." Even small businesses began to pay a good deal of attention to their formal structure, to the design of managerial jobs, and to top management organization. In larger businesses the "management of management" became a central top-management task, with company after company reorganizing and restructuring itself.

The climatic event was probably the massive "decentralization" of the General Electric Company that began in 1952. It became almost mandatory for larger businesses to divide the company into "decentralized product businesses," each with its own general manager responsible for a product line or market and measured by a profit and loss statement as if he were running a separate company.

Other elements were the evolution of staff services; the spread of distinct R & D components throughout industry; the wholesale adoption of personnel-management techniques such as selection, testing, and appraisal; the acceptance of "public relations" as a managerial function—all unknown, even as terms, before World War II, in all but a mere handful of companies.

Management development and management
consulting: accelerators of the boom.

Before 1945 there was only one American company, Sears Roebuck, which had any concern with "management development." And only two others, Du Pont and General Motors, had even attempted to inventory their managerial people—and these primarily for the purposes of compensation. Twenty years later it was the exceptional company which did not at least pay lip service to "management development" as a major and continuing concern.

Before World War II only two universities were engaged in "advanced" or "continuing" management education: New York Unviersity, which first offered evening courses to young managers in New York's financial district around 1920, and M.I.T., which started its "Sloan Fellows" program in the early 1930's. Then, right after World War II, the Harvard Business School organized an "advanced management course" for senior executives—and the rush was on. Today there is no end of "advanced management" and "executive" programs at universities, large or small, of "management seminars," "refresher courses," and so on.

Before World War II such management consulting firms as existed were small—one of the biggest then had a professional staff of thirty-five men and was considered a "giant." Today there are at least one thousand consulting firms (some estimates range much higher); and there are a great many more individuals practicing by themselves, or from a base on a university faculty, as "management consultants." The major and minor accounting firms have developed flourishing management-consulting practices. All the larger, but also a good many of the smaller, firms have gone "multinational," with branches in London and Tokyo, Milan or Melbourne, and clients even in such Communist countries as Yugoslavia or Poland.

But even more indicative of the new awareness of management is popular usage. Before World War II popular rhetoric talked of "capital and labor." Today even the Marxists talk of "management and labor."

How did the boom spread? First triggered in England . . .

It took only a few years for the "management boom" to become worldwide.

It was probably Sir Stafford Cripps, Chancellor of the Exchequer in Britain's first Labor Government immediately after World War II, who triggered the world-wide "management boom," and who also made it a boom "made in America." Though himself a convinced, indeed a doctrinaire, socialist, Cripps concluded that Britain's economic recovery depended upon the systematic infusion of American management into British industry.

Cripps himself was still production-focused; his was a plan for "productivity" teams. But the program almost immediately became much broader. The "best seller" among the reports which the British "productivity teams" published was, for instance, a study of cost accounting and financial controls (the British called it "works accounting"). The Marshall Plan soon thereafter extended Cripps's concept to Continental Europe—and the Japanese began to get into the act in the early 1950's.

. . . it soon became stronger overseas than in the United States itself.

Since then the management boom has become even more effervescent outside the United States than in America itself. The results are spotty—as they are at home. But company after company, often with the help of U.S. consultants, has reorganized itself on the decentralized American model—Britain's Imperial Chemical Industries, Germany's Siemens, Japan's Hitachi, the Bank of England and the British Coal Board, Royal Dutch Shell, and France's Renault, and many more. Interest in and concern with formal management structure became world-wide.

European companies began to accept the principle of making marketing an arm of management. It began to be accorded a status of equality with finance and production. Even in Germany it has begun to draw even with engineering, the traditional elite function. Japanese enterprises had always been concerned with the market, although their viewpoint had a different connotation since they sold primarily through trading companies and not directly. But the new American emphasis on marketing was duly noted and it radically changed the Japanese planning process.

Prior to the boom there was a wide gap between European and American information systems. Americans were developing detailed cost control methods while even substantial European companies still relied on conventional accounting systems largely focused at producing a top level balance sheet. But then came the new British interest in "works accounting" and, with it, a quiet revolution in concepts and methods of information and control. A little later came the adoption of decentralized structures which required profit center accounting and this, too, produced changes in information methods.

Around the world too management development programs have accelerated.

In the 1950's some large European companies began to send a few selected executives to advanced management programs in the United States, e.g., at Harvard. The practice is still growing; in some advanced management programs at American universities, e.g., the Marketing Management Program at Columbia University, four out of every ten participants come from abroad.

But the real change in Europe—and in Latin America—has been the growth of advanced management programs there. Often started under U.S. auspices and, at least in the beginning staffed with U.S. professors (or with nationals who had received their training in the United States), such schools have sprung up all over the world. In Europe alone they are said now to be more than 200. The European schools, for the most part, are not affiliated with universities (though the Latin American ones mainly are). But their approach and curriculum already follow the university-based American model.

The management boom also engulfed the developing countries, and perhaps with even greater vigor. India was among the first countries to set up management institutes and advanced management schools. When, in the 1950's and 1960's, a new younger generation of executives—largely U.S. educated and often "alumni" of U.S.-based multinational companies—succeeded to the top management positions of Latin America's businesses, they eagerly worked for modern management concepts and modern management techniques.

In Mexico, the Technico in Monterey, often called "Latin America's M.I.T.," started an exceedingly successful advanced management program in the 1950's; it is generally given major credit for the tremendous growth of the Monterey industrial area and for Mexico's altogether impressive economic performance. Further south, in Brazil, the management center built around the Getulio Vargas Institutes in Rio and Sao Paulo have played a parallel role. Similar efforts, on a smaller scale but no less powerful in their impact, were mounted in the smaller countries, notably in Colombia.

In Japan the "management seminar"—of a few days' duration, as a rule—has become the height of management fashion. Now there is even an advanced management school in Japan—and that *is* a radical innovation. For, while the Japanese embraced the new management gospel enthusiastically, going back to school after graduation is unheard of. The Japanese university graduate has finished with college. Nor is he being encouraged to mix with executives who work for another company.

But the most unexpected result of the management explosion of these last 25 years—and the one that, long-term, will perhaps have the most important impact —probably occurred behind the Iron Curtain, first in the Soviet satellites of Eastern Europe and then in the Soviet Union itself.

The Yugoslavs, Poles, Hungarians, Czechs,
all have turned to American concepts . . .

The very idea of "management" is anathema to Marxist ideology and is incompatible with it. And, politically, a managerial class with decision-making authority is a far greater threat to the Communist political system than discontented artists and writers. Communist bureaucrats and theoreticians are fully aware of this and have resisted every attempt either to recognize management as a legitimate function or to practice it. That the Czechs were on the point of recognizing managerial autonomy was the final and decisive reason for Russian invasion, the final and unrefutable proof that the Czechs had become "counter-revolutionaries."

Yet today management, in one form or another, has had to be accepted by all European Communist regimes—even, albeit most grudgingly, by the Russians.

The Yugoslavs have gone furthest. Their "decentralization" of industry under which individual companies are organized autonomously to compete on the market, and even to compete for capital, is presented ideologically as "worker control." It is actually "managerial control," and intentionally so. The workers' council is limited to the functions of a strong board of directors and forbidden to manage. Hungary has gone almost as far, and Poland had been moving steadily in the same direction. Even the Czechs have carried out a good deal of the "managerial reform," the prevention of which was a main purpose of the Russian invasion in 1968.

All these countries have gone in for management schools, advanced manager training, accounting and information systems, together with organization planning. Yugoslavia and Poland—and to some extent Hungary—have brought in American consulting firms on a wide variety of assignments. American-designed "management games" are being used to train executives in Yugoslavia, Hungary, Poland, and Czechoslavakia. The Czechs have started a marketing institute, with its own journal, which reprints a wide selection of foreign, mainly American, articles. And all these countries have come to stress the importance of management as a key to economic and social development.

. . . and now the Soviet Union is following suit, but slowly.

The Soviet Union, under Khrushchev, was moving in the same direction. Indeed the essence of the much-heralded "industrial reform" of those years was the establishment of autonomous management and the restructuring of Russia's large industrial complexes along the lines of American organization designs (e.g., decentralization) and management principles.

Under Khrushchev's successors the "reform" has been stalled. Only consumer goods industries, especially clothing and shoes, have actually been set up as autonomously managed enterprises. Heavy industry continues to run on the basis of Marxist denial of the need for, if not of the existence of, such a thing as management, with a central bureaucracy making all decisions through a political process and with the local men in industry confined to technical functions.

Yet the new automobile and truck industries, which are at the heart of Russia's economic plans for the 1970's, are to have their own—apparently GM style—management. And in 1970 two "advanced management schools" for senior executives were opened with great fanfare. Their curriculum so far confines itself to management techniques such as industrial engineering and operations research, and to computer technology and application. But, according to reports, marketing is planned to come into the curriculum within the next few years; and this summer (1972) three Russian government representatives attended the six-week International Marketing Institute program held on the Harvard campus.

Management Realities Outside the U.S.

Management concepts, management techniques, and, above all, management tasks are the same the world over. Management, the years of the management boom proved, is a universal function. But there are very real differences when it comes to management structure and management career ladders, management values and management objectives, management policies and management attitudes; these cannot be divorced from the economy, the society, the political tradition, and the general culture in which business and management live and of which they are a part. Thus, Western Europe and Japan, while using the same management techniques, still have management systems that differ in essentials from those of the United States, and it is these essentials—these fundamentals—that constitute an important part of the realities of the new polycentric world economy.

These fundamentals and realities have much to teach us in America. In important areas, the Europeans or the Japanese do a much more effective job than we do. We could not—and should not—*imitate* them; for our management attitudes and structures are as much part of our society and culture as theirs are of their society and culture. But me might well try to *emulate* them.

And, in any event, there is much that the American manager needs to understand in the fundamentals and realities of management outside the United States. Even if his business is purely domestic, he will increasingly live, compete against, and work with managements that are not American, do not see the same management world he sees, and do not always behave like American managements. And if the American manager does happen to be involved in a "multinational" business—as more and more are apt to be—he will have to accept the fact that his own company will have to embrace divergent management systems, or will at least have to accommodate to them.

Example of American concept followed
with different purposes: management schools.

In retrospect it can be seen quite clearly that even at the height of the "management boom," the new concepts and tools were often used in the already developed countries (i.e., Western Europe and Japan)—and even in many developing ones—to strengthen existing structures rather than to replace them with new, American imports.

One example is the advanced management school in other countries. One reason why it has met with such enthusiastic acceptance in Europe is that it can be—and is being—used as an elite school for a new managerial elite. In France, for instance, there has been since Napoleon the tradition of the *"Grandes Écoles";* the elite schools which provide the leaders in government, business, the universities, and the professions. With the advanced management school at Fontainebleau—for all that it is modeled on the Harvard Business School and uses the same material and often the same instructors the Americans use— French management now has such a *grande école* of its own.

It is a European management school seeking its students in all Common Market countries and Britain. Thus tomorrow's top men—and especially the top staff men—throughout European big business will wear the same "old school tie," will have grown up together, know each other, trust each other, understand each other. And the fact that Europe's *grande école* for managers is located on French soil and run by Frenchmen fits precisely the French idea of France's place in Europe and of the European role of the French language and culture that has informed French cultural policy for 300 years.

To its American originators, on the other hand, advanced management education was largely a means to overcome elitism and cliques. By means of the "advanced course," the promising high-potential man would be able to remedy whatever educational deficiencies his humble origin might have left him with.

And mixing together executives from many industries and companies would overcome parochialism and inbreeding.

Nonetheless, while the French perception of the role and purpose of advanced management education is clearly different, it does fit European tradition and values that most of European society—and by no means only the members of the elite—accept. It fits the way the Germans see the civil service, or the English the graduates of "public school" and of Oxford and Cambridge, just as it fits the French acceptance of the graduates of a *grande école* as superior.

Example of American techniques applied to different philosophies: personnel management.

The fundamental idea underlying the emergence of personnel management in the United States was that of the basic homogeneity of values, expectations, aspirations, and satisfaction throughout the human race, regardless of social condition. As a result American personnel management has tended to develop one comprehensive personnel philosophy and uniform—or at least compatible— personnel policies across a company. And the American labor union similarly strives for uniform labor contracts and across-the-board benefits.

American personnel management has been a major "export product." But it has been used abroad very largely to reinforce a system which assumes that different social groups in business enterprise have different values, different expectations, different aspirations, different satisfactions, and therefore require different personnel philosophies, different personnel policies, different treatment, and different benefits.

Any American would consider this "invidious class distinction." But this is not the way it appears to Europeans, Japanese, or Latin Americans. Rather they see such differentiation the way we have traditionally viewed such differentiated personnel policies as the ban on women and children in underground work in coal mines as being logical and rational consequences of realities of job, need, and capacity. And this view prevails as much in Japan with its very high social mobility by means of a system of national schools and universities, as in the Soviet Union, with its commitment to an egalitarian creed.

Only in Latin countries (Italy, Spain, and Latin America) is the concept of basic differences of different groups within the enterprise embeded in law, with managers, clerical employees, and manual workers each considered a separate and distinct group. But the distinction is even more rigid in Japan where a junior-high school graduate will rarely rise beyond manual worker or low-level clerk, a high school graduate nearly always remains a subordinate white-collar worker; and a university graduate never even starts out except as a management trainee. And though France, England, and Germany are not nearly as rigid in their classification of humanity (indeed actual social mobility in these countries may well be fully as great as in the United States), they too tend to see these three major groups as quite distinct and different from each other.

Outside the United States, therefore, uniformity of personnel philosophy and personnel practices does not necessarily appear as fairness—not even to the most convinced egalitarian (let alone to a labor leader). Accordingly, modern personnel management outside the United States, while using the same tools and techniques the Americans developed, has largely been used to emphasize group differences and to create for each group a different policy with different rights, methods and benefits.

In Japan, above all, modern personnel management as imported from the United States, has largely meant setting up the management people as an even more distinct, even more closed-off, even more differentiated group. The Japanese "salary man"—the catchword for junior and middle manager—is not necessarily "privileged," is indeed, often enough, very poorly paid. But he is considered a different kind of person; and this, to a Japanese, is precisely what "modern personnel management" means.

The management boom nowhere replaced
local fundamentals with American fundamentals.

But far more important than examples of the use of tools and methods "made in America" to accomplish a purpose or fit a philosophy which was quite different from that for which the tools and methods were originally designed, but which was in harmony with the traditions, values, and perceptions of the user, is the fact that the management boom did not eliminate basic fundamentals and realities. It modified them in many cases; but it nowhere replaced them with the fundamentals and realities the American manager takes for granted.

THE DIFFERENT MEANINGS OF ECONOMIC PERFORMANCE

The first, perhaps the most important, of these "givens," is economic reality. Of all the responsibilities of a management, the one for economic performance must always come first.

Due to different capital market structures,
the U.S. goal is maximizing profits . . .

Yet "economic performance" means quite different things within different institutional frameworks. Within the framework of the American—and to a lesser extent the English—manager, profit maximization is a rational objective; and so is rapid earnings growth. But these make very much less sense as objectives for business management within the institutional framework of Continental Europe. And they are almost irrational objectives in the Japanese setting. The reason is not ideology or economic system; it is the different structure of capital markets.

. . . while in Western Europe and Latin
America it is regular dividends . . .

In Continental European countries, equity has traditionally resided in the proprietor and his family for small or medium-sized companies, and with the commercial banks in the case of larger firms. The European commercial bank directly or indirectly holds at least a controlling minority of the shares of most publicly owned, and of many of the larger nonpublic, companies. It has long-term equity positions in large firms. Even where the company's stock is widely held, the shareholders keep their shares in the custody of the banks, who have the right to vote these fiduciary holdings as if they owned them.

Banks customarily acquire their equity interests to be assured of the company's commercial financial business. Providing they receive dividends that are a few percentage points more than the prime interest rate, they are usually saatisfied. Earnings are secondary.

Indeed rapid growth of a company in which the commercial bank holds a major or controlling interest is not in the bank's interest at all. For rapid growth requires constant inputs of new capital. Either the bank in such a case increases its own commitment—at the risk both of becoming overinvolved and of having to cut back and deny capital and credit to other companies within the bank's industrial group; or the bank risks losing its preferred position as the main financier of the growing company and, with it, the company's lucrative commercial-banking business.

Continuity of dividends and long-term stability are therefore of primary interest to the dominant shareholder of Continenal Europe's large public companies. Earnings growth and maximization of profits have to be adjusted—and indeed often subordinated—to dividend requirements. Maintenance of dividends is, as a result, the rational key objective for the European professional manager.

For the privately held business in Continental Europe profit maximization and rapid earnings growth are not only secondary but, in a very real sense, undesirable. Such a business on the Continent is almost always family-owned. Within a few generations, ownership is therefore widely distributed among grandchildren, aunts and uncles, nieces and nephews. Very few of them are actively engaged in running the company. But keeping them satisfied is a survival necessity for the incumbent managers, whether themselves family members or not. And this means maintaining a stable annual dividend. The sum each of these members of the clan receives may be quite small—a few thousand marks or francs each year. But it is considered almost sacred; it is a right rather than a reward. And a management that has to cut or pass the dividends is likely to be in very serious trouble.

Rapid growth for such a business is also far from desirable. It means inevitably need for new capital. The family members are rarely willing or able to supply this. A public issue is rarely possible, in view of the absence of a capital market. Hence rapid growth means, as a rule, becoming the prisoner of a commercial bank and loss of control by the family.

The same situation obtains in Latin America—again for lack of a public capital market. A Latin American company is not apt to be considered creditworthy unless it pays a reasonable dividend. And rapid earnings growth, again, is not particularly desirable. There too, family ownership interests have come to expect dividends. Indeed, the payment of regular dividends is looked upon as a sign of respectability, while not to pay a dividend is regarded as a sign of severe financial crisis. Joint ventures of U.S. and Latin American interests have foundered on differences in dividend policy, since North Americans are likely to want earnings plowed back into the business.

That this is not a matter of ideology or of attitudes but the result of institutional economic structure is shown by the developments in Brazil. Historically, Brazil had the same institutional structure in its capital market as Continental Europe or the rest of Latin America. And managers had just as little reason to focus on profit maximization or on rapid earnings growth. In the last few years, however, a public capital market has developed rapidly in Brazil. It is now possible for a Brazilian company to go public and to finance its growth through publicly held equity capital, and as a result Brazilian businesses are rapidly shifting their objectives to profit maximization and rapid earnings growth.

. . . and in Japan the objective is minimizing the cost of capital.

In Japan, "equity capital," as defined by law, is a small percentage of total capitalization—rarely more than 25%. Although the Swiss commercial code prevails and so, theoretically, the equity holders own the company, nothing could be further from reality. Management controls companies with a very minimum of interference by shareholders, if only because managers, like all Japanese employees, have "lifetime employment" and cannot be fired. The ultimate control, however, lies with the company's bank. The bank has no vote, but the company's dependence on the bank gives the bank what a Japanese manager once described as the "power of irresistible persuasion."

Capital is largely supplied in the form of bank loans. Officially these are short term. But they are automatically renewed. If a bank tells a businessman that his loans are not being renewed, it is the bank's way of saying that the business is finished and, "you'd better merge."

At the same time, the "profit" that matters in the Janpanese business system is the bank's interest income. For the commercial banks *are* the Japanese capital markets. The high degree of dependence upon the bank is fortified by the old tradition that a company cannot raise capital by the sale of new equity shares except at par (a tradition which has begun to change slowly only in the last few years). Since the market value of a company's stock may be many times the par value, the cost of capital through the public sale of securities is prohibitive. Some shares are offered from time to time to present stockholders, but traditionally they have been a form of stock dividend rather than a means for raising capital.

For many years there have been endless arguments between Japanese and American businessmen and economists about the comparative cost of capital in their respective countries. Actually return on total capital employed is pretty much the same in both countries. In the United States, where typically no more than 35% of long-term capital is supplied by fixed interest borrowing, the return on total capital tends to run around 12% (6% on the 35% portion borrowed, 15% pretax on the 65% that is equity). It also runs around 12% in Japan (10% on the 65% borrowed, 15% pretax on the 35% equity).

The Japanese have one decided advantage: interest (their major capital cost) is, of course, tax-deductible; only the very small part that is legally considered "profit" (i.e., the earnings on equity) is subject to corporation income taxes. As a result, an American business may have to earn as much as 50% more than a Japanese firm to show the same earnings after taxes. But that is a cost differential—though a very real one—rather than a difference in the respective earnings base.

The real point, however, is that this institutional structure of the capital market imposes on the Japanese manager a very different set of objectives. His first aim, rationally, is not profit maximization. His main "owners"—the bank and management itself—would derive little or no benefit from rapid earnings growth. His main objective is minimizing the costs of capital, that is, holding down the need for capital and, with it, for profits.

*Differences in medium-term working capital
financing also make a big difference.*

Another capital-market reality with profound impact on management is the totally different situations with respect to medium-term working capital finance in different parts of the world.

The commercial revolution in Great Britain preceded the industrial revolution by about a hundred years, with the result that the commercial bank is not an industrial bank in English speaking countries, but a trade bank. In the rest of the world, the evolutionary process was reversed; the bank is primarily an industrial bank which satisfies the need for a capital market. Working capital credit, so highly developed in America, is much less used in England and is almost unknown in the rest of the world. Lack of intruments for financing working capital needs of average-sized European companies has rendered expansion difficult without, in effect, giving over control to the banks. Only recently have European branches of the U.S. banks begun to fill the need for working capital loans.

In Japan, the lack of a functioning mechanism for working-capital finance largely explains the dominant position of the "Trading Company" even in the domestic market. Very few Japanese manufacturers do their own distribution and selling—and even then usually through a company-owned but autonomous trading company rather than directly. While intensely conscious of the market, the Japanese manager is usually quite remote from it, and has neither experience nor much interest in selling.

The roots of the trading company lie deep in Japanese history. For centuries industry was scattered about the country in thousands of small workshops. It was impossible for them to distribute their wares in the city markets, so trading companies undertook the distribution function. When Japan was opened up to foreign trade, the trading companies assumed the additional task of dealing with the foreigners, with their strange languages and customs—of selling Japanese products in various countries and buying the materials needed by the manufacturers back home.

In addition to their buying and selling functions, however, the trading company soon became the vehicle for medium-term working capital financing. Loans are short-term (e.g., 90 days); but since transactions are continuous, the money is never really paid back and forms a "float," which furnishes working capital financing. Using a trading company keeps a company from being entirely dependent upon the bank.

Japanese domestic distribution costs are very high, to the point that a sort of consumers' revolt occurred in 1971 because prices of some Japanese products were higher domestically than in foreign countries. There has been some movement toward direct distribution but any change is likely to be slow because of the need for working capital finances.

SONY is the one Japanese company that managed to circumvent the traditional financing and marketing pattern by raising equity capital on the New York Stock Exchange to finance itself for expansion, and working capital loans abroad to finance its own international distribution. It serves as a prime example of the molding effect of capital structure upon management goals. For SONY is a vocal believer in basic Japanese ideas in most areas, but being financed very much like an American business, it is the one Japanese company interested in profit maximization.

Japan's wage structure puts a premium on rapid growth in volume . . .

While the Japanese manager sees little sense in profit maximization and rapid earnings growth, he lives, far more than the manager in any other country, with a built-in incentive toward rapid and continuous growth in *volume,* almost regardless of cost and profit.

The reason is that the traditional Japanese wage structure makes rapid volume-growth almost automatically turn into rapid decrease in unit costs and rapid increase in productivity; while, conversely, no growth in volume, or slow growth, means for the Japanese business a rapid increase in unit costs and a rapid decrease in productivity. Here is how it works:

Japanese employees in all categories—right up to senior executives—are paid for seniority rather than for skill or position. A man's salary doubles roughly every fifteen years over his working life, whether he stays on the same job or not—first rising rapidly (doubling every five years in the initial period of employment), then at a steadily decreasing rate. And, except for seniority, it does not, as a rule, change at all regardless of job title, skill, or position. At the same time, employees in all categories—manual worker, clerks, and managerial—are almost never hired except in the entrance position, and at bottom pay. They are also, of course, almost never fired or laid off.

This means, in turn, that personnel costs per employee go up inexorably with the age of a plant or business. But they also go down, equally inexorably, as employment expands. Increasing employment is the one sure way in Japan to decrease costs and to pump up productivity. Any increase in volume short of one requiring new major fixed investment can therefore be costed and priced on an incremental revenue basis. On the other hand, the penalty for not boosting volume, or for raising it only slowly, is to become rapidly a high-cost producer and noncompetitive. The Japanese manager's obsession with volume—seemingly at any price—is therefore perfectly rational, given his objective reality.

*. . . and for the last 25 years this has given
her a tremendous competitive advantage . . .*

The last 25 years were years of high supply of new young workers. Some of them came from a few years of "baby boom" right after the worst of the postwar period when, for a few short years, the Japanese birthrate ran to 35 per 1,000 (at the peak of the "baby boom" in the United States, in the mid 1950's, our rate was only 25 per thousand). But the major source of the abundant supply of young workers for Japan's industry in the post World War II period has been migration from the farm. Whereas almost 60% of Japan's population lived on the land in 1946, the figure now is below 20%—and most of these migrants from the farm were, of course, the young looking to industry for their first—and very low-paid—job.

This has clearly contributed to Japan's steady increase in labor productivity year by year—the very engine of her competitiveness. The world has marveled at such productivity gains, but actually as much as half of this feat may have been the hidden but constant lowering of labor costs resulting from the steady influx of large masses of workers without seniority and thus with very low salaries.

. . . but, with a falling birthrate, it may soon have the opposite effect.

It is therefore of utmost importance to realize that this factor will not work for the Japanese manager in the *next* 25 years, and is even likely to turn against him.

The common Japanese talk of a "labor shortage" is grossly exaggerated. There is tremendous waste of manpower—let alone of womanpower—even in the best-managed Japanese company. But there *will* be a severe shortage of new young entrants into the labor force. Birthrates collapsed in Japan in the mid-Fifties—from 35 per 1000 to 18 per 1000, which is just above the present record-low of the U.S. birthrate and not too far above a long-term population growth rate of zero. And the Japanese birthrate shows no sign of going up again. Each year for the next 20 years, Japan will have 20% fewer young people reaching working age than she had in the 1960's. More important, there is no more reserve of young workers on the farm; that pool has been drained.

Some Japanese experts predict a 50% drop in the number of young employees available to the Japanese business and industry in the next few years. And this may both create tremendous pressures for wage inflation and halve the rate of productivity increase. What effects this will have on the Japanese manager's objective of volume growth as a good in itself is hard to say, but it may drastically change Japanese business reality and, with it, management behavior.

THE DIFFERENT EFFECTS OF SOCIAL STRUCTURE

Every management operates and lives in a society as well as in an economy.

The management boom has had a profound impact on the societies of the developed countries outside of the United States. The biggest impact is perhaps that managers have been accepted in every country—most noticeably in Japan—as full members of society's leadership group. But fundamental social structures have still remained basically unchanged. No matter how "progressive" a management may be, it still operates in its own distinct social reality and within a distinct framework of social norms and social values. This greatly influences not only management structure but also the recruitment and the career ladder for executives, as well as personnel policies generally.

European ideas of top management are a deeply seated heritage containing elements which, if judged by United States standards, appear in some cases regressive and in others advanced. One of the traditional elements is that Europeans have customarily thought of the upper reaches of the business hierarchy as possessing power, almost by divine right. One of the effects of the management boom has been to point out that high position carries with it both power and responsibility.

The Germanic legal tradition has led to a team-type top management . . .

Most of the European companies of the Germanic legal tradition (Germany, Holland, Scandinavia, Austria, Switzerland) have a top-level management format, with a management board, which avoids some of the pitfalls that beset American firms. The company is run, in effect, by a team, each member having clearly defined areas of responsibility, and with the chief executive ("managing director") having full powers but seldom exercising his right to make decisions within any of the responsibility areas. This is by no means the same thing as the American idea of "the office of the president"; it is both more rigid and more flexible.

(This concept of the top management team does not come out of management theory. It springs from a very old Continental tradition of government. Neither the German city-states nor the Swiss confederation had a permanent chief executive. The office rotated among the members of the top council; in Switzerland, the president is still selected in this fashion.)

In these countries following the Germanic tradition, there is also a supervisory board to review performance of the company and to appoint the members of the management board. This board is more like the American board of directors.

Finally, there is a chairman of the managing board—but he is "the executive in charge of company policy" rather than the "chief executive." In respect to company-wide matters he is quite apt to make decisions without even consulting his colleagues. But he rarely, if ever, interferes in the functional areas assigned to them, be it finance or marketing, research or production.

The important fact is that the top executives who make up the management board of the corporation enjoy very nearly final authority in their areas. Each one reports matters to his colleagues if he thinks that they ought to be informed, but he does not usually consult with them on matters which are his responsibility, and he does not usually ask anyone for decisions execpt in carefully defined areas.

. . . while the French concept is a small top group, usually from outside . . .

In France and the countries of the French legal tradition (i.e., Italy, Belgium, and Spain) there is a small top group, rarely more than three, and often there is only one man. They are top management and have powers that go far beyond those of even the most autocratic American chief executive.

But in the larger companies they almost never come out of the company's management. Unless they occupy their positions by inheritance—as does for instance, Gino Agnelli at Fiat—they are far more likely to be recruited directly into the top positions from the outside—from government service, the universities, or the professions, especially law. They therefore know little about the actual work of the business—and are not supposed to concern themselves with operating matters. These are left to functional people with wide authority in their areas but with little say in top management decisions, and often with almost no information about them.

In France, for instance, the typical chief executive of a large company will have attended one of the *grandes écoles,* most often the *École Polytechnique.* Graduating as an engineer, he will, however, not go into engineering work but into government service as a "generalist." After some twenty-odd years in the civil service he will have become an "Inspecteur de Finance" (equivalent to a general's star in the Army) and be freed from departmental duties. Beyond this point, advancement in government service is by political appointment, however, rather than by merit. Some, with the right connections, will continue on, perhaps into the ministry. The others are likely to leave and to enter industry at the highest levels.

The man who goes straight into business is rarely even considered for a top management job. The only—and none too common—exceptions are financial people. Whether the new kind of *grand école* for business managers at Fontainebleau will change this is doubtful; it may send men up through the organization, but not to the very top.

. . . and the Japanese use a seniority pyramid topped by an arbitrator.

In sharp contrast, Japanese top management almost always comes out of the business (the one exception being top civil servants after their retirement from government). And top management and the board of directors are one and the same. The members are chosen from managers who reach age 50 or 55—until then advancement is almost entirely by seniority. But once a man has been chosen for a position as "company director" he is in for life; top executives in their 80's are by no means uncommon in Japan. Within the top group, advancement from "managiing director" to "president" to "chairman" again tends to be largely by seniority.

But all these top people are not expected to work. They are expected to preside, to arbitrate, and, above all, to handle the myriad of complex personal relationships on which Japanese business depends—with the government, with industry associations, with the bank, with sister companies of the same industrial group, and so on. Work is for the younger men. And the center of the decision-making process is a "consensus" of upper-middle managers, the "departmental" (i.e., functional) directors and the "managing directors" (i.e., divisional vice presidents).

Only in England has the management boom changed the traditional pattern.

In the countries of the Germanic legal tradition, the management boom has, by and large, reinforced the traditional pattern and reversed a trend toward an American-style "chief executive" that had been running strong since 1900 and was actually written into German company law under Hitler. In most other countries the management boom has not even had that much impact on top management.

This is not true, however, of England. There, too, exists a specific national tradition for top management. In England the "board of directors" is a company's top management. But under the impact of the management boom the English have come to differentiate increasingly between "executive" and "nonexecutive" board members, that is, between full-time top managers and outside directors. More important, the management boom has made British companies increasingly willing to promote to positions of "executive director" people who actually made their career in business.

Earlier (i.e., before World War II), a sharp distinction was often made between the "board level" and the "working staff," with the latter allowed to rise to positions as "general managers" but usually kept out of the board, that is, out of top management. Today Britain's largest companies—e.g., Imperial Chemicals, Unilever, or Royal Dutch/Shell—are headed by men who have made their careers in business. Even so, British companies often prefer to go, for the top positions, to people who have made their careers in other companies—and in a very large number of cases to people who made their careers in the British subsidiaries of American companies.

Still, Britain is the one country where top management personnel, top management structure, and top management functions closely resemble what an American manager takes for granted.

In England too, there have been the greatest changes in management structure. Decentralization, above all, has been widely adopted there.

Elsewhere, the pattern is mixed. In the larger Japanese companies decentralization prevails. On the Continent, only some large companies—the electrical and the chemical industries in particular—have adopted decentralized organization, with each division an autonomous "profit and loss center." Siemens in Germany, for instance, reorganized itself in the 1960's on lines quite similar to those of the American General Electric Company. Philips in Holland has gone even further with an intricate geometry of worldwide "product divisions" and territorial "companies," each with autonomous profit responsibility. But in other industries older patterns persist, especially the pyramidal "holding company," but also very rigid functional structures.

Marketing alone has experienced a fundamental change across the board.

In most countries the position of marketing has, in fact, changed. While the export sales manager had for a long time been a full member of management, the domestic sales manager was rarely considered a "gentleman," let alone a candidate for top management. As late as 1960 one very large Italian manufacturing company did not even have a domestic sales manager even though 70% of its output was sold in Italy (but the export sales manager was a full member of the top group).

The marketing manager may still not be eligible for the top job in many European companies; but at least there *is* one today, and he is a member of the management group.

DIFFERENT ROUTES TO TOP MANAGEMENT

Even more impervious than top management structure—and even more culturally embedded—are career ladders outside the United States. Again they differ greatly.

Engineering, law, or accounting may be the best career ladder . . .

In Germany, engineering credentials are the quickest route to the executive floor. In the past at least, it was not even necessary for the engineer to be very familiar with a balance sheet or to know much about marketing; others could perform those functions. German excellence in technology—the technological base of many German companies—has been the result (or the cause) of the engineer in the chief executive chair. Second comes the law degree—but not actual experience in legal work.

In France, the law degree is worthless for a business career. But the engineering degree—provided it is from the *École Polytechnique* rather than from an engineering school—is the open sesame. But, in contrast to Germany, work as an engineer all but disqualifies the young *"Polytechnicien."* He goes into government as an administrative assistant. Engineering is prized as training in logic rather than as a profession.

In England, an engineering degree has been something to be lived down if a man is to be a candidate for a high position in business. Engineers used to be regarded as people with dirty fingernails and as good at mechanics rather than at management. There is a major effort under way in England to change this by making technical schools (e.g., the new University of Bradford) the equivalent of such old "schools for gentlemen" as Oxford and Cambridge, as managerial spawning grounds. But the one professional degree and professional career that has really emerged as a career ladder in British business (other than service with a British subsidiary of a U.S. company) has been accounting.

In Japan, finally, *no* functional area is considered career preparation. What matters in Japan is not what you studied but where. Different companies look to different universities for their future top people. The manager who holds his degree from another university will be promoted by seniority like any other—but rarely beyond "department director."

Thus, the Mitsubishi companies, while hiring graduates of practically every one of Japan's almost 400 universities, have only graduates of three in their top management—Tokyo National, Keio, and Hitotsubushi. Rival Mitsui has long favored men from Waseda. Osaka-based companies and groups such as Sumitomo, C. Itoh, or giant Matsushita Electric ("National") look for the graduates of Kyoto, Osaka, and Kobe, and so on. And an undergraduate degree from a foreign university, even Oxford or Harvard, is almost a guarantee of nonpromotion—not because it is not accepted but because there are not enough such graduates in any company to form an effective "clique."

. . . but, in all countries outside the United
States, the "old boys" network pervails.

This example shows another aspect of management outside of the United States—the crucial importance of personal relationships. The old *"Polytechniciens"* in France or the Tokyo University graduates in Japan form an "old boys" network without parallel in the United States. It is through this network rather than through the company's law firm, through the courts, or through bidding on contracts that the manager outside the United States gets his results and exerts his influence. Japan, of course, is the extreme; but other countries follow pretty much the same pattern.

But it is not, as Americans assume, just a matter of "whom you know." The "old boys" network is, above all, a way to know whom you can trust. It is the equivalent of the "Joe sent me" of American prohibition days. And for this reason the sweeping social change of the last half-century did not seriously challenge the pattern.

The French management school in Fontainebleau, the advanced management school founded by Olivetti and Fiat in Torino, the two British management schools that were opened in the 1960's, all aim clearly at creating new career ladders and old boys networks, but they are adaptations, not adoptions; neither the idea of the "right" career channel nor that of dependence on an informal group whose members you know and can trust has been abandoned or even seriously challenged.

RELATIONSHIP BETWEEN BUSINESS AND GOVERNMENT

For the manager and his business enterprise, the area of reality that is most radically different from the one the American manager takes for granted is the relationship between business and government.

Since the very earliest days, American political behavior has been organized as an adversary process. (See also Carey, p. 80, on the adversary society.) The three branches of the Federal Government are so structured as to be in perpetual tension. The relationship between the government and other institutions is largely one of opposition, and particularly so in the instance of the business-government relationship.

The matter is even more complex, however, when it comes to the relationship between business and any one of the specific governmental branches concerned with some phase of business. There is, in fact, an inherent belief that any form of industry-government collaboration is really collusion against which the public must be carefully protected. The prescribed role of the government with respect to the firm is one of regulator, watchdog, and policeman. (Not that this always works; the "regulatory agency," in particular, is often forced into becoming a spokesman for "its" industry, within government, beyond anything a European or even a Japanese bureaucrat would consider proper. But this, then, in the American tradition is considered "malfunction," "dereliction of duty," and a "scandal.")

For United States firms, antitrust laws
work against international business . . .

As a result of the American preoccupation with domestic affairs which obtained for nearly a century and a half, there was no vision of the business firm as an agency of foreign policy. Quite the contrary, the actions of American companies in other nations were popularly regarded as at least immoral and as likely to lead to undesirable involvement. Nor, with the opportunities for opening up new frontiers within the country, was there clearly seen a need for encouraging international trade. Business was not seen as the buttress of domestic security but rather as an enterprise in potential or actual conflict with the individual as well as with a host of other groups, the farmer, the worker, and so on.

These views are reflected in the maze of antitrust laws, so complex that even the experts have great difficulty in unraveling them. They are expressed in the actions of the government in prohibiting or undoing mergers between firms. They are shown in the policy of the United States Government in making it difficult for American enterprises to compete abroad by subjecting them to restrictions unknown to foreign competitors.

Business, in turn, has prided itself—often with little reason—on its total independence from government. It has tended to be contemptuous of the "bureaucrat" and woefully ignorant of the workings of government and of the dynamics of the political process.

. . . but in other countries competition stops at the nearest foreign border.

Outside the United States neither our governmental tradition nor the attitude of American business can even be explained. They violate everything that the Europeans or Japanese—whether businessman, politician, or civil servant—take for granted.

Mention "competition" to an American and he thinks of G. E. vs. Westinghouse, or of Sears Roebuck vs. Montgomery Ward. Mention "competition" to a European—or a Japanese—and he is quite likely to think of the Dutch economy vs. the French, or the Japanese economy vs. all others. To be sure, he knows that industrial firms compete against each other, and (particularly in Europe) the personal relationships between executives of competing firms are often surprisingly bitter and rancorous. But to him such rivalry should stop at the nearest foreign border.

The difference lies in political tradition
(administrative vs. legislative or judicial) . . .

In Continental Europe, and also in Japan, the core of the political process has always been administrative rather than legislative or judicial. And administration is a process of harmonizing and reconciling—of finding a specific solution for a specific case rather than establishing generally applicable principles.

An illustration of the difference is the ITT scandal that rocked the Nixon administration in the spring of 1972, when it was revealed that government officials, including presidential assistants, had been appealed to by the officers and directors of one of America's largest corporations in connection with an antitrust suit against the company, and had discussed the matter with the officials of the Justice Department in charge of the suit.

In any other country it would not have been a "scandal"—indeed it would be unthinkable for top government officials, from the Chief Executive down, not to play an active part in a matter of such importance, and not to have worked out a settlement administratively. Indeed in every other country—regardless of the politics of its government—it would never have been permitted to be dealt with except by the highest officials, if not as a cabinet-level matter from beginning to end.

. . . and in the fact that the rest of the world is basically mercantilist.

But equally important is the fact that only the United States—and to a much lesser extent Great Britain—sees business as something remote from government, and government as something remote from business. Elsewhere, the view is that there is only one national economy, and it is an integral part of national identity and national sovereignty, and essential to both. The other countries, in effect, are basically mercantilist in their view of the relationships between government and business.

On the Continent of Europe, where countries are many and relatively small, where borders may be unmarked by natural barriers, and where armies have marched back and forth for centuries, it became obvious in the early days of the nation-state (i.e., 300 years ago or more) that to maintain physical existence it is necessary to have an army; to pay the army, bullion is required; and to obtain bullion, one must engage in foreign trade. Foreign trade is not only a vital element of the economy; it is also an arm of the nation's foreign policy. The practice of international trade and the mercantile tradition have dominated European thought since the days of Colbert, Finance Minister to Louis XIV, who to this day is more influential as an economist for Europeans than Adam Smith or Lord Keynes.

The American economy, on the other hand, was almost an entirely domestic one, sustained by the constantly opening up of new internal frontiers. Without fear of foreign invasion since 1815, and with opportunities within the country too exciting to ignore, American business has tended, until recently, to look upon foreign trade as merely a fringe benefit. American political tradition sees the economy as one-of-a-kind, free floating in space, connected only by thin strands with the rest of the world, and not in any way affected by it. Even now, Americans are apt to be surprised when they discover the repercussions their acts sometimes cause in the other parts of the world.

In Europe, in other words, a long tradition sees business first and foremost as a national asset deserving protection and support from the state, but also owing support to the state. And the national economy is seen as subordinate to the needs of foreign and economic policy. Neither the attempt of the Socialists to unify the proletariat in all nations (which collapsed in 1914) nor the advent of the Common Market has yet seriously affected the basic tradition. In spite of movements to unify Europe, it is likely to be a long time before the mercantilist habit disappears.

Japan, for historical reasons of her own, is even more mercantilist than Continental Europe. With the opening up of Japan to foreigners and their trade, a little more than 100 years ago, the nation became close-knit in facing a world which it feared and distrusted. Having agreed to become a part of an expanded universe, it was very important for Japan to be strong and to be a great nation like those whose ships touched its shores. It, too, must have a strong army and for that it needed a sound economy. But more importantly, it must export— or else fall in thrall to foreign creditors. To foster national interest, Japanese industry must aid in growth. Profit was secondary. For many years Japan's single-minded national goal has been economic growth and nothing else— every agency in the country has been called upon to play a role in implementation.

Even the labor unions in Continental Europe and Japan are still deeply imbued with the mercantilist spirit—though less so today than they were only a few years ago. They are no more or no less patriotic. But they are keenly aware of the fact that at the border the conflict between management and labor ceases. The customer on the other side is only interested in price and quality; and it is the customer on the other side who matters. And while American radicalism has traditionally been "antibusiness," the radical of the European tradition believed in changing the bosses but retaining the business structure (which explains why the Europeans consider the present-day radicals of the "New Left," who demand that the structures be smashed, as an "American import").

Business is more interfered with, and more supported, in other countries.

As a result of their mercantilist policies, business is far more interfered with in these countries than even now in the United States. For an important business to make any major decision—on pricing, on labor relations, on plant location, or on dropping a product line—without first "clearing" it with the ministry is hardly conceivable.

At the same time, however, it is the job of government to support business— and especially big business, and even more especially big exporting business— all the way. An American ambassador, though perhaps himself an ex-businessman, tends to play hard-to-get when asked to help an American company to get a fat export order. But the French or the Japanese ambassador, though he may consider himself an "aristocrat" and despise businessmen as vulgar clods, does know that he is his country's No. 1 salesman in his foreign country and that it is his job to get the orders for his country's companies.

The attitude of American government is that domestic competition is to be preserved at all costs. In Europe or Japan, domestic competition is not considered particularly desirable. The important thing is to have a strong enough national industry so as to compete with foreign companies. The competitive outlook in France could be expressed as Renault vs. Volkswagen. Consequently a European government which is concerned with an industry situation will exert pressure to force mergers—though not, except as a matter of dire necessity, with a foreign firm.

European governments have for the most part opposed mergers of larger companies with foreign organizations. There have been exceptions when it was necessary to form an alliance to thwart some well-entrenched foreign competitor—for example, Machines Bull in France joining with General Electric to combat IBM. (Other trans-European anti-IBM combinations are being formulated.) Also, associations are sometimes formed to undertake major programs—for example, the British and French collaboration on the supersonic Concorde. Banks have arranged jointly to promote foreign business, but to engage quite independently in their own respective domestic markets.

The attitude of the government in respect to intercompany arrangements is not merely censorious, as would be the attitude of the United States Government, but that of a mother approving or not approving a suitor for the daughter's hand.

Such national industrial husbandry is often ill-advised. In an effort to create an enterprise large enough to compete with a big foreign firm, four small inefficient companies may be combined to form one major inefficient firm. (Yet the resultant company may be so large in relation to the domestic economy that, should it get into trouble, the government has to bail it out or take it over.) Or, while the company may be a monster in its own domestic market, it may still not be large enough for the world economy—and still parochial in its outlook.

French nationalism under de Gaulle's influence has produced a number of such companies that may pose serious future problems. But so may some of the shotgun mergers the Japanese government forced through in order to create a single company without foreign tie-ups and yet big enough for an expanding and competitive world economy—the recent merger between the two largest Japanese steel companies, for instance. Even Great Britain, the least mercantilist government outside the United States, has subsidized, cajoled, and browbeaten its small and ailing computer companies to combine into one big and ailing but all-British computer company rather than permit international mergers.

*The end result: a less anonymous role
for foreign business leaders . . .*

The mercantilist concept of business enterprise as a pillar both of national and of individual security leads to a different role for management in European society than in America. There has been no American business leader for 50 years with the prominence, the power, or the status of a Morgan, a Harriman, or a Rockefeller. Heads of large industrial firms are mainly anonymous.

Indeed, the United States ceased to be a "business society" about the time of

World War I. But in France and in Germany business has become the social elite and the most powerful group in society since World War II. In Japan, business leaders are an integral part of the tripartite "establishment" that runs the nation—business, bureaucrats, politicians.

. . . and a more recognized, purposeful,
role for foreign trade associations.

There is another consequence of the government-business relationship in all other countries—even, though to a lesser degree, in Great Britain. Trade associations are considered semigovernment bodies, and membership is compulsory either by law or in fact. Thus, *Keidanren*, the Japanese industry association, is sometimes called "the first house of parliament." And nothing in the United States compares to the role that the British Federation of Industry plays as spokesman and liaison for business, but also as decision maker for business.

In the United States, trade association activities are heavily circumscribed by the Justice Department, but in Europe or Japan their role is active rather than passive. In Germany, for example, the industry association negotiates the collective bargaining agreement for all companies. In France, it forms the agency for government control of national planning. And while the association manager in the United States is the servant of his members, he tends, especially in Germany, to be more powerful and far more visible than the chief executives of many of his member companies.

American industrial associations provide, almost universally, an opportunity for members to socialize in addition to the undertaking of formal business. This aspect is usually lacking in foreign association affairs. Europeans do not generally have a very high opinion of their competition, and the meetings (perhaps to take a position at the ministry meeting next month) have all of the lightheartedness of an obligatory chapel session at a federal jail.

Related to industry associations are standardizing organizations. In most of the world, these are government agencies, and representation on international bodies is through government nomination. Americans have had to deal with international standardizing organizations in major industrial fields through voluntary representation usually lacking in official support. In recent years European groups have joined together through government-recognized bodies to provide for international "harmonization" of test methods for many kinds of products. The practical effect of this could be to make some imported (uncertified) products unsalable. Such a process by an American association would be an open invitation to a criminal indictment.

Management concepts differ on national
role, industrial ethics, cooperation.

In summary, there are, perhaps, three main areas of divergence in management philosophy between the United States and other countries in respect to the relationship between business and government:

1. *Business, especially big business, is regarded as a national resource in most countries outside the United States.* This makes it the clear duty of government to support and to protect big business. But it also makes it the duty of management to safeguard that resource and to make it as effective as possible. Management is not expected to undertake or even to accept programs which will reduce the effectiveness of the enterprise. Social programs are a matter of government decision after careful consideration.

Japan, of course, has a highly paternalistic industrial system, in which the costs and the benefits have been integrated into the economic structure. Since industry is an element of the national economy, top business management is expected to take part in the formulation of national policies. That is quite different from the American tradition of having businessmen sit on a commission appointed to prepare a report which will not be used for policymaking or for anything else.

Because export trade is considered so vital to the interest of European and Japanese economies, management is expected to be familiar with the various aspects of international problems, with situations in other countries, and with the day-to-day position of world commerce.

2. *The viewpoint on business ethics or industrial morality is different.* American management is hedged in with a variety of taboos stemming from the principle that domestic competition is *good* and that anything which interferes with it is *bad*. Business in other nations is much freer of such restraints. On the other hand, it would be immoral for a Japanese business to undertake programs that might be considered adverse to the nation's economy.

3. *American industry and its own government are adversaries and supposed to regard each other with suspicion and distrust.*

MANAGEMENT BEHIND THE IRON CURTAIN

While the management boom has left almost untouched the realities and fundamentals of the society and economy in which managements in the other developed countries live, it has a profound impact on the very foundation of the European Communist countries—i.e., Russia and the Communist countries of Eastern Europe.

Marxist doctrine has gradually made concessions to the managerial system.

Autonomy of management is a "contradiction within Marxism," as serious as any of the "contradictions within capitalism" on which Marxists pin their hopes for capitalism's collapse. It denotes that the problems of distribution of the benefits produced by the economic machine are not due entirely to its ownership but are a function of the economy.

Over a period of time Marxist doctrine has gradually become bent into new forms in the Soviet bloc by the discovery that some of the elements of the managerial system were needed to make things work. One such change was the acceptance of the profit concept. Every factory manager is now expected to show a profit, and he receives a bonus related to profit achievement.

The next change was acceptance of the "cost of capital" and "interest charges on capital." A factory is provided with a "fund" for which it pays a basic rate of interest. If it needs more funds (for working capital), money will be supplied but at a higher rate of interest. Along with these changes, the factory manager was given a certain amount of discretion in producing his products and in the way they were produced, rather than having the plant run purely as an appendage of the central planning facility. This resulted in some internal strain between the hardliners who saw the changes as a movement away from the purity of Communist philosophy and the pragmatists who felt that it was necessary to make more economic progress.

Then the management boom proclaimed that management should have autonomy. This was resisted in Russia but made a great impression in the satellites which have a Western background. However, even in the Soviet Union, it could not be totally ignored, as pointed out before.

The concept of management autonomy poses a basic threat to the Russians.

The threat to the Soviet system is more insidious than that of the Common Market in that it "bores from within." Management demands an autonomy which undermines the very cohesion of Communist party control and of Lenin's dogma of "democratic centralism." Above all, it is a thoroughly Western notion. This explains its almost irresistible attraction for the satellite countries, which, after all, are (and desperately want to remain) part of Western civilization. In these countries, "management" has become a kind of "counterculture" and the battlecry of the resistors to enforced Russianization.

In the Soviet Union, the impact of the management boom goes deeper and is more traumatic. The concept of management autonomy contains many of the seeds of Western ideas—belief in individual dignity, rational measurement of results, and freedom of individual action—all of which are heretical challenges to Russian tradition long predating the Bolshevik revolution. Russia has had a history of brief flirtations with Western thought, only to be followed by harsh repression. It always produced within the generation involved a severe identity crisis.

As yet, the Russians have not come to terms with the management revolution. They have attempted to contain it. And so, long range, the management boom, and not the resurgence of China, may lead to the fundamental ideological crisis of the Soviet regime.

MANAGEMENT IN THE DEVELOPING NATIONS

Similarly great, and also similarly problematical, has been the impact of the management boom on the developing nations. Management, they would all agree by now, is their best hope for development. But management—and especially the lack thereof—is also their central development problem.

The problem: not failure of capital formation but a management gap . . .

It has often been claimed that the gap betwen the "have" and the "have not" nations is due largely to the failure of capital accumulation in the latter group. Yet the basic problem is not an economic one; it is a management gap. Development is not a function of capital formation; rather, capital formation is a consequence of development. Merely accumulating capital is likely to create unemployment and little else. Management development is a development of markets and of demand, of professional competence and leadership. It is this fundamental need which is at the root of the problem of improving the lot of the developing nations.

It is being said that the economic development programs instituted in these countries have been failures. While progress has been spotty, there has been far more progress than was expected twenty years ago. In many nations GNP has increased rapidly; but—something no one expected 20 years ago—population has grown just as fast, with the result that per capita GNP has grown very little or not at all. Yet without such development programs there would have been major famine.

Historically, nations have never developed at a uniform rate. Even in Europe the pace was irregular. In the current world environment, the three noncommunist, Chinese-populated areas of Hong Kong, Taiwan, and Singapore have grown at an unprecedented rate. Despite everything said to the contrary, in India there is a fast-developing economy of 40–50 million people within a nondeveloping continent of 800 million; this middle-class group is not rich by European standards, but it is a growing one. And Brazil, while it has many remaining sociopolitical problems, may actually be past the point of critical mass for economic growth.

Much of Brazil's economic advance resulted from a diffusion of management competence, often through the multinational company. A second factor has been the systematic export of management concepts and practices from the United States during the management boom. The managements thus produced sometimes look different from the United States model, but many are highly effective.

. . . not just in business, but also in government (except the military).

By now it has also become clear that the creation of improved management in the economic sector is not enough. The greatest problem in a number of developing countries is managerial incompetence in government. In some revolutionary changes, for example, the issues have been less based on the ideologies of conflicting groups than upon the fact that the government was desperately incompetent. It was unable to perform even elementary government tasks.

At least some of the problem has been the result of failure to provide political leaders with even rudimentary ideas of management. In a number of nations leaders have been educated in journalism or law, which are largely areas of individual proficiency. Consequently, no matter how high their ideals, they were unable to cope with the problems of running an organization. As a result, not infrequently, the military have taken over, precisely because they do possess some rudiments of management. Every officer is trained to run an organization, to have regard for resources, to undertake assigned tasks and to report back.

The challenge: to set priorities and find jobs for the exploding population.

One basic management need that few of the developing nations have seriously faced up to is the setting of priorities. The great achievement of the Japanese in the nineteenth century, in moving within a few decades from weakness and poverty to the status of a major power, rested on the decision at the outset to concentrate on a small number of goals. Yet many countries today, though far less developed than was Japan a hundred years ago, are trying to duplicate at once everything done by the richest nations. This policy can lead only to failure. One of the things a good manager knows is to apply his resources to the basic needs; to establish priorities; and to organize to be sure that priorities will be observed.

President Kennedy spoke of the "rising tide of human expectations." In the developing countries it is above all a rise in the expectations from the country's managers, public and private. The management boom—even more so than the display of goods on the TV tube or political propaganda—has made the masses aware of the potential of development and impatient with the traditional mismanagement and nonmanagement of their economies and societies. Management skills have grown apace in many of these countries, especially in the private sector. Whether they can grow fast enough to satisfy the expectations has yet to be proven.

The critical period will be the next decade. After 1980 or 1985 population pressures in most developing countries are likely to decrease or at least to abate. For birthrates in many of these countries (Brazil preeminently), while still high, are rapidly going down. But between now and 1985 jobs will have to be found for all the babies born since the "population explosion" which began in the late Fifties. Some Latin American countries, e.g., Mexico or Brazil, each year will have to find twice as many jobs as in any year during the past fifteen years.

No "ism," whether "capitalism" or "communism," has ever dealt with such a problem or has a theory to tackle it—indeed no existing social or economic theory has ever envisaged such a challenge. Failure to produce job opportunities may create an explosion of disappointment and despair which could rock the world. This may be the most serious of all the management challenges of today.

The Multinational Corporation

While the boom went on, new, interesting, unforseen developments in management came into being—new realities, each with its own management challenge. The most visible of these has been the multinational corporation.

Multinational companies are nothing new, in one sense, for old companies, such as Singer, International Harvester, and Remington Typewriter in the United States, Siemens, Lever Brothers, the German and the Swiss Chemical companies, and many others, were "multinational" well before 1900. What is new, however, is the emergence of a world economy, and of a world market with enough similar demand (regardless of tradition or local culture) to support it. What is new, in other words, is that being "multinational"—i.e., marketing and selling in many countries—has become the rule for the large company since World War II, and it is becoming the rule for a great many medium-sized and even small companies as well.

Most people think of American-based companies when they hear the word "multinational." And indeed the Americans were in the lead. But since the early 1960's companies based elsewhere—in Europe, in Japan, and even in Latin America—have been going multinational faster than the Americans. Today, particularly if extractive industry (e.g., petroleum production or copper mining) is excluded, the multinationals divide rougly 50/50 between American and others (British, Dutch, German, French, Italian, Swiss, Swedes, Japanese, Argentine, Brazilians, and so on).

Most people also think of manufacturing companies when they hear the word "multinational." But nonmanufacturing businesses have gone multinational maybe even faster—especially the big American commercial banks, but also a host of business-service companies, such as auditing firms, management consultants, advertising agencies, and insurance brokers.

Multinationals have aided development,
been the source of good managers . . .

The multinational firm is the only effective nonnational institution in a world increasingly given to paroxysms of nationalism. (There are other "*non*national" institutions—e.g., The World Health Organization—but their role is regulatory or advisory, whereas the multinational corporation acts.) Therein lies its major importance, but also the source of its most central problems. It was the one major social innovation of the post-World War II period which otherwise did not show much political or social imagination. Again, this makes the multinational corporation important and hugely promising, but it also creates the particular problem of relationships with the other social and political institutions, almost all of which are essentially early nineteenth century in their perceptions, their operating methods, and their world views.

In the developing world the multinational corporation has been the most effective carrier of development and the most effective channel for producing good managers for the private as well as the public sector.

A goodly number of "graduates" from multinational companies are, for instance, beginning to be found in positions of responsibility in Latin America, not merely in business but also in government at various levels. Not all of them have a high opinion of the company they left; they could see at first hand some of the relationship problems that will be discussed shortly. Nor would all of them fit into the pattern of the typical American manager. But they are good managers all the same. For they have learned what management is, and why. (This is not always understood in developing countries; for example, there is little awareness of the fact that spending a great deal of time on the preparation of an elegant plan doesn't accomplish much by itself—someone must make it work.)

Thus, these multinational "graduates" know that management is work; it is getting the right things done. They know that the task of management is not to make geniuses out of people, but to get ordinary, highly imperfect human beings to perform. They know that one has to think through objectives and to set priorities. And they know that one measures results—does not allow promises to be substituted for results. These are simple things, to be sure; but they are the essence of good management.

. . . but their very existence makes them a threat to poor countries.

The poor countries, particularly those with newly won independence, are unsure of their national identity, painfully conscious of the limitation of their resources and the endlessness of their problems and poverty.

They feel threatened by the fact that the local subsidiary of a great multinational cannot be very important to the treasurer at the home office in far-off New York, London, or Rotterdam; after all it may produce far less than one per cent of the company's total revenue—less than a single sales district in one of the developed countries. Yet for the country in question this plant is a mainstay of its economy and a main source of desperately scarce jobs. Without the capital from New York, London, or Rotterdam it would not exist; yet to have it depend on decisions made in such a remote place is like having one's head forever in the lion's mouth.

The multinational company is thus a central challenge—both major problem and major opportunity, internally as well as externally—to none of which do we yet have answers.

Example of problem: local government asks
Swiss subsidiary for price concession . . .

The president of the Swiss-owned pharmaceutical company—in, say, Columbia—must be an important man in the country. For his company is likely to be a major employer, a big company by local standards and close to the politically sensitive national health service. (Indeed, it is not unusual to find in such a job a man who has held a high government office as a minister or who has headed the country's leading medical school.) Yet the subsidiary he heads may produce only $1\frac{1}{2}\%$ of the company's total sales, or about the same as the Düsseldorf district sales office.

The President of the Republic is quite likely to call this man to his office and make a direct request—e.g., for a major price concession on a line of widely used antibiotics. The president of the subsidiary must then be able to give an answer—or he and his company are discredited forever. He cannot say that he has to submit the matter to an assistant v.p. in a regional office, who then goes to a regional v.p., who then refers it to an area v.p. for decision—six months later— by the executive committee in Basel.

But the Mayor of Düsseldorf is most unlikely to call the company's district sales manager. And should he do so, he would expect to be told that the district sales manager has to go higher up for an answer or a decision.

Furthermore, a price concession on antibiotics for one country—any country— is simply not a matter the local management can be permitted to decide. It has immediate worldwide impact throughout the entire company and in all its markets. But this is something which the President of the Republic understandably considers quite irrelevant.

. . . or, Italian head of American subsidiary
is offered position in the United States.

Dr. Y, who heads up the Italian company, is one of the ablest men in the whole organization. Because the company is a truly multinational enterprise, Dr. Y is offered the position of International Vice President in Little Rock, Arkansas, which has just become vacant. Dr. Y expresses his gratitude and delight at the offer, but points out that he has two children of school age and does not want them to grow up as expatriates. Further, his wife's parents are living; and she would not wish to abandon them. He may politely hint that his roots are in Rome, which means that he has been to Little Rock and could find nothing— from climate to historical monuments—that could begin to compete with Rome.

Yet if promotion to an American executive post is not an attraction, how can the really good foreign national managers be retained, reporting to four layers of home office executives? Previously, American companies could make the unprecedented offer of making an Italian the head of the company in Italy, even if his father had been a shepherd; and at that time no Italian company would have considered such a move. Now times have changed. There are enough European companies who are willing to accept unencumbered ability, although by no means all of them. Thus the competitive advantage that the American multinational company once enjoyed has disappeared. There also are quite a few European multinationals, and they are looking for the same bright people.

What should managers be: own national, foreign national, dual citizens?

The question of the management career ladder has yet to be solved. How can flexibility and opportunity be provided in the face of cultural diversity? There are several different approaches:

1. Some European (and virtually all Japanese) companies have their own nationals occupy all top spots everywhere. This may work fine for Swiss companies like Nestlés—whoever is afraid of "Swiss imperialism"? But even Unilever has faced growing resistance to its policy of giving Dutchmen preference in filling top jobs in, say, the Unilever companies in Germany. And the Japanese are today under mounting fire throughout Southeast Asia for their "Japanese only" policy in filling local management positions in their subsidiaries.

2. Another approach is that used by IBM (and by a very few others outside the United States). There are very few Americans in IBM companies. The local executives are foreign nationals and have the local traditions. But in addition, whatever they may be, they are IBM men, steeped in an "IBM culture."

3. A third, but less successful, approach is to expect foreign managers to have, so to speak, dual citizenship. They must be loyal citizens of their own nation, observing its culture and methods. But as managers they must be British or Germans following their home country's concepts and methods. Everybody in the management of the Brazilian subsidiary of a certain German multinational is a native-born Brazilian, for instance. But even off the job these men speak only German to each other. Yet no one will ever be a manager in any but the company's Brazilian subsidiary.

The alternatives: systems management or management by jet plane (oxcart).

The future pattern may be "systems management," in which each major market is an autonomous organization reporting *directly* to top corporate management. There may be no need for intermediate levels. (There are, after all, several thousand bishops who report directly to the Vatican; and the system has worked for a great many years.) Such a method requires a great deal more emphasis on objectives, on strategy, and on measurements, but also on executives' personal knowledge of each other.

But the alternative is management by jet plane. The latter is but a variation of Charlemagne's court, which traveled about from castle to castle. But the system didn't last beyond his lifetime—and it left behind an empire falling to pieces. (At that time they suffered from oxcart fatigue; now it is jet fatigue.) That is not to say that there should not be trips for personal contacts with the local management. There should, indeed; but they should be supplements to the system, not the system itself. Trips should be made for establishing personal relationships, for broad consultation, for improving personal understanding, but not for rapid-fire decision making.

Managing multinational companies engaged in producing a variety of different products poses additional management problems. When the complexities of multimarkets are imposed upon multiproducts and multicultured situations, the complexities grow very fast indeed. The most successful multinationals are primarily single product businesses (e.g., IBM). Those with many products and many bsuinesses rarely perform beyond the lifetime of one virtuoso "lion tamer."

Many countries feel that multinationals threaten their national sovereignty.

The external problems are even greater—and even further from solution.

Professor Raymond Vernon of Harvard has recently published a book on the multinational corporation under the title, *Sovereignty at Bay* (New York: Basic Books, 1971). Whether national sovereignty is indeed "at bay" is an open question. But the multinational corporation is a direct challenge, a direct dare, to the whole concept of the sovereign nation state that has dominated political thought and political structure for 300 years and is still the only principle of political organization or international law.

Even a highly developed small country, e.g., Sweden, is worried if its industry is dominated by multinationals based abroad. The often-heard statement which compares the sales of big companies with the GNP of small countries, and then concludes that General Motors has revenues larger than most small countries' GNP, rests on a misunderstanding of economics. The proper comparison is between GNP and a company's "value added in manufacture," which is, of course, only a fraction of the sales figure. But, even so, a big multinational based abroad represents a formidable concentration of economic power for a smaller country.

And it is a serious impairment of such a country's sovereignty to have the power of decision over basic national industries located beyond its political reach. Even the Swiss—the least "anti-business" among all people today—have therefore forbidden foreigners to own control of Swiss businesses.

It may be argued that sovereignty, even of large nations, was closely circumscribed by economic reality long before the rise of the multinational corporation. But it is one thing to be limited, or even to be dictated to, by the forces of an impersonal market, and quite another thing to be the victim—or even the beneficiary—of decisions made by five men sitting around an executive committee table on the nineteenth floor of an office building 3,000 miles away.

But the small country may feel as acutely uncomfortable if its own companies go multinational—as has happened, for instance, in Sweden. Few Swedes, however, believe the old wives' tale that multinationals "export" jobs; they know that they create jobs *and* exports. (Indeed, small countries cannot afford indulgence in such myths.) Most Swedes, including the most vocal critics of the Swedish multinational companies, readily admit that Swedish prosperity is a direct result of the growth of Swedish multinational companies—the most rapid growth, by the way, of all multinationals in the 1960's.

Yet the fact that today there are many more non-Swedes working outside of

Sweden for Swedish-based companies than there are Swedes employed by these companies in Sweden also means that the top management of Sweden's biggest business must put non-Swedish concerns, non-Swedish markets, non-Swedish objectives ahead of Swedish concerns, Swedish markets, and Swedish objectives. Thus, a sovereign government, in the interest of its own economy, may have to subordinate its policy to the needs and welfare of businesses whose main interests are outside the country.

Multinationals are growing so large that they may soon face controls . . .

But big countries too have mixed feelings and vacillate between support of the multinational and hostility toward it. And the big nations, even more than the small ones, refuse to accept its reality and existence and behave as if there were only national economies wth national business.

The United States is probably the most parochial of all governments in its attitudes and policies. It does not even understand why other countries consider it American arrogance, if not "imperialist aggression," when the United States government cavalierly extends its policies and moralities to subsidiaries and affiliates of U.S. companies incorporated abroad—e.g., the ban on trading with Red China and the American antitrust ideas (totally alien to almost anybody else's approach to economic regulation)—or, as has happened a good many times, when it does the same thing to foreign parent companies of U.S. subsidiaries and affiliates.

But in such actions—actually a severe threat to immediate American economic interest and to the American balance of payments—the U.S. Government attitude is by no means atypical. De Gaulle was only more deliberate and more consistent in his refusal to permit any French company to become multinational and thus to extend its business beyond the boundaries of French sovereignty. He knew perfectly well that he took a serious risk of weakening France's economic position (as indeed he did); but that seemed to be a lesser risk than weakening French sovereignty and governmental control of French business.

There are proposals at present for the creation of a special international agency which would charter multinationals, thus making them "a-nationals." There are— perhaps more realistically—proposals for international treaties to spell out the rights and responsibilities of multinationals and to ensure uniformity of treatment. In almost every country, endless congressional or parliamentary hearings on the multinationals generate the most diverse proposals for laws to regulate them, and sharp conflicts of opinion regarding their benefits and their dangers. The next decade is almost certainly to produce substantial changes of the rules under which the multinationals operate.

Indeed the scope and regulation of the multinationals tomorrow may be called the 640-billion-dollar question of the world economy, for that may well be the volume of goods and services the world's multinationals are going to produce in a few more years if they are allowed to continue.

. . . but reality will prevail, and the multinational will become polycentric.

Some facts about tomorrow's multinationals are reasonably clear already. The reality of the world economy is not going to go away—and with it the forces that make multinationalism both economically necessary and economically rational and attractive. The nation state is also not going to go away; there is nothing on the horizon to take its place. But the multinational corporation, like the world economy in which it operates and world management which it represents, will become increasingly polycentric itself—with different situations, relationships, and policies in different countries, with many local variations in respect to regulations, to sources of finance, and even to ownership.

New Management Needs

And now that the management boom is fading, it is increasingly clear that in many areas—and not only in that of the multinational corporation—new needs for concepts, structures, design principles, and even basic management philosophy are emerging. It is also increasingly clear that management will no longer be a one-way street, and that American management has to learn as much from managements abroad as they have been learning from us.

Management, having become multinational,
may now become multi-institutional.

Traditional management has focused on the task of doing well what we already know and understand. But there is equal need for entrepreneurship and purposeful innovation, technical as well as social. (Ansoff, p. 35, refers to the need for entrepreneuring in management.) And for this we have neither principles nor structures as yet.

Nor do we know much about the management of public service institutions, such as hospitals, schools, government agencies, universities, and the like. Yet in every developed country these institutions are becoming more and more important. They are also increasingly becoming more management-conscious. Only a few years ago, for instance, the proud German Civil Service was sure that it knew all the answers in respect to its structures, its organization, and its management. But now one finds, for instance, in the old Free City of Hamburg, a "Management Institute" for the civil service, advanced management courses for senior officials, and such concern with the whole subject that one senior member of the city's governing senate has been put in charge of management.

Similar concern with the management of the public-service institution can be found elsewhere—from Japan to Australia, and from Great Britain to Los Angeles, California. It has even begun to be voiced in the Communist countries. Thus, Poland and Czechoslovakia are searching for new management principles and structures, and for measurements of managerial effectiveness and productivity in their public-service institutions.

And one crying need is for a new kind of institution altogether—the "intersect" institution. (See the chapter by Boulding.) How to set it up, how to structure it, how to set its objectives, how to measure it—in other words how to manage it—are all unresolved questions. Here, by the way, is one area where all of us can learn from the Europeans. The Germans, in particular, have long used such intersect institutions, and have done so more extensively and more imaginatively than anyone else, America included.

In the past, "management' 'has primarily meant "business management." In the future it is likely to concern itself increasingly with managing institutions of all kinds. Just as management has become *multinational,* it is likely to become *multi-institutional.*

Productivity is likely to become again a central challenge.

How can we control the peculiar disease of "stagflation" (i.e., stagnation *cum* inflation) which threatens the modern economy everywhere? Clearly, productivity is the only effective means. At the same time, productivity is becoming a problem because the cost center of a modern economy is shifting from the direct productive worker to the "knowledge worker." In the United States, for example, governments, education, and health care account together for about half of the GNP. Yet they employ few direct production workers.

But even in business the center is shifting. In the 1950's some management pundits said that middle management was becoming obsolete. It was at that point when the great expansion in middle management started; and it has not yet stopped. In the individual company, the shift in employment has been to a professional group corresponding to middle management—the cost accountant, the market researcher, the metallurgist, the quality control man, and now the environmental specialist. For the most part they did not exist in many companies 20 years ago. And this is not an American phenomenon; the same situation exists in most developed countries.

The problem is that to date substantially all the efforts to improve productivity have been focused on the production worker. The formulas that were derived after years of effort simply don't fit the new situation.

It is true that there has been a great increase in the kind of knowledge work which should be classified as "production," such as key punching or routine clerical functions. The fact that no molten metal flows does not change the circumstances, and the standard methods for improving productivity can be applied. The job of the secretary, however, cannot be measured by the number of letters typed per day—at least not if she is truly doing a secretarial job. The environmental specialist is not subject to routine measurement. No one really knows how the manager can be measured. Yet that is where the costs lie. The challenge to management will be to manage the knowledge worker and to make him effective.

New challenge: how to motivate and manage knowledge workers . . .

Altogether, managing the knowledge worker provides a new challenge for which traditional personnel management has few answers. How does one motivate people who have to motivate themselves to be productive? How does one recognize and reward people who neither want nor qualify for the traditional reward—i.e., "promotion" into a managerial job? Above all, how does one handle the central problem of the competent knowledge worker—boredom with his work—after early middle age?

Knowledge workers who do not rise to the top become intensely bored with time. The university professor, who at 29 was so imaginative, is half asleep at 45; he gives the same lecture on the American Constitution. The market researcher, who helped to market new gadgets so successfully 10 years ago, has lost interest by age 40. Yet both the professor and the market researcher are still in the prime of life mentally and physically, and both the university and the company have made substantial investments in them. They have simply had no challenges for years. It is not true that the majority of responsible middle managers are promoted to the level of their incompetence. Rather, they are bored stiff. What they need are second careers.

The military has recognized the problem in a fashion by requiring those above a specified age in a particular rank to quit, or by enabling others to take voluntary retirement. A large number of these men have found useful and responsible positions in a second career.

. . . and other special groups into which the labor force is segmenting itself.

But the knowledge worker is only one—though the most critical one—of the specific groups into which the labor force is segmenting itself, nowhere more than in the United States. There are also the blue-collar workers and the women, the "hard-core unemployable" and the minorities, and a growing number of permanent part-time workers (many with more than one part-time job at the same time). Each of these groups expects different things, needs different things, views its job and its management differently. Yet the traditional American approach, shared by management and unions, is to treat them all alike, have the same benefits for all, the same policies, the same rules. The only result is that benefits, policies, and rules fit no one group, and the one thing which is uniform is discontent.

Here we can learn a lot from others, and especially the Japanese. While the rigidity and hierarchical structure of the Japanese does not, of course, fit American ideals and traditions, the Japanese have evolved employment, pay, benefit, and retirement plans which recognize that different groups have different expectations, and that within each group different individuals have different needs according to their age and the life-cycle stage of their families. This way the Japanese have accomplished a very high degree of *economic* security for most workers—and, above all, almost complete *psychological* security—in glaring contrast with the United States, where very high actual job security for most workers, even nonunionized ones, is accompanied by almost general fear of insecurity.

Yet Japanese labor costs, despite "life-time employment," are amazingly flexible and may actually be more flexible than those of American unionized industry with its "supplementary unemployment compensation," tight job descriptions, jurisdictional restrictions, seniority rules on job placement, and so on—all unknown in Japan.

But there is also the new challenge of satisfying the growing demand for employee participation—the result, above all, of the growing educational status of the work force in all developed countries. It will have to be satisfied. But it should be satisfied in such a manner as to provide for employee responsibility as well as for employee rights.

The concept of decentralization, once so powerful, is now outmoded . . .

Powerful as has been the concept of decentralization, it was never universally applicable, and is less so today. It also is not, by itself, enough to make a company capable of organized purposeful innovation. So there is a whole raft of new needs in respect to management and organization structures.

Decentralization was first developed in the early 1920's (principally by Pierre du Pont at the Du Pont Company and by Alfred Sloan at General Motors) because the traditional functional organization proved unwieldy, rigid, and incapable of communicating, once a business grew beyond modest size. It is still true that functional organization does not work well—and often does not work at all—once a company grows to substantial size.

Yet decentralization in the classical form is often not applicable, either. It works only when individual parts of a business are truly "autonomous businesses" with their own markets and their own products. But this is true only of a minority of companies, and totally untrue in respect to most service businesses— e.g., the big commercial banks. Even in manufacturing it cannot be applied to process industries, such as steel, glass, or aluminum, where all products come out of the same process but go into an infinity of markets.

. . . is being replaced by new design principles, like "simulated decentralization" . . .

Perhaps the most rapidly growing new design principle is "simulated decentralization."

Two glass companies have, for example, set up manufacturing as a profit center having its own responsibility. Similarly, marketing is a separate profit center, and so is even research. This allows for many of the benefits of decentralization in terms of fixing responsibility and measuring results.

But, at the same time, it introduces new difficulties. It is elementary organizational hygiene to keep profit centers from constant frictional relationships. It is also a fundamental principle to minimize allocational accounting, yet in simulated decentralization most expenses must be allocated. It is even more basic to good management not to use transfer pricing because it is wasteful to have much of the energy of the organization devoted to petty metaphysical conflicts. There is nothing which can consume as much time and leave as lasting scars as a fight over a $1.80 allocation for a bottle of waterglass for the research lab.

Yet, despite these difficulties, simulated decentralization may well be the lesser evil in many cases. Thus, in banks and insurance companies, it is being used as the only way in which managers can be brought close to operational results. It is adaptable to establishing cross-functional cooperation, so that managers know to whom they contribute and on whom they must depend to get input. This, in itself, is an increasingly important need.

. . . and "task-force structures" (particularly useful in organizing innovation) . . .

Task-force structures came into being formally in undertaking large defense contracts which involved complex and costly development and production tasks. It was a method of harnessing specialized knowledge located in various parts of the organization for a common purpose. A new and transitory functional task force was created to accomplish the objectives of the particular contract, after which the team was disbanded.

It is now being recognized that the task force is a genuine principle of organization, although a difficult one because of the self-discipline required of all its members. There often are vital tasks to be done within an enterprise that are somewhat incompatible with the formal structure, which of course is designed for its main purposes. In such instances, permanent task force teams may be employed. The task-force team is particularly useful in organizing knowledge work. Top management increasingly is becoming a task-force team. And the innovative organization is, above all, a task-force structure.

. . . and "systems management" (particularly useful in operating multinational companies).

NASA was the prototype of the systems management principle in which a joint effort was carried forward under central direction by a group of separate organizations of many different kinds—government agencies, business enterprises, university labs, even individuals. The NASA effort was a highly specialized one; and putting a man on the moon would appear to bear little relationship to the goals of a business enttterprise. Yet systems management may prove to be exceedingly useful as a method of operating multinational companies.

Systems managements is a most difficult method to put into practice. It requires a great deal of understanding. But it allows for common operational control of a series of enterprises, diversely organized to fit the environmental circumstances.

It is also being recognized more and more that the marketing approach has really not been built into the organizational structure but was grafted onto a pattern which was the heritage of the production era. The basic problem is how to organize the resources so that they will converge upon the customer. To do so is likely to require more of a team approach through the use of organizational principles, such as the task force or systems management. Philips of Holland has taken such an approach in its complex multiproduct, multinational business, which is organized on a two-axis basis.

*The board of directors, as now constituted,
is not functioning effectively . . .*

The top management task and its structure require new thinking and new approaches. Perhaps the most urgent need is that of making top management clearly accountable to someone. The traditional board of directors, no matter how set up in different countries, is not functioning.

In almost every business catastrophe since the 1920's—American, British, German, Swedish, Italian—the directors have been the last to know that the company was in serious trouble. The tendency has been to blame the individual directors. But it is evident that there are serious and fundamental structural defects in the present concept of the board.

The board of directors, as it was conceived in the late nineteenth century, was established on the assumption that the company was small, that it was owned by three or four families, and that it was engaged in making a single product to be sold in one market, so that directors could understand the business. None of these assumptions has much validity in today's big publicly owned businesses.

It was also assumed that the directors would represent shareholders who, since their fortune was their investment in the company, would themselves take a deep interest in its administration. But most shareholders today regard themselves not as owners but as investors, and the last thing they want is to exercise ownership.

*. . . must be restructured to represent new
constituencies, perform its duties better.*

Management, like anyone holding power, must be responsible to a constituency. But the constituency is changing. In the early days of the industrial era there was no doubt as to the constituency—it was the owners of the business who must be satisfied. (Ansoff refers to the needs of various constituencies, p. 61.)

Later, as companies became public, management was considered responsible to the investors. But these days more and more groups consider themselves as "constituencies" to whom management should be held accountable or to whom at least it needs to listen—workers and women, consumers and minority groups, and many others.

Boards are already changing. In Germany there are laws providing for worker representation on the "board of supervisors" and, in some industries, for worker appointment as the company's chief personnel officer. In Sweden government has begun to put its appointees on the boards of big companies. In some Latin American countries laws have been passed for board representation of the "worker's community." In Yugoslavia worker councils are the official "board of directors." And in the United States, without any laws at all, more and more large companies are putting onto their boards representatives of the consumers, of minority groups, of women, and so on.

Yet both the function and the composition of an effective board still have to be thought through. What has been happening so far is largely politics or public relations. But the enterprise, modern society, and, above all, top management need more than a board that "looks right." They need a board that functions effectively.

Management must serve economic and social responsibilities at the same time.

Management, as it was taught and practiced in the management boom, concerned itself with building an effective business as measured by economic performance and economic results. What "economic performance" meant specifically was, as pointed out earlier, heavily colored by the economic realities in different cultures and countries. But few doubted that economic performance was the one appropriate yardstick for management and managers. In that respect there was, and still is, no difference between the "isms," either; the only point at issue between "capitalism" and "socialism" or "communism" is over the definition of "economic performance."

Management therefore could, and had to, be "technocratic," i.e., concerned with effectiveness and efficiencies within economic parameters. Noneconomic considerations were admitted as restraints, as qualifications, and as desirable "extras," but seen as peripheral at best.

Now the demand for social responsibilities is becoming irresistible. Increasingly, social (i.e., primarily noneconomic) objectives are put forth as overriding priorities. Chief among them is, of course, concern with the environment. But ecology is only one of the "qualities of life" for which management finds itself increasingly held responsible.

At the same time, management cannot abdicate responsibility for economic performance. Indeed, economic performance must remain management's first trust and primary concern. On it depends not only the standard of living of ordinary people, but the hope of the wretchedly poor of this world to develop a better economy and society for themselves. On it depends, above all, whether there will be jobs or not. The fact that the wage bill is roughly 20 times the size of all profits means that jobs and wages, rather than profits, are the main "product" of business. Today's profits are tomorrow's jobs; they provide the capital to finance new and better jobs.

Yet the responsibility for the "qualities of life" will have to be built into the management job also.

*In the United States business–government
relations must be tightened; overseas, loosened.*

Finally the relationship between business and government will have to be worked out and restructured in all developed countries.

Here, clearly, the Americans can learn a great deal from others, especially the Continental Europeans and the Japanese. The purely adversary relationship of the American tradition no longer works in the national interest. It is high time that a new relationship is structured, based on recognition by government that business is a national asset and a foundation of national security and prosperity, and on recognition by business that government is the legitimate leader of society. What is needed is a partnership rather than an adversary relationship.

But at the same time the mercantilist countries, too, have outgrown their traditional pattern in which business is an arm of national policy and government an arm of business policy. Just as business and government are too far apart in the American political tradition, they are too close, to cozy, too dependent on one another in the traditional political process of Continental Europe and of Japan. De Gaulle was quite right in his belief that the traditional French system was incompatible with a multinational company. He was only wrong—to the lasting detriment, perhaps, of the French national economy—in his decision to forbid French business from becoming European, let alone multinational, business.

What are needed, and aren't yet available, are new concepts of business-government relationships—concepts, so to speak, of "competitive coexistence" or of "creative tension," in this era of an emerging world economy, of worldwide social and economic needs, and polycentric management.

U.S. MANAGEMENT HAS LOTS TO LEARN—BUT IT'S STILL THE BEST

The management boom is fading. But it is leaving behind a solid achievement: the worldwide recognition of management as a crucial and vital function, as a major responsibility, and as a serious discipline.

Although the management boom was "made in America," one major result was to strengthen traditional and indigenous management concepts in the other developed countries. Even in the European satellites of the Soviet Union the conception of management has served to reemphasize those countries' traditional

Western heritage and to provide a focus of resistance against enforced "Russianization." Only in the Soviet Union itself is the very concept of management likely to bring with it "Westernization," likely to challenge fundamental traditions.

The manager everywhere—and the American manager in particular—will therefore have to learn to look upon management both as *universal*—as concerned with challenges, tasks, and opportunities that are common to modern society, and as possessing a common body of knowledge, generally applicable ways of thought and analysis, and common tools and methods—and, at one and the same time, as culturally conditioned and embedded in *national* values, traditions, perceptions, and structures. There is clearly no one universal management "model."

American management is no longer *the* management. The European manager has recovered self-confidence, and the Japanese manager has acquired (and earned) it.

Yet American management possesses very great advantages. It clearly is still the leader.

Perhaps the greatest management advantages of American business are the much larger number of competent and managerially trained middle managers (approached only by Japan), and the relative ease with which managerial and professional people can move between companies and within the management structure of a given company. Neither the Europeans (with their still quite rigid ideas of the "right" career ladders and their equally rigid, though rapidly narrowing, gap between "us" at the top and "them further down") nor the Japanese (with their strict seniority rules) enjoy these advantages.

Yet the American manager will have to learn from others in many areas—from top managerial structure to personnel policies to government-business relations—where others have a good deal to teach us. He should, however, also learn from management outside the United States, and from their behavior during the management boom, that the productive way to learn from others is not to imitate them. It is to emulate them by adapting their experience so as to make them fit one's own circumstances, needs, and values.

One conclusion stands out above all others: the demands of tomorrow, the new realities, the new needs, fully match what American managers were called upon to satisfy during the last 25 years. The management boom is over. Ahead is the era of management performance.

Contributors

Helpful comments and inputs from the following members of the author's panel are gratefully acknowledged (the author, however, assumes full responsibility for choice of content and interpretation).

MARGARET K. CHANDLER, Professor, Graduate School of Business, Columbia University

THE HONORABLE YASUHIKO NARA, Ambassador of Japan

ANTON PEISL, Board of Management, Siemens A.G., Munich

HOWARD F. VAN ZANDT, Professor, University of Texas, Dallas, formerly Vice President Far East, ITT.

The author wishes to acknowledge the support, encouragement, and counsel of Theodore A. Smith, Associate Director of the Management Study Project.

Management and Man

Methinks I bleed to death,
From so much sudden change.

—Bertolt Brecht
Edward II

THE purpose of this chapter is to sketch some aspects of the social landscape of post-industrial society, not as a blueprint, but as a basis for compelling the reader (whether he agrees with this view or not) to self-consciously examine his own view of our future society in the broadest possible terms.

Precise scenarios of the future are numerous. They range from grey-tone studies in totalitarianism and acute deprivation to utopian landscapes of thera-peutically nurtured appetites and their systematic gratification; from a lushly green landscape reflecting the Romantic tradition's wildest fantasies—a pastoral life without odors, inconveniences, or unpleasantness—to a setting of stream-lined humans in a stainless steel and plastic environment; from a planet suffo-cating with humanity to one emptied of its last vestiges.

To select any one version of the future would be little more than to play in an intellectual lottery of dubious value. What can and must be done is to begin to specify some of the major structural changes, many of which are evident in prototypical form in the world as we currently know it, that will play a signifi-cant role in shaping the future.

We must also bear in mind that among the factors which will shape that future will be the quality of thinking about it which we do in the present. No longer can we think in terms of facilitating or adapting to an inevitable out-come; nor can we, with the innocence of the eighteenth century, think in terms of some ultimate utopia that represents the goal of human history. We must now, with a sense of open-endedness, begin to think about alternative futures and about the intellectual and moral responsibility we have in selecting between such alternatives.

The contents of this chapter fall into three major sections. The first section deals with my own approach to thinking about the future. (Possibly because by its very nature futurist thinking ultimately is both projective and highly specula-tive it also runs the risk of being highly ideological; hence the reader needs to know the perspectives—and perhaps the biases—which underlie my predic-tions.) The second section presents a brief description and analysis of selected current trends within our society that are immediately expressive of the forces that both reflect and shape the new emerging social order, of course including management. The third and concluding section, with the preceding as a context, will deal directly with the future of management.

Thinking about the Future

The preceding decade has seen a growth of thinking and research in the area of the future; indeed it has almost achieved the status of a minor industry in its own right. Thinking on the topic has been in many instances richly and even boldly imaginative. However, the most consistently conservative—as well as the least developed—aspect of most of this work has been the treatment of man himself.

Even where the fact of change is accepted, man has placed that disturbing fact within the context of larger concepts that reinforced the much needed and consoling idea of continuity—i.e., that his existence, his works and inventions, as well as his progeny, would be meaningful and recognizable aspects of the invisible future. He has sought shelter in myths of historical progress and has justified these myths by refashioning history in order to make his time-bound idea of the Human the legitimate heir of the past and, as such, the exclusive gatekeeper of the future. (We learn to conform to divine intent by transforming the essential conceptions of the divine; the vengeful tribal god of the ancient Hebrews is transformed into the stern moral accountant of the Protestant Reformation, and then into the tolerant humanistic psychotherapist of an affluent and secular society.)

We must accept the fact that man is a variable, not a constant . . .

For the most part we still resist the idea of fundamental change, though the attempt becomes increasingly difficult, and surrender to change is, at best, uneven. We learn—however slowly—to accept change in the objects with which we live and the forms of organization within which we live, though there is constant resistance to even that—Consciousness Three being an attempt to prescribe the future through a rear-view mirror, the resurrection of nineteenth century Romanticism. But we avoid the more difficult confrontation with the possibility that man himself changes and can change both rapidly and in very fundamental aspects.

We still continue to construct universal models of man, universal models that look amazingly like our contemporary sense of ourselves. And while a universal model of man may promote desirable social attitudes (particularly through such notions as the brotherhood of man), it also promotes attitudes which create the illusion that there are limits to what man can do on this planet—if not this universe—and these limits rarely wander from images of life within which, at any one moment, we feel most at home.

This has been, to date, almost a universal response to the human condition, vacillating between change and stagnation and accounting for man's illusion that he can control the meaning of the monuments he insists on building at such great cost. For some this tends to be the shape of an enterprise, a name on corporate stationery, or merely the spine of a book. Ironically, the rhetoric of both the traditional businessman and revolutionary converge (both were raised in the same cultural milieu). In the language of a Fidel Castro, both feel that they will be "judged by history," i.e., a future time capable of appreciating their achievements, capable of understanding their motives.

Yet the most primitive understanding of world history suggests that change occurred despite most human societies' assumption of their own permanence—again, not necessarily in terms of costume, object, or architecture, but in terms of what they assumed were the essential and/or natural characteristics of man. Man in the past unself-consciously transformed the world; and, in turn, the world with equal unself-consciousness transformed man. For how many of us over the age of 35 is the world anything like we expected it to be when we were growing up? Indeed, how many of us are what we expected to be when we were growing up? Clearly the world that shaped our characters has been transformed in most critical dimensions.

. . . and also that the nature of change itself changes over time.

Learning to think about change—learning to test what appear to be time-proven and dependable assumptions about the necessary or desirable character-istics of either man or society—is as difficult as it is imperative. The hard fact is that the "wisdom of the ages" may prove to be of little value as guidelines to the future. In a world where almost half of the human beings who have ever lived on the planet are currently alive, the constantly changing nature of the game, the ball park, as well as the most basic rules, may require a more self-conscious abandonment of tradition, however comforting or consoling such tradition may be.

Complicating this problem of thinking about change is that the very capacity to think boldly about macro-social change almost presupposes a recognition of the fact that most currently held theories or models of change are much too simple and too rooted in an attempt to face the future by merely extrapolating from the past. The intellectual journey from the implicitly optimistic perspective of "culture lag" (i.e., problems of social and personality organization lagging behind the changes in technology), to the more ambivalent perspective of the current notion of "future shock" (i.e., the traumatizing effect of rapid techno-logical changes that assault the very capacity of personality and social organiza-tion to cope with change), reflects our increasing but somewhat reluctant recognition that change is a complex, multifaceted process where even the im-pact of various components in the change process changes.

From the vantage point of the *culture lag* concept, changing technology was a predominant and ultimately compelling force for change on the level of institutional organization (e.g., family, church, and government), and upon individuals (e.g., attitudes and values); and it seemed clear that these latter aspects of life would ultimately come to some accommodation with the needs of technology. Some part of this perspective obviously maintains continuing viability. Technology and technological innovation are a compelling force for change and, frequently, create pressure to change within fairly narrow limits. Inkeles's classic essay, "Industrial Man," points clearly to sociocultural convergences observable across cultures where nations with a comparable commitment to industrialization, despite their differing cultural histories, develop fundamental similarities.

In a very critical sense, technology is transcultural, requiring common cultural adaptations. At the same time, however, we have become increasingly aware that such common cultural adaptations may not allow us to describe the kinds of social worlds that will grow up surrounding and using identical technologies. Drucker's contribution to this volume speaks very eloquently to precisely this point. The translation of the pressures of technological development into concrete patterns of social life and individual existence is complex and varied.

Man changes his world and, in turn, is himself transformed.

It is, for example, relatively easy to raise children who look and act much the same way we do *if* we similarly resemble our fathers. To the degree that we do not resemble our fathers, this becomes more difficult because we were in the first instance the end product of a relationship that the very fact of our existence alters.

Much the same can be said of the problems of top maangement. The generations of management over the past century represent a series of expanding perspectives that produced a highly adaptive dynamic. This occurred, however, within the context of relative continuity, particularly in the quality of life in the surrounding society. And that also generated considerable conflict and strain. The changes anticipated for the near future appear to be of even less continuity, with dramatic change occurring both in terms of what man does and of what he is.

One of the major obstacles to predicting, understanding, or even merely describing social change is that it occurs unevenly. In the complexity that is modern urban-industrial society, we find the past, the present, and the future competing for space within the same historical moment. A casual stroll through any major American city will bring the walker to sights and sounds that with few differences could be found in Dickens's descriptions of Victorian London; and in many instances these will be found in close proximity to an alternate set of sights and sounds that resemble the best dreams, or worst nightmares of our utopian thinkers.

We must all be familiar with one or another company that maintains and is sustained by the twenty-first century technology, operating within the context of organizational structures and principles that developed during the present era and are presided over by a management that could be charitably described, in terms of mentality, as nineteenth century. There also are some young people whose characters and sense of what the world ought to be is still locked into the mold of the nineteenth century, while some of the most extreme innovators in personal and social styles are men and women of advanced age.

The future often becomes familiar while the past still is viewed as permanent. As a result, little one way or the other can be proven by recourse merely to example; it is critical that we learn to look at social change in the way that it happens—historically, and in a multifaceted and highly interactive context.

The Social Landscape

The term "post-industrial" describes more than the changing character of technological processes, and even more than the changing character of the organizational structures that transform mute technology into social and economic enterprises. It necessitates a concern for potential changes in the entire fabric of social life. It is not unreasonable to assume that the full emergence of post-industrial society will occasion changes as vast and profound in their implications as those that accompanied the emergence of industrial society.

In the Post-Industrial Era, even the "unchangeables" are subject to change.

A number of major aspects of social life, all in the process of transformation, and all highly interactive (some perhaps being little more than different ways of looking at the same phenomena), constitute the "master trends" we must consider in order to fill in gross outlines of the emerging post-industrial society. We will begin with those seemingly most rooted in the "unchangeable": (1) *the life cycle,* (2) *sex or gender roles,* and (3) *the family.*

THE LIFE CYCLE: BEING RECYCLED

Freud observed that one of the three aspects of the human condition that constituted the basis of man's permanently tragic existence was his inability to control his own biology—the inability to stop the process of birth, growth, and inevitably decay that is life as we know it. While this in its ultimate sense remains unquestionably true, it really tells us very little about just how the period intervening between birth and death will be divided.

Chronological age in different societies, as well as in different periods in the history of the same society, suggests vastly different capacities. The contemporary upper-middle class female of 15 or 16 years is unprepared, at least psychologically, for sexual intercourse, while her counterpart no more than 200 years ago might well have already been married and possibly had her first child. The life cycle as a series of distinct stages, often associated with biological change, turns out to be rather flexible.

For industrial societies the most dramatic and possibly the most significant of several recent modifications of the life cycle was the invention of youth. Still undergoing the vagueness of continuing change at both ends and somewhat unevenly granted to different segments of our population, youth generally runs from mid-adolescence well into the years of young adulthood. This is a time when young people are allowed to begin to experiment with serious activities and experiences without the necessity of serious consequences, a phenomenon that Erikson has defined as a "psychosocial moratorium." Partly expressive of the affluence generated by industrial societies, the main job of this age and social group, Kenniston argues, is to play. This new, or relatively new, social form has many consequences, one of which is of singular importance for our present concern.

For the first time in human history, we have generated a significant part of a generation who have been allowed to experiment with and develop a repertoire of adult gratifications without having to first earn the right to such gratifications.

It also must be noted at the outset that this phenomenon occurs precisely among that segment of the society from which managerial elites have generally been recruited. The effects of this development, as we are already beginning to observe in our own children, are numerous. The single most important effect, given our present purpose, is to alter the motivation to achieve. Access to such gratifications—travel, exotic experience, frivolous consumption, etc.—were previously the rewards selectively allocated to those who "succeeded," frequently after years of striving, self-denial, and hard work.

Indeed, for previous generations, the very attractiveness of such gratifications had little to do with their intrinsic qualities and could become the focus of a great amount of energy merely because they stood as public symbols of achievement and success. In worlds where there was great competitiveness and limited access to distinguished success, the availability of such gratifications was secondary to that for which they stood.

The theme has become: "different strokes for different folks."

Now many young people experience them directly and test their worth existentially—not as symbols of something else, but as experiences. The criteria for evaluation increasingly become personal rather than social; i.e., activities become important, not because they stand for something in society, but because they are "their thing," and relevance increasingly refers to the personal and immediate rather than the social and programmatic.

The organizing time-frame of reference of the society—or of critical sub-populations—begins to shift from future-oriented to present-oriented; similarly, the pivotal metaphors that organize a sense of self shift from predominantly social (i.e., "What does the world expect of me?") to predominantly personal or privatized (i.e., "What do I expect of the world?"). In the very testing of the rewards that society used to hold out to its achievers—testing in a context where their value was not inflated by the implicit price tag of time spent in pursuit—many of them were found wanting. Included in this were many things that were previously labeled "conspicuous consumption." Others were found to have been attractive, but not worth the price a society seemed to demand for their legitimate possession.

As a result, work or careers or vocations are increasingly seen not merely as a means of achieving ends—power, money, status—but as a state of being that has to have its existential or experiential pay-offs in the here and now.

This shift calls into question the motivations to work, how individuals will work, and for how long they will work. The very notion of a career where duties at any one point are partially evaluated in terms of some ultimate destination, central to most conceptions of "careers" in professional management, is also called into question.

Implications for management: The new
generation of managers will be nonconformist.

It may be this development that becomes a major factor in the creation of a managerial "generation gap." There are three aspects of this potential problem:

1. There may have to be a greater emphasis upon the activities of work itself as an experience that affords an opportunity to develop and display individual competence, as against a more traditional apprenticeship approach of "learning the ropes." We must also expect a more critical response, one that less immediately accepts the wisdom of previous experience.

2. Outside of work, the potential managerial cadres will also be more experimental with regard to life-style commitments. Just as work itself is viewed in terms of the quality of experience that it affords in the here and now, the full range of social activities that make up one's life will be measured in terms of experiences afforded. In a curious way, the impulse to experiment outside the world of work, and its attending capacity for nonconformity, may create a wider gap than that which occurs in the job context.

3. The effect of these changes upon an older generation of executives can only be intense and, unfortunately, highly defensive. The very effect of such changes will be to appear to radically devalue the price tag of success. A part of a generation of top managers that paid for advancement by "toeing the line" both on the job and in their private lives cannot help but be threatened by and resistant to such changes.

SEX ROLES: ABOUT TO MERGE

If any one aspect of life appears more rooted in the stabilities of "the laws of nature" than the life cycle, it is the distinctions we make in terms of gender or sex role differences. "Man's natural tendencies . . . woman's characteristics . . . the mothering instinct . . ." Phrases like these and many more continue to characterize much of popular speech and too much of scientific discourse. However, as with the life cycle, there is just too much cross-cultural and historical variation in the components of gender roles (masculinity and femininity) to maintain a position in which there are critical differences between the capacities of men and women that are fixed by nature.

Possibly because gender identification is fixed at very early ages (as the best recent studies suggest), possibly because sex or gender role distinctions permeate almost all of the activities that constitute the mundane details of hour by hour existence, possibly because they are linked to unchanging attributes of the body, gender roles may be the slowest changing of all the dimensions of social or psychological life we will be considering. However, given the dramatic changes that the history of industrial societies contains, plus the changes that continue to occur (some as delayed responses to changes that have already occurred), this may be the very aspect of social life where the pressure to change may be the greatest.

The myth of "eternal man and eternal woman" is being challenged.

Most industrial societies—indeed perhaps all societies—have reached a point where they can ill afford to have approximately half their populations feel that they are only fulfilling nature's fixed destiny for them when they are wiving and/or mothering. The specialization of work, the growth of child care institutions, and the "automating" of household activity increasingly empty these roles of too much content; in the near future this conception of a woman's place will command only the resigned, the needlessly dependent, or the defective.

Men's situation is little better. Many of the attributes of masculine role performance were linked to the requirement of struggle for survival that consumed massive amounts of both energy and time—a quality of struggle that industrial society fundamentally changed and that post-industrial society promises to render almost obsolete. As the dimensions of the social worlds within which men live (the communities they live in, the organizations they work for) increase in size, it becomes harder to experience them as social realities; and, as a result, personal aspects become increasingly salient. For example, as the amount of time and energy required for their "breadwinning" activity diminishes, they must turn to social situations where many of their most significant masculine attributes become not only inappropriate but potentially crippling. This will become more apparent in our discussion of the changing family.

An additional factor contributing to this impending revolution in sex role stereotyping is the emergence of youth and youth culture. Previously, one of the main reinforcements of sex role stereotypes or identities was their ability to facilitate the realization of important sociocultural goals. A man had to be a man among men in order to earn or legitimate his possession of the good life. Similarly, females in a world where men believed the lyrics to "the girl that I marry must . . ." had to be feminine-plus in order to "hook" the man who would provide access to that good life.

Now the world of the middle class young permits both sexes greater amounts of cross-gender activity. The males are too young to work, and the females too young to marry; together they share and develop increasing appetites for activities, behavioral styles, and emotional expressions that are not segregated by sex—e.g., males rational/females emotional; males object-oriented/females interpersonally oriented; males aggressive/females passive. Such rigid sex distinctions, while still evident in our society, show signs of weakening among just that part of present-day youth who may be most prototypical of the future.

Implication for management: more women
in men's jobs, more men dissatisfied.

Most management roles, as with all except specially defined occupations, tend to be designed to reinforce stereotyped concepts of what masculinity involves. At one time, these occupational definitions may have actually represented requirements of the job—but no longer. Increasingly, and particularly on the level of the executive, we masculinize job descriptions, not because they require men, but in order to allow the occupants to feel like men. In a sense, we have not masculinized those jobs; we have over-masculinized them.

An upcoming generation may not only provide increasing numbers of women capable of handling such positions, but also an increasing number of talented men who will be unwilling to pay the price of being harnessed to a narrow and constraining definition. Moreover, those that do both fit the over-masculinized definition *and* want it, may in fact be among the least sensitive to the needs of new styles of management.

THE FAMILY NO LONGER "NUCLEAR"

Once again, while the family appears among the most enduring of all human institutions, we also sometimes tend to mask a dramatic amount of variability behind that simplifying label. As we have already suggested, a transformation of basic family structure was one of the major consequences of the emergence of industrial society, altering both its composition and its relationship to the economy. With diminishing moral and economic supports to family life (as post-industrial societies heighten existing tendencies towards both secularization and affluence), the family unit may become in one sense less important and in another sense more important.

It will become less important as it ceases to be the central economic unit (already true for productive activity and increasingly true for consumer activity), the central social welfare unit; and even the basic socializing institution (as the number and importance of extrafamilial socializing agents, such as schools, peer groups, and mass media, intervene earlier and earlier in the lives of young people). On the other hand, it will become more important as the context within which personal needs can be expressed—needs which are generated by the movement towards post-industrial life styles.

The family now has time to attend to one another's needs . . .

We see this problem as already part of the contemporary social landscape. Industrial society, which was accused of taking people away from the family, actually increased the amount of time people could spend within the family, and particularly increased the amount of time that was not bound up with routine activities, but time free to attend to one another's needs.

Indeed, this freedom shapes the most basic problems in family life and in the maintenance of family stability. Previously families were bound together by economic necessity, the need to maintain social status, and a round of trivial or banal activities; now families must face having to be meaningful people to one another (being an adequate breadwinner or a competent household manager may not be enough), and that is something we were rarely trained to handle. Now husbands and wives and children, as the latter approach adolescence, must really learn to be intimate in a psychological rather than a physical sense. More than fulfilling societal expectations with regard to being a good spouse or a good parent, we learn—however painfully—to ask (much like the young): What's in it for us? Does my wife really know me? Do my children?

Additionally, effective learning of narrowly formulated sex roles, which made women and men appear complementary, becomes insufficient, as both are encouraged to express a much broader range of emotional or personal needs and modes of expression. Among the affluent and well educated in the current population we can see expressions of the strain engendered by this transitional stage as many find themselves drawn to the "encounter movement," and other variants of the humanistic psychologies, in order to overcome traditional training that served to constrain rather than facilitate the expression of feelings.

It is not only the surviving aspects of social life that remain from remote history which prove inadequate to the demands of the new society; those that represent the expression of very recent history also are deficient. An excellent example is the case of the "nuclear family," itself an invention of urban-industrial life.

The "nuclear family," generally consisting of the marital pair and their pre-adult children, effectively freed many from the constraints of an extended family appropriate to rural, small-town settings.

But it also depended upon a new order of stabilities; it was assumed that there would be limited career and residential mobility and that personalities would remain comparably stable. Much of psychology, reflecting the historical moment, developed ideals of personality development that pointed to the development of a stable and fixed identity as being normal, healthy, and necessary for the full realization of adult status; similarly "scientific" approaches to marriage focused upon learning how to match psychological attributes of potential marital partners as if such attributes of personality or character were relatively permanent.

Moreover, the assumed stability and universality of sex role distinctions informed and shaped a sense of complementary or matching needs that would bind a husband and wife as if each were incomplete without one another.

However, major shifts in the very organization of social life will call much of this into question; indeed, it is already being called into question as there appears general agreement that the nuclear family is "in trouble," is in many ways inadequate to meet the social and psychological needs of many living today.

. . . and will share more and more
experiences (but very flexibly).

One solution offered to this growing crisis in the contemporary family, as recently suggested by Margaret Mead, is a return to the extended family that we knew in a more agrarian or pre-industrial society. This solution is utopian, since it requires moral, economic, and social pressures alien to both industrial and post-industrial society. As post-industrial society increasingly frees people from narrow sex role alternatives and a limitation on the number of roles one can play both in work related and in non-work related spheres, it will be the more ephemeral life style commitments that will bind individuals together; and the possibility that two or more individuals will maintain sufficiently identical profiles of such commitments is fairly low. A great deal of middle-class divorce American-style seems to involve two adults who, while still liking each other, come to realize that they in fact share very little in common, having grown either at different rates or in different directions.

The family will grow larger, we suspect, in the sense that more individuals will be sharing experiences on an intimate basis; it will grow more flexible as the ways men and women "put their games together" will increase, as "where their heads are at" becomes more a dynamic process, and will reflect a capacity or desire not merely to select from this increased number of alternatives, but to sample many of them.

Just as man learns to live with change, with temporary objects, temporary housing, temporary community, and even a temporary sense of himself (learning to accept and utilize his essentially unfinished nature), he will also possibly learn to live comfortably with temporary or provisional relationships at the very core of his social life. The family, then, may also become more temporary, resembling somewhat the "serial monogamy" currently so common, though, hopefully, with far less economic, social, and emotional dislocation than is presently observable.

*Implication for management: the family will demand
more of the executive's commitment.*

Changing patterns of family life have both a general and a very specific implication. The general implication deals with social change in a most fundamental way: the forms of change most likely to become a firm part of our collective future are those that are transmitted through and reinforced by the family. The family will remain for the conceivable future that major character-forming agency even of post-industrial society.

Specifically, this concerns the role of the family in the life of the executive. It is, after all, only recently that management theory took into account the role of the family in determining success or failure on the executive level. Even then, the family was viewed in terms of its ability to facilitate the career of the husband/father; family life and styles were to be organized with the husband/father's career needs as pivotal. The future may provide us with a situation where the family, despite (or perhaps because of) its unpredictability, commands more of the executive's commitment, as it provides more of his immediate rewards—a situation that reverses so much of the present, where careers are evaluated in terms of the strains they create for family life.

While this might well produce lower levels of commitment (though not necessarily), as well as requiring greater flexibility in the load placed upon executives, it also mitigates against the executive who is married to his job, a style frequently associated with the dangerously obsessional.

But this may be enough to establish that more than mere change of organizational styles and strategies alone must be considered; that we must begin with a sense of change potential in the most critical of all variables—man himself. Additional examples of changes and their implications could have been cited— for example, the extension of viable capacities at the farthest end of the life cycle; or the possible narrowing of generational differences as the period of years during which individuals can share comparable activities, friends, and social locations increases at both ends. It might result, for example, in children and parents spending much of their lives sharing comparable interests.

Human Vision and Social Values

Though social historians continue to argue the question of the predominant direction of influence in the relationship between technological change and changes in values and ideologies, most agree that the emergence of industrial capitalism and Protestant or Puritan values occurred coincidentally. Central to this value orientation was the "Protestant work ethic" and the extension of that ethic to non-work spheres of social and personal life. As Max Weber observed, the Protestant Reformation destroyed the walls of the monastery, and made the entire world a monastery. That is, almost all activities—including all activities previously defined as profane—were charged with moral significance and became occasions when the individual's moral worth was being tested.

The "Protestant work ethic" persisted as
the Western World became more secularized . . .

With increasing secularization, the basic content of this value orientation was translated into appropriately secularized language: the notions of *prudence* (husbanding carefully that with which one was endowed by God), and of *success* (finding concrete evidence of one's state of grace), became transformed into *adequate super-ego formation* (the capacity for delayed gratification) and *fulfillment of achievement need* (the underachiever no longer being a sinner, but merely a psychological casualty). In a world where industrialism created new standards of living and where the role of consumer became almost as important as the role of producer, new capacities for pleasure were accepted; but the Puritan spirit persisted in that such pleasures had to be earned and, if possible, justified by being made to serve the serious aspect of life.

Central to this approach to life is the idea that men (particularly men) should have serious work to do in the world and that, if possible, they should leave their mark upon the world. Thus, it is not sociologists alone who ask, "What do you do for a living? What is your occupational label?" And, as the history of sociological research over the past third of a century abundantly demonstrates, once we know that, we also know a great deal in addition about the person. Occupation is how men and families are linked to an industrial society. For the middle class, work is defined as a career, a calling, a vocation, something that would serve as an organizing pivot for the bulk of one's adult life, providing the markers by which basic worth is to be measured.

"Making it," as a major part of the ethos of industrial society, tied together the need for prudence (or delayed gratification) and a commitment to work, as the ultimate goals we project into an uncertain future that would exhaust a lifetime's effort. Much of what one did, including a substantial amount of self-denial (indeed, the greater the self-denial, the more heroic the effort), had to be justified in terms of some future reward.

. . . *but now it faces a tug-of-war between*
self-discipline and self-gratification.

One problem on the human level, however, was that it was difficult to train individuals to both self-discipline *and* a capacity to experience directly the rewards of achievement. Waiting and struggle often make the reward more significant than it can ever be as an experience. We are all familiar with one or more acquaintances who have been utterly demoralized by their inability to translate their achieved statuses into an effective life style. In previous periods this may have been less of a problem, since the mere effort to achieve frequently consumed so much of the individual that there was too little "leftover life to live" to give rise to that demoralization. Or, in a world where too few actually "made it," one could bask in the self-satisfaction that derived from the large numbers surrounding one who had not yet made it.

This Puritan work ethic also facilitated capital formation; not only did it celebrate the value of accumulating a capacity for pleasure and self-indulgence (wealth), but even more it celebrated the greater display of self-discipline and moral worth expressed by not spending that capacity frivolously. It was all right to endow good works (most typically, buildings carrying one's name into the future), but even more desirable was the training of one's heirs to carry on and expand that burden of unspent capacities for pleasure, with an equal commitment to seeing it grow and multiply.

However, as I have already suggested, the very conditions of life make it more difficult for the young to willingly accept this burden, which becomes one of the strains creating pressure for change. Growing numbers of the young have now come to reevaluate traditional conceptions of work and its significance as they first learn to work at their play (and it is significant how seriously and energetically they go about it) and, subsequently, expect the right to seriously and energetically play at work.

The individual worker can be effective
in narrow areas, change jobs often . . .

There are three factors increasing pressures for change: (1) the changing character of technology, (2) the growth of knowledge, and (3) the ways both technology and knowledge are organized. All three combine to make general competence difficult to achieve; even in relatively specialized areas, subspecializations proliferate esoteric requirements.

However, all three also make it possible to be effective with relatively narrow competencies. This is not unlike the model of the assembly line, where workers quickly trained to limited skills effectively participate in what is a relatively complex process. Thus, workers within complex technologies or science factories find themselves, while on an absolute level possessing profoundly more skill and knowledge than the assembly line worker, relatively in much the same relationship to the larger organizational structure within which they work.

This will not be true of all jobs, but it is, or is in the process of becoming, true for a predominant number of workers on all social levels. This, in turn, should make it more difficult to sustain the notion of a single career either in the same job and/or with the same employer; labor-force histories may well take more of a horizontal profile than a vertical one, with a single individual working at a number of dramatically different jobs during his life. Even where agreement with this possibility occurs, it is not uncommon that some seek exemption, preserving an existing position in one or another profession—usually one's own. Some professions, such as law, medicine, as well as top management, do pose special problems (as well as greater powers of resistance), but it is hard to conceive of these not being touched by this kind of development.

. . . but he will feel that the importance of work per se *is diminishing.*

Much of the current discussion about job dissatisfaction focuses on how to enhance the "humanization" of work. Strategies most frequently suggested involve a rejection of technical efficiency for greater personal involvement in larger processes; a reduction of the size of organizations to a point that allows for participatory democracy; or "meaningful" participation in decision making at *all* levels of organization. The entire approach assumes that work would remain central to most people's lives, as well as occupying the largest amount of time.

What we have been suggesting, on the other hand, is that the potential diminishing of the importance of work *per se*—through a man's being less chained to any one job, and the weakening of the relationship to other aspects of life style—will not only make this a less urgent question; it will also pose in equally urgent ways the problem of humanizing the non-work aspects of life.

It must be remembered that we have been "trained" for a long time to work; we have rarely, if ever, been trained to fully live in other ways. (One wonders, for example, how much of the expressed discontent of younger workers is not wholly a response to the job as such, but also includes a frustration with having to cope with the larger social world and new kinds of opportunities and demands made upon them and for which they have been ill trained to respond.) And, returning to an earlier theme, many of these opportunities and demands involve responses that are inconsistent with their own fairly rigid and equally narrow sense of sex role expectations.

MEN AND OBJECTS

Even more offensive to the Puritan spirit than having something less than a serious commitment to one's vocation is disregarding the intrinsic value of things. As John McHale, one of the authors of the present volume, noted some time ago, man's characteristic environment has been one in which objects were assumed to be more enduring than he was; and only recently, possibly since the end of World War II, has this been significantly reversed.

Clearly, the landscape of Post-Industrial societies will represent an increase in man's durability over the things he creates. For industrial societies and before, the greater durability of things gave to those things the ability to express moral significance and to bestow that significance upon their possessors. Things as possessions could, in many instances, become the measure and significance of life itself, justifying an entire lifetime's labor. And the possession of these attributes powerfully shaped our motives, even those seemingly linked to our primordial origins, such as sex. For two or more generations in American society, the automobile significantly played this kind of role.

Needless to say, it was the symbolic value of things that created the very strong relationship between occupation or social status and life style. However, the very technological capacities of a Post-Industrial society, as it produces more and better at lower cost, tends to reduce the significance, particularly the moral significance, of things or objects. Objects being more replaceable, having a potentially shorter existence, are less likely to serve this moral function, and they are far less likely to serve as powerful motivating forces in their own right.

In the same process, Post-Industrial society also alters substantially the traditional relationship between work and life style, as individuals with different occupations can increasingly share comparable life styles. In addition, as objects lose some of their moral significance, both work and income become even less able to predict life styles. The plastic nature of the objects generated by post-industrial technology—which should include not only the things or objects we live with, but also the larger structures around us—makes life styles as flexible and varied as the jobs it creates. Men and women need no longer be locked into single careers, into narrow sex-role definitions of what one can be or do—or, for that matter, into the house one lives in, the furtniture one fills it with, or even the community or region where one resides.

The result may be the release of man from the totalitarianism of society.

The picture that emerges suggests both a new kind of man in the future and a continuing crisis for man as we currently know him.

The possibility of a social life that can be holistically experienced (or even fully comprehended) becomes impossible or nearly impossible in a social order that increasingly is organized on a global and potentially superglobal basis, though many of our traditional values insist that this is precisely the arena within which serious man realizes his destiny. The earlier image of mass society tended to be more frightening to intellectual aristocrats who had this commitment to serious work (leaving your mark upon the world) than it did for more ordinary people.

As the scope of social life expands, the need and ability to organize lives in more personal terms increases. What could happen is the potential release of man—particularly serious man—from the ultimate totalitarianism that has characterized most of human history: the need to serve society, to live at ease in a world where there may not be any purposes larger or more compelling than his own. A world begins to emerge where things, relationships, environments, and even other people become freely substitutable; and the closest things man may be able to treat as a constant he may have to find within his own changing character; a temporary society containing temporary people—as if we have ever been anything else. These represent challenges to management—on all institutional levels—more complex than any yet known.

Management in the Future

Across institutional spheres such as industry, commerce, government, and education, industrial society has already pushed management toward becoming increasingly abstract or, in a sense, content-free. Thus important managerial levels of industry X once reflected the specific content and history of X, and were trained to that capacity by the experience within industry X. Managers generally found themselves having more in common with other workers on many different levels within that industry (having shared a common history) than they did with persons of comparable position in other industries or institutional settings; in effect, the frame of reference was vertical, and the basis of identification specific.

Industrial society has already altered this pattern (and Post-Industrial society should witness a further step in the same direction); now the frame of reference is more horizontal and the basis of identification specific not to the enterprise but to the more general attributes of the particular job. The contemporary professional manager increasingly learns competencies that are applicable to a wide range of industries and adapts them to the specific content of that industry. What we are describing is a situation where the individual finds that he has more in common with people doing the same things in other settings (and possibly more loyalty to their problems) than he has with those within the same organization.

The future is for managers who only know how to manage . . .

As organization becomes both more complex and sub-specialized, the major function of management is to make committing decisions, while the range of possible alternatives from which decisions must be selected is narrowed by the very complex structure of the surrounding organization and the resultant dependence upon others for information and knowledge. This is why, to paraphrase Einstein, the closer to the board room one gets, the emptier the world becomes.

There is an almost direct analogy here with the practice of medicine, where the elaboration and rate of growth of specialized knowledge make it virtually impossible for a single doctor to have meaningful general competence and, simultaneously, where technological and scientific developments have made it possible for persons with limited knowledge and, possibly, limited training to carry out important and, in some aspects, relatively complicated medical tasks. What is already happening is a recasting of the role of the physician; he is becoming a medical tactician who manages a medical health system composed of specialized professionals (perhaps trained only in their particular specialization), paraprofessionals, and technicians, and who, like many of today's managerial cadres, is competent not because of what he knows, but because of his ability to assimilate and utilize the immediately relevant knowledge of others.

. . . and who would rather be right than chairman of the board.

Such developments should, on the one hand, create a managerial role of somewhat diminished importance—one in which there is maximal substitutability, as well as one that requires limited specialized training and can be prefaced or followed by a large number of career patterns. On the other hand, within somewhat narrowed confines, there is also greater freedom to innovate.

At this point, we come very close to Ansoff's notion of the Post-Industrial managers as having a greater capacity for "risk taking" (see p. 22ff.). The sources or potential sources of this "freeing up" are several. One such factor is the lessening of the monetary or status incentives, as well as a commitment to a vertical career. This, in turn, allows the individual to approach his task in terms of the experiences it provides rather than in terms of its utility as a staging area for his assault on the next rung of the ladder; he will be potentially less self-protective. (For some there is continuing belief in the notion that it would be the incentive aspects of work that would produce innovation. However, experience dictates that, rather than producing innovation, more often it has produced conformity and timidity.)

Another aspect of a changing attitude toward work should be a greater willingness to accept change in the very changes for which one had previously been responsible. A deemphasis of status achievement is also likely to make it difficult for the individual to passionately organize his life around a single enterprise, such that his mark upon it becomes "his" monument, if not "his" tombstone. This does not necessarily mean less responsibility, but a different kind of responsibility. Such executives will be freer to admit mistakes or, more importantly, admit that yesterday's right answers may be today's wrong answers.

THE STYLE OF MANAGEMENT

A major component in the development of management science during our not too distant past involved a concern for the self-conscious recognition of "human relations" factors. Man, we discovered, had to be approached as self-consciously as we learned to approach the organization of technology during an even earlier period. To understand the style of management to come requires a comparison of the motivation to work in Industrial and Post-Industrial societies.

Management in Industrial society could predicate its approach to its employees upon the following assumptions (though some of these may have already begun to shift for particular segments of the population, particularly among the young): (1) there was a monetary incentive, i.e., one worked in order to live with comfort and dignity; more importantly, (2) one worked—particularly males—because having a vocation was important to his own sense of worth and seriousness, because this was linked to his very sense of self as a man, and because he was rarely trained to do anything else. There was additionally a commitment to long-term career goals, such that potentials or prospects in the distant future could be powerful incentives to energetic conformity in the present. These assumptions, however, may well be increasingly called into question by the environment of Post-Industrial society both as it emerges and as it is already part of our collective existence.

The goal is to "humanize" work, but this may turn out to be impossible.

Many view this as the almost impossible (and, potentially, extremely expensive) task of "humanizing work." In the language of Erich Fromm, a major critic of industrial society, work must be both democratized and eroticized; it must represent a context where the worker can experience the "joys" of free and meaningful cooperation and also self-actualization. But this is only partially valid. It assumes—as has been historically true—that work remains the central core of personal and social life. And this need not be the necessary pattern for Post-Industrial society *or the forms of social life that will follow it.*

As (or if) we develop a capacity to find non-work both personally and socially important and gratifying, the effects we require from the work experience can radically shift. In such a context, a great deal of what presently is defined as dehumanizing can be tolerable and for some—during all or parts of their work history—even attractive. It may become even more acceptable or attractive in a context where such work does not too restrictively define access to life-style alternatives, or where it is not necessarily defined as permanent.

These potential motivational changes will undoubtedly create new problems for management and, indeed, to some degree may already be occurring and creating new problems. The absence or lessening of economic sanctions, status distinctions, and new expectations should produce work groups who are far harder to discipline, but who also have a comparably greater, *though less overdetermined,* involvement with the job.

Management approaches will have to be in most instances far less arbitrary. The general effect of hierarchy alone should be less effective in realizing compliance. Authorities, on all levels, may have to be prepared to explain and defend orders *to* subordinates. This, of course, increases the risk that some part of the time they may be proven wrong or in error. They will be in effective command less, and lead more. But this may be seen as another aspect of the new "risk-running" capacity of Post-Industrial management; risk running must be seen not only in terms of establishing goals, but also in the very process of activity. This also assumes greater involvement on the part of the managers—

involvement not in the sense of involvement in a long-term career, but involvement in the activity in question.

In fact, elitism may replace democracy on all but trivial matters.

Much of what we have said would appear to support the contention of Bennis and Slater that what we have been calling Post-Industrial society becomes by definition a democratic social order, as well as meeting Fromm's requirement for the democratization of work. This fact is partially true: democracy, or its appearance, on all work levels undoubtedly will increase; the work group—be it on the level of the production floor or the executive suite—will be more collegial, casual, and provisional, with competence and cooperation replacing the arbitrary exercise of authority.

At the same time, however, unless the retrogressive impulse toward decentralization without regard to integration is accomplished and work remains the predominantly important and serious focus of adult life, increased elaboration of technology should require the size of organizations correspondingly to increase in size and geographical spread (though the size of subunits may remain small or become smaller). This, in turn, will require integrative decision-making at increasingly remote levels. This clearly represents a considerable pressure toward elitism with respect to important decisions, leaving democracy to flourish on immediately personal, but somewhat trivial, levels. It may be possible to democratize these larger structures, but that remains, at best, problematic.

Men and societies adapt; they transform themselves more often than they disintegrate. Men will learn in new ways to manage new situations. And if our particular vision of aspects of that transformation turns out to be inaccurate, one thing is still clear: that the emergent form which management takes may no more resemble the contemporary version than that version resembles its nineteenth century predecessors. Which brings us to our final question, the role of present-day management in "managing" the continuing transition.

MOTIVATION TO MANAGE

Given the potential validity of our description of Post-Industrial man, the life styles available to him, and the structure of values that Post-Industrial society generates, it is probable that the management role will be dramatically transformed, particularly in ways that make it more accessible to those sharing some of the dominant values of the society. This means, in turn, that it will allow for effective performance despite wide varieties of previous experience and limited prior training, and that it will call for something less than a predominant and nearly lifelong commitment.

This redefinition of the executive function would clearly deny it much of its present claim for significance and glamour; moreover, it would deny much of its claim for special privilege or wealth. Indeed, it would take from the position many of the attributes that others argue are necessary to attract high-caliber aspirants.

The motivating factor will be less materialistic, more spiritually satisfying.

What, then, might serve as a motivating factor once traditional conceptions of ambition lose their effectiveness? The one possible motive that makes sense is the sometimes characteristic of man to seek confirmation of his own competence—competence being, to follow the approach of Harvard psychologist Robert White, a need to constantly extend one's mastery of one's environment. (I suspect that societies have generally worked harder at channelizing, and even repressing the impulse to competence more rigorously, than they have the sexual impulse.)

The motivation to perform in critical decision-making roles, then, may derive from a type of commitment where responsibility, not power, is sought.

THE CHANGING OF THE MANAGERIAL GUARD

The institutions or organizations most resistant to change are those that are self-perpetuating, where those that control the institution or organization also control access to positions of control—the difference, perhaps, between an elected political administration and a self-perpetuating public commission. Moreover, in almost all organizations we have known to date, control over the organizational apparatus, however it is vested, also produces resistance to change; the "iron law of oligarchy" does operate—even among those organizations "dedicated" to "liberation."

This creates a number of dilemmas as current experience, more than ever before, requires that managers self-consciously learn to manage change—change either within their own structures or within the context within which the organization is located. Thus, even if, as some suggest, the rate of technological change may be slowing down (which I believe to be unlikely), the previously slower rate of change in other sectors of social life will continue to place significant change high on the executive agenda.

The change in management will be as agonizing as it is inevitable.

The contemporary executive remains a serious man, in the serious pursuit of traditional goals—objective achievement and recognition, status and wealth as something to be used either to gain still further increases in wealth and possessions, or to win still further recognition of one's worth. His primary commitment is to work, which is seen in terms of a career, and sometimes as a calling. In order to get where he is, he not only had to work at things and in ways that found their meaning primarily in where they might carry him, but, having submitted himself to personal characterological and moral examination premised upon a fairly narrow range of tolerances, he is not about to *not* demand the same from those that seek to follow his path.

In many ways, managerial elites still formed by the culture of Industrial society (and still more influenced by pre-industrial values than many would admit) will increasingly be in the difficult position of being a father who is asked to raise and encourage a child who in many basic regards will neither resemble him nor confirm his values (honor him)—a serious father raising what he must find to be a frivolous child; an over-masculine figure who must cope with what he must define as a feminized son or masculinized daughter; a Puritan evaluating a self-indulgent child; a father with a child who shares his father's permanent commitments, if at all, only partially, only provisionally. This is a great deal to ask of the best of men.

There is no easy programmatic solution to this problem—no easy design, no fast executives' weekend seminar. However, even managerial elites are far from being homogeneous. Possibly, some element may have quietly already moved in this direction; unfortunately, many of these in moving away from traditional postures have also moved out of the executive suite, committing themselves to other activities. But, no matter how, change is bound to come.

Perhaps merely raising the issues to greater self-consciousness is the most that can be expected at present, with the hope that this increased tolerance may, in turn, facilitate new and necessary changes in both managers and styles of management.

In the transition from the Industrial to the Post-Industrial Era, Americans generally and top management specifically would do well to seriously consider the implications of the following three possible developments:

1. Widespread and extended resistance to change on the part of top management, born of satisfaction with the familiar and fear of the unknown, may so slow our forward thrust relative to other nations and so incite resentment on the part of those disadvantaged thereby as to fuel anti-capitalist sentiments. The net effect over even a relatively short time might be to force U.S. leadership into a defensive and therefore reactive posture at home, hinder the United States from exercising its most constructive influences in the development of global management systems, and in effect do this country's leadership position in the 1970's and 1980's irreparable harm.

2. A hallmark of the Post-Industrial Era will be the very extensive refashioning of our patterns of organization, goals, management, and control within the economic, political, and social systems of the United States. For example, networks and systems and the interrelationships and management thereof may become more important than the organization and management of single institutions and organizations. The Industrial Era concepts of profits and profitability are already being enlarged or redefined to factor in the costs of social responsibility or social management at all levels. The less isolated and more involved nations become in the global framework of policy making, the greater the influences that are present to act and react upon each other.

3. This increasingly integrative and interactive condition of society almost certainly will make for a period of instability and impermanence, will force Americans and top managers to alter their perceptions, values, attitudes toward themselves and each other, and will force them to reformulate and gain a new understanding of what really constitutes "progress" and "management"; for nothing in this world is constant except change itself.

In short, management is just a part of the larger question of the future of man.

Ten

JOHN McHALE with
MAGDA CORDELL McHALE

Management: The Larger Perspective

THE current debate regarding change has been dominated by the recording of exponential curves of growth in many areas of our environmental and social interactions. Population, pollution, violence, crime, etc., are all shown to have reached explosive "saturation" points indicating that human society is on a collision course with disaster. Recent studies have stressed that undue material and economic growth in itself may indeed be a principal evil. Some have suggested that our minimal survival will require the abnegation of many of our sophisticated sociotechnical means and the return to a more arcadian and stable type of society.

The major emphases of this debate, even if qualified, have significant import for management in a changing world. Though much of the evidence is not in, nor wholly validated, we may assume that we are at a critical juncture in human affairs.

This part of the study attempts to place the changing role of management within a larger historical context, to identify those sets of fundamental and structural changes which have occurred in the immediate past, are under way in the present, and may most influence the social, economic, political and cultural climate of society in the next twenty-five years.

To this end, both the major study papers themselves, and various external sources,* have been drawn upon to assemble various synoptic and cross-sectional views of the overall context. The charts and diagrams which are used should be looked upon as conceptual aids—rather than as being substantive data compilations; i.e., even where numbers are used, they are not intended to reflect measurable accuracy.

We tend to focus on current, readily measurable trends . . .

The warnings of impending catastrophe, the analysis of diminishing resources, of population pressures, etc., certainly have their place and value—not the least

---

* For reading convenience, quotations from the major panel papers in the study are identified only by the author's name in parenthesis, e.g. (Ansoff), (Drucker), etc. Other sources are numbered and footnoted in the usual manner.

of which has been the alerting of the general public and its legislators to the vast range of problems which the past century's accelerated development has brought about. But they may also be used to increase despair, to paralyze action, and to force artificial and repressive stabilities.

Growth, size, and change are all relative measures. What look like separate rates of increase of abnormally explosive growth in one narrow frame of reference may be a more slowly changing distribution in a wider context or longer time span. Exponential curves do not grow in isolation. They are related to other growths and values—as one factor increases, another may be in decline.

Adequate statistical compilations are of quite recent origin and in many areas are still crude approximations. Many recent and alarming curves may only be evidence of better bookkeeping as change patterns become more precisely identified and documented. Other statistical increases often share the same defect: social "problems" and pathologies are as you label and count them.

. . . ignoring more basic, longer-range patterns of change.

It may be, indeed, that what we now view as an explosive increase in many human factors is *not* in fact abnormal—that the norms which we read as stability for most past history are not now applicable to the human condition. What we read as exponential is an abrupt series of discontinuities which constitute a radically new human context for which there are few viable historical precedents.

It might also be underlined that the negatives inherent in the range and complexity of the problems which now face us are balanced, in many ways, by the positive capabilities for human action which have been concomitantly developed. We have a greater variety of choices and options available to us, and greatly enlarged capacities to act decisively in many areas which have hitherto been beyond our control.

The changing context for management in all sectors of society requires a shift of viewpoint from considering one problem or one issue as isolated phenomena in time towards a more systemic "process" orientation in which events, trends, changes may be seen as interactive aspects of the whole. Igor Ansoff, in his chapter of this study, refers specifically to the need of the business manager for a "Keplerian perspective" in confronting the emerging world changes:

It is a world which lost little of the original competitive complexity and acquired many others; a world of discontinuity in which it is dangerous to predict the future through reliance on history; a world full of novel problems and challenges for which past experience is a poor guide. In this world, the business firm has lost its Ptolemaic centrality: it is no longer the social sun around which revolve other less important planets. It has become a part of a Keplerian system of many interacting and independent planets (Ansoff).

Historical perspective: change from the Renaissance . . .

The longer view for such mapping of change might well go back to the evolutionary origins of humanity. But, for a more synoptic and Western perspective, we may choose the Renaissance as a convenient and recent benchmark. Though this "watershed" period is more generally regarded as an intellectual and aesthetic rebirth marking emergence from the medieval period, its pragmatic basis lay also in the rise of the mercantile classes in the city states and ports of Europe. Trading ventures to the Near and Far East brought not only new knowledge and techniques but also the material wealth to encourage and sustain the artistic and intellectual expansion of the period. The scientific and aesthetic exploration which characterizes the Renaissance was intertwined, in no small measure, with more practical developments in mining, metallurgy, engineering, and commerce. The inventions in optics and geometry aiding astronomy were accompanied by the improvement of the mariner's compass which, in turn, assisted the risk-capital exploration of the "new worlds."

The conjoining of these manifold changes represents one of the major waves of "discontinuities" in the West. From this time on many of the material, economic, and technological changes in our present world may be traced to common origins in the "conceptual shift" which occurs during this period—e.g., with the systematic derivation of scientific principles from the direct observation of natural processes. Both the date and the discipline mark the end of one kind of culture of long established dominance and the beginning of a new and relatively unprecedented form. Since that time, virtually every notion and cherished belief about the nature of the physical universe, of society and the nature of man which had subtended earlier cultures, has been slowly eroded, modified and, in many cases, swept away.

The central dialogues of the Renaissance still echo in our own period—around our relationship to the physical world, the relationship of the individual to society, the relations between individual and individual.

. . . through the Industrial Revolution . . .

At first, the material changes wrought in society by the new scientific orientations were relatively slow. They gained rapid momentum only when discovered principles began to be applied to industrial technologies less than one hundred years ago. Though the social and intellectual bases of society were grossly affected by new "ideas," the full effects of the scientific revolution are not parallel with the Industrial Revolution but occur late in the nineteenth century. The emergence of the scientist as a "professional" is almost coincident with those specific discoveries which form the springboard of modern science—the extension of experimental and measurable ranges into the hitherto invisible subsensorial world of atomic, molecular, and radiation phenomena. We are still wrestling, in much of our present thinking, with the difficulty of orienting ourselves towards this new knowledge—of a world in which many of our major physical transactions are now invisible and untouchable but their negative effects, e.g., nuclear weapons, may be devastatingly apparent.

The favored benchmark for the development of modern technology, the Industrial Revolution, occurs somewhat independently of later specifically scientific developments produced within, and for, industry. The lineage is much more that of a craft-technology tradition which pursued its course through technical inventions conceived in terms of immediately practical ends—predating the discovery and elaboration of scientific principles, e.g., of energy dynamics, chemical transformations, etc., which more properly constitute the basis for later, specifically industrial evolution. They belong more, also, with the intensification and routinization of the craft and cottage industries incident upon the increased mercantile and colonial expansions of the seventeenth and eighteenth centuries.

Many of the features that have been considered as enduring characteristics of the scientific and technological industrial process are actually the end phases and adaptations of the older craft production tradition, such as the human factory system, the sweatshop assembly of manufactured components, the routinization of work, and the concentration of populations and production centers in close association with raw materials and energy sources.

The later evolution of the Industrial Revolution occurred towards the end of the nineteenth century when the craft-based phase was well under way. As Peter Drucker has particularly analyzed, it is to this period that we owe much of our major industry today—the automobile, aeroplane, steel making, electrical generation, etc.—all have been in continuous development from their late nineteenth century origins:

> Most industrial technology today is an extension and modification of the inventions and technologies of that remarkable half-century before World War I. This continuity, in turn, has made for stable industry structure. Every one of the great nineteenth century inventions gave birth, almost overnight, to a new industry and to new big businesses. These are still the major industries and big businesses of today.[1]

The closing interdependencies of science, technology, and industry are roughly coincident with the two world wars. The first, related to World War I, spurred developments in high strength alloys; energy conversion; air, surface and undersea transport; telecommunications.

. . . and the Second Industrial Revolution, after World War II . . .

The next phase, during and after World War II, has been called the Second Industrial Revolution, and marked a new relationship between basic scientific research, technical development, and social usage. The major tools, and change agents, of our present period—electronics, automatic control systems, and computers—emerge from this relation, plus the new "software" tools of operations research, decision theory, and systems analysis. Within this latter development, the methodologies of physical science are applied to the organization and planning of the research development itself, that is, organized innovation. From the fusion of these "tools," and the more direct application of scientific procedures to human affairs, comes automation and, as some have phrased its latest development, the emergence of "Post-Industrial" socioeconomic forms.

A point to underline here is that, in many ways, much that we regard as being part of a new "Industrial-Modern" order is, in fact, the tail end of an older phase of development. The change to a new and unprecedented kind of world reality occurs during the period towards the end of World War II to around 1950. This includes two events whose "managerial" challenges are of the greatest magnitude and longest range consequence—the first use of nuclear weapons, and the first electronic computer. Both events awesomely magnify our capabilities for both negative and positive purposes.

. . . and finally to the Post-Industrial Period.

At some unmarked point during the last twenty years, we imperceptibly moved out of the Modern Age and into a new, as yet nameless, era. Our view of the world changed; we acquired a new perception and with it new capacities. There are new frontiers of opportunity, risk and challenge. There is a new spiritual center to human existence.[2]

Used to express the notion of a continuous smooth developing socioeconomic structural process, the term, "the industrial society," is in many ways a misnomer. As the phenomenon of scientific * industrialization develops, it is less directly constraining upon the form of society than were the pre-industrial agricultural, craft-industrial phases that preceded it. Rather than becoming a more visibly identifiable determinant of the societal and physical environ, its processes shift over into relatively invisible metabolic functions. This is particularly the case as it evolves successfully through later chemical, electromechanical, and electronic phases. At the same time, the major institutions and social forms shift also from emphases on materially productive activities and economically determined relations toward a wider range of human concerns.

At this point in our perspective review, we might usefully compress our categories of major structural changes in society into three main phases—*the Pre-Industrial, Industrial* and *Post-Industrial (Post-Modern)*. Though this compression and its labeling could be exhaustively qualified, it may be useful for present purposes in indicating some of the changes in managerial or organizational forms which have occurred or will be required in the next period.† Daniel Bell has succinctly characterized the three phases of society as follows:

---

* A criterion of difference from craft to technological to scientific industrialism would be the institutionalization of innovation. Whereas craft evolution is more determined by traditional precedent, and early technological development by isolated invention, the scientific tends to have change and innovation *built in* as a working premise.

† This categorization is also used in Igor Ansoff's paper, "Management in Transition," Chapter 2 (pages 22–63) in this volume; and the use of these terms may facilitate cross reference.

We can think of society in terms of pre-industrial, industrial and post-industrial. Most of the world today is essentially pre-industrial, in the immediate sense that at least 60 per cent of the labor force is engaged in extractive work: mining, fishing, timber and agriculture. Industrial societies are essentially those few . . . where the majority of the labor force is engaged primarily in industry and manufacturing. The United States, to some extent, is the first post industrial nation in which the majority of the labor force is not engaged either in agriculture and extractive industries, or manufacturing industry, or a combination of both, but essentially in services—that is, trade, finance, real estate, education, research, administration and government. But this is not just a change in sectors, a change only from extractive to industrial to services. It is a change equally in the character of the societies themselves. . . . A pre-industrial society is essentially one based on raw materials as a game against nature, and in which there is diminishing returns. An industrial society is organised primarily around energy and the use of energy for the productivity of goods. A post-industrial society is organised around information and utilization of information as a way of guiding the society.[3]

These phases are, obviously, not abrupt or initially exclusive and homogeneous. Many elements of one will continue into another intact or marginally transformed. In some respects, aspects of Post-Industrialism may resemble the Pre-Industrial phases more than the Industrial, etc. Also, and importantly, though we concentrate mainly on the U.S. and Western society in this study, the changes in other socio-cultural contexts will be different.

Moving from the Industrial form to the Post-Industrial does not mean that the society is less technologically or industrially based—but merely that the "production/manufacturing industries" are less salient as the prime motive force and wealth generating sector. Agriculture provides a useful analogy. In the U.S., the agricultural sector still remains a vitally productive component of the economy—but its relative importance has declined as a motivating and goal setting force in the society. It requires fewer and fewer workers to maintain and increase its productivity but it is no longer the major focus for innovation and plays a lessening role in shaping the values, attitudes, and ways of life in the society.

However, if we view the over-all change from Industrial to Post-Industrial forms as a more or less peaceful change to a service "economy" with the major social institutions remaining intact, this would be oversimplified and misleading. The fundamental transition is much greater than merely a change in the industrial and economic bases and will entail a more massive revision and more conscious restructuring of society with accompanying redefinition of roles, status, values, rights, privileges, etc.

"Watershed" Charts: A Synoptic View

In the series of charts which follow, the division of changing phenomena into fixed and dated periods is arbitrary and approximate—many of the trends, events, and processes flow across the time periods. One might also qualify "time's" arrow, in this case, as seeming to imply a qualitatively linear progression from one phase to another—as onwards and upwards with technology! Bias is displayed in the assumption that the range, quality, and expansion of human life has improved over time, and that much of this has been due to increased material means. This is not to suggest that we are moving toward some Post-Industrial, or Post-Modern, utopia. The main thrust is to underline that we do now possess enormously developed physical means and resources to improve the material existence of more people. The central challenge lies with the social management of our capabilities in the larger public interest for all people.

THE WATERSHED

The term "watershed" has been used as descriptive of the way in which various separate strands of development begin to flow together and to interact with one another in the approximate time frame under review.

This first chart shows the underlying expansion pattern of various physical and intellectual capabilities, e.g., the opening up of the electromagnetic spectrum, growth in accuracy of physical measurement, the extension of "monitoring" and control into the subsensorial ranges of the environment at the miscroscopic and macroscopic levels, human expansion into space and into the oceans. Over these expansions has been placed the growth curves of population, energy, etc. Many more of the latter curves could have been overlaid. The point to be made, however, is that just at the stage in human affairs when such exponential indicators suggest a "runaway world" of such interdependent and large scale complexity as to be beyond direct human intervention and control, we have, with seeming spontaneity, developed precisely those tools and capabilities which are required to manage its order of systemic complexity. Latent within this relatively invisible development is a pattern of human conceptual expansion, which underlies, with its longer amplitudes and lower frequencies, the more directly perceptible curves of physical "problem" curves. In many senses the underlying expansion patterns of human control are the expression of new "management" capabilities and challenges which have begun to emerge only in the past few decades and form the basis for new industries, new modes of governance, and new configurations of social and organizational forms.

The *rise in efficiency of energy conversion* and dramatic gain in over-all energy available is one of the key transition points from pre-industrial to industrial societies. It is impossible to raise and maintain advanced material standards, for the most people, in economies whose energy converters are limited to animal and human muscle power and simple mechanical converters—windmills, sailing ships. The rise in energy conversion is also paralleled, in many cases, by internal industrial efficiencies; e.g., in the generation of electricity, the amount of fuel necessary for the production of one kilowatt-hour, in the U.S., declined from 6.85 pounds of coal (or coal equivalent) in 1900 to 3.0 pounds in 1920: to 0.95 pounds by 1955. This shows an increase in thermal efficiency more than sevenfold in fifty

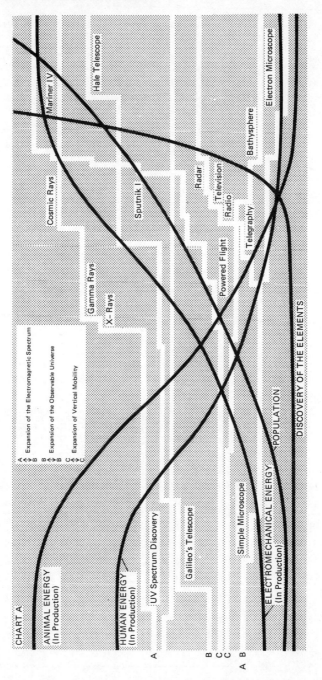

CHART A:

ANIMAL ENERGY (In Production)

HUMAN ENERGY (In Production)

A ↔ B   Expansion of the Electromagnetic Spectrum
B ↔ B   Expansion of the Observable Universe
C ↔ C   Expansion of Vertical Mobility

UV Spectrum Discovery

Galileo's Telescope

Simple Microscope

ELECTROMECHANICAL ENERGY (In Production)

POPULATION

DISCOVERY OF THE ELEMENTS

X-Rays

Gamma Rays

Cosmic Rays

Mariner IV

Hale Telescope

Sputnik I

Radar

Television

Radio

Bathysphere

Electron Microscope

Telegraphy

Powered Flight

CHART B: STAGES OF TECHNOLOGICAL DEVELOPMENT

PRE–INDUSTRIAL

ECONOMY	Agriculturally Based Marginal Economies of Scarcity
POWER	Human and Animal Muscle, Wind and Water, Wood-Burning
WORK SKILLS	All-Around Skilled Craftsmen and Unskilled Manual Workers
MATERIALS	Wood, Iron, Bronze, Lead, etc.
COMMUNICATION	Word of Mouth, Drum, Other Signals Messengers and Newspapers
TOOLS	Tusk, Horn, and Bone Hand Tools Bronze Age Iron Age Hand-wrought Iron and Wooden Tools

PRE–INDUSTRIAL
Stage 1
Stage 2
Stage 3
INDUSTRIAL
Stage 4
POST–INDUSTRIAL
Stage 5
	Adaptation———
	     Domestication———
	          Diversification—

TRANSPORTATION	Walking, Use of Animals, Canals, Sailing Ships

In this period, which comprises most of recorded history, societies were agriculturally based, marginal survival economies—many still are. Survival in these terms, for the individual or the group, was essentially a zero sum game. There was a basic limitation and insufficiency of material resources to share. One survived or "won" by securing advantage over opposing individuals or groups in competition for scarce means. As one side won, the other lost. Stored surpluses in such societies were rarely sufficient to maintain more than a fractional elite in relative long term security.

Life in pre-industrial society was largely framed in either/or terms—either work, as social rules prescribed, or starve; either conform or be variously censured, ostracized, or killed; either marry or burn, and so on.

Material wealth and physical power resided in the visible domain of land to grow crops, in control over animals and men to provide the work muscle power, and in material property assets. Authority was hierarchical, based most often on punitive physical coercion; organizational and managerial forms were organized around the control of material means and the regulation of scarce resources according to traditional, often "sacred," precedent and fixed routines.

INDUSTRIAL			POST-INDUSTRIAL	
Industrial Economies of Abundance			Non-Resource-Depletive: Economies of Abundance	
Steam Engines, Gasoline Engines, Electric Motors, Atomic Fission and Fossil Fuel Conversion, Fuel Cells			Atomic Fusion, Solar, and Other "Income" Energy Sources	
Subdivided Manufacturing Processes Replace Skilled Craftsmen with Semi-skilled Machine Operators	Human Feeder or Tenderer Replaced by Skilled Inspector/Mechanic	Highly Trained Engineers/ Designers, Skilled Maintenance Technicians, Systems Specialists, and Programmers	Human Skills Emphasis in New Service Organizations and Managerial Forms	
Iron, Mild Steel, Copper	Alloyed Steel, Light Alloys, Aluminum		Plastics, Composites and Super-alloys, New Materials Used, e.g., Magnesium, Titanium	
Mail by Train and Ships Mechanically Printed Newspaper	Telegraph Telephone	AM and FM Radio, Movies, Microfilm, Television, Magnetic Tape, Transoceanic Telephone	Video Phone, Data Phone, Telstar and Syncom World-Wide Communication Satellites, Graphic Computers	
Mechanical Energy Conversion e.g., Steam Engine	Beginning of Machine-based Mass Production		Post-manufacture Industrial Base: New Electronic, Biochemical, Bioengineering, Communications Technologies	

Mechanization ──►

Automation ──►

Horse and Buggy, Steam Trains	Automobile, Diesel Trains and Ships, Airplane	Rocket and Jet Vertical Takeoff Aircraft, Atomic Submarines, Ground Effect Craft, Helicopters, High Speed Monorails

The specifically industrial form of society is one based (a) on the acquisition of mechanical, and latterly electro-mechanical conversion of energy in excess of that previously obtainable via human, animal, and other relatively low energy converters; (b) on the concomitant increase in the range of raw materials which may be processed with higher temperatures, more powerful forming techniques, etc., with wider availability of materials due to expanded transportation capabilities and increasingly precise knowledge of the nature and properties of materials themselves.

The Industrial Revolution is marked—by the first large-scale application of inanimate mechanical energies to productive use—as the period in which human society begins to move from marginal survival to forms based on possible machine-aided abundance. Beginning with the steam engine, mass production technologies, with division of human labor in repetitive machine tending, assembly tasks, highly specialized professional roles and occupational definitions, and its aggregation in large urban clusters close to materials extraction, production, and distribution facilities, began to transform society economically, socially, and culturally. The typical concentration of "heavy industry" forms evolving in this period are also characterized by being highly resource depletive with gross environmental impacts through their wastes and effluents, and with correspondingly high impact on human resource misuse and spoliation.

Salient features of the emergence of the post-industrial society are:

(a) industrial productivity may be sustained, and increased with less direct inputs of manpower. The "labor force" moves into service industry sectors with supervisory and managerial functions, into the knowledge and human services "industry"—research and development, education, welfare, recreation, etc. The emphasis within the production sector itself is a shift in concentration from the manufacture and distribution of products only, toward products as part of a larger "service process," e.g. towards service/maintenance for life time of product supplies or its end use provision in rentable and serviced forms. Advanced industrial systems, e.g., airlines, diversify into service networks of motels, hotels, resorts and other full service forms; the communications industry expands from personal message service towards larger systemic services in health, education, resource communications, etc., towards "Comsat" forms. Such process-services systems as they extend become less measurable within the strictly economic, rationally efficient terms of older product-oriented industrial forms.

(b) New industries emerge based on different sets of energy, material, and technological requirements. We earlier referred to atomic power, to the new electronic technologies based on new uses of larger areas of the electromagnetic spectrum. We may note also that these new industries tend to be relatively non-resource-depletive forms compared with the highly resource-depletive environmentally impacting

CHART B: Continued on the following pages.

CHART B: STAGES OF TECHNOLOGICAL
DEVELOPMENT (CONTINUED)

PRE-INDUSTRIAL

Organizational scale was relatively small, e.g., in terms of urban aggregates, few cities went far beyond the million mark, due to the constraints of the inadequacy of food supply, public health maintenance, communications, etc., to manage large numbers above this number. The large formal organizational forms were typically armies, religious groups and, to a lesser extent, governmental units. Such societies were oriented toward slow rates of change, to geographic remoteness and relatively isolated local autonomy.

The World
1500–1840

The Best Average Speed of Horse Drawn Coaches on Land and Sailing Ships at Sea Was Approximately 10 M.P.H.

Man on Foot = 3 m.p.h. Caravel = 5 m.p.h.   Horse Coach

Guttenberg Printing Press, 1441

Life styles were closely tied to work role, hierarchical position, and mode of life as relatively unalterable at birth and for the given life span. The peasant had a fixed style of life (in clothing, food, housing, mobility, language) much different from that of the soldier, the merchant, the noble or prince. Ethical values in such societies tended to confirm the prevailing survival modes and "quality of life" and to be constrained within fixed systems of belief and conformity which limited possibilities for more individual choice and action.

The long historical conditioning to such realities, which effectively limited any appreciable widening of expectations for most people, produced most of the socio-political and economic definitions of man and his relation to society. It still underlies much of our present outlook on work, economy and the function of social institutions in the West— and equally, but differently, in the East.

1830

years. (See also Chart A, p. 305, for changes in the *kinds of energy* used in production.)

The *labor force shift,* which was earlier referred to, demonstrates the reallocation of human energy and time within the economy. Machines can now create most of the product wealth with less direct human involvement both in industry

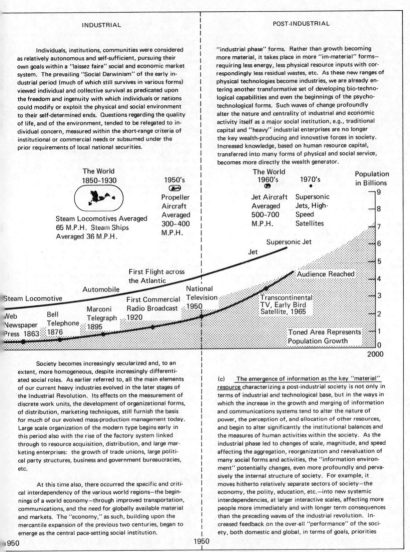

INDUSTRIAL

Individuals, institutions, communities were considered as relatively autonomous and self-sufficient, pursuing their own goals within a "laissez faire" social and economic market system. The prevailing "Social Darwinism" of the early industrial period (much of which still survives in various forms) viewed individual and collective survival as predicated upon the freedom and ingenuity with which individuals or nations could modify or exploit the physical and social environment to their self-determined ends. Questions regarding the quality of life, and of the environment, tended to be relegated to individual concern, measured within the short-range criteria of institutional or commercial needs or subsumed under the prior requirements of local national securities.

The World
1850-1930

Steam Locomotives Averaged
65 M.P.H. Steam Ships
Averaged 36 M.P.H.

1950's
Propeller
Aircraft
Averaged
300-400
M.P.H.

First Flight across
the Atlantic

Automobile

Steam Locomotive

First Commercial
Radio Broadcast
1920

National
Television
1950

Marconi
Telegraph
1895

Web
Newspaper
Press 1863

Bell
Telephone
1876

Society becomes increasingly secularized and, to an extent, more homogeneous, despite increasingly differentiated social roles. As earlier referred to, all the main elements of our current heavy industries evolved in the later stages of the Industrial Revolution. Its effects on the measurement of discrete work units, the development of organizational forms, of distribution, marketing techniques, still furnish the basis for much of our evolved mass-production management today. Large scale organization of the modern type begins early in this period also with the rise of the factory system linked through to resource acquisition, distribution, and large marketing enterprises: the growth of trade unions, large political party structures, business and government bureaucracies, etc.

At this time also, there occurred the specific and critical interdependency of the various world regions—the beginnings of a world economy—through improved transportation, communications, and the need for globally available material and markets. The "economy," as such, building upon the mercantile expansion of the previous two centuries, began to emerge as the central pace-setting social institution.

1950

POST-INDUSTRIAL

"industrial phase" forms. Rather than growth becoming more material, it takes place in more "im-material" forms—requiring less energy, less physical resource inputs with correspondingly less residual wastes, etc. As these new ranges of physical technologies become industries, we are already entering another transformative set of developing bio-technological capabilities and even the beginnings of the psycho-technological forms. Such waves of change profoundly alter the nature and centrality of industrial and economic activity itself as a major social institution, e.g., traditional capital and "heavy" industrial enterprises are no longer the key wealth-producing and innovative forces in society. Increased knowledge, based on human resource capital, transferred into many forms of physical and social service, becomes more directly the wealth generator.

The World
1960's   1970's

Jet Aircraft   Supersonic
Averaged   Jets, High-
500-700   Speed
M.P.H.   Satellites

Supersonic Jet

Jet

Audience Reached

Transcontinental
TV, Early Bird
Satellite, 1965

Toned Area Represents
Population Growth

Population
in Billions

9
8
7
6
5
4
3
2
1
0
2000

(c)   The emergence of information as the key "material" resource characterizing a post-industrial society is not only in terms of industrial and technological base, but in the ways in which the increase in the growth and merging of information and communications systems tend to alter the nature of power, the perception of, and allocation of other resources, and begin to alter significantly the institutional balances and the measures of human activities within the society. As the industrial phase led to changes of scale, magnitude, and speed affecting the aggregation, reorganization and reevaluation of many social forms and activities, the "information environment" potentially changes, even more profoundly and pervasively the internal structure of society. For example, it moves hitherto relatively separate sectors of society—the economy, the polity, education, etc.—into new systemic interdependencies, at larger interactive scales, affecting more people more immediately and with longer term consequences than the preceding waves of the industrial revolution. Increased feedback on the over-all "performance" of the society, both domestic and global, in terms of goals, priorities

1950

CHART B: Continued on the following page.

and in agriculture. Service—as product maintenance, as services industry, as direct human service—creates more social wealth. Though requiring more labor initially, many areas of routine service also become augmented by machines, or direct human labor is wholly replaced by machines.

CHART B: STAGES OF TECHNOLOGICAL DEVELOPMENT (CONTINUED)

INDUSTRIAL	POST-INDUSTRIAL
The later developments of industrialism incident upon World War I and II bracket this specific phase of an industrial society whose major work energies, attitudes, economic values, etc., are geared toward production and manufacture of goods and to the pervasive measures of social interactions in "economically" justifiable terms—roles, status, life style, etc., are closely related to work. Though its rationale was being eroded, the "zero sum game" syndrome was dominant throughout the industrial period and became crystallized in the image of "economic man" which is still latently operable today. The measure of "rational efficiency" of production of goods and services—in terms of lowest costs, least material and labor inputs, and largest volume output at highest speed—is a dominant characteristic of the industrial phase. Originating in, and appropriate to the mass production economy, it is also displaced and "reified" to become the measure for developing, evaluating, and managing other social sectors and institutionalized activities—where its expanded usage may not only be inappropriate but constraining and even undermining their "effective" management. Many of the latest modes of social and value accounting, with their terminology of "cost-effectiveness," "risk-benefit," "program budgeting," etc., apart from extending efficiency criteria into areas where it may actually increase inefficiency and corrode effectiveness, often reveal underlying "scarcity" anxieties which impose strictly economic priorities where, indeed, they may be quite useless. We may note that such recent accounting terms have originated in the military sector—which is hardly a viable model for the economic and accountable allocation of resources. Neither the images nor the anxieties fit the emerging types of energies, materials, interconvertibility, and organizational capabilities which are at our disposal. One of our key managerial challenges is the avoidance of such obsolete socioeconomic models, and their reformulation in terms of the new systemic models which more clearly fit current reality.	and the satisfaction of "value preferences" of its members introduces new modalities of social, economic, and political interaction wherein the information process in itself becomes the prime "social navigation" instrument in the guiding and shaping of the forward course of the society. Importantly, also, as information and organized knowledge become the major resource base for society—one which does not decrease or lose in value through wider sharing and use but may actually gain—the character of the "zero sum" survival game is profoundly changed to a "non zero sum enterprise." "Winning" is no longer based on the other losing—and tends more and more to be predicated on a system in which maximal gain in life advantages, the quality of life in widening choices of life strategies, may only be obtained in due ratio to the degree to which more and more people reciprocally share the same advantages. In terms of physical resource and product wealth, potential abundance makes this not only feasible but the only realistic strategy. The older form of exclusively owned material property and artifacts no longer applies to the larger "process systems" in society. An airline service, telecommunications system, electrical or other advanced service network only works optimally with the largest number of users sharing the system. In similar ways, intrinsically unique value and wealth are no longer so attached to material objects. In many cases the objects of common utility are identical or only marginally differentiated. Material ownership as necessarily conditioning the terms of access to, and use of, products and processes perceptibly declines as rental and other service relations increase. The supposedly acquisitive materialism of "the technological society" becomes contradictory when the post-industrial trending appears to be toward less acquisition, attachment, and domination by the "value" of physical possession. Beyond a certain level of material development, it seems obvious that material value, in the sense of pursuit of exclusive ownership, declines as possessions become more freely available—and as less time and human energy are exacted for their availability. With the devaluation of material gains and rewards, "human capital," the development of psychically rewarding organizational forms and the over-all quality of life issues come to provide the core directions for managing society in the post-industrial period. To an increasing extent, the "hard" science and technological means are "as given," the more urgent challenges, problems, and priorities lie with the invention of socially innovative means with which to re-form our major institutions and to redevelop our societies in more humanly meaningful ways.

The *shrinking work week* is another way of displaying this interrelationship of wealth and work. Employment as such becomes less directly attached to actual product wealth available. This point will be referred to, in different ways, in other areas of this text. As other observers have noted, the decrease in work hours doesn't always mean that the worker uses the extra leisure time for non-work activities—but will often just "moonlight" on some other job. This is, in part, a transitory phenomenon. Most of our training, our acquired roles and status, etc., have been occupationally linked for so long that it may take a generation to decouple them.

Also, with "productive economic work" regarded as occupying the central part of human life, leisure was considered as a fractional in-between period, i.e. non-work. The devil finds work for idle hands! We now begin to view this

MATERIALS AND TECHNIQUES

PRE-INDUSTRIAL

An important corrective may be entered here, in that the term "pre-industrial" does not mean "pre-technological." The earliest hunting and herding societies used highly developed techniques—the discovery of fire, the invention of the wheel, the lever, bow and arrow, food preservation, etc., are no mean feats. The range of "behavioral technologies" used to train and domesticate sources of animal energy and food are tremendous technical advances. The trading and mercantile societies of the sea coasts also developed sophisticated navigational, accounting, and building techniques. The long history of the agriculturally based society is a complexly technical development not only of the physical techniques of agriculture itself but of language, number, symbol and image systems accompanied by the "invention" and development of many of the social organizational institutions and cultural forms which still largely constitute the basis of contemporary society.

Pre-industrial means rather more simply those societies which have not developed the range of "industrial" materials and inanimate mechanical energies which characterize emergence into the recognizably industrial phases of the more immediate past period. Their level of energy conversion was low and the range of metals and non-metallics were also used at relatively low levels of functional efficiencies, and their production and use of such materials was correspondingly much less. Their tools and materials use systems tended also to be more localized in origin and source of supply, smaller in scale and maintainable in relatively autonomous economic terms. The industrial phase characteristically develops towards the use of globally distributed materials and markets and the evolution of globally interdependent economies.

INDUSTRIAL

The first phase of industrialization was marked by the localized growth of iron and steel production when large scale-mechanical industry developed in those countries where supplies of iron ore, coal, etc., were available close to power sources. The swift "take-off" of the industrially advanced countries owes most to these locally convenient factors.

The second phase occurs in the late nineteenth/early twentieth century when new steels and other alloy production required access to a greater range of resources which were relatively scarce in the then industrial countries, e.g., manganese, tungsten, nickel, cobalt, etc., were unevenly dispersed around the globe. This phase is marked by intense competition for control of these resources particularly in the underdeveloped countries. The key concentration of industrial power was in steel production paired with heavy dependence on coal and oil fuels as a major energy resource.

POST-INDUSTRIAL

The post-industrial phase which we are just entering is characterized by the increasing displacement of steel as the prime industrial material (for structural, machine, transport and other uses) by other "light" metals, composite materials, and plastics. The forward pattern of industrial development lies (1) in the pairing of the light metals with electrical power from hydro or nuclear sources (2) in the increased use of metallics and nonmetallic composites and plastics with similar power sources. These developments could swiftly alter the present industrial power balance and, importantly, may turn the present "prior investment" advantage of the older established industrial regions into a restrictive disability.

somewhat differently as leisure becomes identifiable as a major life component. We may call it "optionally reinvestable time," or simply discretionary time, which may be used in many ways—travel, education, voluntary service, etc. Many of the more creative human activities which had been related as marginal spare-time interests, or even hobbies, may become the central life interest for individuals.

The gain in *expectancy of life-time* is a not inconsiderable feature of advanced industrial economies. Though much play has been made of the physical and mental ills accompanying industrialization and urbanization, the available data tend to suggest that this is hardly so; for most people, the process has been a gain in both life-time available and health. The "quality of life" enjoyed by a

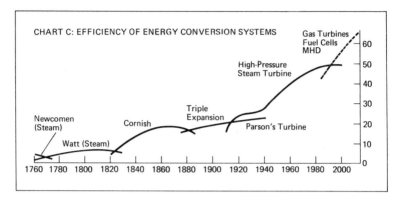

CHART C: EFFICIENCY OF ENERGY CONVERSION SYSTEMS

CHART D: GROWTH OF UNITED STATES GNP

CHART E: TYPICAL DEVELOPMENT OF THE LABOR FORCE BY BRANCHES OF THE NATIONAL ECONOMY

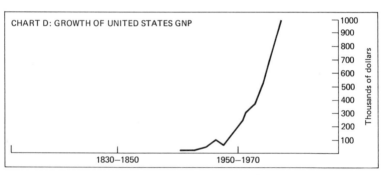

BEGINNING OF INDUSTRIALIZATION		PROCESS OF INDUSTRIALIZATION		BEGINNING OF SCIENTIFIC AND TECHNICAL REVOLUTION	
Mining	2–3%	Mining	3–5%	Mining	2–4%
Construction	2–3%	Construction	5–7%	Construction	8–10%
Transport/Comm.	2–3%				
Commerce	7–8%	Transport/Comm.	4–6%	Transport/Comm.	6–8%
		Commerce	4–6%	Commerce	11–16%
Services	8–12%	Services	10–14%		
				Services	20–35%
Manufacturing	8–12%	Manufacturing	25–35%		
				Manufacturing	25–30%
Agriculture	60–70%	Agriculture	25–45%	Agriculture	3–20%

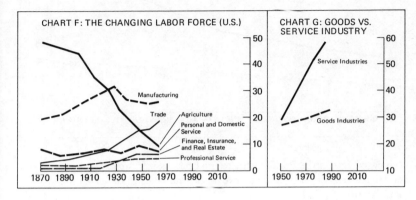

CHART F: THE CHANGING LABOR FORCE (U.S.)

Manufacturing

Trade

Agriculture

Personal and Domestic Service

Finance, Insurance, and Real Estate

Professional Service

1870 1890 1910 1930 1950 1970 1990 2010

CHART G: GOODS VS. SERVICE INDUSTRY

Service Industries

Goods Industries

1950 1970 1990 2010

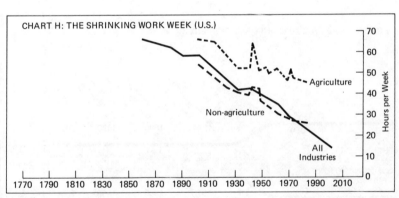

CHART H: THE SHRINKING WORK WEEK (U.S.)

Agriculture

Non-agriculture

All Industries

Hours per Week

1770 1790 1810 1830 1850 1870 1890 1910 1930 1950 1970 1990 2010

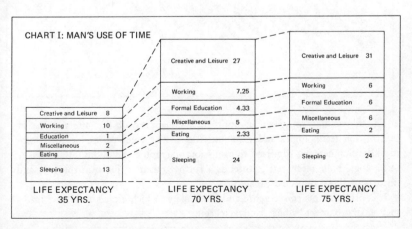

CHART I: MAN'S USE OF TIME

Creative and Leisure	8
Working	10
Education	1
Miscellaneous	2
Eating	1
Sleeping	13

LIFE EXPECTANCY 35 YRS.

Creative and Leisure	27
Working	7.25
Formal Education	4.33
Miscellaneous	5
Eating	2.33
Sleeping	24

LIFE EXPECTANCY 70 YRS.

Creative and Leisure	31
Working	6
Formal Education	6
Miscellaneous	6
Eating	2
Sleeping	24

LIFE EXPECTANCY 75 YRS.

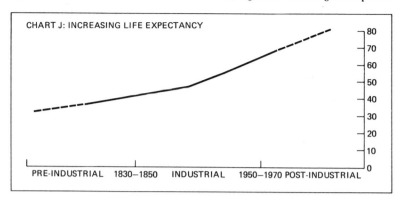

privileged few in the Pre-Industrial period may now be regarded by some as a
nostalgic goal, but one can hardly extend that nostalgia to the given life span of
the majority of people.

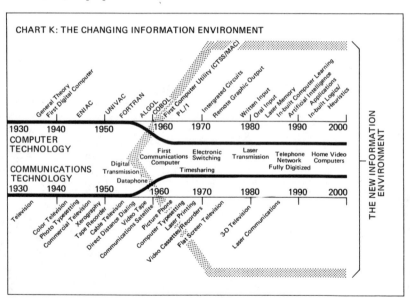

The above diagram gives an approximate mapping of the intersections of
information technologies and communications. The combination of such technical developments as digitized transmission of graphic and audio inputs, image
technology, holography, etc., portends a further quantum jump in the uses and
impacts of these amplified capabilities.

It is precisely this convergence and interlinkage which creates the "new information environment" which is now emerging.

As is not unusual in socio-technical innovation, we are dealing with a phenomenon in which the characteristics of any one set of technical aspects considered in isolation, e.g., *just* the computer or just the communications satellite, may not enable us to predict the potential consequences of interactive combinations of the various developments. The behavior and impacts of the whole is more than the sum of its parts.

In less than a decade, a service industry that was based on relatively short telegraph messages and person-to-person telephone calls has been transferred into a data pipeline that is carrying more and more of the nation's vital information. The new technology of communications makes possible a flow of digital data that bursts over electronic circuits from computer to computer, streaks through the air between microwave relay stations and is bounced off satellites from continent to continent.[4]

The impacts and challenges of this "new environment" on management, on decision making, on organizational policy, etc., are touched upon in various areas of this text.*

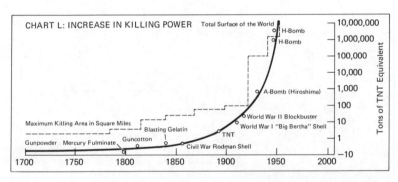

CHART L: INCREASE IN KILLING POWER

The *increase in killing power* at longer ranges and manifold increase in destructive force is certainly a significant "hallmark" of our period. Again—for the first time in human history—we have developed, in our period, the capability to destroy all life on earth through the use of nuclear weapons. It is a curious paradox that the most advanced and sophisticated "global management" systems are those in support of military prediction, planning, and control procedures.

For example, ICBM's can be launched to strike anywhere in the world in less than 30 minutes. The "managerial" aspects of handling information, men, and machines are enormous in terms of "more than 15,000 aircraft, over 1,000 missiles, a quarter-million personnel. Aircraft in flight can be contacted swiftly anywhere in the world, direct telephone contact can be made immediately through

* For more specific and detailed discussion, the reader should refer to The Conference Board study, "Information Technology; Some Critical Implications for Decision Makers 1971–1990," 1972.

CHART M: SOCIAL STRUCTURE

PRE–INDUSTRIAL

PEOPLE	Low life expectancy at birth, little formal education Most employment in agriculture, rudimentary specialization
PHYSICAL RESOURCES	Hand labor, aided by tools and animals Little development of natural resources Large construction mainly monumental
SUBSYSTEMS	Extended family Large organizations, intermingling of army, church, and state "Anomic" associations Villages and small towns
EXTERNAL RELATIONS	Colonialism and imperialism
INTERNAL RELATIONS	Localism and sectionalism
CODES AND VALUES	Passivism Survival and other-worldliness Religious law and "law of the jungle"
SYSTEM GUIDANCE	Restricted elites

— TRANSITIONAL PHASES —

one handset with more than 70 subordinate centers spread around the globe." *

Against this enormous negative capability, our positive systems for global co-operation, for creative rather than destructive purposes, are still rather puny. They are not, however, negligible. The almost invisible development of specifically transnational agencies and organizations has gone on steadily from their beginnings, in many cases, only a century ago, e.g.:

1. The Universal Postal Union, which we take for granted as a world public utility.
2. The International Telecommunications Union concerned with communications standards, wavebands, and use of the frequency spectrum.
3. The regulation of air, sea and other world transport within a framework of transnationally enforced codes and standards.
4. The intricate network of World Health Organization agencies—monitor-

* As reported in an Information Release, U.S. Strategic Air Command (402) 294-2544/4433.

INDUSTRIAL	POST-INDUSTRIAL
Rising life expectancy, much more education, Specialization of labor force, declining agriculture	Life expectancy above 75 "Learning force" surpasses total employment Professionalization of labor force, with at least 70% in services
Power-driven machines in large aggregations Natural resources more developed, depleted, and wasted Expansion of built environment with vast urban slums	Cybernation and computerization Resources more protected and conserved More rapid and concentrated growth of built environment
Nuclear family Larger and more differentiated organizations, including the factory system Growth of associations and pressure groups Urban and metropolitan areas Clearer differentiation of governmental sector	Highly capitalized family Complex, mixed organizational constellations New kinds of associational networks—Megalopoli and metropoli Blurred line between government and non-government
From empire to bloc or commonwealth Informal penetration and infusive diplomacy	Polynuclear world society Extensive transnational, intersecting, and interpenetrating relations
More integration, with growth of nationalism Vast communication and transportation networks Class and group conflict	Decline of both sectionalism and nationalism The "mobiletic revolution" New forms of intense conflict
Cosmopolitanism and nationalism Constitutional, statutory, judicial, and administrative law Activism and secularism	Megalopolitanism and transnationalism More organizational and professional codes Decline of scarcity Decline of scarcity values Secular humanism
Multiple elites National planning systems	Dispersed elites, greater circulation Transnational planning systems

TRANSITIONAL PHASES — TRANSITIONAL PHASES

The table above, by Bertram Gross, presents succinctly some of the major changes in social structure in the transition from pre-industrial to post-industrial societies.

By comparing the various elements in the first column with those in the second column one may get a general impression of the kinds of structural change in the many preindustrial societies now in transition to industrialism. Neither column, however, presents a "general" or "ideal" type . . . Let us now compare the second column with the third column. Here we find tremendous changes. The most dramatic ones, of course, are the "mobiletic revolution," . . . and the transformation of the old-time factory system into a system of goods production in which machinery replaces not only manual labor but even large amounts of mental labor . . . We must also note the growth of "complex, mixed organizational constellations" and "megalopoli and metropoli," . . . In addition, the following structural changes may be briefly touched upon:

1) Increased life expectancy is creating a social structure in which there is more "generational intertwining" than ever before in history, that is, more active older people around to compete with—and try to impose their values on—younger generations.

2) The learning force—composed both of those enrolled in full-time formal education and those who take part in educational "refresher," "extensions" and "development" programs while working—is growing so fast that it will sooner or later become as large as the employed labor force.

3) Professionalization of the labor force, with over 70 per cent in various kinds of services, will bring into being new elites and new orientations in labor unions, trade associations and ranking systems in organizations.

4) Secular humanism in values will be based on material abundance, as contrasted with (a) "zero sum" non-redistributive values of pre-industrial societies (based on their limited productive potentials) and (b) the "scarcity economics" and "zero sum" redistributive ideologies in industrial societies (increasingly out of keeping with growing productive potentials).

One may again underline, as is evident from the table, that we presently have societies with different components at each of the "stages" above. Even within developed nations such as the U.S., characterized as having entered the post-industrial phase, many elements of the social structure still remain pre-industrial and industrial—and may well continue to do so. Though the various tables used may suggest abrupt discontinuity between each phase, the development is, in reality, much more uneven.

ing and controlling the spread of plague, smallpox, cholera, etc., on the global scale.

5. The World Weather Watch, etc.

This area of transnational "human service network" management certainly offers an executive challenge which may be larger, and ultimately more socially rewarding, than even the largest multinational corporate undertakings.

The table above, by Bertram Gross,[5] presents succinctly some of the major changes in social structure in the transition from Pre-Industrial to Post-Industrial societies.

One may again underline, as is evident from the table, that we presently have societies with different components at each of the "stages" above. Even within developed nations such as the U.S., characterized as having entered the Post-Industrial phase, many elements of the social structure still remain Pre-Industrial and Industrial—and may well continue to do so. Though the various tables used may suggest abrupt discontinuity between each phase, the development is, in reality, much more uneven.

The Post-Industrial shift is still in transition.

The Post-Industrial hypothesis should neither be taken as negating all previous period values, institutions, etc., or as wholly desirable in some of its aspects, or as accomplished fact! In terms of developmental time, all major contemporary societies are still in varying stages of transition from agriculturally based forms to fully industrialized. For example, it is only in the past seventy years, approximately, that the United States has become an industrialized society, and it is only in the past few decades that it has begun to display trends of moving into a Post-Industrial stage. Though we refer glibly to "scientific and technological" societies, we have as yet no such examples; no one society is scientifically or technologically based to the extent that its operating premises, institutions, and goals are congruent with scientific principles or take full cognizance of technological capabilities. Again, at our present stage, this may not be wholly desirable or practical.

One overriding set of facts, however, is arrayed around the ways in which scientific and technological development have forced us into the reality of a relatively small global community with the beginnings of a world economy and some outlines of the sets of international and transnational institutions which may be required to operate at this level.

THE GLOBAL BALANCE OF HUMANITY AND ENVIRONMENT

We have also arrived conceptually at the point where we regard the global situation of humanity as being sustained within a delicately balanced and complex set of environmental relationships. From this time on, all major elements of the human enterprise are now seen to be closely interlocked via a man-made eco-system which has to be considered as an integral "organic" subsystem of the planetary ecology. Recent emphases have been on the modification of this over-all system by human action in large-scale undertakings—through physical transformation of the earth to economic, technological, and other purposes. Such transformations have also been occasioned by politico-ethical systems, by needs for social contiguity and communications, by art, religion, etc.

The range and magnitude of our technological intrusions into the planetary biosphere is now such that all of our large-scale techno-industrial undertakings need, increasingly, to be gauged in terms of their long-range consequences and implications for the global community.

In similar fashion, the scale of many of our global technological systems—i.e., of production, distribution, transportation, and communications—has gone beyond the capacities of any single nation or group of nations to sustain and wholly operate. They require, and are dependent upon, the resource range of the entire earth for the metals and materials of which they are built and the energies to run them—in which no single nation is now self-sufficient.

The whole planetary "life-support system" increasingly relies upon the global interchange not only of physical resources and finished products, but of the "knowledge pool"—of research, development, and technical and managerial expertise—and the highly trained personnel who sustain and expand this.

In these combined senses, and at this scale, there are few "wholly" local problems anymore—such as may be left entirely to the short-range "economic" expediency or temporary ideological preference of some exclusively national concerns.

Many of the decisions affecting the disposition, use, and operation of our large-scale technologies go far beyond the relatively brief commercial, economic, or political mandates of local decision making. Air, water, and soil pollution are not local—the air is not restrained within municipal or national boundaries, nor are the oceans.

The "managerial" implications of organizing, regulating, and developing at the scale and complexity of this global enterprise far outweigh many of the internal problems of management in any of the sectors of our local societies.

Advanced vs. developing nations: a managerial challenge.

In terms of managerial challenges and problem definitions and priorities, the continued disparities between the so-called advanced nations and the lesser developed may be viewed as the gravest threat in our immediate future.

The explosive rises in population, the pressures on food lands and other resources, the scale of human wastage, environmental destruction, and the social disorganization and pestilence accompanying even our limited wars, are also linked in due measure to the revolutions in human expectations which now circle the globe.

These disparities between the *haves* and the *have nots* may also be defined as part of a growing ecological imbalance in which the "hyperactive" advanced economies extract, produce, and consume more, with more waste by-products, than the lesser developed—and by their increased dependence on raw materials from the latter now exist in a directly parasitic relationship to them.

In terms of energy use, the more fortunate individual in the industrial countries consumes more than fifty times that of his counterpart in the poorer regions —and contributes in due measure much more than fifty times the by-product pollutants now critically affecting the global environ systems.

Over-all, in the past decade, the advanced countries—far less than one quarter of the world's population—consumed:

> 77% of all the coal
> 81% of the petroleum
> 95% of the natural gas

with one nation alone, the United States, specifically using one third of the world's total industrial energy, and consuming approximately 40 per cent of the world's output of raw materials.

In round terms, approximately 20 per cent of the world's population enjoys 80 per cent of the world's income—using more than half of all the earth's resources and producing a concomitant balance of the biospheric pollutants which now threaten the viability of the planet.

This gap between rich and poor has other salient features which make it one of the most critical problems facing man in the next two decades.

The internal managerial problems of the "advanced" societies will certainly not vanish with the transition to post-industrialization. In important ways, this transition changes many of the ground rules upon which such societies have operated, and they will face increasingly social, economic, and political turbulence if necessary responses to these changes are resisted or inadequately conceived.

Complex service systems will require new management techniques.

We have already noted the decline in wholly economic and material measures of human activity. The expansion of interest and investment in human services provides a model of longer term concern with the quality of individual and collective social life rather than with its merely quantifiable and economic aspects.

In relation to such a human-services oriented type of society, it is evident, already, in the U.S. that full participation in the society might no longer be predicated on private enterprise and the so-called market system as we have traditionally regarded it.

Apart from food, clothing, housing (and many areas of these are already heavily subsidized)—the large scale services of the society—education, communications, transportation and health, etc., tend to go beyond "economic" provision by private corporate concerns. They are increasingly government provided or heavily assisted by public funds.

We may note also that, as many complex service systems (e.g., light, heat,

water, housing, refuse disposal) become vital to the actual survival of large concentrated populations, they will increasingly need to go beyond the short-range
profit orientation and expediency of private concerns and will require different
managerial, regulatory, and administrative systems. As people become more
vulnerable to service breakdown, repairs, and maintenance of these systems, the
issue of ethical contractual bases for their efficient and equitable provision becomes more acute. More services, more goods, and their control in the public
interest, will pass over into the realm of public utilities.

The critical role of public institutions and voluntary agencies in this kind of
transition need hardly be underlined, nor need it be much stressed that such expanded needs for public service will, in turn, have to be based on new conceptual
attitudes, motivations, and rewards for such service.

Public institutions face nonmanagement problems.

As we go forward into the next two decades, the social composition of the
polity will also change with new value orientations and consequent new pressures upon the administration of public institutions. There will be a much more
heterogeneous and diverse spectrum of interest constituencies than ever before.
Previously marginal groups and classes are already asserting their specific identities and degrees of autonomy, e.g.: (1) what has been termed the new property class: those who carry their property around in their heads—professionals,
students, technicians, and "idea people"; (2) the emergent class/ethnic groups:
blacks, Spanish/Americans, Indians, etc.,—those who have come to value and
elaborate their own cultural position, language, and social locus as positive
life style (with concomitant demands for recognition and respect), and
(3) women, who have also begun to redefine stereotyped roles and now
seek to engage on their own terms, in their own right, as a separate but equal
group—a majority group—requiring new rules, social postures, and identities.

The changing information environment, with more access by individuals and
groups to information systems and communication channels, will enable many
of these diverse constituencies to form swiftly into coalitions and pressure groups
with which to pursue their particular needs. A continuing problem, however, will
be the currently fragmented and piecemeal approach to institutionalized public
service and its uneasy linkage to wholly political expediency in decisions and
policy formation.

All of these changes have their dangers and uncertainties—and place the
role of management in all sectors in the most critically exposed position in society.
There will be the need, for example, to work out more consciously and deliberately the relationships between the sectors—government, business, education, etc.
If all the assumed directions toward increasing governmental provision and control of major services were correct, this would, obviously, make for enormously
centralized power in the society. The "corporate state" may be more or less

efficient, its other proclivities for control over more areas of individual and social life are certainly less desirable.

New attitudes toward work will have serious consequences.

Shifting our level of attention and returning to one of the "ground rules" referred to above, we may note another problem area which may be specific to the emerging Post-Industrial phase. The core activity of work itself becomes progressively detached from those statures and roles which "locate" and inter-relate members of the society and largely provide much of the meaning and purposeful direction of its institutionalized activities.

With access to material (and, to an extent, spiritual) means of gratification no longer measured by the yardstick of "gainful labor," many of our institution-alized reward and incentive systems become less and less effective; and in turn this begins to threaten those sets of institutionalized relationships which provided the cohesive basis for many societal undertakings. This dysjunction is not only reflected in the youthful dropout but increasingly leads up through worker dis-affection with the quality of work and its environs to the executive dropout. Having, in the industrial period, largely substituted material rewards for more intangible "psychic income," we now face a decreasing repertoire of institutional "sticks and carrots" with which to engage people in various sectors of the social system. Both the internal and external aspects of managing the core enterprises of the advanced society will be increasingly impacted with this phenomenon.

Far from being a utopian steady-state phase of society, the Post-Industrial transition carries with it its own specific set of problems and "managerial" chal-lenges.

Two Views of Future Change

As no one may accurately predict the future for the next twenty years with much certainty or internal consistency, two viewpoints regarding broad societal changes are presented. The first is based upon the assumptions made by the authors of the major chapters in this report; the second, upon a more gen-eralized framework of overarching assumptions, more directly concerned with the nature of change itself.

AS VIEWED IN PRECEDING CHAPTERS BY THE AUTHORS

Amongst the initial assumptions which were discussed, there was considerable divergence on the need to cast such a study within the future. A strong case was made for dealing with the problems which the executive faces "now." It was underlined that:

(1) while future trends may alter circumstances, forecasting has frequently been highly inaccurate;

(2) decisions made upon long-range assumptions alone can be dangerous—in overconstraining and distorting current issues and problems;

(3) there are built-in barriers which do prejudice managers against considering long range (for example, most reward systems are based strictly on the attainment of short-range results); and

(4) the practice of management, not only in business but in most of our institutions, tends to be inherently insensitive to "future" trends.

This may be best summed up in the following quotation from the study, which states the problem of how the business institution, specifically, must deal primarily in the present—but may also flexibly adjust to emerging forces which change present circumstances:

"We will be tomorrow what we are becoming today." This approach to judging an *individual's* future performance by his past achievements is based on the notion that an individual is not likely to change his characteristics or capabilities. Our experience shows that many business firms have the same incapacity to change. People get grooved in conducting the same old business in the same old way, so the future course of the enterprise is very much an unfolding of the present.

"It is not necessary, however, that a business firm be in the future what it is becoming today. The people making up any business are responsive to decisions and leadership in changing the goals, objectives, organization structure, policies, programs, and style of managing the enterprise. . . .

"Thus dealing with the future calls for an almost continuous flow of *present* decisions as the outlook is assessed and re-assessed in the light of new forces. Many such decisions will have an influence throughout the business; and some may commit resources with considerable finality. Some decisions may foreclose the making of others. So part of the skill in coping with change is to keep the options open as long as that can soundly be done." (Bower and Walton)

The current or "now" decisions are, of course, not only decided by future possibilities and consequences but also by those sets of conscious and unconscious assumptions about both the present and the past which provide the perceptual and conceptual framework—the images, premises, and value sets—through which we selectively screen, assess, and evaluate impinging changes.

The value image is enormously important in its effects. . . . Incoming messages are not admitted to the image free. At the gate of the image stands the value system demanding payment. . . . We now know that what used to be regarded as primary sense data are in fact highly learned interpretations. We see the world the way we see it because it pays us and has paid us to see it that way.[6]

We may presume that these sets of implicit assumptions will vary from one managerial sector to another, from individual to individual, and, to a considerable extent, by the accumulated experience set, and the position, status, class, and role of the individual—as manager or managed.

An important divergence: the nature of change itself.

This divergence was polarized around several propositions:

1. *That all the major changes in society had already occurred,* that there is no longer an accelerating rate of change comparable with that of the past fifty years, and that we were now entering a plateau period with specific regard to major technological changes. This did not rule out socio-cultural changes. Major changes in this area may be expected—but with emphasis on the key role of *social innovation* as more important than additional sophisticated technical advances.

While suggesting a leveling out of change rates, this view did not discount the need to plan for the future—"what are the plausible crises which may occur and how can we better anticipate their occurrence and the other contingencies we might expect," i.e., the future as anticipated surprise. It also stressed the need for in-depth "hindsight" study of bad decisions and how they were made.

2. *That we were now in an acute transitional period of fundamental structural change in society* which, though it might not exhibit the range of technological advance of the immediate past would, in itself, constitute a multifold and accelerating change wave of comparable dimensions. The significance of this specific set of changes for management is succinctly stated below:

A major premise is that . . . [the] developed countries of the world are going through a period of major social discontinuity which heralds arrival of a new era increasingly referred to as Post-Industrial—an era of major restructuring of social values and institutions. The result of this structuring will be a widening of the gap between the best of current managerial practice and the type of practice which will be required for continued successful organizational behavior. (Ansoff)

3. *The third propositional focus suggested that a further wave of technological changes may be expected* through (a) the fusion and convergence of existing and developing "hard" technologies, e.g., the combination of information and communications technologies, and (b) development of new "soft" technologies, e.g., the bio-physical and bio-chemical ranges in health and environmental areas and in areas of bio-technologies relating to agriculture, to new bio-technical substitutions for existing technical processes, etc. Also, and importantly, this focus implies that the older divisions and presumed "linear" causal linkages between physical technologies, economic change and social, cultural, and political change will no longer obtain—that we are entering a period whose systemic interlinkage and interdependence of change agencies themselves will be quite different from the immediate past—and will, therefore, not only challenge current management practices in each sector but eventually change the nature of management itself in many fundamental ways.

We may note that though these viewpoints may appear to be polarized, they, in reality, are related through a spectrum, or continuum, of assumptions and attitudes which overlap and interweave. They exhibit a considerable degree of unanimity that, indeed, "uncertainty may be elevated as a management principle" in confronting the next few decades!

A more critical divergence: the definition
(explicit and implicit) of management itself.

One viewpoint tends to hold that management is, in many senses, a neutral instrumentality—a body of ascertained principles which operate in much the same way whether we are discussing the management of a business, of government, of education, or of a voluntary association. Associated with this would be some well-defined set of expectations regarding managerial "efficiency," the fusion of management with "administration" and, to a certain degree, regarding the underlying premise that there was an implicit hierarchy of the manager and the managed—that strategic objectives are set by top management and these are then implemented "tactically" by successive lower levels of management.

The image is one of the professional manager skilled in the principles of scientific management and able to deploy his skills efficiently within any given organizational form or situation. Division between "the manager" and "the managed" is maintained, and even though turbulence and uncertainty may be assumed as external to the organization managed, there is the underlying assumption of continuity, stability, and compliance within the complex series of linkages relating individuals in organizational forms. This somewhat unidimensional view of the manager also avoids various current dilemmas of the manager as person, e.g., as parent, as citizen, as concerned participant in the affairs of his community and society, often in conflicting roles and with divided conscience and moral attitude between the demands of each role.

Somewhat in distinction from this position, Drucker, while adhering to the over-all development of sets of management principles, suggests in his analysis of the changes in management conditioned by different socioeconomic and cultural contexts that, with reference to the future development of European and Japanese management:

> It is clear that there will be no universal management model. The next decade is likely to see an adaptation and a further development of managerial principles within the predominant cultural and economic traditions of each area. It is, therefore, important to examine the underlying differences and to indicate their consequences.

Where our initial definition of management was drawn from the business area, it is of interest to compare this with the somewhat polar position stated within the "New Perspectives on Governance":

> To perceive public management as administrative technology is to miss the essence, because this does not have much bearing on the spirit or quality of the govern-

ing process. . . . The eventual test of the managerial process in governance is its ability to satisfy—that is to say, its capacity to cope with the expectations, stresses and perceptions of its tangled consistency. Its role is not merely to mind the store, nor to provide an institutional priesthood, but to *comprehend the potential* of the society and, thus comprehending, to construct and execute strategies which realize that potential within limits and safeguards. . . . It will no longer be taken for granted that governments are licensed to act in the stead of the governed and at low risk of interference. The opposite expectation will prevail, that public consent is not to be presumed but to be sought. Election to office will not be a blanket license to govern but an indicator of conditional confidence. (Carey)

Within the two polar positions may also be detected some further implicit assumptions on the criteria of efficiency and effectiveness. Without detailing the internal managerial efficiency objectives, the different institutional sectors of business, government, education, etc., one may note the continuance of the somewhat folkloric assumption that business is "more efficient" than the other sectors and the accompanying exhortation that they may be better run by its principles.

This confusion of short-run "efficiency" with longer-run "effectiveness" may, indeed, lead to considerable and very real inefficiency when the former operating standards are applied to institutions, whose managerial goals may not be clearly defined in wholly economic and "administratively convenient" terms.

The contribution of the "voluntary sector" in society, a major subject in this study, highlights the above discussion. This sector, specifically, in certain of its growth directions tends to take on the tasks which are not performed or have been relegated by other social sectors for various reasons, amongst which we may often find that they cannot be economically performed nor meet the more rationally efficient criteria. Though it may obviously strive for greater managerial capability and efficiency in carrying out its tasks, the voluntary organization cannot be measured within the same management efficiency criteria of, say, business or government. Its constituencies are more diverse and flexible; they are more directly participative and "unmanageable" by their very nature. Their goals and objectives may vary from the immediately practical ends of the welfare mission to the more transcendental of the religious order—and, more often than not, may combine both in the same organization.

It may be useful at this point to conclude this cursory review of the internal assumptions of the study with a selection of some stated trends and assumptions from the three chapters dealing directly with the major sectors of society. In each case, these are summary "headline extracts"—without the specific qualifications and implications for their management which are treated at length in the original texts.

Changes in viewpoint represent shifts away from traditional perspectives.

From the above selection of stated trends in three major institutional areas, we may note some considerable shifts away from traditional perspectives. For

AUTHORS' VIEWS ON TRENDS

Forces for the Future: Business (Bower)

1. Erosion of religious standards and moral values
2. Broad and urgent demand for improvement in the quality of the environment
3. Expansion of consumerism
4. Rising level of education
5. Continued increase in leisure time
6. Changing social attitudes and values
7. Further growth in the size and dominance of our major institutions
8. Continued rapid internationalization of the world and growth of the multinational (or international) corporation
9. Pressure for zero population growth
10. Increasing dominance of the service industries
11. Continued increases in foreign competition
12. Continuation of the forces that retard increases in the productivity of labor
13. Increasing tempo and impact of technology
14. Continued increases in the speed and effectiveness of transportation and communications
15. Accelerating impact of the computer in information handling
16. Growing sense of social responsibility in business decision-makers
17. Increasing lack of realism and balance in dealing with complex technological, social, and political issues

General Assumptions and Trends: Governance (Carey)

1. In the next twenty-five years, accepted distinctions between political governance and the governed will be less apparent . . . trend towards sharing of power, blurring of distinctions between political governance and the governed.
2. Emergence of a "social criticism industry"—increase in voluntary and intersect organizations for critical policy analysis, environmental conservation, ombudsmanship and citizen advocacy . . . information technology (will) enable such groups to mount continuous watch on public management performance.
3. (Consequent) decrease in flexibility: increased pressure for decisions, implementation, and disclosure; lead times become shortened as well as reaction times.
4. Trend towards the designing and shaping of institutions with features of openness and "self destruct" mechanisms.
5. As the nation's aggregate influence and affluence grows and economic poverty decreases, the inequities and inequalities in the distribution of income, power, and wealth will become more visible and less acceptable . . . government will be increasingly expected to correct for these distortions.
6. To accommodate rising demands, government will be obliged to divest itself of unmanageable operational activities . . . to spin off responsibilities and resources to other levels of government through strategies of devolution and revenue sharing.
7. a) Likelihood that roles of national government will partially reverse to what they were at the start of the century . . . via regional clustering to set decentralized goals and priorities.
   b) Beyond this (however) central government will be more deeply engaged in problems of income support and economic regulation . . .
   c) Public management "hived off" via quasi-governmental institutions as contractors and grantees entrusted with delivery of services and governed by user groups.
8. Estimate that not less than 40% and up to 50% of GNP will be committed to public purposes—through aggregated demand of government contingent liabilities, subsidies, credit guarantees.
9. Altered calculus of American power in world affairs:
   a) diminution of political and military leverage
   b) rise of combination economies constraining our bargaining power in world markets.
10. Crisis of values and perspectives on goals and uses of power relative to the human condition . . . efficiency criteria will carry governance part of the way but only part . . . Not power but humanism is the chief hope for the new governance.

Some Major Future Trends in Voluntarism and Nongovernmental, Nonprofit Organizations (Dixon: Horton Smith)

1. Increasing importance of voluntary organizations as devices for social navigation and problem-diagnosis/solution-experimentation.
2. Increased pressure on the free and participatory nature of the voluntary, nongovernmental, nonprofit sector because of the increasing size and complexity of voluntary organizations.
3. More rapid turnover in voluntary group memberships and more rapid changes in the membership composition.
4. Increases in the more temporary, ad hoc, short-term and problem-focused voluntary groups/nongovernmental organizations which will form, be active, and quickly disband as the need or problem they addressed is dealt with or recedes in importance.
5. Increased tendency for various types of communication media and communication participation networks to become informal functional substitutes for voluntary organizations/nongovernmental organizations.
6. Increases in the number and variety of voluntary groups and . . . as average education levels, occupational specialization, and discretionary ("leisure") time increase . . .
7. . . . development of nongovernmental organization/voluntary organization/volunteer administration as an independent profession . . .
8. Increasing challenges to the economic viability of the voluntary sector or specific portions of it in a world of increasing competition for resources of all kinds.
9. . . . substantial increase in the number of "intersect organizations," hybrid types of quasi-voluntary, also quasi-governmental, quasi-business organizations . . . indicating a search for new organizational forms suited both to the complexity of our problems and growing sophistication of population.
10. Broad changes in the relative composition of the voluntary sector, as issue-oriented and advocacy groups continue to come to the fore and intensify their demands for justice, equality of opportunity, power, etc. Declining emphasis on traditional service-oriented voluntarism as more of these tasks and goals are taken on by business and government.

example, the forces for the future viewed from business are less concerned with the internal management and boundary problems of the firm than those external forces which might previously have been concerned as relatively marginal to business—changes in social attitudes, moral standards and values, social responsibility, population growth policy, etc. In governance, the major preoccupations are with the devolution of governmental administration, in its conventionally hierarchic and politically oriented forms, towards more open, directly participative, and flexible structures which depart considerably from governmental development as we have known it. Even if it is not an assumed "withering away of the state," there is an underlying assumption of changes in the dominant role and centrality of political governance, as such, which are antithetical to the conventional wisdom. Though the voluntary "associational" sector has been a major institutional component in American society from the founding of the Republic, its explicit recognition as a viable and dynamic agency for larger social change has not been generally admitted within discussion regarding the over-all management of that society. As we may now note, the growth, and expansion of interests and objectives, of this sector assumes that its traditionally passive, non-political and, to an extent, non-ideological, posture has been already changed towards more direct, concerted and activist, concern, not only with the social and ethical aspects of societal welfare, but with the broadest range of economic, political and socio-cultural issues.

The most salient assumption, common to all of the contributions in this study, is the increased convergence and interpenetration of all major social institutions —and, implied within this, an emergent commonalty of their goals and objectives.The general direction may be summarized within four major trend patterns:

Trend towards pluralism

Increase in shared and decentralized governance

Growth of voluntary sector towards more over-all societal involvement

Governance function expanded to nonpolitical organizations

Decrease of political and military leverage as centers of power

Growth of multi-constituent social processes

Growing investment in broad social needs diversified to user requirements needs

Trend towards social responsiveness

Increasing accountability of decision makers in all institutions

Environmental pressure on firm

Nonprofit organizations become more "market" or "general constituency" oriented

Increasing responsibility of business beyond business as such

Trend towards convergence of public and private organizations

Business and government intersects widen

Convergence of public and private institutions

Less differentiation between profit and nonprofit, governmental and nongovernmental organizations

Freedoms of nonprofit organizations increase

Changes in the character/nature of management

Decrease in hierarchic, authority-oriented, managerial forms

Shift from "tactical" short-range to "strategic" long-range management

Increase in participatory role of external "user" and internal "managed" groups

Shift of basis of authority from economic coercion to consent of managed

Management by experience less valid

Shift of attention from management of others to self-management

Emergence of group management

Even where the above trends underline convergence of institutional function, etc., it is, however, still tacitly assumed within the over-all study that the power and centrality of the major institutions will continue as relatively unchanged within the next two decades. With the exception of the growth in influence of the voluntary sector, the balance and division of power between the economy, the polity, etc., is regarded as essentially similar with minor caveats. In most important senses, the over-all profile of American society is held fairly constant within a national and international climate of increasing turbulence and uncertainty.

Given the degree of convergence, interpenetration, and increased interdependence of our institutions assumed, it is still essentially true that those who run the major enterprises of the society in effect run the society. And, although considerable attention is accorded acute managerial crises and challenges to institutional legitimacy, at different levels and in different sectors of the society, the central debate of the past few decades remains somewhat obscured—*who does the managing; on whose behalf; and to what ends and purposes?*

CHANGE . . . AND THE RESPONSE TO CHANGE

Rather than attempting to provide a definitive set of facts, predictions or forecasts, this review is intended to focus more upon questions regarding change itself. Its main function is to complement the sets of internal assumptions above, and to indicate broadly: those changes which have already occurred in the recent past (i.e., how did we get to where we are now?), and those which we might expect to impinge, directly or indirectly, upon the management of our major institutions and organizations in the next 25 years (i.e., what assumptions can we make about where we are going).

Even where we cannot accurately predict significant events for the next period, the premises for prediction do play a role in determining the occurrence of events and how we may respond to the changes as they occur.

Many of our current dilemmas stem from critical changes in the immediate past.

Many of our current dilemmas result from a situation in which we have had, possibly, more radical transformations in the human condition in the past 75 to 100 years than at any comparable period in history. Within three generations, there has been a series of scientific, technological, social, and economic changes impacting one upon the other.

One major discontinuity in our own period, as Drucker [7] and others have underlined, originates with developments in science in the late nineteenth century—the extension, as earlier noted, of experimental and measurable ranges into the invisible subsensorial world of atomic, molecular, and "radiation" phenomena. One singular resultant of this development, the use of nuclear weapons at the end of World War II, is an obvious discontinuity which still continues to reverberate throughout our societies. The more direct application of many of these discoveries into the industrial process, occurring during and after World War II, marked the emergence of a new relationship between basic scientific research, technical development, and socio-industrial use. The major tools, and change agents, of our present period—electronics, automatic control systems, and computers—emerge from this relation, plus the new "software" tools of operations research, decision theory, systems analysis. A major accelerator of this discontinuity was, therefore, the "organization of the invention" or the innovative or change process in itself.

Referring back to Drucker's point, however, about the past half-century as being essentially chaarcterized by continuity—as measured by the yardsticks of the economist—one might qualify this in other areas and by other yardsticks. The very continuity of growth and expansion has possibly engendered many social discontinuities or major changes—for example:

1. The change from socioeconomic arrangements based on scarcity to those of relative abundance—from the alienation of poverty to the alienation of affluence.

2. The break in the transmission of relevant "experience," of norms and mores from one generation to another with its corresponding changes and conflicts in values; the change from production/deferment of gratification to attitudinal sets of consumption/immediate gratification.

3. Cultural changes via the growth of the mass media and the relatively enormous increase in output of mass entertainment, leading again to the wide diffusion of rapidly changing models, images of viable human con-

duct, discontinuous changes in expectations, life styles, etc.; changes in cultural products in the fine art sector which represent major discontinuities in painting, sculpture, literature, etc., and in the climate of ideas within which these are produced.

In short, there appear to be areas of discontinuity and crisis in many socio-cultural forms—institutional, psychological, interpretative, aesthetic, etc.

Some of these may, indeed, be traced back to the same set of scientific dis-coveries (both in physical and social sciences) beginning in the Renaissance, and gradually diffusing throughout Western society till their clearer formulation and synthesis in the late nineteenth century and early twentieth century. Many of our "conceptual" difficulties regarding change may still stem from the emergence of relative indeterminacy and intangibility which began to erode our models of the physical universe itself and of human society within it. From being a relatively contained, fixed and "rationally" apprehendable Newtonian world to the gener-ally educated person, the whole order of reality began to shift its outlines, become ambiguous and unfused, with relationships which were neither visibly nor logi-cally apparent before. The context of present change still reflects this dichotomy between the older "world view" of relatively fixed series of logically connected linear cause-and-effect mechanisms, and that world view in which ends/means, issues/questions, problems/solutions all interpenetrate, loop back upon one another in interweaving sets of feedback patterns.

Changes in the twentieth century have been bigger, different.

They differ not only in their quantitative aspects from those of the past but also in the quality and degree of their interrelationships. They are no longer isolable sequences of events separated in time, in the numbers of people affected, and in the social and physical processes which are perturbed. They may be further characterized by their simultaneity of occurrence—by their swift inter-penetration, by increased feedback upon one another and, hence, by the greater interdependence of one group of changes upon another.

1. Increased Frequency. New relationships and narrowing intervals be-tween scientific discoveries, technological development, and large-scale usage have become dramatically visible particularly in the last twenty-five years. For example, where it used to take five to ten years for a product to move from the research to the production stage, this process has often been shortened to one or two years. Many of the products now made by industry did not exist twenty-five years ago.

In part, this may be specifically attributed to the institutionalization of the change process itself, i.e., the deliberate organization and management of inno-vation which emerges during and immediately after World War II.

This increased frequency of change in the research, development, and produc-tion cycles has been matched by similar changes in market and consumer demands—many more consumer product areas have moved into more rapid obsolescence cycles and degrees of expendability, e.g., from buildings and refrigerators to paper towels.

2. *Range and Scale.* Many of the longer range and larger scale effects of various types of changes, e.g., on the physical environment, on social relations on health, etc., have only become measurably apparent in the last two decades. More attention has been given to the adverse effects of such changes, but equal emphasis could be placed on their positive effects, e.g., gains in public health through improved diet, sanitation, medical advances, etc.; gains in the quality of living standards through improved housing, product control and maintenance, access to wider ranges of products and services, etc.

3. *Size and Complexity.* In 1903 the Wright brothers could introduce a new technology, the aeroplane, at a level where it could be designed, built, and tested by two men. A comparable technological development in the past decade was the Apollo project requiring approximately 300,000 people, thousands of parts, and over one million times the cost—and representing in itself many significant advances in managerial innovation.

With the increased size of systems, and wider distribution of products and services, has also come increases in the potential numbers of people and institutions who may be affected by systems breakdown and product malfunctions, e.g., from the relatively "minor" hazards of appliance breakdown or the occurrence of botulism in a two- or three-thousand batch of a processed food, to "large" aircraft crashes or major power failures over large regions. These have given rise to managerial questions of "accountability," of the ethical bases for contractual services upon which millions of persons may depend, etc. Recently, as in the SST, the adoption, large-scale development, and use of a new technological advance is no longer left to the market mechanism but increasingly exposed to debate regarding its possible socio-physical and socioeconomic consequences.

In similar vein, power utilities are now required to file "environmental impact studies" to secure approval for new large-scale installations. In terms of managerial accountability in the public interest, might we also envisage requirements of "social, cultural, and individual impact studies" for similar approval of the introduction of comparable products and services in other areas of the economy?

4. *Expanded Impact and Awareness.* Through increases in the speed of communications and transportation, the agencies of change (artifacts, ideas, techniques, images, and attitudes) are now diffused more rapidly and penetrate more swiftly into more aspects of human life.

The "management of information" brought the Vietnam war into almost every living room—and, in turn, affected the management of the war itself. The local impact of the introduction of a new soft drink or a supermarket in world terms may have as much cultural impact as any series of ideological messages. Changes in life styling—from clothes, to art, to houses and "styles of protest"—are now diffused on the world scale in a manner which is unprecedented historically.

The swift communication of information sharply decreases the "time cushion" between the emergence of "an issue" into public prominence and the concomitant public pressures for legislators and public administrators to deal with it. Many aspects of the "managerial crisis" might be attributed to this specific aspect of change. The amount of information, in itself, and the increased numbers of information stimuli also impose new strains on management and decision making.

5. *Differential Rates.* Changes in technologies, in ideas, institutional and social changes occur at varying rates and have different time spans of integration and acceptance causing dissonance and discontinuity in and between various sectors of society.

The combination of the above factors gives less and less time for "managerial" assessment of specific changes in themselves, and for individual and social adaptation. At one extreme, change becomes the preferred norm; at the other, when it is associated with disruption and uncertainty, resistance to change becomes the mode. As we have been historically accustomed to slow and sporadic change, our latent assumption is that change is abnormal, that stability is the obverse of change—and "control" lies with alternation of these two states. More effective understanding and management of the change process lies with the recognition that change and motion are constants, and that stability may be accommodated within change.

What are the future connotations of today's critical changes?

GLOBAL ASSUMPTIONS

1. *Increase in Population.* There are approximately 1.2 billion more people on earth.

In 1900, there were 1,571 million people on earth; in 1945, 2,300 million; in 1971, 3,706 million; we have added 2.1 billion to our numbers since 1900. In the U.S., estimates of population increase show 82 per cent of this between 1965 and 1975 will be among persons under 35 years—between 1975 and 1995, the proportion will be about 70 per cent. Between now and 1980, persons between 20 and 40 years of age will increase in number at a rate twice that anticipated for the total population.

More people not only require more in quantity of goods and services but demand more in far greater diversity and quality than in any previous period. To keep pace with these requirements we have, in many cases, measurably extracted more materials, metals, minerals and fuels from the earth and atmosphere in the past century alone than in all history. This increase in numbers and needs has refueled and widened the debate about the overall "manageability" of both national and world populations in terms of available resources and energies. Most recently, one feature of this debate has concentrated on the concomitant amounts of "pollution" this engenders and its implications for future growth. Whether one agrees, or not, with this negative aspect of the debate, it has already impacted upon the management and forward planning of major components of the industrial complex.

In dealing with our assumptions for the next twenty-five years, this area of population/resource relations will be a crucial aspect, e.g., affecting future markets for goods/services, the balance between public and private interests, questions of the uses of "the commons," of regulatory practices, etc.

2. Growth in Large Urban Concentrations. In 1945, there were 41 cities in the world with over one million inhabitants.

Today, there are 83 such cities. Accompanying this concentration, there has been, particularly in the U.S., an out migration from the central city to the sub and exurbs. Apart from the managerial challenge of the "governance" and maintenance of such large human aggregates, there are a series of ancillary questions which should enter into our future assumptions, e.g.:

1. The development of new physical and social technologies of urban services in housing, health, transportation, security, communications, etc.
2. The rise of new goods industries and service forms to accommodate the enlarged scale and complexity of urban living.

3. Larger Organizational Employment. In the U.S. particularly, more people are employed in large organizational systems, e.g. educational and corporate complexes, government—local and Federal—and its ancillary semi-government and private agencies, etc. These are not only large in numbers but in their geographical scope and in their heightened degree of interconnectivity and interaction at different levels. For example, only about 15 per cent of total sales in the economy are from small individual enterprises even though these may be identified as 85% of the number of businesses. "In 1935, there were 6.8 million farms. Now there are less than 3.7 million. By 1980, there may be less than 1 million . . . Today the top 3 per cent of all farms produce more than the bottom 78 per cent . . . by 1959, these big units . . . had acquired 49 per cent of the land (and) produced 31.5 per cent of all crops and livestock." [8]

The top 500 largest U.S. industrial corporations account for almost two-thirds of all domestic industrial sales and 120 of these have annual sales exceeding $1 billion.

In general work terms, there is a somewhat parallel picture. "Between 1950 and 1960, for example, private enterprise accounted for only one out of every ten new jobs that were created in the economy. All the rest were generated by the public or the private not-for-profit sectors. . . . Today, a third of the labor force works for some employer other than a private businessman, compared with only 5% in 1929." [9] The relation between government and private enterprise is further obscured by the indirect and direct subsidy patterns and by more direct dependence by some enterprises, e.g. in the defense sector, on public financing.

More than two-thirds of the 10 million new jobs created between 1960 and 1970 were generated by the expansion of governmental expenditures, half of the jobs directly on the public (especially the state and local) payroll, and half of the jobs indirectly on private payrolls created by government purchases. . . . The pay check, however, now certified a declining percentage of the population as consumers of the abundance. Massive income transfers by social security and welfare checks qualify more than 30 million payees with purchasing power; that is more than twice the number of people who earn their livings on the public payroll. Taking these 45 million public-sector people, adding those employed by public purchases in the private sector, and counting the dependents of all of these, we come to . . . a watershed number of more than 100 million . . . more than half of the American people now depend for their daily bread on money laid out for public purposes.[10]

This is not to say that such a trend towards larger organizational employment may persist in the next few decades or that there may not be greater decentralization of production, and particularly new service entities, with more diversity of both large and small operations. A concealed point in the above may be, more importantly, the overall-role of the public sector in generating credit, etc., for quasi-public services provided by the private sector.

4. The World Economy. Though still characterized by varying degrees of national autonomy and competitiveness, it has been trending towards more interdependent and cooperative practices within which the national units operate as members of various trading and political blocs, e.g., OECD, COMECON, EEC, CACM, LAFTA, etc.

Recent monetary readjustments at the world level confirm one growing aspect at this level. The growth of the multinational corporate entities is another aspect. During the 1960's, the ten largest multinational corporations expanded at some 8 per cent per year, nearly double the growth rate for many national states. Of the 100 largest economic entities in the world, just over half are corporations. This is tied directly, in some ways, to larger scale technological developments in communications, transportation, manufacture and distribution—to the need for international regulatory and organizational standards, etc. Also, many of our advanced industrial products need to draw upon the total available range of globally distributed resources for their processes. No one developed nation is now entirely wholly self sufficient in such resources—and probably never was since full industrialization got under way.

In some cases, large-scale technological developments have gone beyond the capacity of individual nations to build, maintain, and develop further, e.g. the Anglo-French Concorde, the linkups of the European electrical distribution grid,

"Large economies of scale require enormous costs and resources for utilization . . . Most European companies are incapable of producing the huge transformers needed for the increasing voltage demands in their networks. This development has forced even such giants as Siemens and Telefunken to join forces in the heavy electrical field. In the U.S., five producers supply the entire market, while in Europe, there are as many as thirty." [11]

In many cases, also, product planning is done on a worldwide basis, e.g. IBM comments on the planning of a new computer, "Final specifications reflect inputs from at least twenty countries . . . so that it may meet the needs of virtually every market; handle decimal as well as sterling . . . print output not only in Indian or Japanese Katakana—but in type faces for any of 22 different languages." To such specifications we may add internationally exchanged technicians, standardization of instructions and programs, etc., plus the fact that the manufacture and assembly of various components may be thousands of miles apart.

5. International Disparities. There persist major world disparities between rich and poor nations—with accompanying world problems of population pressure, food, and other resources shortages, etc. These may tend to be "managed" in our conventional piecemeal fashion until a critical emergency arises, e.g., massive socioeconomic collapse of one of the larger, lesser developed nations which then threatens the more fortunate nations with its secondary repercussions —local warring, dislocation of world communications and trade, health service breakdown with possibilities of epidemic disease, etc. This will also be exacerbated by the tendency for levels of expectation and aspiration in both rich and poor nations to continue to outdistance the capacity to satisfy them—underlining the critical dysjunction between our developed scientific and technological capabilities and our apparent incapability to deploy them effectively in terms of human priorities.

A managerial challenge here lies with the role of governmental and nongovernmental organizations and, importantly, the multinational corporate entities— to the extent that they may perceive the implementation of solutions to these major world problems as a major function of their over-all policies.

6. Supplies and Services. Internal socio-physical maintenance services for advanced societies, e.g. health and environmental services, transportation, energy supply, etc., have vastly increased in size and complexity. Many begin to go beyond the point of "economical" provision and control solely by private enterprise and, in some cases, begin to outreach local national resources. This has already led to varying degrees of "nationalization" in many countries—often without any specific gains in performance and quality.

As complexity feeds on growth and growth feeds on complexity, the decisions of large organizations affect more and more people, and those affected begin to wonder why they should not therefore participate with the organization's managers in making those decisions. It is already true in the United States that the line between "public" and "private" can no longer be drawn between government and private enterprise, because all private enterprise has some degree of public responsibility—the larger and more complex the enterprise, the more public responsibility it is expected to carry. And this means that more and more private executives must simultaneously serve as public executives, whether they like it or not.[12]

There is a leading "managerial" initiative here regarding the invention of new forms of public/private entities to provide these kinds of services and to anticipate emerging needs in this area. To date, industrial corporate entities have been the most productive form of enterprise for providing goods and services to the largest number of people at lowest cost. The question is, that as we are now reordering major priorities in society according to our changing perceptions of needs and problems, can the corporate form be mobilized in new ways to deal more directly, for example, with social problems—in education, urban areas, environment, etc.?

7. *Environmental Changes.* Large scale human operations in the environment have grown in the past fifty years to the point where they have begun to affect the global environment on a large enough scale to warrant serious attention towards the identification of various aspects of environmental imbalance at the world level. While we are still wrestling with national and local regulation of environmental quality, the debate has now moved to the need for international regulation, e.g. the U.N. Conference on the Human Environment, etc. Although some of the "ecology" flurry has lost its apocalyptic tone, there is evidence for continuing public concern—and "managerially" the problem of environmental impact control and cost would appear to be here to stay.

Linked to this concern with environmental quality are questions of resource depletion, of the need for increased resource reuse, etc. Some of these questions have been raised at regular intervals for over 100 years, but their expression has now taken on a more apocalyptic tone. But although the scale of technological and other intrusions in the biosphere are now of considerable magnitude, all the evidence, on needs for "a steady state society," limitations on resouce availability, and cutbacks on the use of resources, etc., is not yet in. We may presume, however, that both this widening concern and its formulation in terms which are often directly "anti-growth," "anti-technological," etc., will affect the allocation of public fiscal resources in R & D, the internal development of science and technology itself and the ways in which these will be integrated into industry. Both private and public management seem to have been taken relatively unaware by this change in the climate of ideas, and of resultant sets of new questions regarding accountability and responsibility for their operations. Though there has been much talk, in recent years, about the technological "system," the industrial "system," etc., in most cases, we are really describing relatively piecemeal aggregates of different kinds of enterprises which are neither systematic in their own sectors nor operated as systems in relation to other enterprises and other sectors.

8. *Changes in Resources.* These will take two forms:

1. A reevaluation and "reperception" of our resource range as more knowledge and information accrues on resource substitution and "convertibility,"
   the discovery of new synthetics, and of the basic recyclic nature of many of
   our major resource use patterns, i.e., from single use and discard to multiple use and recycling patterns. Though partially forced by the emergence
   of critical shortages in key metals and minerals, it will also be part of a
   more systemic reorganization of industry as the trend toward automated
   extraction, processing and manufacture continues.

2. The emergence of "information" viewed as a major resource—with its
   unique characteristic of being non-resource depletive in use by comparison
   with other resources, e.g.:

   a. in many ways, its value and quantity does not diminish by distribution
      and sharing but may be increased;

   b. combining information and communications technologies in new in-
      dustries operating more in terms of the electromagnetic spectrum ranges
      is characterized by lessening inputs of physical resource per unit per-
      formance or product and by drawing upon nondepletive "spectrum"
      energies.

Also, as noted above, all other resources are actually determined by the state of
our information and knowledge about the physical environment. Providing, in
effect, a new resource base for society, this will powerfully affect many value orientations which emerged from earlier resource use patterns. Competition for the
allocation of scarce resources, linked to the depletive nature of physical resources
themselves, has formed many of the major premises for our social institutions,
organizations, and regulatory practices. The increased dependence upon informa-
tion/communications as a major resource could move society toward new configurations of institutions and organizations which may be as different from our
present "industrial phase" forms as these were from pre-industrial forms.

In addition to the above, we may assume that our attitudes to, and evaluation
of human resources will undergo major changes. As direct human labor, in routine and repetitive functions, becomes of decreasing importance, social roles and
status in this and other areas will also become increasingly detached from economic and "productive" measures and from work itself. Where we have traditionally accorded "work" such a central function in determining a variety of
social relations and "identity sustaining" roles for active participation in society,
we may no longer be able to do so.

One does not suggest the decline of work as such but its reevaluation, in other
than strictly economic and market terms, toward self fulfillment for the person,
toward the measurement of the value of the activities of individuals and institutions in ways other than by their "fiscal" value. In effect, there is vastly more work
required, more individual and collective commitment required over longer periods, in the larger "human services" challenges in the society. The traditional
economic calculus is no longer a necessary or sufficient measure for these tasks

nor can it wholly provide the necessary incentive and motivational structure. This issue is already impacting upon institutions and is likely to continue to do so.

Labor and reward—Corollary to the foregoing is the claim that, "people won't work if you give them something for nothing." This is a common ground for argument against wage increase, public relief, and foreign aid. Again, this belief imputes an intrinsic value to work, and an especially high status to material acquisition. It overlooks the activities and contributions of the very rich, most of whom are anything but drones although they are under no financial compulsion to work, and it overlooks the contributions made by members of monastic types of religious orders, members of the traditionally under-paid world of academia, and the better part of the world's peoples, who receive little more for their work than subsistence. In those few cultures that have such a natural abundance that work is unnecessary, people are still observed to be normally active. Rather than there being a direct relationship between the amount of work a person does and the financial reward he is given, it is probable that in reality the opposite condition holds. In terms of sheer, routine, day-to-day energy output, it is the lower occupational status groups who work hardest. It is they who must man the fields, the foundries, and the mines, and it is they who live closest to the line of economic marginality.[13]

This problem of changing attitudes toward work also impacts on the feelings of "identity" and "legitimacy" of the manager. As the business ethos comes under pressure and the distinction between public and private responsibilities becomes blurred, the individual executive will find it harder to maintain directional "certainty" about his own goals and those of the enterprise which he manages:

Even compared to a generation ago, our private enterprise system is just as enterprising but not nearly so private. The growing sense of public responsibility in American business—verbalized at inspirational lunches but also increasingly in evidence during office hours—can be seen as the search for legitimacy by managers of properties whose "ownership" is no longer the key to executive responsibility.

It is now commonplace to observe that the diffusion of property divorces ownership from control of the economic system. Managers of productive enterprises, and managers of pension funds, mutual trusts, bank-held trusts and funds, and other large-scale forms of organized "private property," are each year harder put to it to say to whom they are effectively responsible. If the question is, "Who owns General Motors or A.T.&T.?" the honest answer is so vague an entity ("the public") that it leaves the collective leadership of managers in control of what is owned. To the more operational question, "Who is responsible for the actions of General Motors or A.T.&T.?" the answer is clear enough: a large and growing number of their executives. But to whom are they responsible?[14]

9. *War*. War has become increasingly costly, "uneconomical," and "risky," particularly for the larger and more powerful nations. While this may have always been so, the change in "cost" which is suggested here, using the example of U.S./Vietnam, and similar types of interventions, is that the social costs and internal socio-political repercussions of this kind of war on the U.S. have been disproportionate to economic costs and gains. Where "the other side" has been

physically bombed, the U.S. has been "psychologically bombed" domestically to a degree which renders war more costly in a way that is different from World War I, World War II, and even the Korean conflict. With more sophisticated weaponry, smaller wars between smaller nations may also be cheaper and economical in conventional terms, but even here the posture of the great powers has been to contain and limit these—even where, paradoxically, they have helped build up the war-making potential for either side. Dealing with local civil war type violence, as in Northern Ireland, has become more costly to the more powerful side than to their adversaries. Though we are not directly concerned with the "management of war" or "conflict resolution," there may be much that is relevant in the psychosocial dimensions of this area for management in general.

10. Social Changes. Western patterns of prolonged education, extended vacations, shorter work week, etc., are possible indicators of the extent to which we have moved from a work-centered culture or economy. It is not merely that more people may have more leisure, but there has been some decline of work as the yardstick of socially and individually gainful activity with the concomitant decline of exclusively economic measures for human activities. In the U.S. specifically, there has been an emphasis on the redefinition of social, civil, and political rights which has been paced by changes in the individual and group's perception of their social roles, responsibilities, motivation, and measures of achievement. Various dissident social groups have coalesced and intensified their demands for more equable participation in society, e.g., the minorities, women, youth, the disadvantaged, the marginal, and the "socially deviant," etc.

However we characterize this emergence of specific pressure groups—as transient phenomena or evidence for continuing social movements—they have already contributed to perceptible changes in social values, norms, and mores, and have brought forward challenges to the legitimacy of established institutional arrangements. The management of various institutions, e.g., education, public administration, corporate industry, etc., has been impacted by these challenges and has demonstrated various degrees of ability to deal with such pressure by accommodating more flexibly to reasonable change demands—as well as by avoidance, exclusion, or repression of dissident groups. In some cases the latter strategies have been effective for the time being, but one could envisage that they could reinforce styles of managerial rigidity which may be internally damaging to the institutions themselves. Even if we assume a downward trend in this area, it may be important for us to reassess our traditional institutional responses to internal and external changes in themselves in the many different forms which these can take, and their significance for the future of institutional management.

11. Political Climate. Though directly related to the above, we may note additionally that the developed nations run the greater risk of increased internal fragmentation within the next decade as the basis for "national consensus" via traditional party systems becomes more eroded. The lesser developed nations may still find some temporary cohesion through nationalist movements and alliances within their "Third World" groupings.

The major ideological blocs, whether Communist or Free World, were never as homogeneous or cohesive as their respective images suggested, so we may assume that they will not escape fragmentation and division into a plurality of coexistent ideological groupings. But the latter process could take time, and we can expect strong attempts through the next decades to shore up local national divisiveness in either of the major blocs by channeling the insecurities and fears of their societies into ideological outlets.

ASSUMPTIONS SPECIFIC TO THE UNITED STATES

Many of the global assumptions above are also applicable, in varying degree, to the U.S., but there are several characteristic trends and developments which are uniquely important for consideration.

In general, we may note that the U.S.A. emerged most significantly in the past twenty-five years as the major world power. Having come out of World War II as the nation least physically damaged by the conflict and with its vast productive capacities in no way impaired but enhanced, it has now enjoyed a long period of economic, political, and socio-cultural leadership. This, with its earlier tradition of rapid growth, relatively boundless expansion, and optimism, has enabled it to proceed, until recently, with a confidence in its own power and "manifest destiny" to assume the role of major world policeman and goal setter. It has tended to remain success oriented, impatient, unwilling to compromise, and, generally, to go its own way with security and certainty based on its visible advances in material standards, political and military power, and internal national cohesion.

1. Externally, the U.S. will face increasing economic, scientific and technological competition from other major nations or "common market" groups, e.g. Japan, the European Economic Community, the COMECON bloc, etc. This will include intensified competition for physical resource access and control in critical areas where the U.S. is no longer self-sufficient. Its position of political and military leadership in the Free World has been considerably eroded by the Vietnam conflict and by its supportive relationship to various "less than free" regimes in other world regions.

The shift from being *the* major power, whether illusionary or not, to being one of a number of relatively coequal major powers may be a difficult change of role. The need to compromise, to live within less certainty, security, and faith in one's own unilateral power, and to tolerate ambiguity both ideologically and socially, could be stressful.

2. Internally, the nation's apparent prosperity and belief in social progress has already been called into question. Its physical environment is now beginning to show the scars of unregulated growth, overexploitation, and lack of foresight and planning. Though paradoxical, in a nation which is still the most materially advanced in the world, its "quality of life" is also now called in question as it shows signs of dislocation and obsolescence in many areas of its socioeconomic, educational, and political structure. Faced with these symptoms of disorder (which are not peculiar to the U.S.), one may summarize the internal situation as a "crisis of social management." Philosophically, the idea of planning and management has been alien to the American experience—except in business. Other sectors of the socio-political system have been carried along on the principle that the balance of competing interests, the separation of various powers, and the operation of a kind of socio-political "free market" would result in optimal present decisions and short-run policies which could be left to work themselves out in the long range. We are now in the long range—and the consequences of this view are apparent. It has been suggested that the "social managerial" transition will be from a short-run *tactically* oriented "means" society toward more concern with longer range *strategic* goals and "ends."

3. *Total U.S. population may be expected to be approximately 250 million by 1995—though projections vary considerably and are often inaccurate.* While approximately one sixth of this number will be over fifty five, the major proportion—approximately 63%—will be under 35. It will be a relatively "young" population en masse.

Importantly, if the current population growth profile is maintained, we may expect that the non-white population will grow almost twice as fast as the white population. With our time scale of twenty years, this suggests that current racial tensions in the society could persist and intensify considerably during that period.

Though we may not assume that present educational trends will remain constant or that the present segmental "educational-career-retirement" pattern will obtain, it is likely that the proportion of this population (particularly those under 35) who have experienced some form of higher education will be over 50%. This will still leave a considerable number who have not had access to such education and/or have dropped out. Therefore, though a more educated populace by today's standards, it may be assumed to contain a substantial number of people who are not "educated" to those standards.

The above pattern also suggests that unless present educational practices and structures are reformed considerably, the gap between the educated and the non-educated elements in the population may be greater than it is presently. This could have important consequences for the general organization of the society e.g., in creating more divisiveness, a less egalitarian social structure, the persistence of disadvantage and poverty, etc. In general, however, one of the more important points may be the increase in actual numbers—as requiring accompanying increase in goods, services, social maintenance systems, etc., with corresponding demands on governmental and institutional systems.

4. Given that many of our major cities no longer function as viable population centers, we may expect continued movement to the suburbs and further out to the exurbs.

Apart from the buildup of large conurbation groups over the major city belts in the East, Mid West and Western Coast, we can also assume a greater migration towards more dispersed population aggregates. The latter may not become communities or cities within our present definition but will be made possible by increased transportation and communication. In terms of "community" of the older face-to-face personal contact form, they will not be communities but will be part of various identifiable community networks "at-a-distance." Also, with a shorter work week and "staggered" or personally selected work periods, there will be an increase in seasonal migrations of the type now called vacations—but occurring at different times in the year and work cycle. This will add a further "community" dimension of increased transience in certain areas, by different social groupings.

5. From assumed population trends and current growth rates of materials and energy consumption, it has been estimated that in contrast to the past twenty years, the U.S. society will "require" variously from 200–500 per cent rises in goods production, electric power and other consumption, construction, etc.

Many of these areas of demand will at least double or triple in the next ten to twenty years. To assume this as possible at present rates of use and discard practices and piecemeal organization of industries and services may be quite unreal in terms of resource availability—apart from the major consideration of environmental impacts.

Within the next twenty years, it will be critically necessary to redesign many of our production and consumption practices so that their resource and energy usage becomes more efficient and systematic in relation to materials and energy conservation. Such redesign and reorganization will, in itself, be a considerable challenge to management in the various institutional sectors.

6. Not withstanding external competition and internal strains, it may be assumed that current economic growth per se could be sustained for at least the next ten year period. After that period, it seems open to conjecture. The more important question for management seems to be that redefinition of growth in itself, i.e., growth of the firm may not always be congruent with, or wholly measurable in economic terms. More generally, growth in the society can have multiple meanings, outlets, and measures—in neither wholly material nor economic terms.

. . . growth, as measured by our present economic accounting, tends to generate more and more "spillovers" which become costs borne directly by other private parties or distributed among the society as a whole. . . . The result is a social cost (though frequently a social benefit, too). The most obvious example of a social cost is air pollution—the result, in part, of the increasing number of private cars in the society. In every elementary economics textbook, air was once the classic illustration of the "free good." Yet the irony is that in the next 30 years one of the most scarce resources we may have (in the sense of proportionately sharply rising costs) will be clean air. The costs of automobile disposal are not charged to the automobile owner; similarly, the costs of salvaging a depressed coal mining community are not charged to the companies selling the competing fuels which may have driven coal off the market.

. . . in assessing public services we do not have a means of estimating actual benefits or values. In items that are sold in the market, such as automobiles or clothing, we have market prices as the value individuals place on the products. But how do we value publicly provided services such as health, or education, or protection? Our accounting system does so only by the "input" costs, not by the output values.[15]

a. Continued shift to service oriented economy with more than half the work force in service occupations—these will account for more than half of the-man hours in all goods production. This shift is also important in the nonprofit service occupation, e.g., the Federal, state, local government, educational, health, and other sectors will account for an increasing proportion of employment. With fewer workers in the goods industries and a major proportion in specifically nonprofit service sectors, corporate organizations whether in service or manufacturing will employ substantially less of the labor force—but that lesser number will be increasingly professional technical personnel.

b. New "business" complexes will emerge in response to increasing demands in the environmental, social, health, and urban systems need areas. Some of these new entities will be a mix of both private and public enterprise and will exhibit different organizational and managerial forms and responsibilities as a result of this—and of their new market orientations.

Underlying both (a) and (b) above, there are assumed changes also to a more pluralistic mix of private profit, nonprofit; public/private consortia, and public enterprises. Changes in the concept of wholly economic profit will play an important role here as the operational definition of profit evolves to embrace wider terms of social profitability, social costs, social investments.

These trends have connotations outside the economic sphere where they impinge upon changes in larger societal values and goal orientations, e.g., when the agricultural sector declined in economic dominance, there was a corresponding shift from agrarian values and goals to an intrinsically different industrial set.

7. *Changes in the economy above will be reflected in the re-allocation of political support, participation and power influences.* Where the two-party political process with its short-term mandates and undue exposure to special interest groups is seen to militate against the management of social and economic issues in the larger public interest, we may expect that many of the more vital social services may be removed from direct political pressures and influence and ad-

ministered via other structures—or "hived off," in Carey's phrase, to various mixes of private and public enterprise. This will require the reorganization, redesign, and development of many areas of governmental and quasi-governmental units at various levels.

With the increase of information and communications in the society and a more educated population generally, there will be a larger amount of diversity in individual and group attitudes. Given that a more centralized and authoritarian political regime is avoided, this will lead to a plurality of "constituencies" and pressure groups seeking access to, and participation in, the governance process.

The above trend may be generalized to include similar demands for access to the decision making, policy planning, and governance process of other major institutions in the society—which in turn suggests that they will evolve towards such new participative modes or face disruption and turbulence in their organizational climate.

8. One of the main challenges for social management will lie in the relative decline of "work" and occupational roles as providing major areas of identification and social involvement for larger numbers of people.

Our industrial society, in the past century, has so evolved that the majority of our status values, our economic, political, social, and gender roles, and their major institutional linkages which provide social cohesion, are hinged around productive work and occupational roles in the society.

With the decreasing need for a large "routine" work force, this linch pin will be weakened or withdrawn. Though this may not reach critical proportions within our time frame of reference the consequences may be far-reaching, for we have, at the present, few ways of institutionalizing and rewarding various forms of nonwork. Most of our goals, reward systems, incentives, and value premises for social action are "work" and "achievement" oriented.

Classical economics has been responsible for a great deal of misunderstanding about the nature of human motivation. If a monetary system is postulated to be a natural and major aspect of all advanced economic systems, it may follow theoretically that the desire for monetary gain (or for material acquisition) will be the basic driving force within advanced societies. However, under searching examination, even in Western society there is no regularity in the relationships between effort, reward and occupational status. To attempt to go further and apply the financial incentive "axiom" to all undeveloped societies, many of whom have little or no monetary orientation, is the grandest of follies. It can be demonstrated rather easily that in all societies people work out of motives far transcending sheer desire for material gain.[16]

Where "unemployment" is the name we presently use for enforced leisure, this only exposes this area more as a "problem orientation." The problem may be temporarily dealt with by decreasing the work week in various sectors, by increased vacations, sabbaticals, and other devices, but one of the challenges for our institutions in the next period will be to develop, invent, or deliberately design new ways of "valuing" to ranges of human activity which are not productive work as presently defined.

The possible diversity of values, life styles, social movements, and social groupings evolving in the next period may present similar problems of social cohesion. Again, the challenge to our institutions will, in many cases, be obverse of their principal role in the past—which was to optimize conformity and stability. Their future task will be the optimization of diversity—in a social climate of continuing change.

Underlying both of the above assumptions is the emergence of a different conception of man and woman, their relation to each other, to their children, and to society. It will be much less dependent on socially ascribed or prescribed roles and statuses, but determined rather more by individually shifting (and individually idiosyncratic) needs and desires at various stages in the life cycle. Much of our prescribed conformity to consensual norms was dictated by the earlier group survival requirements of pre-industrial and industrial society. As advanced nations, such as the U.S., move in the next twenty-five years into Post-Industrial forms, based on possible material abundance rather than marginal scarcity, we may no longer require that large areas of our social behaviors be prescriptively contained within majority norms.

9. Strains in many areas of social and institutional organization have various complex causal reasons, e.g., lack of responsiveness to change leading to withdrawal of support by participants, questions of legitimacy in the exercise of their influence and power to sanction or reward behavior, increased divergence of values, etc.

Institutional strains and breakdowns are in themselves only symptomatic of the set of larger questions which various groups in the society are addressing in different ways. Some of these questions we have already alluded to, e.g., the decline of role identification with work, changes in the allocation of power and values, increases in population and organizational size. The central question is that much of our social and institutional dialogue within the next twenty (or fifty) years will be intrinsically concerned with a redefinition and reformulaton of the meaning, purpose, and function of human beings in society. Though we may phrase this in terms of "the critical management requirements for our major social institutions," the deeper philosophical question remains the same. We cannot manage without meaning or purpose, nor can we ignore the larger satisfaction of changes in human needs and desires.

Towards a Managerial Taxonomy

It may be suggested that the over-all set of papers in this study indicate, and illustrate, sets of new perspectives on the managerial function in ways that suggest a changing taxonomy of the managerial process itself and the organizational environments in which it operates. It would be neither possible nor desirable to attempt to crystallize this taxonomy here—with its multiple configurations and interpenetrations of sector institutions, its redefinitions of the roles, responsibilities, etc., of the manager. We may seek, however, to complement and expand the taxonomic approach via several diagrammatic and tabular arrays drawn in part from the study and from other sources.

MANAGEMENT STYLE

The operations of the individual manager may be variously qualified by the organization environment, the kind of business, and the social sector in the society. These factors will, therefore, vary in their "style" of execution. According to Bower and Walton:

> Management style . . . may be defined as "the way we run the business.". . . As outsiders who get behind the scenes of many well-managed companies, we have observed the power of style as an unwritten law governing quite precisely how people shall make decisions and conduct themselves generally within the company.
> "The way to run the business" usually develops as a matter of practice and of following example, rather than through the conscious development of guidelines for decision making and personal conduct. Everyone down the line watches for "signals" from top-management executives as to how he should conduct himself; and these signals are not what the CEO and those reporting to him *say,* but what they *do.*
> . . . the style with which a business is managed can have specific value in coping with particular forces, and broad value in keeping executives sensitive to change.

Drucker, on the other hand, points out the influence of the environment on management style:

> Management, as it was taught and practiced in the management boom, concerned itself with building an effective business as measured by economic performance and economic results. . . . Management therefore could, and had to be, "technocratic," i.e. concerned with effectiveness and efficiencies within economic parameters. . . . Now the demand for social responsibilities is becoming irresistible . . . at the same time management cannot abdicate responsibility for economic performance . . . yet the responsibility for the "qualities of life" will have to be built into the management job also.

Though we earlier contrasted two major positions on managerial function —(a) as relatively invariant in its principles throughout the range of organizational forms (Bower), and (b) as varying considerably in the future according to social and cultural contexts (Drucker)—we may insert a middle ground position which indicates more commonalty in managerial style in terms of function. While management may vary from sector to sector, and not, in itself, be wholly constrained with any well defined set of "management science" principles, it does exhibit some standard characteristics.

Clearly there is much in common in the management of, say, a government department, a public corporation, a private manufacturing enterprise, a law firm, a professional body, a public-administered hospital and a private charity. What is it? The most obvious common characteristic of all these organizations is that they are all "open systems." They maintain a form more enduring than their constituents by constantly drawing from and returning to the world around them materials, money and men. This is most obvious in a manufacturing industry as it converts raw materials into finished products and scrap . . . but is equally true of a newspaper or a city government or a charity. . . . Thus the management of every organization involves a balancing function of great complexity . . . "optimizing-balancing," the regulation through time of a host of relationships, not fully attainable, often sharply conflicting, as to realize an acceptable combination of them with the resources available.[17]

The one style which seems to be granted universal criticism is the vertically organized, centrally controlled bureaucracy mode—one may note, however, that the persistence and resilience of this form also make it one of the more universal styles still employed.

Organizational Forms

The newer organizational forms will also have their own problems. Though adopted as managerial styles which "optimize human relations" in organized work, they also generate new anxieties due to this more ambiguous, adaptive, and temporary quality. Both managers and managed will feel less secure and more liable to social strains and psychological tensions. Generalizing this "temporary" form of associational and work life to the larger society, which also exhibits similar shifts, will obviously require specific education and training in living with ambiguity and without the certainties which more traditionally stable forms have given. Though this trend has been on the way for some time, it may take a "generational" shift to replace the older more or less bureaucratic forms. In its description as a major organizational trend, it also begs the question that many organizing and managing functions will remain hierarchical and authoritative by their nature; e.g., the medical operating room, though characterized by strong teamwork, will still be a situation in which authority and decision making is vertically oriented. Also, though the "participatory" style may be in vogue, in many cases people in some of their overlapping work and professional activities may not wish to be involved in each decision, each change in policy, etc. More obviously, perhaps, *there will be a continuing spectrum* of both managerial styles and organizational forms ranging from the vertically authoritative and stable mode to the more temporary "mission or task oriented" and participatory forms.

In focusing more directly on the possible changes in management capabilities, it may be useful to revert to the earlier categorization of the shift from Pre-Industrial to Post-Industrial forms.

349

CHART N: MANAGEMENT CHARACTERISTICS

PRE-INDUSTRIAL	INDUSTRIAL	POST-INDUSTRIAL
1. Personal profit and advancement, but often contained within a "transcendental" organization form; e.g., priesthood, royal court, etc.	1. He is profit minded, relates all of his decisions and actions to the over-all profitability of the enterprise.	1. He is globally profit-minded both in time and space. His concern is with both immediate and long-term profitability. No business is his business. All opportunities are to be weighed against the over-all profitability of the enterprise.
2. Individual entrepreneur. Single man operation varying within the above settings. (1)	2. Equates his personal success with the success of the enterprise.	2. Tempers his devotion to profitability with social awareness. He is a reasonable citizen who does not believe that what is good for business is good for the country.
3. Authority is positional, hereditary, and taken as accepted right. (2) Freedom to exercise power was frequently absolute and nonaccountable.	3. Experienced and familiar with the traditional business of the firm and has developed a feel for the critical variables which affect the success of the enterprise.	3. Finds satisfaction not only in the extrinsic satisfaction of money and power, but also in the intrinsic rewards of creative managerial work.
4. Use of expert advisors (4), but in keeping with above settings, management was often a given prerogative; decisions were rarely questionable by subordinates.	4. Problem-solving perspective is primarily a technological and economic one. He has had little exposure to the political, societal and cultural variables which affect business decisions.	4. Familiarity with his business firm is less in terms of what it has done and more in terms of what it can do: its resources, strengths, weaknesses, and the constraints on its behavior; has a continuing interest and broad knowledge of the opportunities outside the traditional business of the firm.
5. Innovating entrepreneur (3), but entrepreneurial behavior was constrained by rigid social structures.	5. Within his perspective, he is an incisive convergent problem-solver. He is quick to relate a problem to a previous precedent, to isolate the critical variable, to devise an appropriate solution.	5. Problem-solving perspective is broad: technological, competitive, economic, political, cultural, sociological . . . a man of many archetypal talents: entrepreneur, planner, administrator, systems architect, politician, and statesman.
6. Managed by traditional rules and precedents, modified by personal motivation towards gain and advancement.	6. Preconditioned to prefer the familiar solution to the novel one, an incremental change to a large one, a familiar risk to a gambler's plunge.	6. A divergent creative problem-solver . . . continually searches for new alternatives; he is a habitual learner, quick to assimilate new information and isolate the controlling variables and devise novel solutions procedures.
7. Use of divide and conquer strategies (dealing with subordinates separately and erecting barriers between self and subordinates); paternalistic; distributor of charity and patronage; hereditary position and absolute power required less human relations management.	7. A skillful communicator and leader of men. In exercising leadership, he is preconditioned to exploit the historical dynamics of the organization. He is skillful in timing the introduction of a needed change in the organization. He is a skillful crisis manager so long as the options available to him include familiar solutions.	7. A skillful leader of group and organizational problem-solving. Where lacking personal expertise, he is skilled in the art of using experts.
8. As the managerial context was more limited in organizational size, numbers of people, and activities managed, etc., the assumed managerial skill was relatively unrestricted and multivalent . . . within the above bounds.	8. Has only limited skills in solving novel problems which have no precedent in his previous experience. Nor is he skilled in leading the organization on major departures from historical organizational development.	8. Risk propensities are not biased in favor of the familiar, nor is he a habitual gambler on the unknown (but) attempts to develop a balanced portfolio of risks which is commensurate with probable gain.
		9. Leadership skills lie in including the organization to take bold departures from the past tradition.
(Ref. N)		(Ansoff)

THE MANAGER AS AN INDIVIDUAL

In discussing all of these kinds of changes, we tend to treat the manager rather abstractly. One of the important ways in which change is effected in practice will be through the specific perceptions and evaluations of individual managers —who they are, what age, sex, class, etc.

It is clear that the individual manager's personal attitudes, experience, values, and position in society will color and influence not only the acceptance of change but the actual perception of the need for, the pressures to, change. Hence, the need to ground our conception of the manager in terms of social and cultural location.

There is a strong tendency to assume the manager as trained professional, as identifiable with a particular age, class, position in society, etc. This tendency extends towards a system of shared values, attitudes, and attendant motivations. How far this may hold for the future in the advanced societies is possibly debatable. For the lesser-developed countries, for example, it may, indeed, be a problem where their urgent requirement for managerial capability leads them to select managers whose training and education may be more appropriate to advanced developmental stages—and disadvantageous to the lesser developed.

Ansoff particularly discusses the need for a radical widening of the "selective screening" process, to include social consequences in the longer range and broader context, if the business manager, specifically, is to retain his entrepreneurial posture in society.

. . . the shift to a "Keplerian perspective" requires expansion of entrepreneurial behavior beyond markets and technology, to include government and society. It is no longer acceptable to argue either that the "business of business is business" or that behavior other than single-minded pursuit of profit-maximization is socially subversive. The role of government, both positive and constraining, on the behavior of the firm will grow and must be dealt with explicitly by a doctrine other than minimum interference. Consumers and the public will become more vociferous and better organized in making their dissatisfactions and desires felt by the business sector. The workers and the managers themselves will be decreasingly willing to work for a firm which pursues profit to the exclusion of their personal aspirations and of the social consequence of business actions. Thus, entrepreneurial activity must increasingly include explicit concern with non-business decisions and with the development of new kinds of strategies for dealing with society. (Ansoff)

Implicit within the "ideology of management," for example, is that it is non-ideological, yet the central problem for management in, and of, society is always viewed as that of "keeping it going without disruption," [18] i.e. by maintaining the balance of activities so as to avoid major discontinuities whilst, paradoxically, pursuing short range objectives which are often productive of discontinuity and disruption in the longer run.

The ultimate goal of industrial societies is taken as given: to maintain economic advance on the basis of a dynamic science and technology, while adjusting the existing social system *ad hoc,* as the requirements and consequences of this advance unfold, and sufficiently to contain social dissensus and conflict to a manageable level. . . . The status quo is changed only gradually. . . . There is thus one important and inescapable implication of a political character; namely that the stuff of politics, both theoretical and practical, is effectively reduced to questions of an instrumental kind—to questions, that is, of a kind which may be appropriately determined by the "technocracy" without their discussion in public of even their full communication to the public. The crucial questions are defined as ones which require special expertise for their proper comprehension . . . it follows in turn, then, that participation in the democratic process must, for the mass of the population, necessarily be of a decidedly restricted and indirect kind. It becomes in effect limited to joining in organised groups which can seek, via their own officials and experts, to influence key decision makers; and to periodic voting on alternative sets of national political "leaders," who will tend increasingly to bid for electoral support on the grounds of their superior technical or "managerial" competence.[19]

One of the specific impacts of information and communications technology on business management will be to make important changes in the managerial function used—changes in the number and magnitude of decisions to be made, and in the time scale of challenge and response in decision making. On the one hand, there will be more decentralized decision making where the "local" manager has access to more information, etc., but there will also be increased electronic proximity to the head office with consequently swifter feedback on decisions made. Errors in judgment may be more visible and bring swifter retribution!

Management will also be forced into more dependence on new modes of predictive market information to govern their output of goods and services to fit more rapidly changing profiles of consumer/market needs and preferences.

CHART P: EMERGING MARKET CONTINUUM

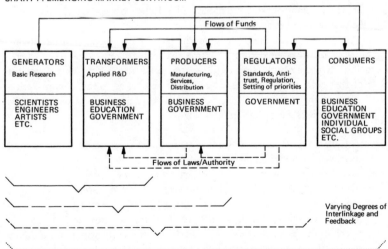

The diagrammatic representation of this expansion of the market continuum (Chart P, p. 351) shows the developing interlinkages of feedback between different areas. We may note some recent and ongoing developments relevant to this diagram, e.g.:

1. The environmental issue where many businesses were directly impacted by increased consumer information and its more rapid and wider diffusion in the communications media—coupled with the enhanced capacity to mobilize consumer groups and legislative pressure through the same information means.
2. The auto safety, durability, repair and maintenance debate has followed much the same pattern.
3. The interlinkage of the above with other areas, e.g. air and water pollution and its consequent market and consumer pressures on the electrical utilities and energy industry generally.

We may presume that Ansoff's new entrepreneurial manager would perceive these, not necessarily as pressures and challenges to change and modify existing practices only, but as new business opportunities for ventures into new environmentally oriented, and more socially oriented, enterprises!

Managers and management are located within organizational forms and the styles of management, the personalities, attitudinal characteristics, motivational patterns and systems of sanctions, rewards, and incentives of individual managers, will vary according to the organizational form and social sector in which it is located.

One way to view this is in our familiar "shift" table from Pre-Industrial to Post-Industrial which gives some grasp of the changing characteristics over time, according to the implied socioeconomic and cultural changes which have been described earlier. (See diagram opposite.)

This mode, of course, sets up a somewhat artificial temporal division among the different organizational forms, hinting that earlier forms disappear, whereas, in fact, they show surprising resilience and survival capacity. This is not the fault of the table, which is oriented to show the change towards more appropriate and optimal forms for larger scale business and other activities in the three societal phases. Such a model might show:

1. The changing dominance of one organizational form over another as their social environmental climate changes.
2. The "ecological niche" characteristics which allow for the survival (or nonsurvival) and viability of forms over time in a variety of changing conditions.
3. The interdependent linkages which between organizations and the ways in which quite disparate forms may affect, influence, and partially determine the viability and efficiency and effectiveness of one another.

CHART Q: ORGANIZATIONAL ENVIRONMENT

PRE-INDUSTRIAL	INDUSTRIAL	POST-INDUSTRIAL
1. Authority derived through custom and/or tradition with extended family and paternalistic organization serving as base.	1. Managerial authority based on its economic power over employees, managerial allegiance to the organization based on the concept of surrogate.	1. Managerial authority is based not on power but on knowledge, in which work is designed to the dual criteria of task effectiveness and intrinsic motivation of the individual.
2. Organizational patriarchal; dominated by family and nepotism. Monolithic in power and authority. Early mechanisms of administration in the forms of scribes and officials.	2. An organizational structure (typically a multi-divisional structure) designed both to take advantage of economies of scale and also to be responsive to transient changes in the marketplace	2. An organizational structure which accommodates both stability of competitive behavior and fluidity of entrepreneurial behavior: a combination of efficiency-seeking bureaucracy and innovative "adhocracy."
3. Individual ownership of property. Family considered as the only source of capital and a reservoir of trusted manpower. Close linkage between various organizations.	3. A profit-center oriented substructure which assigns to a manager commensurate authority, responsibility, and accountability.	3. A decentralized substructure of "strategic business units" matched to the distinctive segments (demand-technology life-cycles) of the firm's environment, with maximum entrepreneurial freedom for managers of each segment.
4. Low level of economic and organizational democracy.	4. An efficient but highly selective information system which reports past performance in financial language. Environmental data is limited to the traditional markets of the firm. Direct environmental scanning is focused on economic trends and behavior of competitors.	4. A top-level corporate substructure devoted to balancing the firm's strategic portfolio or distinctive segments and to integrating entrepreneurial and competitive activities.
5. Lack of mobility; inability to meet requirement for skilled manpower.		5. A surveillance system scanning the environment beyond current business and major trends, projects these into the future, translates them . . . for the firm, and injects this information into appropriate action points. A forecasting system not assuming the future to be an extrapolation of the past, but exploring structural changes underlying current trends.
6. Rational administrative structure developed through formal rules. Development of modern nation state as result of expanded system of government administration as well as of joint stock companies and factory method of industrial manufacturing. Interest in large scale organizations resulting from religious ideals.	5. A lag control system which uses past performance to pinpoint deficiencies and institute prompt corrective action.	6. An information system which is rich beyond current operating data, which communicates "up" and "down" as well as laterally, to link people according to common tasks.
	6. A long-range planning system which extrapolates past trends into the distant future and provides a basis for financial and capital budgeting.	7. A reward and motivation system rewarding both current profitability and investment in future profitability, . . . tolerant of meaning failure and risk-taking behavior. . . builds rewards into the content of jobs and recognizes the changed personal values of both workers and managers.
7. Family role in direct economic production; family benefits. Emphasis on wisdom and goodness on the part of the family. Motivation to increase family fortunes.	7. A reward system which rewards the manager for the performance of his unit as well as for its contribution to the overall goals of the firm. Cooperation is rewarded; deviation from organizational norms is penalized. The incentives are economic as well as for prestige and power.	8. A control system which is future-oriented, based on "remaining cost to complete and remaining performance to accomplish" rather than on historical performance.
8. Lack of mobility due to hierarchal structure of society and relatively fixed division between sectors.	8. A management development system which prepared managers for positions of higher responsibility through experiential progressive exposure to various functional areas of the firm.	9. A closely controlled management system (similar to PPBS) based on entrepreneurial analysis of multiple alternatives, which matches planning, programming, budgeting, implementation, and control into a coherent whole.
		10. Career-long management development combining career planning, job rotation, and education, . . . married neither to promotion from within nor hiring from without . . . develops managers through exposure both to the current operations and to the opportunities/challenges of the unfolding socio-political-cultural environment.

(Ref. Q)   (Ansoff)

4. The ways in which specific organizational forms are related to the range of social institutions.
5. Some measure of the "requisite variety" of organizational forms and "niches" which may be needed to satisfy the requirements of social systems at different levels both of complexity and at development stages.

Organizations can be ranked along a good many dimensions. Many of these dimensions constitute a fairly continuous spectrum without clear dividing lines. Some of them have sharper divisions or pigeonholes. Theoretically, it would be possible to locate any particular organization in the n-dimensional matrix of these various dimensions. Then perhaps by cluster analysis, we could identify the empirical clusterings, which would give us at least an empirical taxonomy. In practice, however, this task is so enormous that it may be doubtful whether it would be worthwhile. (Boulding)

Following upon the above suggestion, Boulding notes some of the classification criteria for such an approach. These may be summarized as follows:

1. *The market/non-market dimension* as measured through the proportion of the total revenue of an organization derived from sales and the proportion derived for grants, or one-way transfers from other organizations or persons.
2. *The operating/regulating continuum* where the measure could be the proportion of output of goods or personal services, by contrast with information; i.e., output of regulatory organizations consists of information transmitted to the parties that constitute the environment of the organization.
3. *The coercive/noncoercive continuum* with coercive organizations invoking police power when legitimate, or unofficial sanctions when they are illegitimate like the Mafia, and noncoercive forms on the whole utilizing the market environment for their survival.

The chart of organizational characteristics does encompass some of these questions, but it is still relatively superficial and linear in its selection of types and criteria. Again, in order to establish and group categories together, some indication of evolutionary development is implied which may or may not, be correct in its underlying assumption of increase in organizational efficiency.

In the educational sector, the university presents an interesting and "peculiar" case of an organizational (and institutional) form containing at least three different kinds of memberships constituency in a special kind of "pluralistic collectivity." Its three main constituencies—administration, faculty, students—each exhibit different internal structural arrangements with varying degrees of formal and informal organization. Though approximately pyramidal and hierarchic in formal structure, its internal allocations of means, etc., is split between two main groups whose motivational and incentive and goal systems are often at variance. Without engaging in too close an analysis of these factors, the following notes may be helpful as exploratory of another type of form—which is now undergoing relatively extensive restructuring!

Some Comparative Relations in University as Organization

A. ADMINISTRATIVE	B. ACADEMIC (FACULTY)
1. Well-defined hierarchy of authority	1. Less-defined hierarchy
2. Written rules (explicit)	2. Few written rules (implicit)
3. Division of labor (specialized)	3. Less division of labor (specialized by discipline field)
4. Impersonality in human relations (universalistic)	4. Personal relations (particularistic)
5. Role as "job" not career in lower levels—nonpervasive Commitment extending into other relationships—according to rank	5. Role as career—highly pervasive Commitment—not correlated with rank
6. Separation of means	6. Less defined, e.g., separation from *physical* means: personal ownership of *"intellectual"* means
7. Coercive punitive oriented	7. Rewards oriented
8. Promotion and selection at lower levels based on examination (e.g., Civil Service employees)	8. Promotion and selection in various ways—indirectly on technical competence (external exams: professional codes, etc.), seniority
More bureaucratic—as defined by its function, i.e., a collectivity of offices.	*Less bureaucratic*—more "egalitarian," pluralistic association of professionals.

C. STUDENT BODY exhibits no specifically bureaucratic form of organization: positions are manifestly ascribed by a seniority system whose goal orientation is outside the system, i.e., implies no internal authority—of senior vs. freshman. Student role expectations change in the educational process, which is by definition an "enlargement" of role alternatives as part of the socialization process in which the university has functioned as extended familial authority.

The widespread social ferment in the universities in recent years may be traced in part to challenges to this structure of internal "power" arrangements and have led to many new forms of over-all governance and management of higher education. This latter direction accords with developments towards more participatory, human relations oriented and nonhierarchical structure in other organizations. We may certainly expect that the whole system of higher education will undergo further changes particularly where: (a) its student constituency is no longer exclusively tied to the standard age cohort but is extended towards a "lifelong" educational mode with multiple entries and exits into the educational process; (b) the educational process itself goes "beyond the walls" via new information and communications technology, e.g., the British "Open University" and other European and U.S. directions of this kind.

The voluntary, quasi-governmental and "intersect" organizations. Though not wholly descriptive of a new genus or type of organizational form, these do represent, in some cases, a leading edge of change in organizational form, style of management, and constituency. One aspect of change is in the rapid growth of

CHART R: ORGANIZATIONAL CHARACTERISTICS

STYLE	FOCUS	ORGANIZATIONAL FORM	INFOR-MATION FLOW	CONCEPTION	ORGANIZATI Purpose of Des
TRADITIONAL STYLE	Maintaining a tradition			Historical institution	Preservation of status quo
CHARISMATIC OR INTUITIVE STYLE	Pursuing an intuition			Spontaneous creation	Implementing intuition
CLASSICAL OR BUREAUCRATIC STYLE	Running an admin-istrative machine			Mechanistic structure	Maximizing efficiency
HUMAN RELATIONS OR GROUP STYLE	Initiating and leading groups			Network of personal relationships	Maximizing personal satisfaction
SYSTEMIC STYLE	Survival of a system in a hostile environ-ment			System of flows of information and materials, devel-oped in response to opportunity	Maximizing su vival potentia and growth o system
NETWORK STYLE	Adapting to emerg-ing conditions			Dynamic evolving networks of per-sonal and organiza-tional units, living system or organiza-tion	Maximizing re vance to per-ceived proble

ORGANIZATION Source of Momentum	DURATION	MEDIA	DECISION MAKING PROCESS		
			Main Concerns	Goals	Degree of Consciousness
Force of tradition	"Permanent" throughout a historical period	Mainly written	Recurrent items	Unquestioned, possibly implicit	Non-reflective
Dynamism of intuition	"Permanent" for the lifetime of the leader and his immediate disciples		Critical issues	Highly explicit	Spontaneous
Leadership drive and allocated funds	Undefined duration		Efficient performance of voted programs	Objective and evaluated quantitively	Conscious; calculated
Group synergism	Undefined short duration	Written Telephone Facsimile copies Etc.	Elaborating group goals	Subjective and emergent	Articulation of feelings
Individual self-advancement through organizational unit success in achieving system milestones	For as long as is useful for owners and employees	As above, but significant introduction of computer use at each level speeds up feedback	Adapting system to changing conditions	Outlined centrally; defined and refined by decentralized executant units	Highly conscious of rational perspective
Stimulus of individuals and organizational units by new problems and possibilities	For as long as is useful in terms of problem relevance	As above, plus more extended use of interactive communications modes, remote terminals, video conference techniques, etc., enabling widely distributed decision centers to interact swiftly	Maintaining balance between adapting to environmental change and creating a fulfilling environment	Defined interdependently	Conscious balance between value and rational perspectives

CHART R: ORGANIZATIONAL CHARACTERISTICS (continued)

STYLE	DECISION MAKING PROCESS		LEADERSHIP		FUNCTIONAL CHARACTERISTICS
	Type of Decision		Dominant Personality	Functions of Leaders	
TRADITIONAL STYLE	Affirmation of new custom	Transmission of heritage	Elders; wise, sacred	Voice of tradition; source of wisdom nurturer; guardian	Implicit consent Intuitive accord Agreement under obligation or coercion
CHARISMATIC OR INTUITIVE STYLE	Proclamation of intuition	Magnetic, persuasive influencing	Enlightened	Prophetic, inspirational	Vertically oriented hierarchical bureaucracy Organized by expertise
CLASSICAL OR BUREAUCRATIC STYLE	Production of orders	Detailed directions	Aggressive, domineering	Directive; organizing	Written communications with "fixed" decision rules and chains of command with centralized decision points
HUMAN RELATIONS OR GROUP STYLE	Formulation of consensus	Shared	Sensitive, cultured	Permissive, non-directive, creation of "atmosphere"; draws out	Horizontally organized by "function" areas Mixture of fixed decision rules and autonomous functional rules Shorter chains of Command with more decision points Participation consent
SYSTEMIC STYLE	Initiated by experts and evaluated by team	Initiated by experts and evaluation team	Expert, technician	Interprets system environment; clarifies goals, monitors change	Network-type organization with mission or objective foci which set flexible decision rules Information flow includes critical man/machine interfaces (e.g., systems analysts, programmers, and comptrollers) which feedback from bottom to top More autonomous decision making Team consent Modified by team in response to local conditions
NETWORK STYLE	Participative with representatives of all concerned bodies	Outline directives	Network link catalyzers, generalist	Interprets psycho-social environment, clarifies goals and organizational complexes required; monitors change	More diffuse and geographically separated network type, with a high degree of adaptability and change in organizational configuration Information and decision flows evolve in response to perceived needs rather than predefined and preset objectives or programs Increased feedback at swifter rates enables previously autonomous decision-making to be integrated into whole system directions

| CENTRAL PROCESSES | ORGANIZED RELATIONSHIPS | | PERSONNEL CHARACTERISTICS | RELATIONSHIP TO ENVIRONMENT | |
	Intra-organizational	Inter-organizational		Social Environment	Problem Environment
trength of tra-ition little wareness of lternatives	Coherent, stable traditional hierarchical structure	Traditional contacts; other organ, irrelevant; federations of organizations stable under supreme authority	People trained for highly specialized and limited functions

Little job mobility | Component part of static society | Docile, isolated problems in an orderly environment |
| udgmental haracter of ntuition poten-ial withdrawal f adherents | Emanations of the central intuition | Contacts initiated and maintained if they accept superiority of central message and help disseminate it | Pyramidal authority structure with fixed procedures for access/appeal to higher levels | Rejection of status quo; articulates change | Identification of a new fundamental problem underlying previously isolated problems |
| pecific stand-rds set by top nanagement | Procedural routinized linkages based on document transfer; jurisdictional disputes | Relations governed by policy of recognition in which superiority of the recognizer is considered implicit | | Machine for managing extensive but uncomplex environment | Docile problem groups characterized by their number and variety rather than their complexity and interrelationship |
| dividual sense responsibility; swerability to nstituents | Fluid; informal based on mutual empathy | Ad hoc unstructured contacts; organization for project level collaboration; organization groupings racked by fear of "organization" | Transitional form of organization sharing characteristics of stages 1 and 2

Mixture of line and staff functions with corresponding organizational roles well defined—but flexibly adjusted to allow for more autonomy via both formal and informal access to higher levels of decision-making

Job mobility more confined to upper level organizational tasks—other workers tend to remain tied to stated work descriptions and rankings | Reflection of cultured democratic society | Dynamic interactive problems, the consequences of some solutions to problems constitute new problems |
| Conscientious-ess of expert; orrective of goals; threat of non-survival of ystem | Interacting, constant evolution of new authority structures | Links between complementary or competing organizations committed to survival of same macro-system; dictated by cost effectiveness | Skills less tied to specific sets of tasks within organizations

Worker less tied to a single work situation: with developing competence and more flexible skills less attached to specific employing organization

Organizations tend to arrange work to develop capacities of people rather than use the capacities to accomplish work

Growth of serial careers—with multiple entry paths into different careers, etc. | Attuned to those features of its environment which might constitute a potential threat to its continued growth | Aggressive interactive problems; considerable strategic skills required for central planning |
| Conscientious-ness of those with network roles; counter-balancing objec-tives of organi-zational units; threat of non-survival of human society | Interdependent; dynamic emergence of cross-linking authority centers of short duration | Interdependent; dynamic emergence of cross-linking authority centers of short duration, distinction between intra- and inter-organizational links considered academic | As above—mix of diverse specialties flexibly adaptive to changes in task and policy directions

The managerial executive becomes the prime interface and coordinator of "temporary" systemic clusters of specialized project groups—with multiple, mobile, and overlapping memberships

Ranking according to competence in flexible performance rather than by hierarchic position in organization | Attuned to those features of its environment which might constitute a potential threat to its continued activity and to those which might be threatened by its continued activity | Very aggressive interactive problems; centralized strategy abandoned in favor of decentralized response by a network of inter-dependent organizations |

this type of organization in the past few decades. An important stimulus for the emergence of these forms is that which came into existence to satisfy needs, and interests, and as responses to problems, which older structures fail to provide, or where its managerial constraints do not allow it to handle the problem effectively, or they are themselves older forms whose function has been superseded causing them to move into different areas of need. For example, the traditional operational areas for many of the voluntary organizations has gradually been taken over by governmental and other quasi-official structures in areas of "charity" and "welfare," so that they are forced to redefine their mission and seek new service constituencies. Often this process will not only transform the organization's profile of interests and support, but the new range of "problems" may attract more and different memberships and so regenerate and accelerate organizational growth.

The voluntary organization also, and obviously, has a different managerial style from, say, the entrepreneurial firm or the government agency. Its type of leadership, efficiency or effectiveness criteria, structure of rewards, incentives, and objectives are also quite different. The fact that its working membership is "voluntary" and "unpaid" does in itself provide one salient difference from most other organizational forms in requiring more internalized and "affective" satisfaction from its support of, and involvement in, such voluntary work. Its efficiency and effectiveness is measured more by the quality and extent of services it is able to perform for these kinds of "psychic income" return than almost any other kind of organization.

> . . . voluntary associations in American life . . . seem to satisfy two basic social needs. They offer the individual an opportunity for self-expression, and they provide a means through which he can promote his interests or beliefs, or satisfy his altruistic impulses, by way of collective action. Most voluntary associations fall into one of two types, the expressive and the instrumental, or in some cases represent a combination of the two. An example of the former might be an amateur choral group; of the latter, a national health agency; and of a mixture of the two, a national sports society.[20]

One may note that the voluntary sector continuum runs from the more fixed and traditional types at one end to the temporary ad hoc groups at the other. The age range, class, minority, and socioeconomic diversity now represented on the continuum is a fairly recent phenomenon. Earlier studies have always ranked traditional membership in voluntary associations directly with higher income and class level. The interpenetration of traditional voluntarism with issue-oriented public interest groups, with consumer and marginal groups, and with those concerned with the exploration of "alternative life styles," combined with the more discretionary time and income available in the affluent society, could turn this sector into one of the more cohesive "bridging" agencies in society—capable of merging and mobilizing diverse group interests, and of channeling social energies into concerted action. This could provide the institutionalized "social criticism sector," which Carey outlines. It would also constitute an elaboration of what Vickers has termed the "appreciative system" in society—a vital component for over-all social management.

Paralleling the growth of the voluntary sector has been the proliferation of *quasi-nongovernmental organizations.* These have mixed private and public component policies, memberships, and constituencies. They have been established to fulfill a number of specific purposes which (as with the voluntaries) neither wholly private nor wholly public institutions could satisfy.

. . . In each instance there was a convincing basic reason for (their) establishment. An urgent national need had been identified that no other institution in the society was meeting, or, seemingly, could meet.[20]

In common with the voluntary association, the management of the quasi-governmental agency has, and will continue to have, difficulties in maintaining its independence where it may increasingly require direct or indirect support from public funds—either as "grants" or in the form of funding for specific projects. With public fiscal support, there is also, in turn, the problem of "accountability." To whom is the organization accountable and how does this affect the independence and freedom with which it sets its own goals and purposes? This is a salient question regarding the freedom of all private or semipublic organization, e.g., if a "dependent" quasi-governmental agency is created to take over a social task or mission which has already been initiated by a private voluntary association, the latter suffers a loss of function and, in some measure, a loss of freedom to operate in this task area.

We may note also that the quasi-governmental form is part of the array of "intersect" organizations reviewed in the study and defined briefly as follows:

In the twentieth century many societies have witnessed the development of "peculiar" organizations which do not fall into any of the well recognized categories. They are not quite government, although they are usually the result of some kind of government action. They are not quite business, although they perform many business functions. They are not educational or charitable organizations, though they may also perform some of these functions. They frequently occupy "cracks" or interstices in the organizational structure of society. It is often hard to say what is a structure and what is a crack. They have been named "intersects" perhaps because they are intersector organizations, participating in some sense in two or more sectors of society. (Boulding)

Again, as with voluntary and quasi-governmental organizations, and particularly where certain of these are definable as intersects, they present different managerial challenges than the traditional firm and "official" governmental and educational forms—even where the latter are also changing. One might expect many of the intersects, e.g., research organizations, "professional" administrative, and regulatory forms, etc., to exhibit multiple management strategies internally which would resemble more the educational/university model than the business firm. Others may be closer to the voluntary form where more "accountability" constraints are placed on management by the nature of their volunteer constituencies, etc. Where intersects have been "hived off" from government to accomplish purposes which traditional "civil service" management could not deal with as effectively, one may presume that they might come closer to business management forms. Still others may be looked to for the emergence of new managerial technique where their "purposes" and needs are so new as to have no organizational precedents to follow, e.g., where they deal specifically with new technologies and man-machine relationships. One may qualify the latter statement obviously to the extent that they will always have the one governing precedent—that they are "human" organizations composed of, and dealing with, people and their coordinated actions towards some variably shared end goal.

Social Management

Given the diffusion, interpenetration, and convergence of managerial objectives and end goals suggested in the major papers, and that much of the convergence is directed towards an assumed commonalty of changes in goal orientations and attitudes toward the "quality" of organizational and work environments and toward the over-all quality of life in the society, we may assert that "social management" will be one of the major directional changes in management itself. This includes not only new concepts of social costing, of social profitability and responsibility for the firm, new orientations in political governance, in education, etc., but also that in a more general sense that all *managerial practice*—from prisons to factories to voluntary help agencies, etc.—will begin to be recast in social forms, i.e., in which the "effective" satisfaction of human needs, desires, and "end purposes" becomes the overriding operational criterion for organizational performance rather than narrower and compartmentalized goals of organizational efficiency in itself.

Practically speaking, the larger challenges and more transcendental ranges of rewards, incentives, and responsibilities for the manager now reside in concern with the social management of the larger and more complex maintenance and service systems of the society. This doesn't mean just more governmental or political management. As is implied throughout this study, it is suggested that the future of management itself lies with the reorientation of all managerial and organizational directions towards their evaluation in terms of their wider impacts upon, and longer range consequences for, the whole society—economically, socially, and culturally. This may seem initially impractical for the business manager who is most accustomed to, and skilled in, the shorter range and limiting constraints of the market with its central evaluative criteria of economic profit. The narrower definition of profit, in wholly economic terms, may no longer be viable in itself. Vickers addresses this point rather cogently:

Later ages may wonder, as other cultures may wonder now, how anyone in a highly developed society like our own can cherish the belief that undertakings operating for profit in a market can escape the embarrassing value judgments inherent in the multi-valued choice. This belief rests on two assumptions, both of which are less true today than they used to be. One is the assumption that managing a business can be *fully* described as managing an investment and that, therefore, *all* the criteria which determine success in business management can be reduced to or derived from those which determine success in managing an investment. The other . . . is that companies operating for profit in a market can leave the multi-valued choosing to the individual buyer . . . Few people today accept these assumptions in the unqualified form which was acceptable to their grandfathers but even fewer, I think, realize how far they have been eroded or how far their residual truth is itself a cultural artifact, subject to cultural change. They have been eroded by changes in economic conditions. (Free) markets barely exist today in any important field . . . These assumptions have also been eroded by political changes. In an even wider field—for instance, in the land and property market—the preferences and values expressed by individual buyers and sellers represents so small a fraction of the social valuing and preferring which is involved, that the missing element is increasingly expressed either by public regulation of the market or by the entry of government, central or local, as buyers and sellers, to express political choice. An increasing volume of individual needs can be satisfied only by political choice . . . The social costs and values of all activities demand entry into a calculus far beyond that of the market.[21]

Social management involves longer range planning in normative terms and may be best served not only by the redesigning and redirection of our older organizations but by more deliberate attention to, and investment in, new institutional and managerial forms. These will be concerned with anticipating, and planning for change, with measuring the social planning for change, with measuring the social progress of the firm, the institution, and the society, and with the analysis and coordination of "preferred value outcomes" at these many different levels. Our sketch of taxonomic approaches to organizational forms here has addressed this via a beginning selection and classification of modes already extant, with some attention to those which might be more appropriate in dealing with various aspects of change.

Types of Institutions

We may usefully add one more dimension to this taxonomy which is more future oriented in its concern with "integrative" and "adaptive" modes. Jantsch, describing the "changes in institutional concepts over the past few decades . . . distinguishes between three basic types [22] (see page 364).

In a further study [23] the author recognizes three further characteristics for determining the types of *future* institutions required:

  1. "*Integrative,* implying the need for institutions to plan and operate on a system wide basis—planning for change in a complex dynamic system involving simulation on the basis of multivariate inputs characteristically

TYPES OF INSTITUTIONS [22]

INSTRUMENTAL

Instrumental institutions are primarily geared to the deployment of more or less rigid sets of material and non-material resources for innovation (or conservation) and not to the innovation process as such. They preserve linearity of planning and action, are insufficiently sighted on future objectives and outcomes and attempt systemic consistency mainly with regard to quantitative problems of resource deployment, and usually not going beyond pseudo-rational "decision-istic models" which may be considerably influenced by the interaction of pressure groups. Frequently, instrumental institutions are characterized by the absence of planning altogether. Examples in the areas of science and technology are the National Science Foundation and the National Institutes of Health, the proposed Department of Science revived now after ten years of dormancy, the European-type university, and many fundamental research set-ups within and outside the university. The broad instrumental character of the latter, especially research institutions in "big science," has encouraged the fatal linking of fundamental research to higher education, and has, thereby, enforced the application of instrumental criteria to both areas.

PRAGMATIC

Pragmatic institutions are geared to action leading to well-defined objectives, usually accepting a medium-range look into the future (as far as the "freezing" of such objectives permit). They are not, or are little concerned with defining the objectives of such action. Pragmatic institutions may, therefore, be regarded as ad hoc arrangements for effective tactical (operational) planning and implementation, corresponding to a specific strategy. They become a problem when they tend to become permanent. Examples of pragmatic institutions in the area of science and technology are the modern Institute of Technology, industrial product line development and project management. Pragmatic institutions have been vehicles for the enormous acceleration of technological, and thereby social change in our time, and for our academic and industrial excellence in technological disciplines. They constitute a propitious framework for linear growth goals, not for integrative planning and socio-technological system engineering.

ADAPTIVE

Adaptive institutions are geared to the flexible process of continuous search and modification, which is the essence of planning at the strategic and policy levels. They may include, and make use of "building blocks" which are, in themselves, pragmatic in nature. Adaptive institutions, or inter-institutional structures, permit the systematic consideration of high-level objectives and alternative means to meet them. Long-range forecasting and planning over a time scale of several decades can be practised in the fullest sense only within their framework. Examples include the gradually introduced Planning-Programming-Budgeting System of government—once it will have achieved its full impact—to a certain degree the National Aeronautical and Space Administration (NASA) and the use of flexible "innovation emphasis structures" in advanced-thinking industry.

social, political, economic aspects of problems pertaining to the joint systems of society and technology must be dealt with.

2. *Normative* institutions to assess and forecast value dynamics, to establish and sharpen concensus where appropriate.

3. *Adaptive* (as referred to in the above table) institutions relating continuously planning objectives and potentials to the changing environment and to provide suitable information systems. For the avoidance of "over-planning" or fixed centralized planning, which would be constrained upon the development of new initiatives and alternatives, it is suggested that "futures creative" planning process would be based on decentralized initiative and centralized synthesis, that it would not necessarily be responsible for decision making but rather for providing the full information base for decision making in a systematic manner."

CHART S: LIFE CYCLE MODEL	Legislative	Judicial	The President	Executive Office of President	Department of State	Defense	Justice	Interior	Agriculture	Commerce	Labor	Health, Education, Welfare	Housing and Home Finance	Atomic Energy Commission
−1 to 0 Conception, Prenatal, Birth														
0 to 5 Infancy														
6 to 12 Childhood, Puberty														
12 to 18 Adolescence														
18 to 30 Young Adult														
30 to 42 Prime of Life														
42 to 60 Middle Age, Menopause														
60 to 100 Old Age, Death														

Parts of this anticipatory planning model are already evident in the "technology assessment" activities already under way in the "social indicators" and "social accounting" procedures being introduced, and in the newer requirements for institutional assessment mechanisms now under discussion.

Amongst the models for such managerial planning, we may adduce the life cycle model on page 365.

This gives another perspective for assessing the impingement of institutional management on the individual at various life stages. It may be viewed in several ways.

1. *As indicating which institutions, agencies, etc., impinge most directly on which stages of the life cycle.* The federal agencies range could be replaced by other institutional ranges.

2. *As a projective planning model* for allocating resources so as to effect change over time. For example, if some desirable change—in health, attitudes, motivational values, etc.—was projected as to be required optimally in twenty years' time, then the best life-cycle range for effectual investment would be in the earliest phases from birth to twelve years, i.e., those who would be adults at this time. The least effectual range would, obviously, be in the later years of the life cycle.

3. *As a budgetary analysis tool,* it might enable one to judge the effectiveness of past allocations in hindsight fashion.

4. Viewed somewhat differently it suggests, of course, a "totally institutionalised" and technocratic model of individual development which may be over-constraining and restrictive on individual development, freedoms, etc. But it also recognizes that this process has already been under way for some time. From birth to death, we are caught up in a web of institutional processes—familial, educational, medical, commercial, governmental, etc., which do influence directly and indirectly our life directions. The "self determination" dimension which is missing in this sketch model, would be the specific allocation of the degrees of freedom, of participation in the decision-making process, of rights, etc., within which the individual may operate. It not only poses important questions regarding the management of the given institutional means indicated, but has underlying implications regarding the "managed society."

Managers in all sectors must face up to the problem of managing change.

The over-all charge for this study has been to explore the various changes, challenges, and opportunities for management which will occur within the next two decades. One of its major challenges and opportunities in all sectors will be to engage more deliberately and consciously with the impact and assessment of its own actions within the larger context of the society. Conversely, it must also contribute more directly towards the shaping of the value attitudes and goals of the large society in more positive ways.

Beyond Optimism and Pessimism . . . Nothing less than this, as I believe describes the demands which are made on us, both as doers and as done-by in the politico-economic systems which history has bequeathed to us. We may be biologically incapable of meeting these demands; or, if theoretically capable, we may yet be unable to make the cultural change required in the time available. The prospect could not be more dark or uncertain. But to such situations neither optimism nor pessimism is appropriate. The situation is beyond both—as all serious situations are—and our proper response to it was well defined two centuries ago by an American whose utterance will never be bettered. In 1780, while the House of Representatives of the State of Connecticut was in session, the noonday sky was so strangely darkened that some members, anticipating the approach of Judgment Day, called on the Speaker to adjourn the session so that they might prepare to meet their God. The speaker ruled—"Gentlemen, either this is the end of the world or it is not. If it is not, our business should proceed. If it is, I prefer to be found doing my duty. Let lights be brought." [24]

We can no longer afford to take an exclusive view of managerial and organizational responsibilities as limited by the boundaries of the firm, institution, or association that is managed. All of our major decisions eventually feed back upon one another and influence the large collective decisions which shape the goal directions of the society. We can either engage more closely and consciously with the management of change—or be faced with a change of management. Our current ability to evaluate and determine our future goals, in the larger sense, lags far behind our potential managerial capacity to fulfill any specific goals which we may set ourselves.

Chart References

A. John HcHale, "Conceptual Revolutions," Working Paper No. 2, 1972.
B. Adapted from:

    (1) International Industrial Development Center Study, Stanford Research Institute, 1961.
    (2) Hugo Boyko, *Science and the Future of Mankind,* Dr. W. Junk, ed. (issued by World Academy of Art and Science, The Hague, 1961).
    (3) Change/Challenge/Response, Office of Regional Development (Albany, 1964).

C. Hans Thirring, *Energy for Man* (Bloomington: Indiana University Press, © 1958), used with permission.
D. (1) U.S. Department of Commerce, Bureau of Census, *Statistical Abstract of the U.S. 1971,* p. 305.
    (2) U.S. Department of Commerce, Bureau of the Census, *Historical Statistics of the U.S. Colonial Times to 1957,* p. 139.
E. Radovan Richta, *Civilization at the Crossroads* (Prague, International Arts & Sciences Press, 1969), p. 325.
F. Delbert C. Miller and William H. Form, *Industrial Sociology: The Sociology of Work Organizations,* 2nd edition (New York: Harper & Row, 1964), p. 51, © by Delbert C. Miller and William H. Form.

G. Report of National Goals Research Staff, *Quantity with Quality,* U.S. Government Printing Office, 1970, p. 183.

H. Hiller and Farm, *Industrial Sociology,* p. 815.

I. R. B. Fuller and John McHale, *Human Trends and Needs,* (Carbondale: World Resources Inventory, Southern Illinois University, 1963), p. 16.

J. Metropolitan Life Insurance Company, 1964, plus other sources.

K. John McHale, *The Changing Information Environment: A Selective Topography,* Chapter in the study, "Information Technology; Some Critical Implications for Decision Makers 1971–1990." (New York: Conference Board, 1972).

L. (1) Allen, et al., *Technology and Social Change* (New York: Appleton-Century-Crofts, 1957).

   (2) Robert U. Ayres, *Technological Forecasting and Long Range Planning* (New York: McGraw-Hill, 1969), p. 22, used with permission.

M. Bertram M. Gross, "Space-time and Post-industrial Society," in *The Spatial Aspects of Development Administration,* ed. James Heaphey (Chapel Hill: University of North Carolina Press, 1972).

N. Bertram M. Gross, *The Managing of Organizations* (Glencoe: The Free Press, and London: Collier-Macmillan, 1964).

P. McHale, "The Changing Information Environment: A Selective Topography," p. 28.

Q. Gross, "The Managing of Organizations."

R. Anthony J. N. Judge, "The World Network of Organizations," *International Associations,* January 1972.

S. John Dixon, "Man the Measure: Human Processes and National Policies," Working Staff Paper; Office of Planning, National Institute of Mental Health (Washington, D.C., 1965).

Notes

1. Peter F. Drucker, *The Age of Discontinuity* (New York: Harper & Row, 1969), p. 8.

2. Peter F. Drucker, *Landmarks of Tomorrow: A Report on the new "Post-Modern" World* (New York: Harper & Row, 1965), p. xi.

3. Daniel Bell, *The Management of Information and Technology.* Paper prepared for 11th meeting of Panel on Science and Technology, Committee on Science and Astronautics, U.S. House of Representatives, 1970, Moderator's Remarks, p. 14.

4. Manley Irwin, "A New Policy for Communications," *Science and Technology,* April 1968, p. 77.

5. Bertram M. Gross, "Space-time and Post-industrial Society," in *The Spatial Aspects of Development Administration,* ed. James Heaphey (Chapel Hill: University of North Carolina Press, 1972).

6. Kenneth Boulding, *The Image: Knowledge in Life and Society* (Ann Arbor: University of Michigan Press paperback, 1961).

7. Drucker, *The Age of Discontinuity,* pp. 8–9.

8. Edward Higbee, *Farms and Farmers in an Urban Age* (New York: Twentieth Century Fund, 1963), p. 3.

9. R. L. Heilbroner, *The Limits of American Capitalism* (New York: Harper & Row, 1965), p. 52.

10. Gerard Piel, *The Acceleration of History* (New York: Alfred A. Knopf, 1972), pp. 356, 357.

11. Victor Basiuk, "The Impact of Technology in the Next Decades," *Orbis,* vol. 14, No. 1 (1970).

12. Harlan Cleveland, *The Future Executive: A Guide for Tomorrow's Managers* (New York: Harper & Row, 1972).

13. Stanley A. Hetzler, *Technological Growth and Social Change: Achieving Modernization* (London: Routledge & Kegan Paul, 1969), pp. 25, 26.

14. Cleveland, *The Future Executive.*

15. Daniel Bell, "The Corporation and Society in the 1970's," *The Public Interest,* No. 24, Summer 1971.

16. Hetzler, *Technological Growth,* p. 23.

17. Sir Geoffrey Vickers, *Towards a Sociology of Management* (New York: Basic Books, 1967), pp. 67, 68, 69.

18. Clark Kerr, *Industrialism and Industrial Man* (Cambridge, 1960).

19. John H. Goldthorpe, "Theories of Industrial Society: Reflections on the Recrudescence of Historicism and the Future of Futurology." Paper for the 7th World Congress of Sociology, September 1970.

20. "The Quasi Nongovernmental Organization," reprinted from 1967 Annual Report of the Carnegie Corporation of New York.

21. Vickers, *Towards a Sociology of Management,* pp. 71, 72.

22. Erich Jantsch, Integrative Planning for the "Joint Systems" of Society and Technology—The Emerging Role of the University. Report while Visiting Research Associate, Alfred P. Sloan School of Management, Massachusetts Institute of Technology (Cambridge, May 1969), pp. 68–71.

23. Erich Jantsch, "Adaptive Institutions for Shaping the Future," "Prespectives of Planning." Proceedings of OECD Working Symposium on Long Range Forecasting and Planning (Bellagio, Italy, October/November 1968), published by OECD (Paris, 1969).

24. Geoffrey Vickers, *The Demands of a Mixed Economy,* based on a Howard Crawley Memorial lecture given in the University of Pennsylvania under the joint auspices of the Wharton School and the School of Social Work, September 23, 1970.

Contributors

Input papers of the following panel chairmen and colleagues who participated in The Conference Board Study influenced the preparation of this section (the authors assume full responsibility for choice of content and interpretation):

H. IGOR ANSOFF

HENRY M. BOETTINGER

KENNETH E. BOULDING

MARVIN BOWER—C. LEE WALTON, JR.

ERNEST L. BOYER

WILLIAM D. CAREY

CHARLES M. DARLING, III

JOHN DIXON—DAVID HORTON SMITH

PETER F. DRUCKER

WILLIAM SIMON

THEODORE A. SMITH

Staff Members on this study:

ERIC BARTELT

ROSALIND FORSE

DARRELL MCINTIRE

DAN RADELL

Senior Executives Council of The Conference Board

Senior Executives Council members at the time of the study were:

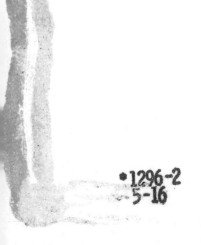